The Relevance of Romanticism

The Relevance of Romanticism

Essays on German Romantic Philosophy

EDITED BY

DALIA NASSAR

OXFORD
UNIVERSITY PRESS

OXFORD
UNIVERSITY PRESS

Oxford University Press is a department of the University of Oxford.
It furthers the University's objective of excellence in research, scholarship,
and education by publishing worldwide.

Oxford   New York
Auckland   Cape Town   Dar es Salaam   Hong Kong   Karachi
Kuala Lumpur   Madrid   Melbourne   Mexico City   Nairobi
New Delhi   Shanghai   Taipei   Toronto

With offices in
Argentina   Austria   Brazil   Chile   Czech Republic   France   Greece
Guatemala   Hungary   Italy   Japan   Poland   Portugal   Singapore
South Korea   Switzerland   Thailand   Turkey   Ukraine   Vietnam

Oxford is a registered trademark of Oxford University Press
in the UK and certain other countries.

Published in the United States of America by
Oxford University Press
198 Madison Avenue, New York, NY 10016

© Oxford University Press 2014

Library of Congress Cataloging-in-Publication Data
The relevance of Romanticism : essays on German romantic philosophy / edited by Dalia Nassar.
   pages cm
ISBN 978-0-19-997620-1 (hardcover : alk. paper)—ISBN 978-0-19-997621-8 (pbk. : alk. paper)
1. Philosophy, German—18th century.   2. Philosophy, German—19th century.
3. Romanticism—Germany.   4. Romanticism—Germany—Influence.   I. Nassar, Dalia,
editor of compilation.
B2748.R64R45 2014
141'.60943—dc23
2013034627

9 8 7 6 5 4 3 2 1
Printed in the United States of America
on acid-free paper

CONTENTS

ACKNOWLEDGMENTS

I would like to thank the contributors to this volume, from whose work I have learned and with whom I have enjoyed working. I would also like to acknowledge the support of the Australian Research Council Discovery Early Career Research Award (DE120102402), which enabled me to undertake and complete this project. Finally, I wish to thank Ryan Feigenbaum for his invaluable help and editorial work on the manuscript.

ABBREVIATIONS

Frequently cited works have been identified by the following abbreviations.

Johann Gottlieb Fichte

GA   *Gesamtausgabe der Bayerischen Akademie der Wissenschaften.* Edited by Reinhard Lauth et al. Stuttgart: Frommann-Holzboog, 1962–2012.

FW   *Fichtes Werke.* Edited by Immanuel Hermann Fichte. Berlin: W. de Gruyter, 1971.

Johann Wolfgang von Goethe

FA   *Sämtliche Werke* (Frankfurter Ausgabe). Edited by H. Birus et al. Frankfurt am Main: Deutscher Klassiker Verlag, 1985–1999.

LA   *Die Schriften zur Naturwissenschaft.* Edited by D. Kuhn et al. Weimar: Hermann Bölhaus Nachfolger, 1947.

MA   *Sämtliche Werke nach Epochen seines Schaffens* (Münchner Ausgabe). Edited by K. Richter et al. Munich: Carl Hanser, 1985–98.

WA   *Goethes Werke* (Weimarer Ausgabe). Edited by P. Raabe et al. Weimar: Hermann Böhlau, 1887–1919.

Friedrich von Hardenberg (Novalis)

NS   *Novalis Schriften: Die Werke von Friedrich von Hardenberg.* Edited by Richard Samuel, H.-J. Mähl, P. Kluckhorn, and G. Schulz. Stuttgart: W. Kohlhammer, 1960–88.

Johann Gottfried Herder

HW   *Johann Gottfried Herder: Werke in zehn Bänden.* Edited by Ulrich Gaier et al. Frankfurt am Main: Deutscher Klassiker Verlag, 1985–2000.

Friedrich Hölderlin

HSW *Hölderlin: Sämtliche Werke (Kleine Stuttgarter Ausgabe)*. Edited by Friedrich Beissner. Stuttgart: W. Kohlhammer, 1962.

HFA *Sämtliche Werke. Historisch-kritische Ausgabe* (Frankfurter Ausgabe). Edited by D. E. Sattler. Frankfurt am Main: Stroemfeld/ Roter Stern, 1975–2008.

Immanuel Kant

AA *Gesammelte Schriften*. Edited by Preußischen Akademie der Wissenschaft. Berlin: de Gruyter, 1900–.

Friedrich Wilhelm Joseph von Schelling

HKA *Werke: Historisch-kritische Ausgabe*. Edited by H. M. Baumgartner, W. G. Jacobs, and H. Krings. Stuttgart-Bad Cannstatt: Frommann-Holzboog, 1976–.

SW *Schellings Sämmliche Werke*. Edited by K. F. A. Schelling. Stuttgart: Cotta, 1856–1861.

Friedrich von Schlegel

KA *Kritische Friedrich-Schlegel-Ausgabe*. Edited by E. Behler, J. J. Anstett, and H. Eichner. Paderborn: Schöningh, 1958–.

Friedrich Daniel Ernst Schleiermacher

FSSW *Friedrich Schleiermacher's sämmtliche Werke*. Edited by O. Braun and J. Bauer. Berlin: G. Reimer, 1835–1864.

KGA *Kritische Gesamtausgabe*. Edited by Günter Meckenstock et al. Berlin: de Gruyter, 1980–2005.

All citations will contain volume and page numbers. In cases where there are separate parts to a volume, the volume number will be followed by a "/" and then the part number.

CONTRIBUTORS

Karl Ameriks is the McMahon-Hank Professor of Philosophy at the University of Notre Dame. He is the author of *Kant and the Historical Turn* (Oxford, 2006), *Kant and the Fate of Autonomy* (Cambridge, 2000), and editor of the *Cambridge Companion to German Idealism* (Cambridge, 2000). He is a founding coeditor of *Internationales Jahrbuch des Deutschen Idealismus* (*International Yearbook of German Idealism*), and since 1994 he has served as a coeditor of the approximately seventy-volume series Cambridge Texts in the History of Philosophy. Professor Ameriks was elected a fellow of the American Academy of Arts and Sciences in 2009. He is also the recipient of several fellowships from the National Endowment for the Humanities, the Earhart Foundation (most recently in 2010), and an Alexander von Humboldt Fellowship. He is a former member of the American Philosophical Association Board of Officers (2003–2005) and past president of the Central Division of the American Philosophical Association (2004–2005) and the North American Kant Society (1991–1994).

Frederick Beiser, one of the world's leading historians of German philosophy, is Professor of Philosophy at Syracuse University. He has also taught at Harvard, Yale, Pennsylvania, Indiana, and Wisconsin. His book *The Fate of Reason: German Philosophy from Kant to Fichte* won the 1987 Thomas J. Wilson Prize for the Best First Book. He is also the author of *German Idealism: The Struggle against Subjectivism* (Harvard, 2002), *The Romantic Imperative* (Harvard, 2003), and more recently, *Schiller: A Re-examination* (Oxford, 2008).

Brady Bowman is Assistant Professor of Philosophy at the Pennsylvania State University. Before coming to Penn State, he was a research associate in philosophy at the Friedrich Schiller Universität Jena (2000–2007). His recent publications include *Hegel's Metaphysics of Absolute Negativity* (Cambridge, 2013); *G. W. F. Hegel's Heidelberg Writings. Translation and Commentary*, ed. and trans. with Allen Speight (Cambridge, 2009); "Spinozist Pantheism and the Truth of 'Sense Certainty': What the Eleusinian Mysteries Have to Tell Us about

Hegel's *Phenomenology*," *Journal of the History of Philosophy* 50 (1): 85–110; and "Goethean Morphology, Hegelian Science: Affinities and Transformations," *Goethe Yearbook* 18: 159–82.

Laure Cahen-Maurel is the author of a number of articles on the aesthetic interactions between German idealism and romanticism, and has published the first complete translation of the main text of Caspar David Friedrich into French, titled *En contemplant une collection de peintures* (Paris: José Corti, 2011). She has prepared the French editions of some of the principal writings of the German art historians: J. J. Winckelmann's *Pensées sur l'imitation des œuvres grecques en peinture et en sculpture* (Paris: Editions Allia, 2005), Aby Warburg's *La Naissance de Vénus et Le Printemps de Sandro Botticelli* (Paris: Editions Allia, 2007), and *La légende de l'artiste* by Ernst Kris and Otto Kurz (Paris: Editions Allia, 2010). She is a collaborator on the forthcoming collection of essays on German philosophy called *L'idéalisme allemand* (Paris: Le Cerf, 2014).

Richard Eldridge is the Charles and Harriett Cox McDowell Professor of Philosophy at Swarthmore College. He is the author of *The Persistence of Romanticism: Essays in Philosophy and Literature* (Cambridge, 2001), *Literature, Life and Modernity* (Columbia, 2008) and editor of the *Oxford Handbook of Philosophy and Literature* (Oxford, 2009). He is the recipient of numerous awards, and has been a guest Professor in Erfurt (2005, 2007) and Freiburg (2009–2010).

Michael N. Forster earned his PhD in Philosophy at Princeton University. In March 2013 he became the Alexander von Humboldt Professor, holder of the Chair in Theoretical Philosophy, and Codirector of the International Center for Philosophy at Bonn University. Previously, he was the Glen A. Lloyd Distinguished Service Professor in Philosophy and the College at the University of Chicago. He is the author of six books on German philosophy, as well as many articles on German philosophy, ancient philosophy, and contemporary philosophy of language. His most recent publications are *German Philosophy of Language from Schlegel to Hegel and Beyond* (Oxford, 2011) and *After Herder* (Oxford, 2010).

Manfred Frank is Professor Emeritus of Philosophy at the University of Tübingen. He has published numerous books on romanticism, idealism, and the philosophy of mind, including *Einführung in die frühromantische Ästhetik* (Suhrkamp, 1989); *Unendliche Annäherung: Die Anfänge der philosophischen Frühromantik* (Suhrkamp, 1997); partial English translation, *The Philosophical Foundations of Early German Romanticism*, trans. Elizabeth Millán-Zaibert (SUNY, 2004); and *Selbstgefühl: eine Historisch-systematische Erkundung* (Suhrkamp, 2002).

Kristin Gjesdal is Associate Professor of Philosophy at Temple University. Her work has appeared in journals including *Kant-Studien, Hegel-Studien, Journal of the History of Philosophy, History of Philosophy Quarterly*, and *British Journal of the History of Philosophy*. She has written the "Novalis" and "Hermeneutics" entries for the *Stanford Encyclopedia of Philosophy* (the latter coauthored with Bjørn Ramberg). Her book *Gadamer and the Legacy of German Idealism* appeared with Cambridge University Press in 2009. She has been a visiting scholar at the Goethe-Universität, Frankfurt, and Columbia University, as well as a postdoctoral Fulbright Fellow at the University of Chicago. In 2009 she received a fellowship from the Alexander von Humboldt-Stiftung in Germany.

Amanda Jo Goldstein is Assistant Professor of English at Cornell University. She works on European romanticism and the life sciences, with special interests in rhetoric and figuration, pre-Darwinian biology, and materialist theories of history, poetry, and nature. Her book project, *Sweet Science: Romantic Materialism and the New Sciences of Life*, shows how writers from Erasmus Darwin to Percy Shelley revived ancient materialism to cast poetry as a privileged technique of empirical enquiry—an experimental practice fit to connect the biological problem of living form to the period's pressing new sense of its own historicity. Goldstein received her PhD in Comparative Literature (English, German, French) from the University of California. Before joining the Cornell English department, she was a Mellon postdoctoral fellow in biopolitics at the University of Wisconsin, Madison.

Keren Gorodeisky is Associate Professor of Philosophy at Auburn University. Her primary research areas are Kant, philosophical aesthetics and eighteen- to nineteenth-century German philosophy. She is currently working on two projects. The first is a book-length interpretation of Kant's view of the special form that characterizes aesthetic judgments. The second is a reconstruction of the philosophy of the "Early German Romantics," particularly Friedrich Schlegel. Her publications include "A New Look at Kant's Account of Testimony Concerning Beauty," *British Journal of Aesthetics*; "A Tale of Two Faculties," *British Journal of Aesthetics*; "(Re)encountering Individuality: Friedrich Schlegel's Romantic Imperative as a Response to Nihilism," *Inquiry*; and "Schematizing without a Concept—Imagine That!" *Kant and Philosophy in a Cosmopolitan Sense* (Berlin: Walter de Gruyter, 2012). Gorodeisky is the recipient of the 2012–13 Philip Quinn Fellowship for Young Women in Philosophy at the National Humanities Center.

Jane Kneller is Professor and Chair of the Department of Philosophy at the Colorado State University. She has published *Kant and the Power of Imagination* (Cambridge, 2007) and translated Novalis's *Fichte-Studien* (Cambridge, 2003).

She has received several fellowships from the National Endowment for the Humanities and is past vice president of the North American Kant Society (NAKS), and current member of the advisory board for NAKS, as well as a member of the editorial board of the *Kantian Review*.

Bruce Matthews is Professor of Philosophy at Bard College, and has been a Visiting Professor at Tübingen University (2004) and Freiburg University (2011). He is the recipient of numerous awards and grants, including the Hans Jonas award, two Fulbright Senior Scholar awards, two University of Chicago Teaching awards, and a National Endowment for the Humanities grant. His books include *F. W. J. Schelling's Berlin Lectures: The Grounding of Positive Philosophy* (SUNY, 2007); *Schelling's Organic Form of Philosophy: Life as the Schema of Freedom* (SUNY, 2011), and the forthcoming *Schelling: Heretic of Modernity* (SUNY). Founding member of the Schelling Society of North America, he is also a member of the International Schelling Society, the American Philosophical Association, and the Society of Intercultural Philosophy.

Dalia Nassar is Assistant Professor of Philosophy at Villanova University, and Research Fellow of the Australian Research Council at the University of Sydney. She is the author of *The Romantic Absolute: Being and Knowing in Early German Romantic Philosophy 1795–1804* (Chicago, 2013). Her article "From a Philosophy of Self to a Philosophy of Nature: Goethe and the Development of Schelling's *Naturphilosophie*" (*Archiv für Geschichte der Philosophie*, 2010) was awarded the prize for "Best Essay published in 2010" by the Goethe Society of North America. She has been a recipient of research awards from the DAAD (2003, 2004), the Thyssen-Stiftung (2009), and, most recently, the Australian Research Council (2012–2015).

Paul Redding is Professor of Philosophy at the University of Sydney and a fellow of the Australian Academy of the Humanities. He works mainly in the areas of Kantian philosophy and the tradition of German idealism. In particular he is interested in the relationship of the idealist tradition to the later movements of analytic philosophy and pragmatism, and in issues in idealist logic, philosophical psychology, and philosophy of religion. He is the author of *Hegel's Hermeneutics* (Cornell, 1996), *The Logic of Affect* (Cornell, 1999), *Analytic Philosophy and the Return of Hegelian Thought* (Cambridge, 2007), and *Continental Idealism: Leibniz to Nietzsche* (Routledge, 2009).

John H. Smith is a professor of German in the Department of European Languages and Studies at the University of California, Irvine. His books include *Dialogues between Faith and Reason: The Death and Return of God in Modern German Thought* (Cornell, 2011), and *The Spirit and Its Letter: Traces of Rhetoric in Hegel's Philosophy of Bildung* (Cornell, 1988). He was also coeditor of "Goethe and Idealism: Art, Science, Religion, and Philosophy—1790 to 1817," a special issue of the *Goethe Yearbook* (2011). He is the recipient of research awards from the Humboldt Foundation (1991–1992, 2004, 2010) and the Fulbright Commission (1998–1999), and was guest researcher at the Freie-Universität, Berlin in 2010–2011.

David W. Wood received his PhD in Philosophy jointly from the Sorbonne, Université Paris IV and the Ludwig-Maximilians-Universität in Munich. From 2009 to 2011 he was a postdoctoral researcher at the Bavarian Academy of Sciences, where he collaborated on the *Johann Gottlieb Fichte Gesamtausgabe*. He is the author of *"Mathesis of the Mind": A Study of Fichte's Wissenschaftslehre and Geometry* (Rodopi, 2012); editor and translator of Novalis, *Notes for a Romantic Encyclopaedia: Das Allgemeine Brouillon* (SUNY, 2007); coeditor and cotranslator (with Michael G. Vater) of J. G. Fichte and F. W. Schelling, *The Philosophical Rupture between Fichte and Schelling: Selected Texts and Correspondence, 1800–1802* (SUNY, 2012), and joint editor of the forthcoming *Routledge Handbook of German Idealism*. With Daniel Breazeale he is currently preparing an edition of J. G. Fichte's earliest philosophical writings entitled *From Kant to the Wissenschaftslehre: Zurich Writings, 1793–94.*

Introduction

"The romantic imperative," Friedrich Schlegel wrote in 1797–1798, "demands the mixing of all genres. All nature and science should become art—[and all] art should become nature and science.... Poetry should become ethical and ethics should be poetic" (KA 16, 134, no. 586). The attempt to bring together (to "mix") various disciplines and ways of knowledge, to make philosophy poetical and poetry philosophical, to introduce poetic insight into ethical norms, to bring art and science together—these were the aims of the movement that has become known as *romanticism*. Science and art, philosophy and poetry, the romantics repeatedly proclaimed, should become one. The various disciplines, as Schelling put it in the introductory remarks to the inaugural edition of his *Zeitschrift für spekulative Physik* (1800–1802), must "enter into one another in the most precise and closest alliance, in order to bring forth the highest, where the interest of art and poetry with science and vice versa begin to become absolutely one and the same" (HKA 1/8, 250–51). Hölderlin, Goethe, Novalis, Schelling, Schlegel, and Schleiermacher each sought to realize this ideal in his practice as a poet, philosopher, and scientist. Their aim was nothing less than developing a new way of knowledge and a new compendium of knowledge, a "bible" or an "encyclopedia," as Schlegel and Novalis called it, in which the different disciplines are united by common insights and goals.[1]

At a time of greater disciplinary specialization and rigid distinctions between ways of knowing, the romantic imperative seems both anachronistic and undesirable. Yet the last two decades can be described as nothing less than a genuine revival of interest in German romantic philosophy. Philosophers working in a variety of areas have embraced the ideas of the German romantics, disentangling them from false or misunderstood legacies, and reexamining them in light of contemporary debates. While this increase of interest began in Germany—with the publication of Manfred Frank's lectures *Einführung in die frühromantische Ästhetik* in 1987—since the 1990s, philosophical interest in romanticism has become an even stronger current within the Anglophone context.[2] What are the reasons behind this (apparently) sudden and (largely) unprecedented interest in philosophical romanticism?[3] Why have philosophers

from a number of fields—aesthetics, epistemology, social and political philosophy, philosophy of religion, philosophy of science, hermeneutics—turned
to romanticism?[4]

The general historical interest in romanticism is, perhaps, not surprising.
After all, the so-called romantic movement, which began in Germany in the
1790s, has had a lasting effect on Western culture. Romantic theories of literature, romantic conceptions of nature, and romantic interest in non-Western
culture (especially Indian culture and language) have played significant roles
in shaping both the nineteenth and twentieth centuries. However, the recent
revival does not simply have to do with a desire to understand the past, or an
attempt to grapple with the "romantic legacy." For it is a specifically *philosophical* revival, motivated by philosophical questions.

Before discussing the reasons behind this philosophical interest, I want to
note that, at least within the Anglophone context, philosophical romanticism
has generally been regarded in the *wider sense* of the term "romantic."[5] This is in
contrast to the narrower sense that is usually associated with the Jena romantics,
or *Frühromantik* in Germany, and specifically denotes the circle of friends and
acquaintances in Jena who congregated around Friedrich and August Wilhelm
Schlegel and their journal, the *Athenäum*.[6] The recent (Anglophone) reception
of romanticism almost always includes Hölderlin (who was only associated
with the Jena group indirectly through Schelling and Hegel) and often includes
Schelling,[7] as well as figures who were directly connected to the Jena romantics, but did not contribute to the *Athenäum*, such as Goethe.[8] Thus, the term
romantic—at least within the Anglophone context—means something like an
extended family of thinkers rather than a smaller coterie.[9]

There is, however, a second reason for widening the connotations of romanticism. A philosophical investigation into romanticism seeks, first and foremost,
to understand the concerns of the romantic movement and its philosophical
aspirations, as epitomized in the "romantic imperative." The focus is thus on the
questions, methods, and aims that a number of thinkers—spread throughout
the German-speaking regions of the late eighteenth and early twentieth centuries—share and that speak to us today.

Philosophers working on romanticism generally concur on its contemporary
significance. Frank, for instance, has argued for the relevance of romantic theories of self-consciousness for the philosophy of mind, theories of individuality,
and conceptions of the self.[10] While Frederick Beiser's approach differs from
Frank, he agrees that "many of the aims and problems of romantic philosophy
are still vital today" such that philosophical romanticism is not only historically significant but also, as he puts it, carries "contemporary relevance."[11] What
are these aims and problems that underlie romanticism and remain (or have
recently become) relevant?

The aim of this volume is to answer this question. By situating romanticism both in its historical context and in ours, the volume seeks to shed new light on romanticism as a distinctive movement in the history of philosophy as well as offer important insight into today's pressing questions and concerns. By drawing together the fruits of the intensive recent engagement with romanticism, the volume aims to stimulate and facilitate a dialogue on the significance of romantic philosophy and its continuing relevance for contemporary debates.

The volume is divided into four parts. The first consists in a debate between Frank and Beiser, in which they elaborate their differing interpretations of romantic philosophy and address their disagreement. Frank's "What Is Early German Romantic Philosophy?" recounts some of his key claims regarding both the development and the character of philosophical romanticism, by situating it within a realist and skeptical critique of Fichtean and Reinholdian foundationalist philosophy. Frank thus introduces an English-language audience to his long-held and influential understanding of romanticism as a distinctive philosophical movement that should not be identified with idealism. In contrast, Frank contends that romanticism was a realist movement that was opposed to the view that the "absolute" is knowable or attainable.

Beiser's chapter directly challenges Frank's interpretation of the romantics, particularly in relation to idealism. Beiser illustrates, contra Frank, that the romantics and idealists held many similar views, and argues that the differences between the two movements are not essential. Thus, these two chapters serve to situate the contemporary interpretations of romanticism and thereby introduce the reader to some of the most important questions concerning the meaning of romanticism and its significance in our time.

Each of the three following parts of the book focuses on a central concern of the German romantics: Part 2 considers history, culture, and education; Part 3 concerns aesthetics and mythology; and Part 4 investigates science and nature. As each of the chapters demonstrates, the "romantic imperative" motivates the romantic project, and guides the romantics' conceptions of truth and knowledge, beauty and reality. In every insistence, the romantics insist on uniting a poetic and philosophical way of knowing, of bringing aesthetic insight into our understanding of social and natural phenomena, and scientific knowledge into human life and art.

Part 2 focuses on romantic views of human culture and education. The romantic conceptions of history, language, and sociability, as well as the idea of *Bildung*, are considered in light of contemporary social and political thought. Karl Ameriks's "History, Succession, and German Romanticism" investigates the romantic notion of a "progressive universal poetry" and argues that it provides a useful framework for defining a distinctively romantic conception of history, one that is all at once political, philosophical, and aesthetic in a broadly religious sense. Ameriks contends that, especially for our late modern age, this early German romantic conception has advantages over merely linear, circular, or chaotic conceptions. By situating the romantic model in the context of debates about the teleological and providential nature of history, as understood by Kant, Reinhold, and Hegel, and comparing it with views developed in later antiteleological writings by figures such as Burckhardt, Nietzsche, and Heidegger, Ameriks illustrates the ways in which the romantic model remains the most promising.

Michael N. Forster's "Romanticism and Language" challenges the common misconception that the German romantics were theoretical lightweights, by looking at their views on language. Building on Herder's revolutionary views about language—especially, his principles that thought is essentially dependent on and bounded by language, that meanings/concepts consist in word-usages, and that thoughts, concepts, and language vary profoundly between periods, cultures, and even individuals—Schleiermacher and Friedrich Schlegel, Forster argues, made vitally important and new contributions to the philosophy of language, linguistics, hermeneutics, and translation theory.

Kristin Gjesdal's "Hermeneutics, Individuality, and Tradition: Schleiermacher's Idea of *Bildung* in the Landscape of Hegelian Thought" sheds critical light on the view that there is a sharp, unbridgeable division between the romantics and Hegel, and between the emphasis on individuality, on the one hand, and the commitment to a philosophy of *Bildung*, that is, education in and through culture, on the other. She begins with an examination of Friedrich Schleiermacher's theory of interpretation, which is often viewed as a proto-example of aesthetic-romantic attitudes. In contrast to this view, Gjesdal illustrates that Schleiermacher's model addresses meaning and thought as expressed in the communal medium of language and thus regards *Bildung* and understanding as two sides of the same coin. Thus, Gjesdal shows that the chief difference between Hegel and the romantics is not that Hegel has a notion of *Bildung* and the romantics do not. Rather, the difference has to do with alternative conceptions of *Bildung*. Gjesdal examines these alternative conceptions and argues that while Schleiermacher's view differs from Hegel's, it in fact offers a necessary complement to Hegel's scheme, and is, as such, deserving of rehabilitation—be it within the field of interpretation studies or within the larger philosophical discourse of *Bildung*.

Jane Kneller's "Sociability and the Conduct of Philosophy: What We Can Learn from Early German Romanticism," describes the model of sociability developed by the early German romantics with the aim of showing its relevance to academic discourses that seek to be more diverse and inclusive. Kneller begins by linking the early romantics' conception of "symphilosophizing" to the art of "reciprocal communication" hinted at by Kant at the end of the "Critique of Aesthetic Judgment" and to the transformation of academic discourse in Jena during that period. She goes on to discuss the ways in which the work of three of the central figures of early German romanticism—Friedrich Schlegel, Novalis, and Friedrich Schleiermacher—developed Kant's notion of a "sociability that befits our humanity" by socializing Kant's account of genius, thereby giving rise to a theory of genial conversation that is still worthy of study and emulation.

Part 3 offers highly innovative accounts of and responses to romantic contributions to aesthetics. Richard Eldridge's " 'Doch sehnend stehst/Am Ufer du' ('But longing you stand on the shore'): Hölderlin, Philosophy, Subjectivity, and Finitude," serves as an apt segue into a discussion of romantic aesthetics, as it considers the significance of art (particularly poetry) in illuminating the human condition. Eldridge begins with a survey Hölderlin's mature philosophical sense of the human subject as caught ineluctably between abstract reflection and concrete receptivity, and contrasts that sense briefly with the stances taken by Kant, Schiller, and Hegel. He then traces the consequences of this sense for Hölderlin's poetology, and concludes by showing how both this philosophical sense and this poetology are enacted in Hölderlin's late, major fragment "Rousseau."

Brady Bowman's "On the Defense of Literary Value: From Early German Romanticism to Analytic Philosophy of Literature" argues that doubts about literature's cognitive relevance are shaped today in part by the institutional fate and ambivalent legacy of early German romanticism. While the romantics succeeded in bringing modern literature to the university as an academic discipline, their attempt to revolutionize traditional scientific cognition failed, rendering literary studies a conceptual orphan within the university. Bowman contends that German romanticism has generated two competing views of the relation between literature and the overtly truth-seeking disciplines. The *Schlegelian* legacy of skepticism, antirealism, and antifoundationalism, still vital to poststructuralist thought, he argues, is powerless to give a positive account of literary value; it offers no principled justification of the institutions on which it nevertheless depends. In contrast, Bowman locates a *complementarist* legacy associated with figures like Schiller and Schelling, which emphasizes literature's cognitive *priority* to discursive knowledge and its role as the cognitive *fulfillment* of such knowledge. This tradition, Bowman maintains, offers important resources to aesthetic cognitivism for articulating and defending the value of literature and the institutions that support it. Drawing on John Gibson's 2007 work *Fiction and the Weave of Life*, he goes on to argue that the expanded romantic space of cognition is best understood in terms of a complementarity between propositional knowledge and Cavellian "acknowledgment." When viewed in these terms, Bowman concludes, German romantic theories of aesthetic experience can provide systematic orientation for current analytic philosophy of literature.

Keren Gorodeisky's " 'No Poetry, No Reality': Schlegel, Wittgenstein, Fiction, and Reality" continues the consideration of romantic aesthetics in relation to analytic aesthetics but, in contrast to Bowman, finds in Friedrich Schlegel's conception of poetry and its relation to truth significant resources for clarifying and overcoming confusion in contemporary discussions of art and its value. Gorodeisky notes that Schlegel's remarks about poetry and reality have often been regarded as outlandish, "poetically exaggerated," statements. This is the case, she argues, because they are taken to suggest that there is no difference between poetry and reality or to express the view that there is no way out of linguistic and poetic constructions. In contrast to these views, Gorodeisky illustrates that Schlegel's remarks are philosophical observations about a genuine confusion in theoretical approaches to the distinction between fiction and reality. The confusion at stake involves the assumption that this distinction *is* and *must be* fixed independently of the ordinary practices of using these terms to mean certain things in specific situations—an assumption that is grounded in a confused picture about the way language works. She contends that this confused understanding of the distinction between fiction and reality is not an object of the past, but a picture that is still shaping a central strand in the contemporary debate in philosophical aesthetics on our emotional responses to fiction. Although she does not use Schlegel's approach to argue against this view directly, Gorodeisky suggests that his philosophical method offers resources for unraveling a central confusion in this contemporary debate.

Laure Cahen-Maurel's "The Simplicity of the Sublime: A New Picturing of Nature in Caspar David Friedrich" shifts the attention from poetry and literature to the visual arts, by considering the meaning of the sublime both in the romantic era and in contemporary painting. Her underlying question is: given Hegel's famous philosophical dismissal of the notion of the sublime, and in a postmodern age deprived of theological doctrines, why has the romantic notion of the sublime resurfaced in contemporary art, particularly in the work of British artist Anish Kapoor? To answer it, she turns to the painter whom Kapoor names as his most significant inspiration, Caspar David Friedrich, and asks whether Friedrich supplies a distinctive notion of the sublime that is not identifiable with the Kantian sublime. Cahen-Maurel investigates the role assigned to the sublime by Friedrich and offers a detailed analysis of Kapoor's use of the Friedrichian sublime and its meaning in his art.

In "The New Mythology: Romanticism between Religion and Humanism," Bruce Matthews argues that it is essential to develop the romantic notion of a "new religion," which, he maintains, seeks to unite with humanism in order to create and sanction new normative values. Precisely because this proposed union of religion's divine necessities and the freedoms of humanism was never consummated by the romantics, Matthews argues, the problem that troubled the romantics remains with us today. Matthews identifies the environmental crisis as the most obvious and troubling example of our failure to create new values and argues that Schelling's "organic form of philosophy" offers a viable alternative to this destructive course. Schelling's alternative course, Matthews maintains, suggests a new mythology of nature whose utopian potential may, both in formal and in substantive terms, provide the emancipatory power capable of liberating an engaged hope from its bondage to the ideology of irony that currently emasculates transformative political action.

Part 4 offers rigorous examinations of romantic conceptions of science that seek to demonstrate the ways in which the romantics understood mathematics and natural philosophy and developed new and significant methods of investigating natural phenomena. In "Mathematics, Computation, Language, and Poetry: The Novalis Paradox," Paul Redding challenges the stereotypical view of Novalis as the romantic poet par excellence. He begins by establishing Novalis's serious interest in mathematics and goes on to show that his view of language is founded on a mathematically based computational approach, which can be traced back to Leibniz. Redding then examines Novalis's approach to language, and his attempts to bring mathematics to bear on poetry, in light of debates that developed later in the eighteenth century concerning the relation between language and thought—debates that continue to be relevant today.

John H. Smith's "Friedrich Schlegel's Romantic Calculus: Reflections on the Mathematical Infinite around 1800" offers a new interpretation of the romantic notion of *unendliche Annäherung* or "infinite approximation," by exploring the significance, context, and consequences of discussions in the latter part of the eighteenth century around the "mathematical infinite." Smith begins by looking at Salomon Maimon's 1790 *Essay on Transcendental Philosophy*, which introduces the notion of the infinite into philosophy, and argues that by replacing Kant's radical distinction between the faculties of sensibility and understanding with a view of their infinitesimal difference, Maimon opens new avenues for idealism and romanticism. By pursuing the relevance of these discussions for philosophy around 1800, Smith specifically deals with the mathematical conceptions of that period, while arguing that although these earlier conceptions are considered "wrong" or ambivalent by (some) mathematicians today, they nonetheless provide powerful tools for rethinking the nature of both reality and consciousness.

In agreement with Redding's assessment of Novalis's grasp of mathematics, David W. Wood's "The Mathematical *Wissenschaftslehre*: On a Late Fichtean Reflection of Novalis" offers an analysis of Novalis's neglected *final* philosophical fragments, particularly those found in the concluding sections of the

Romantic Encyclopaedia (1798/99) and the *Fragments and Studies* (1799–1800). He argues that in his late writings Novalis was one of the first thinkers to positively grasp the underlying mathematicity of Fichte's *Wissenschaftslehre*. While recognizing differences between the two thinkers, Wood argues that they are united by a number of shared commitments. The fact that mathematical elements of Fichte's system only became more widely acknowledged in the twentieth century by philosophers of mathematics such as Hermann Weyl, Andreas Speiser, and Jules Vuillemin, Wood claims, should be considered as a belated but independent confirmation of Novalis's original insights on the relationship between mathematics and philosophy in Fichte's *Wissenschaftslehre*.

The final two chapters of the volume focus on what the authors have called "romantic empiricism," which, as Amanda Jo Goldstein puts it, emphasizes "the scene of empirical observation." In her "Irritable Figures: Herder's Poetic Empiricism," Goldstein challenges the "two culture" framework that has shaped the pursuit of knowledge over the last two centuries, and argues for a reappraisal of romantic philosophy of science, as developed by Johann Gottfried Herder. Goldstein begins by tracing the development of Herder's philosophy of science, its relation to the legacies of New Scientific experimentalism and classical empiricist psychology, and its engagement with the emergent sciences of life. She then elucidates Herder's account of perception and cognition, which grounds his understanding of scientific knowledge and truth. Herder recognizes, Goldstein explains, the essentially *figurative* and *analogical* process of knowledge and, on that basis, develops a philosophy of science that accounts for the figurative aspect of scientific representation and truth, and reciprocally, the scientific aspect of figurative representation. In this way, Herder does not only anticipate twentieth-century views on the metaphorical nature of knowledge, but also offers one of the most rigorous explanations of the relationship between poetic and scientific truth.

In the concluding chapter, "Romantic Empiricism after the 'End of Nature': Contributions to Environmental Philosophy," Dalia Nassar similarly distinguishes an empiricist tradition within romanticism, which she identifies with Herder's close friend and ally, Johann Wolfgang von Goethe. Following the various recent proclamations that the idea of "nature" is no longer desirable or plausible, Nassar argues that environmental philosophy has arrived at an impasse: without any notion of a world other than the human world—or the world manipulated by human action—environmental philosophy is unable to justify itself or explain its aims. In contrast to the abstract or vague conceptions of nature that contemporary theorists reject, she offers Goethe's grounded, empirical approach to phenomena, which, she argues, offers a rigorous and nonreductive method of inquiry that seeks to grasp the integrity of natural phenomena without undermining their differences. Furthermore, she contends that Goethe's claim that knowledge involves transformation implies that it cannot be divorced from ethical responsibility. For it is in remaining *open* to what is before me, and *allowing myself to be transformed by it*, that I come to grasp it. The act of knowledge thus demands an honest engagement with reality, with the phenomena. While this is not a thorough and comprehensive environmental ethics, the claim that we are under an epistemological obligation to what is before us, Nassar maintains, provides an important first step in that direction.

NOTES

1. Schlegel writes that "the encyclopedia must be constructed out of a synthesis of the science of knowledge [*Wissenschaft*] and the science of art [*Kunstlehre*]" (KA 18, 374, no. 652). Novalis describes the encyclopedia as "the book of all books" and as "producing a living *scientific organon*" (NS 3, 558, no. 21; NS 4, 263).

2. Two recent articles enumerate this (to many, surprising) course of events. See Elizabeth Millán-Zaibert, "The Revival of Frühromantik in the Anglophone World," and more recently Peter Thielke, "Recent Work on Early German Idealism 1781–1801." Although Thielke's article looks at new work on German idealism, he devotes several pages to detailing the rise of interest in romanticism within the Anglophone context and recognizes that many of the English-language works on so-called idealism (such as Frederick Beiser's *German Idealism*, and Paul Redding's *Continental Idealism*) contain a number of chapters on the romantics. As we shall see, within the Anglophone context in particular, the term "romantic" describes a much wider phenomenon than the German *Frühromantik*, which specifically denotes the circle around the Schlegel brothers and their journal, the *Athenäum*. The fact that the word "romantic" remains contested is elegantly demonstrated by Frank and Beiser's debate in Chapters 1 and 2 of this volume.

3. The reasons why the romantics have been long overlooked by philosophers have been elaborated at length by Beiser, "Introduction: Romanticism Now and Then," in *The Romantic Imperative*, 1–5.

4. See Robert Richards, *The Romantic Conception of Life* (2002) for views of science and nature; Richard Eldridge, *Leading a Human Life* (1997) and *The Persistence of Romanticism* (2011), on the significance of romantic thought for epistemology; Michael Forster, *German Philosophy of Language* (2011) and Kristin Gjesdal, *Gadamer and the Legacy of Idealism* (2009), for hermeneutics; Paolo Diego Bubbio and Paul Redding, ed., *Religion after Kant* (2012) and John H. Smith, *Dialogues between Faith and Reason* (2011) on romantic religion; Jane Kneller, *Kant and the Power of Imagination* (2007) on theories of imagination and their significance for social thought.

5. The meaning of "romantic" has long been contested. Arthur Lovejoy was one of the first to challenge the notion that the word represents a specific movement: "the word 'romantic' has come to mean so many things that, by itself, it means nothing" (Arthur Lovejoy, "On the Discrimination of Romanticism," in *Essays in the History of Ideas*, 235). Beiser offers an account of the various responses to Lovejoy, and also his own response in "The Meaning of 'Romantic Poetry,'" in *The Romantic Imperative*, 6–22. For the variety of meanings of the word in the German context

(and its various historical sources), see Hans Eichner, "Germany / Romantisch— Romantik—Romantiker," in *'Romantic' and its Cognates*.

6. Philippe Lacoue-Labarthe and Jean-Luc Nancy claim that the "romantic period" can only be identified by a place—Jena—and a journal—the *Athenäum* (*The Literary Absolute*, 12). Although Frank does not explicitly identify romanticism with Jena and the late 1790s, he excludes Schleiermacher (who was in Berlin) and Hölderlin (in Tübingen) from his major examinations of romanticism, *Einführung in die frühromantische Ästhetik* and *Unendliche Annäherung*. However, as he argues in Chapter 1 of this volume, *Frühromantik* encompasses a large number of (lesser known) figures, and should be grasped in terms of its questions and concerns, rather than in terms of its location.

7. Schelling's place in romanticism is a topic of debate. Beiser, for instance, includes him in his *German Idealism*, but in so doing considers the romantics to be idealists. See his Chapter in this volume on the relation between romanticism and idealism. For Schelling's place in *both* romanticism and idealism, see Dalia Nassar, *The Romantic Absolute*. Schleiermacher is another figure that ambiguously fits into the group, as he was a close friend of F. Schlegel's while the latter was in Berlin, but did not live in Jena or contribute regularly to the *Athenäum*. On Schleiermacher's romanticism, see John H. Smith, "Living Religion as Vanishing Mediator: Schleiermacher, Early Romanticism, and Idealism."

8. Goethe did, however, have editorial input on the journal. See Nicholas Boyle, *Goethe, the Poet and the Age*, vol. 2, 646ff. In the German context, the time period which in English is often described as "romantic" is identified as the *Goethezeit*, the time of Goethe. This more inclusive term might be a better translation of the Anglophone use of *romantic* than *Frühromantik*, which is much more limited. For recent investigations into Goethe's philosophical contributions and his relationship to romanticism and idealism, see the special edition of the *Goethe Yearbook* (vol. 18; 2011), co-edited by Elizabeth Millán and John H. Smith, *Goethe and German Idealism*, and Nassar, *The Romantic Absolute*. Finally, Herder has also received more attention in the context of romanticism in the Anglophone context. See Michael Forster, *After Herder* and *German Philosophy of Language*, and Amanda Jo Goldstein's contribution to this volume, Chapter 15.

9. It is important to keep in mind that those usually associated with romanticism (Friedrich Schlegel and Novalis) never identified themselves as romantics, but rather used the verb "to romanticize" (*romantisiren*) to describe a way of seeing the world. Thus, Novalis famously writes "the world must be romanticized" adding that "romanticizing [*romantisiren*] is nothing more than a qualitative involution. In this operation the lower self is identified with a better self... When I give the commonplace a higher meaning, the customary a mysterious appearance, the known the dignity of the unknown, the finite the appearance of the infinite, I romanticize it" (NS 2, 545, no. 105). And in his famous fragment in the *Athenäums-Fragmente*, Schlegel speaks of romantic poetry as "universal progressive poetry" (KA 2, 182, no. 116). The meaning of romanticism, then, should not be determined by a place or a time period (for, importantly, even Novalis was not in Jena at the time), but by particular philosophical questions and concerns. Thus, this volume in part aims to

rethink romanticism in terms of questions and concerns, rather than in terms of a specific time and place.

10. See Frank, *Das individuelle Allgemeine; Das Sagbare und das Unsagbare; Selbstgefühl: eine historisch-theoretische Erkundung.* Beiser's interests, although primarily historical, nonetheless affirm the relevance of romanticism. See especially, "Introduction: Romanticism Now and Then," in *Romantic Imperative*, 1–5.

11. Beiser, *The Romantic Imperative*, 3–4.

PART ONE

German Romanticism as a
Philosophical Movement

1

What Is Early German Romantic Philosophy?

MANFRED FRANK

1.1. THE REALIZATION OF "CONSTELLATION RESEARCH"

According to a general belief, it is a fundamental trait of modern philosophy to have conceived of itself as grounded in the certitude of self-consciousness. Pioneered and launched by Descartes, multifariously diversified by Leibniz, this thinking, after an empiricist intermezzo, is said to have achieved its highest manifestation in Kant and, even more so, in Fichte's philosophy, since in it subjectivity finally becomes the principle of a deductively unfolding system of knowledge, whose elements receive their peculiar objective justification by virtue of their derivability from the Self.

Following in Heidegger's footsteps, several thinkers working within the spectrum of what has been called "poststructuralism" or "postmodernism" have put forth the view that subjectivity's absolute seizure of power (*Machtergreifung*) is the peak of the occidental forgetting of Being or *différance*. Because perennial prejudice stylizes Fichte as the developmental climax of subjectivistic dazzlement, and because we are accustomed to reconstructing early romanticism in Jena as dependent on Fichte, it has become common practice to label leading philosophical figures such as Friedrich von Hardenberg (Novalis) and Friedrich Schlegel as developing a kind of "subject philosophy." This might explain why in the context of feuilletonistic writings one often finds catchwords like "early romantic subjectivism" and "occasionalism," or even references to the "arbitrariness of romantic theory."

These descriptions are, however, deeply problematic and even nonsensical. Following the research undertaken by Dieter Henrich and his students, we can afford to boldly turn our backs on these misunderstandings and misconceptions of romanticism. By extensively combing through new textual sources from the period between 1789 and 1796 in Tübingen and Jena and using the method of *Konstellationsforschung*, their research has shed surprising new light on the philosophy of early romanticism.

What do the dates 1789 and 1796 refer to? They demarcate a space of thought (*"Denkraum"*) that *Konstellationsforschung* has been studying in detail with hitherto unknown precision and thoroughness. The beginning of this epoch is marked at one end by Reinhold's *Essay towards a New Theory of the Human Faculty of Representation* (*Versuch einer neuen Theorie des menschlichen Vorstellungsvermögens*) and by the second (and considerably reworked) edition of Jacobi's *Letters on Spinoza's Doctrine (Briefe über die Lehre Spinozas)*. At the other end, the years 1795/96 mark the time in which Hölderlin developed his important sketch "Judgment and Being" (*Urtheil und Seyn*), Novalis completed his "Fichte Studies" (*Fichte-Studien*), and Friedrich Schlegel began his "Philosophical Apprenticeship" (*Philosophische Lehrjahre*). These various writings considered Fichte's approach in the "Science of Knowledge" (*Wissenschaftslehre*) to have been superseded. The intervening years between 1789 and 1795/96 were molded by long disputes with the legacy of orthodox theology, by Kant's revolutionary spark in Tübingen, by Reinhold's attempts to systemize Kantian philosophy, and by the first emergence of doubt in Jena and Klagenfurt concerning the feasibility of a philosophy that pretends to derive and develop its whole content from and out of a single first principle. This type of philosophical project was introduced by Reinhold's "Elementary Philosophy" (*Elementarphilosophie*) and by Fichte, who soon joined him and adopted the programmatic label.

In 1794, when Fichte first presented himself in Jena as Reinhold's successor, he was initially "enthusiastically" acclaimed as a "Titan"—as Hegel reports to Schelling at the beginning of 1795.[1] Fichte seemed eager to celebrate before his audience all the refinements of the project of the Elementary Philosophy he had elaborated. He was not aware of all the nagging questions that Reinhold's pupils, such as Novalis, had been focused on since 1791— questions that challenged the usefulness and sense of such an undertaking. In fact, by the time of Fichte's arrival, the debate was deemed to be passé and superseded in those circles. Nonetheless, Fichte's arrival in Jena and the presence of many of Reinhold's pupils among his audience managed to spark new interest in the debate. For instance, Niethammer (who was Hölderlin's cousin, a fellow student of Novalis's in 1790–1791, and later Friedrich Schlegel's mentor in Jena), talked about the "dispensability of a highest and single principle of all knowledge."[2] In fact, it was the patron and Maecenas of the Reinhold circle, Franz Paul von Herbert (1759–1811) from Klagenfurt, who, by a remark of his own, had stimulated Niethammer to express himself in such a way. Herbert writes,

> From now on I declare myself an irreconcilable enemy of all so-called first principles of philosophy, and he who thinks he needs such a principle, I declare to be a fool, who deduces and syllogizes everything from these principles whenever he suffers from paroxysmal attacks... How much is lost for philosophy only because of a stupid envy of Kant's fame; look at Kant's first principle in the *Critique of Reason*; and if this does not seem sufficient to you, there is no remedy.[3]

Von Herbert left space at the end of the letter, in order to invite Johann Benjamin Erhard (1766–1826), the leading intellectual figure of the Reinhold circle, to add some personal remarks. A few years later, in 1797, Novalis described Erhard as "the only true friend" of the Reinhold circle (NS 4, 202). Erhard agrees with Herbert's portrait of the situation and specifies the shared anti-Fichtean conviction it expresses:

> From one point of view Herbert's position regarding the *one* principle is justified. A philosophy that starts out with one principle and pretends to deduce everything from it will always be nothing more than a piece of sophistry; only that philosophy which is capable of climbing to the highest principle and manages to show how everything stands in harmony with that principle without being deduced from it, only that philosophy is the true one.[4]

It is not difficult to see how in this letter Erhard already starts the move, motivated by the sterility of Elementary Philosophy, that will lead him to a reaffiliation with the Kantian theory of ideas and the systematic use of teleological principles embedded within it.

As a lawyer and liberal enemy of Fichte, another one of Reinhold's pupils, Paul Johann Anselm Feuerbach (the father of the famous philosopher Ludwig Feuerbach and a fellow lodger with Friedrich Schlegel), spoke of the "impossibility of a first absolute philosophical principle."[5] Friedrich Carl Forberg, another former pupil of Reinhold's and a dear friend of Novalis's, who later became the catalyst and then, alongside Fichte, the victim of the Atheism Controversy in 1798, similarly proclaimed the impossibility of philosophical foundations.[6] Both Novalis's "Fichte Studies" and Feuerbach's text were most likely requested by Niethammer as contributions to his journal, to which Schlegel also contributed.[7] It was essential for the newly founded *Philosophical Journal (Philosophisches Journal)* to serve as a forum for discussing the legitimacy or futility of a philosophy starting from a first principle.

Consequently, subsuming early German romanticism under the project title of a so-called "Philosophy of the Subject" is inaccurate for a number of reasons. This has become clear, however, only after a series of groundbreaking investigations and archival findings in the 1960s and 1970s, which include the publication of Hölderlin's "Judgment and Being" in 1961, the publication of parts of Schlegel's "Philosophical Apprenticeship" in 1963 and 1971, and, finally, the first complete and critical publication of Novalis' "Fichte Studies" in 1965.[8] Scholars working on Hölderlin, Schlegel, and especially Hegel, were unaware of these texts or of the letters commenting on them. Again, Dieter Henrich and his students were the first to realize the importance of these editions and findings. Thus it became clear that although subjectivity remained a significant topic for the early romantics, this was only as a result of the critique of Elementary Philosophy, which led Fichte's students to deny the status of absoluteness to subjectivity. Instead, they considered subjectivity to be a derivative phenomenon that only becomes accessible to itself under a condition or presupposition (*Bedingung, Voraussetzung*), which is beyond its (subjectivity's) control. In turn, the elusiveness (*Unverfügbarkeit*) of this condition can only be clarified through the structure of self-consciousness. By choosing this path of reflection, early romanticism swiftly departed from a type of speculation that the history of ideas associates with the names of Fichte, Schelling, and Hegel and is usually cataloged under the lemma "German idealism."

Before I go on to elaborate on the highly opaque concepts and problematic issues mentioned in this introduction, I should say something concerning the viable strategies for developing a theory that conceives of subjectivity as being derived from a transcendent ground. A first strategy (section 1.2) consists in clarifying the relation of dependence, which above all means specifying the object of that dependency. Additionally, there is a second strategy that draws Kantian consequences from the irrepresentability of the Absolute and redefines striving after the infinite as an endless striving. (In the above passage quoted from the letter by Erhard, we could already get a glimpse of that strategy.) I will pursue this strategy in section 1.3. According to this second strategy, the Absolute is transformed into an idea in the Kantian sense of the term. In what follows I will show that Novalis and Friedrich Schlegel were quickly driven from the first to the second consequence. But to begin with, I will consider the first consequence.

1.2. IDENTITY AND EXISTENCE PRECEDE REFLECTION

I have already mentioned the conception of a transcendent presupposition of self-consciousness, which, as transcendent, undermines its ability to ground a deduction. The term "transcendent" in this context means that the subject merely presupposes this condition without having it at its epistemic disposal. In 1795 Hölderlin and Novalis refer to this presupposition (independently yet almost indistinctly) as "Being" or "absolute identity." But what is the link between the two terms "Being" and "identity"?

With respect to the latter: in the play of appearance and reflection, self-consciousness manifests an identity that it cannot represent as such. In Novalis's words: the bipartite *form* of judgment denies the monadic *content*. The nominalized reflexive pronoun "self" stands for this detour or indirect representation: "We abandon the *identical*," writes Novalis in September 1795, "in order to represent it" (NS 2, 104, no. 1). Hence self-consciousness is the representation of something that is in itself nonpresentable. He writes,

> In order to render *a* clearer [*a* being the constant of identity], A is divided. *It* is posited as general content, *a* as determinate form. The essence of identity can only be presented in an illusory proposition [*Scheinsatz*]. (NS 2, 104, no. 1)

In order to be clear on the necessity of this obstructive detour, it is helpful to note that what we usually refer to as self-consciousness is the result of a *return of* consciousness to itself. Philosophical terminology has coined the word "reflection" for this particular kind of returning or turning back onto one's self. Two things are implied here: first, it implies what Hölderlin in *"Judgment and Being"* calls the "primordial division" of something that is essentially united, namely, the subject and the object, into two relata. Second, this immediately leads us to the question of how it is possible to learn from the duality of reflecting and reflected the fact that, originally, the self was *one* (although it seems impossible to doubt that this unity is a characteristic trait of my conscious life). "The I is one and at the same time divided," observes Novalis (NS 2, 136, no. 32). And in his private lectures delivered in Cologne in 1804, Friedrich Schlegel remarks, "this is the actual contradiction in our I, that at the same time we feel ourselves to be finite and infinite" (KA 12, 334).

In the expression *reflection* there is another layer of meaning which was already prefigured in Novalis's notion of an "illusory proposition." Even if consciousness emerges only through reflection, it is only a perverted and apparent one. The reason for this view becomes clear when we take into account the fact that Novalis thinks of consciousness as an "image" or "sign" of "Being" that transforms Being into appearance. Indeed, another meaning of "reflection" is an inverted mirroring (*verkehrende Spiegelung*). Our original consciousness—Novalis speaks of a "self-feeling" or "sense of self"—stands in an inverted position to reality. It is inverted because by reaching from out of itself, consciousness encounters the world *secundo loco*, as something secondary. "Our theory has to proceed from the *conditioned*," Novalis writes, and not, as is the case with Fichte's philosophy, from the unconditioned (NS 2, 147, no. 86). That which depends on Being, namely, consciousness, is not itself that of which it is conscious (namely Being), but only copies or "represents" it through a "sign" (NS 2, 106). Nonetheless, consciousness detects in itself the means by which to correct this inversion by a second inversion (*"ordine inverso"*) (NS 2, 127f., 131ff.). "There is always an alteration between image and Being. The image is always the inversion of Being. What is located to the right of the person appears in the image on the left" (NS 142, no. 63; cf. 114ff.). The reflected mirror image or the self-reflection restores the original order, so that the I becomes conscious of its ontological dependence on Being.[9] Fichte, according to Novalis, did not perform this self-reflection and consequently, in a Berkeleyean vein, conceived Being as something dependent on a thematizing consciousness or rather as some kind of inert condensation of an antecedent act. Consequently, for the idealist, Being is neither understood as something positive nor as a Kantian "absolute position," but rather as a *"negative* concept" that only demarcates itself against the truly positive concept of conscious action (GA 1/1, 498f.). But Novalis did not want to be an idealist.

Let me return to the first meaning of "reflection," as it is present in Hölderlin's thesis of judgment as primordial division. The first person to analyze the problem in this way was Reinhold, who was Hölderlin's teacher in 1790–1791 and with whose Elementary Philosophy Hölderlin was acquainted (by reading Reinhold's work and through reports from Niethammer). Through Niethammer, Schlegel—who had been a follower of Fichte—also became familiar with the objections raised by Reinhold's pupils. In Jena, Schlegel immersed himself in the intellectual culture, assimilated the criticisms of a philosophy based on a first principle developed and radically revised his views.

In his *Attempt at a New Theory of the Human Faculty of Representation*, Reinhold asked how we can conceive of "the *identity* of the object of consciousness with the subject," if subject and object are determined by completely different conditions of cognizability?[10] It might be the case that representation in self-consciousness is de facto identical with the represented. But from the objective presentation of one relatum *only*, its identity with the other relatum is not yet *intelligible*. Hölderlin, with insurmountable conceptual precision, gets to the heart of the matter in April 1795:

How is self-consciousness possible? By opposing me to myself, through self-separation, and, regardless of this separation, nonetheless perceiving myself *as* the *same* in the opposed. (HFA 17, 156; emphasis added)

The implicit reference to Reinhold should not be overlooked. Reinhold was the first to illustrate that self-consciousness does not merely consist in the presentation of a self, posited as object, but also consists in a presentation of the self *as* self. The term *as* must be employed if self-consciousness is to be explained. One might have consciousness of her- or himself without, however, knowing that it is *herself* of whom she is conscious. (I might be ignoring a mirror or mistaking myself for someone else.) Indeed, it would be completely pointless to expect the instruction that *I* am this alien thing, from a stranger or somebody identified as a stranger. However, as soon as I recognize the alien thing *as me*, this cognition of the self as object—in Novalis's words—must occur and be certified through a nonobjective self-feeling—or a "sense of self" (NS 2, 113, no. 15).

But what is a self-feeling? The insight that Novalis achieves in a few steps leads from the presupposition of an absolute identity to the presupposition of *Being*, and, in so doing, to a second concept, whose meaning we have yet to clarify. Hölderlin and Novalis are directly referring to Jacobi, and indirectly referring to Kant and his famous thesis on Being.

Kant first presented this thesis in his early text *The Only Possible Argument in Support of a Demonstration of the Existence of God* (1763). The indeterminate verb "being" has a "completely simple" meaning, namely, position ("*Position*") (AA 2, 73; see also 70). Kant's thesis resounds in Hölderlin's discussion of "Being, in the only sense of the word."[11] Position is nearly the name of the genus or class "Being," which is—Kant maintains—conceptually almost irresolvable or unanalyzable ("unauflöslich") (AA 2, 73). *Almost* unanalyzable because there is nonetheless a double specification we can wrench from it, which distinguishes relative and absolute positing. The relative position of a concept is one that poses a general term in relation to a subject. This is the case in usual predicative sentences. A concept is posited absolutely, by contrast, when something general corresponds to it, and when the concept's class of reference is not empty, as in the following nonpredicative sentences: "There is a God" or "I am." Strictly speaking, the meaning of "Being" (qua existence) is restricted to the meaning of the absolute position.

But how are Being and predication connected? What makes them conceivable as varieties of position or positing? The synthesis in judgment (the "relative position") must be grasped as an inferior type of what Kant calls "absolute position." This seems to be exactly what Hölderlin envisioned as he jotted down the following in the spring of 1795:

Being—expresses the union of subject and object... Judgment. is... that kind of separation by which object and subject become possible, the primordial division [Seyn—drükt die Verbindung des Subjects und Objects aus....

Urtheil. ist… diejenige Trennung, wodurch Object und Subject möglich wird, die Ur-theilung]. (HFA 17, 156, 19–22)

In exactly the same way, Novalis conceives of the manner in which existential Being—embedded in the form of a judgment—mediates itself to consciousness, as Pseudo-Being, or, as he drastically puts it, as "improper Being," adding that "improper Being [*unrechtes Seyn*] is an image of Being" (NS 2, 106, no. 2). In the language of Kant: the relative position, which is constitutive for consciousness, displays the absolute position in the form of judgment.

One might have noticed that Hölderlin and Novalis articulate the primordial division in both semantic and epistemological terminology; they use "subject" and "predicate" as well as "subject" of consciousness and its "object" in parallel to "predicate" which is singular. This has to be seen in light of the fact that this generation (unlike Kant) interprets the predicative "is" as an indication of identity. In so doing they follow the Leibnizean thesis that all true judgments consist in an analysis of what is comprehended in the subject term: "*praedicatum inest subjecto.*" Moreover, the group operating in Tübingen was influenced by the view, espoused by the logician and metaphysician Gottfried Ploucquet, that predication is a statement of identity. Ploucquet's writings were canonical in the Tübingen Seminary and for a long time served as the basis for the theses and dissertations produced there.[12] If we want to bring this view (of predication as identity) to some kind of convergence with the Kantian one, then predication simply consists in a relative identification, while Being is an absolute identification. By superimposing Kant's famous thesis on Being and the conception of predication as a statement of identity, a distinctive view emerges—one that was shared by both Hölderlin and Novalis, and incidentally also by Schelling—namely, the notion of the essence of absolute identity as enclosing a ground that repels all consciousness. Being, the late Schelling will say, is prior to thought ("unvordenklich"). In other words, there is no thought—no real predicate—that can be inserted or presupposed in order to function as a ground for deducing or grasping existence (SW 2/3, 227f., see also 262).

Now that the nexus between Being and identity has become clearer, we can take the next step and ask: how can Being refer to a specific feeling, as Novalis maintains? Again, the decisive inspiration stems directly from Jacobi, and indirectly from Kant. It was Jacobi who, with the term "feeling," moved the focus to an expression that is closely connected to the semantic domain of sensations and the a posteriori given. Jacobi explains that it was the French language that suggested to him "the expression, le sentiment de l'être"[13]—an expression that he deems to be "purer and better" than the German "Bewußtsein" (consciousness). Following a widespread tradition (of empirical psychology of the late eighteenth century), Jacobi also speaks of the "sentiment de soi-même," literally, the "feeling [or sentiment] of one's self."[14] Sentiment of Being and self-feeling are two faces of the same coin. "*Sum*," "I am," and not "*cogito*" or "I think," was the name of the first cognition, Jacobi claims.[15] Thus the primordial experience of the self is an experience of Being, or rather an experience of actuality "that immediately displays itself in consciousness and verifies itself through the deed."[16] The mode of this kind of consciousness is feeling: "Even of our own existence we only have a feeling; but no conception."[17] A conception would be a "real predicate." However, existence is not grasped with concepts, it is felt.

1.3. REINTERPRETING THE "HIGHEST POINT OF PHILOSOPHY" AS A "KANTIAN IDEA"

I will now turn to the second consequence of the early romantic approach. Its unfolding redirects us once more to Jena in the years prior to Fichte's appearance and leads us into the lively debates of Reinhold's pupils. It gravitates around the idea that Being or absolute identity was not even the passively acquired content of a sentiment or, as Hölderlin says, "of intellectual intuition" (HFA 17, 156). Rather, they are thought to be unreachable targets, or even rational projections, much like an idea in the Kantian sense. Such an idea can only be infinitely approximated, without ever being achieved. We saw that this goes hand in hand with a deeply rooted skepticism in the face of first principles, which Fichte's "I" or Reinhold's "fundament" claimed to be. This skepticism is quite deep in the cases of Novalis and Schlegel. In the second part of his "Fichte Studies," Novalis describes concepts that guarantee the unity of the system of beliefs and its justification as "necessary fictions" (NS 2, 179). Unlike a feeling, a fiction is not something found (*Findung*), but something created (Er*findung*).

> The highest principle must not at all be something given, but something freely produced, something *fabricated* [Erdichtetes], *devised* [Erdachtes], in order to lay down the foundations for a general metaphysics. (NS 2, 273)

This not only offers a strong response to the foundationalist context of absolute idealism, but also illustrates the will to radically break with a philosophy based on first principles and demonstrates an unexpected high regard for poetry.

But let us proceed step by step. The early romantic definition of philosophy as "yearning for infinity" emphasizes the nonpossession, the lack, of a principle.[18] If there is no safe foundation that presents itself to our consciousness as evident, then it is possible to doubt each of our beliefs: "the clinging, the being glued to the finite," maintains Schlegel, "is the true character of dogmatism" (KA 12, 51). So-called romantic irony allows for that; it is not a particular feature of the content, but a trait of the style of speech. Something is uttered ironically when the *way* of saying it neutralizes the determinateness of the content, brings it into suspense, or sets in motion a withdrawal from it in favor of an infinity of options that might as well have been uttered in its place. Ironic speech keeps open the irrepresentable location of the infinite by permanently discrediting the finite as that which is not intended.

One of the deep convictions of the young intellectuals, who were later called the Jena romantics, was that beliefs cannot be ultimately justified, but—as Schlegel ironically puts it—"are eternally valid only for the time being" (KA 2, 179, no. 95).[19] Like Reinhold's students, the Jena romantics dismissed epistemological foundationalism as the Scylla, without throwing themselves into the arms of the Charybdis of skepticism, or "intellectual anarchism" as they also called it (NS 2, 288–89, no. 648).[20] At the beginning of July 1796, during a visit with his former fellow student Forberg,[21] Novalis again takes up the question that marks the beginning of his "Fichte Studies."[22] He writes, "What do I do when I philosophize? I reflect on a ground... All philosophizing must result in such an absolute ground" (NS 2, 269, no. 366).

Why must philosophizing result in an *absolute* ground? Because a relative ground would place itself within a chain of further grounds, which would not lead to a final link (or ground). But it is precisely this which seems to happen, and which leads Novalis to pose the following question:

> What would it be like if this absolute, all-embracing ground were not given, if this concept contained an impossibility: the drive to philosophize would be an infinite activity—and therefore without end, because an eternal need for an absolute ground would exist, which can only be partially sated—and therefore would never cease. (NS 2, 269, no. 366)

The problem of infinite regress was brought up by Jacobi in the seventh supplement to the expanded second edition of his book on Spinoza: if we go on to describe knowledge as justified belief, as has been the case in a time-honored (and still lively) tradition, then, he explains, we fall into an infinite regress.[23] We base our knowledge claims on propositions, which express knowledge only under the condition that they are themselves justified by other propositions that express knowledge and so on. This regress could only be terminated by a proposition whose validity is *un*conditioned. "Unconditioned" thus means not depending on a higher condition. The validity of an unconditioned proposition ought to be clear without further elucidation: "neither in need nor capable of further justification."[24] This proposition must thus be (self-)evident, since "(self-)evident" literally means that which is clear in and through itself.

With an unconditioned transformed from a possession of knowledge into a regulative idea that can only be infinitely approximated, Reinhold's "consulship of the ground-seeker," now inherited from Fichte, loses its stabilizing function (KA 18, 19, no. 5; KA 2, 155, no. 66). First of all, Reinhold's students contested the possibility of basing a system of beliefs on an evident cognition, since cognitions of that kind, they argued are private experiences of consciousness. By invoking them it should remain impossible to give an explanation of the formation of an intersubjective consensus. The formation of such a consensus is a criterion of what we call knowledge. Furthermore, a more accurate analysis shows that evident cognitions are hard to distinguish from the claims of common sense.[25] The latter must also be grounded in so-called intuitions, that is, we must believe in them. Propositions of belief have a character similar to that of Euclidean axioms (an axiom literally means "something believed"). Were it possible to demonstrate them, they would suddenly lose their status as ultimate principles, since a proposition that is justified by another cannot be ultimate. The justification of knowledge thus becomes an article of faith. Novalis thus states that "it is a product of imagination in which we *believe*, and which, according to its and our own nature, we will never be able to cognize" (NS 2, 273, no. 568). But the most serious and far-reaching objection turned out to be the third one: Reinhold's highest principle is not as independent as it claims to be. Rather it presupposes other propositions to justify it, ones that allegedly ought to be deduced from it. This criticism was most strongly established by Reinhold's colleague in Jena, Carl Christian Erhard Schmid, and by the former repentant at the Tübingen Seminary Carl Immanuel Diez, who later studied medicine in Jena.[26]

Should this critique be legitimate, it would have disastrous consequences for Elementary Philosophy. Indeed, as a result of it, Reinhold soon felt compelled to revise his position.[27] Furthermore, Novalis's fundamental critique is only comprehensible in light of his familiarity with the critics of first principles in Reinhold's circle and in light of his proximity to the views of his former tutor, Schmid.[28]

I shall forgo the details of this claim and only anticipate the conclusion at which Novalis arrives. Searching for an ultimate concept from which all the others can be derived, he claims, is "nonsense" and leads us into the "areas of nonsense." "Representation" (*Vorstellung*) is the highest mental concept (i.e., concept concerning mental entities). However, it is—just like all other concepts—achieved through comparison between and abstraction from singular mental acts and experiences. This means that if it is derived from these mental operations, it cannot be their source. In other words, the pretension of foundational philosophy is based on a circular argument: what is purportedly derived from the highest principle is in fact already presupposed by it.

I hope that my sketch—in spite of its gaps—has been successful in showing the objection that induced Reinhold in the early spring of 1792 to remodel his system, the only difference being that Novalis does not use this argument against Reinhold, but against Fichte. In so doing, he can once again refer to his old teacher Schmid, who criticized a technical mistake in deductions proceeding from the I: a logical deduction typically proceeds from a universal major premise to a singular minor premise, which is logically independent of the major premise.[29] Yet Reinhold's "principle of consciousness"—exactly like Descartes's or Kant's "I think" or Fichte's "I am"—does not state something general, but a singular fact. In order to produce the consequences presumed by the followers of First Principle Philosophy, the logical support of a major premise was needed, which, however, could only have been discovered inferentially (which proposition could do the job?). In short, Fichte's derivations display only the characteristics of a *hypothetico*-deductive procedure, in the same vein as Kant's derivation of the regulative ideas of reason or Popper's essentially fallible derivations. As Schmid puts it, "but that which is accepted only as a hypothesis [and not—as asserted—as immediate *evidence*] cannot in this respect lay claim to universality, because there is freedom of choice concerning the question, whether this, that, or no hypothesis at all is required to explain the indubitable fact."[30] Finally, the set of premises from which an explicandum follows according to one or several general rules is unlimited. In other words, the set of premises is not sufficiently determined by the existence of this concrete explicandum.

1.4. ROMANTIC REALISM

The undesirability of the first consequence was vividly exemplified to these independent thinkers by Fichte's foundation of his idealism on an "I" that was boosted into something absolute. However attractive this solution might have appeared, it yielded several problems, just like the dualisms at the root of Kantian philosophy. In turn, however irresistible the solution of absolute idealism might have appeared in the face of the systematic burdens inherited from Kant, the early romantics deemed this way unviable and looked for loopholes out of the idealistic fly bottle.

In light of the comfortable Fichtean liquidation of the external world and the thing-in-itself, which Forberg had witnessed in Jena, he wrote in his *Fragments from my Papers* that in the presence of Fichte he had "not felt differently than in the company of a conjurer," adding that he only begs God to save Kant from his self-declared friends, since "as far as his enemies are concerned he probably will be aware of them personally."[31] Like many of Reinhold's pupils, Forberg stuck to the motto: Better to fail with Kant, than to win with Fichte.

Did Kant not emphasize with all the desirable clarity that, according to his theory, "representation in itself does not produce its object in so far as *existence is concerned*," but ought to receive it from the world (*KrV* A125)? Novalis simply offers a twist to this when he writes, "consciousness is a Being outside of Being within Being." He continues:

> Being outside Being must not be proper Being [*kein rechtes Sein*].
> An improper Being outside Being is an image—Hence Being outside
> Being must be an image of Being inside Being.
> Consequently consciousness is an image of Being within Being. (NS 2, 106, no. 2)

Images are representing entities. As such they are ontically dependent on whatever they represent: as a representing entity the image is dependent on the represented: "wherever there is cognizing—there also is Being" (NS 2, 402). But the opposite does not hold. In contrast to Fichte, and in agreement with Kant, Novalis professes an ontological realism. Such a realism is perfectly compatible with the view that the unity of being and consciousness is the transcendent presupposition of our self-consciousness, an unachievable idea of reason in the Kantian sense. Such an idea, according to Novalis, can only be realized aesthetically:

> We *strive* everywhere for the unconditioned, but always *find* just conditions. (NS 2, 412, no. 1)
> The attainment of the unattainable is, according to its character, inconceivable. (NS 3, 413, no. 745)
> When the character of a given problem consists in the impossibility of solving it, we will solve it by representing its insolubility as such. (NS 3, 376, no. 612)
> The sense for poetry...presents the nonpresentable. . (NS 3, 685, no. 671)
> The highest-ranking works of art are absolutely *unobliging*. They are ideals that can—and *should*—please us only approximately: aesthetic imperatives. (NS 3, 413, no. 745)

Around the time that Novalis was jotting down his thoughts about infinity, or rather about the impossibility of philosophy as a search for knowledge, he received a visit from Forberg in Jena, who, as Novalis remembers, "after a longer interruption of our friendship showed...a heart full of tenderness toward me" (NS 4, 187). As previously mentioned, Forberg had studied with Novalis under Reinhold. Apparently Forberg was so taken by Novalis's views, quoted above, that a year later, in his *Letters on the Newest Philosophy*, he wrote:

> Thus it will be something like an ultimate therefore [Darum] or ground that I will have to look for, in order to meet the demand of my reason.
>
> But what if such an ultimate ground were impossible to find... ?
>
> Nothing else would follow than this: that the demand of reason could never be completely met—that reason would have to continue its investigations into the infinite, without bringing them to an end even into eternity. The absolute thus would be nothing more than the idea of an impossibility.
>
> But: is a goal that is unattainable less of a goal? Is the view towards the sky less enchanting, only because once and forever it remains a VIEW?[32]

NOTES

1. Manfred Frank and Gerhard Kurz, eds., *Materialien zu Schellings philosophischen Anfängen* (Frankfurt am Main: Suhrkamp, 1975), 122.

2. Niethammer to von Herbert (June 2, 1794). *Friedrich Immanuel Niethammer: Korrespondenz mit dem Herbert- und Erhard-Kreis*, ed. Wilhelm Baum (Vienna: Turia + Kant, 1995), 86.

3. Ibid., 75f. The letter from von Herbert to Niethammer is dated May 6, 1794.

4. Ibid., 79.

5. This is the title of his 1795 essay, which appeared in the *Philosophisches Journal* 2, no. 2 (1795): 306–22.

6. See Mähl's comment in NS 2, 32f.

7. See Niethammer's preface to the first edition of the *Philosophisches Journal*.

8. Hölderlin's "Urtheil und Seyn" ("Judgment and Being") appeared in HSW 4, 226–7. Schlegel's "Philosophische Lehrjahre" ("Philosophical Apprenticeship") appeared in KA 18. Novalis's "Fichte-Studien" ("Fichte Studies") is in NS 2, 104–296.

9. See also Schelling for a similar conception: SW I/4, 85ff.; SW I/9, 230ff.

10. Reinhold, *Versuch einer neuen Theorie des menschlichen Vorstellungsvermögens* (Prague and Jena: C. Widtmann & J. M. Mauke, 1789), 335; Reinhold, *Beyträge zur Berichtigung bisheriger Mißverständnisse der Philosophen, Erster Band, das Fundament der Elementarphilosophie betreffend* (Jena: Michael Mauke, 1790), 181f., 197, 222.

11. Friedrich Hölderlin, *Vorstufen zum Hyperion*, in *Sämmtliche Werke, Kritische Textausgabe*, ed. D. E. Sattler (Darmstadt: Luchterland, 1984), 163.

12. See Manfred Frank, *Auswege aus dem deutschen Idealismus* (Frankfurt am Main: Suhrkamp, 2007), 13–14; Gottfried Ploucquet, *Logik*, trans. and ed. Michael Franz (Hildesheim: Olms, 2006), xxxff.

13. Jacobi, *Ueber die Lehre des Spinoza in Briefen an Herrn Moses Mendelssohn*. Neue vermehrte Auflage (Breslau: Löwe, 1789), 193f. The new critical edition

reference is Friedrich Heinrich Jacobi, *Werke*, vols. 1/1 and 1/2, *Schriften zum Spinozastreit*, ed. Klaus Hammacher and Irmgard-Maria Piske (Hamburg and Stuttgart-Bad Cannstadt: Meiner and Frommann-Holzboog, 1989). The old pagination is provided in the margins of the new critical edition.

14. Jacobi, *Briefe* (1789), 109; cf. Manfred Frank, *Selbstgefühl. Eine historisch-systematische Erkundung* (Frankfurt am Main: Suhrkamp, 2002).

15. Jacobi, *Briefe* (1789), xxivf.; similarly NS 2, 268, no. 559.

16. Jacobi, *Briefe* (1789), xxxvif., no. xxix.

17. Ibid., 420, n.

18. See for instance KA 12, 7, 51; KA 18, 418, no. 1168; KA 18, 420, no. 1200.

19. This is an allusion to Niethammer's essay "Von den Ansprüchen des gemeinen Verstandes an die Philosophie," in *Philosophisches Journal* 1, no. 1 (1795): 1–45; here: 41ff.

20. See also Friedrich Schlegel: KA 18, 80, no. 614.

21. See NS 4, 187.

22. See NS 2, 113, no. 15.

23. Jacobi, *Briefe* (1789), 424ff., 430ff.

24. Ibid., 215.

25. Niethammer, "Von den Ansprüchen des gemeinen Verstandes an die Philosophie."

26. Schmid, *Empirische Psychologie* (Jena: Cröker, 1791), 57f.; cf. Dieter Henrich, *Grundlegung aus dem Ich. Untersuchungen zur Vorgeschichte des Idealismus Tübingen-Jena (1790–1794)* (Frankfurt am Main: Suhrkamp, 2004), 316; 600ff.; Immanuel Carl Diez, *Briefwechsel und Kantische Schriften. Wissensbegründung in der Glaubenskrise Tübingen-Jena (1790–1792)*, ed. Dieter Henrich (Stuttgart: Klett-Cotta, 1997), 912 (from a report from Reinhold to Erhard dated June 18, 1792).

27. Reinhold, *Allgemeine Literatur-Zeitung* no. 53 (May 1792): 425–27; Reinhold, "Ueber den Unterschied zwischen dem gesunden Verstande und der philosophierenden Vernunft in Rücksicht auf die Fundamente des durch beyde möglichen Wissens" (composed in summer 1792), in *Beyträge zur Berichtigung bisheriger Mißverständnisse der Philosophen, vol. 2, die Fundamente des philosophischen Wissens, der Metaphysik, Moral, moralischen Religion und Geschmackslehre betreffend* (Jena: Johann Michael Mauke, 1794); Henrich, *Grundlegung aus dem Ich*, 910ff.; ch. VI, esp. 230, 298ff.

28. Schmid, *Empirische Psychologie* I, 18f. (§ VI of the "Introduction").

29. Schmid, "Rezension von Reinholds *Fundament des philosophischen Wissens*," *Allgemeine Literatur-Zeitung* nos. 92 und 93 (April 1792): 49–60; here: 52f., 57ff.

30. Ibid., 59; cf. his argument against Fichte: Schmid, "Bruchstücke aus einer Schrift über die Philosophie und ihre Principien," *Philosophisches Journal So the Journal was quoted earlier and later.* 3, no. 2 (1795): 95–132; here: 101.

31. Forberg, *Fragmente aus meinen Papieren* (Jena: J. G. Voigt, 1796), 74, 42.

32. Forberg, "Briefe über die neueste Philosophie," in *Philosophisches Journal* 6, no. 1 (1797): 44–88; here: 66f.

2

Romanticism and Idealism

FREDERICK BEISER

2.1. THE QUESTION, A WINDMILL?

Whenever we think of the great German cultural revival of the late eighteenth and early nineteenth centuries, we are bound to have in mind two intellectual movements: romanticism and idealism. These movements are clearly fundamental for an understanding of German culture in this epoch, and so both have been studied in depth by generations of scholars. It is somewhat surprising to find, therefore, that the relationship between them has been so understudied. What they have in common, and how they differ, is still very obscure. They are indeed so obscure that some scholars have begun to dispute their proper relationship.

Two such scholars are myself and Manfred Frank. Over the years we have formed antithetical conceptions of the relationship between idealism and romanticism. In his *Unendliche Annäherung* Frank has seen the early romantic movement as fundamentally opposed to idealism.[1] He has stressed the opposition between these movements for two reasons: the romantics were realist in their ontology, and they were antifoundationalist in their epistemology, unlike the idealists, who were foundationalists. In my *German Idealism* and *Romantic Imperative* I have placed the early romantic movement within German idealism,[2] which Frank and others see as a terrible mistake because it seems to attribute Fichtean idealism and foundationalist concerns to the early romantics. Recently, Frank has declared our differences on this score in a prominent place,[3] and so it is imperative that I try to clarify the issues. The point of this article will be to do just that.

But before I go into details, it is necessary to clarify the main issue. Someone might object, quite understandably, that the quarrel between Frank and myself is a storm in a teacup, a mere dispute about words. Why not just declare with Humpty Dumpty that words mean what we want them to mean, so that Humpty (Beiser) gets to call romanticism one thing and Dumpty (Frank) gets to call it another? The relationship between romanticism and idealism is understudied and disputed, the objector will say, for the simple reason that the terms "romanticism" and "idealism" have no definite meaning. Since they have no precise meaning, there is no such thing as a fixed or definite relationship between romanticism and idealism. What relationships scholars find just depends on the meanings they give the terms. And so it seems the better half of prudence to regard the whole question as a purely verbal one, a trap for scholars unwary and naive. It was on just these grounds that, nearly a century ago, Arthur Lovejoy bid us to abandon the very concept of romanticism.[4] That concept had been given so many different, even opposing, definitions, Lovejoy complained, that it was better to talk about "romanticisms" in the plural than "romanticism" in the singular. Since idealism is in no better shape than romanticism, perhaps we should abandon that concept too, and so drop the whole question about its relationship with romanticism?

Such advice has its point, of course. There is a real danger that discussion of the relationship between romanticism and idealism gets bogged down in mere words. Some of the dispute between Frank and myself, I have to confess, is verbal, revolving around the different meanings of the term "idealism." Still, it is a mistake to think that the issue is *entirely* verbal, as if there were no substantive issues at stake. The fact of the matter is that the denotation or extension of the terms "idealism" and "romanticism," though not their connotation or intension, has been fairly well fixed by generations of scholars. The term "German idealism" generally refers to the tradition of philosophy from Kant to Hegel, and more specifically to the doctrines expounded by Kant, Fichte, Schelling, and Hegel from roughly 1781 to 1801.[5] "Romanticism" in those years means the period known as *Frühromantik*, and it refers to the circle of poets and philosophers in Jena and Berlin, which includes the Schlegel brothers, Schelling, Novalis, Schleiermacher, Hölderlin, and Tieck. If we limit ourselves to these dates, the terms "romanticism" and "idealism" do have a definite extension. The question of the relationship between idealism and romanticism during this period then becomes twofold: (1) What do the thinkers in *each group* have in common? (2) What do the two groups have in common and how do they differ? These are not verbal questions at all, but very complex and very difficult substantive ones. They involve the comparison of many thinkers, many writings of each thinker, many of which are very obscure.

So, to this extent, the obscurity of the question does not derive only from the obscurity of the words but from the very subject matter itself.

Granted that we have a real question before us, it seems to me to be eminently worthwhile to try to answer it. This is first and foremost because, by common consent, these movements are so important, and important not only for German cultural history but the history of philosophy in general. But there is another less important, but still pressing, reason why we should try to answer it: namely, the old standard theory about their interrelation, which has prevailed for generations, has broken down utterly. According to this theory, which was put forward by Rudolf Haym, H. A. Korff, and Nicolai Hartmann,[6] romanticism was essentially a parasitic form of idealism, and more specifically a poetic form of Fichte's *Wissenschaftslehre*. It was, as Haym put it, "poetically exaggerated Fichteanism."[7] This interpretation has failed not simply because of more careful interpretations of old texts but also because of the publication of many new texts, materials that had not been available to Haym, Korff, and Hartmann. It has only been since the 1960s, with the publication of the new critical editions of Hölderlin, Schlegel, Novalis, and Schleiermacher, that scholars have been in position to examine, in all their variety and depth, the many philosophical writings of the early romantics. These show us clearly that the romantics were not disciples but critics of Fichte's *Wissenschaftslehre*, and that one of their major aims was to overcome what they perceived as the inadequacy of Fichte's idealism. The early romantics rejected not only Fichte's methodology and conception of nature, but also his idealism, which seemed to trap the self inside the circle of its own consciousness. For them, Fichte's idealism was not the solution to be celebrated but the problem to be avoided.

So, given that the old theory has collapsed, it is necessary to rethink the whole question of the relationship between idealism and romanticism. There are two ways of going forward. One would be to stress the difference between idealism and romanticism, to make a sharp distinction between them. The other would be to continue to emphasize the affinity between them but to hold that Fichtean idealism is only one part or aspect of idealism in general. Manfred Frank has gone down the first path; I have gone down the second. Over the years I have tried to convince Frank to go down the path of salvation and righteousness, but he has stubbornly resisted. Rather than recanting and renouncing the error of his ways, he has challenged me in public. And so he has, in effect, thrown down his gauntlet. In full recognition of such a worthy opponent, who has taught me so much over the years, I now pick it up and prepare to joust.

Joust? A sense of occasion demands an appropriate metaphor, and this occasion is a romantic one. So I ask the reader to imagine the following: a tournament between two aging knights in rusty and creaky armor, fighting for the hand of a beautiful mistress, who holds in her hand a blue flower. Call her

Mathilde, if you like, or even better Dulcinea. Following chivalrous custom, I will abandon my claim to her if my opponent knocks me off my horse, my trusty steed Rocinante. That said, ladies and gentleman, let us commence. *Arre! Rocinante, arre!*

2.2. ROMANTICISM AND FORMS OF IDEALISM

To begin, let me briefly summarize the *status controversiae*. The basic difference between Frank and me is that I firmly place early romanticism *inside* the tradition of German idealism while Frank places it equally firmly *outside* that tradition, and indeed *against* it. Frank and I agree that the old Fichtean interpretation of early romanticism is obsolete; but he regards this as a sufficient reason for distinguishing early romanticism from idealism *in general*, whereas I think that such reasoning is a non sequitur because Fichte's idealism is only one part of the idealist tradition as a whole. I see my differences with Frank as partly verbal, stemming from the different meanings of the term "idealism," but also as partly substantial, reflecting our different approaches to and interpretations of the texts.

Regarding the verbal issue, it is necessary to be precise about the meaning of "idealism." Frank and I differ in our use of this term, and it is the source of half the difference between us. We can avoid a lot of confusion if, at the outset, we make a very basic distinction between two forms or kinds of idealism. Very crudely, there is "idealism" in the *subjective* sense, according to which "the ideal" denotes the realm of consciousness of the self-conscious subject (whether that subject is empirical or transcendental, individual or universal). There is also "idealism" in the objective sense, according to which "the ideal" denotes the realm of the archetypical or intelligible.[8] The subjective idealist holds that everything within our experience—though not necessarily everything that exists—is only for some self-conscious subject. The objective idealist maintains that everything within our experience—and indeed everything that exists— is the appearance, manifestation, or embodiment of some archetype or ideal. Taken in such general terms, it should be clear that these forms of idealism are conceptually distinct. A subjective idealist need not hold that everything in experience is an appearance of some ideal or archetype; for he might be a nominalist who denies the reality of archetypes and who affirms that everything that exists is particular. An objective idealist need not claim that those particular things that embody or instantiate the archetypical are perceived by or exist for some self-conscious subject; for they could still be embodiments or instantiations of the ideal even if no self-conscious subject existed to perceive them.

Any adequate account of the German idealist tradition has to be broad enough to accommodate both these senses. A narrow univocal account will not work if only because the paradigmatic thinkers that we place in this tradition—Kant, Fichte, Schelling, and Hegel—use "idealism" in both these senses. As all students of the tradition know, there was a fundamental break around 1800 between the "subjective idealism" of Kant and Fichte and the "objective idealism" of Schelling and Hegel. That break appears in Schelling's correspondence with Fichte, and then in Hegel's *Differenzschrift*, which defends Schelling's break with Fichte. Schelling and Hegel argued that their "objective idealism" is superior to the subjective idealism of Kant and Fichte because it accommodates the independent reality of nature and because it does not reduce nature down to the experience of the self-conscious subject alone. That was, as I read it, the point behind Schelling's famous *Durchbruch zur Realität*, which he makes in his 1799 *Allgemeine Deduktion des dynamischen Prozesses*.[9]

Given that subjective and objective idealism have such different senses, and given that there was such a deep and self-conscious break between its chief protagonists, one might well ask why or how there is one idealist tradition at all. Why not speak of two traditions, or "idealisms" in the plural, as Lovejoy advises us to do with "romanticism"? I would do so if it were not for the fact that a hard and fast distinction between these idealisms, as if they have nothing in common, is equally problematic. There is still one general sense of "idealism" common to both strands of the tradition insofar as both regard the realm of thought or the ideal as the key to understanding experience or reality, and insofar as both oppose materialism. The basic difference between these strands is simply whether we *attach* or *detach* the ideal—the realm of thought or meaning—from the self-conscious subject: subjective idealists attach it, objective idealists detach it. What the common principle of these idealism might be is a difficult question that I cannot pursue here. But, quite apart from how we formulate that principle, there is still another reason to write of a single tradition from Kant to Hegel. Namely, Schelling and Hegel themselves self-consciously continued to place themselves within the Kantian-Fichtean tradition. It is noteworthy, for example, that Hegel, in his *Differenzschrift*, still sees himself as completing the Kantian revolution in philosophy.[10] No account of German idealism is complete or adequate, I believe, unless it can explain this apparent paradox: that Schelling and Hegel broke with Kant's and Fichte's idealism yet both placed themselves within the Kantian-Fichtean tradition.

Now my major difference with Frank regarding the concept of "idealism" is that he narrows its meaning down to subjective idealism alone. According to his definition in *Unendliche Annäherung*, "idealism," "crudely put" (*grob gesagt*), denotes the view that "the basic givens of reality are mental [*geistige*] entities or can be reduced down to them."[11] This is a passable definition for *subjective* idealism all right; but it does not work at all for *objective* idealism, which does not hold that the basic givens of reality are mental. If we were to adopt Frank's definition for the idealist tradition as a whole, we would have to limit it down to Kant and Fichte and leave aside Schelling and Hegel. It would become impossible to make any sense of "objective idealism," not to mention Schelling's and Hegel's break with Fichte and their advocacy of an idealism that takes into account the independent reality of nature. There are passages in *Unendliche Annäherung* where Frank does talk about "absolute idealism," a synonym for "objective idealism," which he defines in terms of the doctrine that an absolute ego creates all of reality.[12] But this is still "subjective idealism" in my terms because it does not matter whether the realm of consciousness belongs to a transcendental or empirical, universal or particular, subject. In any case, absolute idealism in this sense—a supersubject creating the entire world of empirical reality—is not a useful term to describe anyone in the idealist tradition. It is an old misconception that is better laid to rest.[13]

The different meanings Frank and I attribute to idealism are decisive for the dispute between us. Because he defines the concept in subjective terms, he distinguishes it from early romanticism; because I define it more broadly, not only in subjective but also objective terms, I place it under the general heading of idealism. But in an important sense Frank and I agree. Namely, *if* one were to define idealism in the subjective sense, then the romantics are *not* idealists, and they were indeed opposed to it. It was this narrow subjective sense behind the old Fichtean interpretation of early romanticism, which Frank and I both reject. Furthermore, Frank and I are at one regarding the realism of early romanticism. In *Unendliche Annäherung* Frank argues that the romantics were not idealists but realists in holding that the realm of being exists independent of the self-conscious subject. After Fred Rush complained about the vagueness of Frank's use of "realism,"[14] Frank made some fine distinctions in *Auswege aus dem deutschen Idealismus*.[15] We need not pursue these distinctions here, useful though they are. The relevant sense of realism for the romantics Frank calls "ontological realism," according to which "there are things existing independent of consciousness and whose independence is denoted by the term being."[16]

Though it might surprise Frank and others, I have to stress that I agree with him entirely that the early romantics were committed to just such a realism. It is important to add that this realism was meant to be full and robust, allowing for the existence of being or nature independent of any subjects whatsoever (empirical or transcendental). It is not reducible, therefore, to the "empirical realism" that Kant and Fichte tried to accommodate under their subjective idealism, for that empirical realism, though allowing for the intersubjective existence of objects "outside us" in space, still saw space itself as "transcendentally ideal," that is, as forms of intuition of the self-conscious subject. This form of realism would not have satisfied the romantics, who wanted, as Friedrich Schlegel put it, "a higher realism" that would give an independent reality to nature apart from any subject, whether empirical or transcendental.[17]

Granted that the romantics aspired to a higher realism, which is indeed the kind of ontological realism that Frank attributes to them, it is tempting to conclude that they were opposed to idealism. This is indeed just the inference that Frank makes. It is misleading, however, because it fails to distinguish between subjective and objective idealism. While the higher realism is indeed incompatible with *subjective* idealism, it is perfectly compatible with *objective* idealism, and the whole point of objective idealism is to accommodate that realism. Even if there were no self-conscious subject, it is still possible to hold that everything that exists in nature is a manifestation of the ideal, where the ideal is the archetypical or intelligible.

If we accept that the romantics held such an objective idealism, then it becomes possible to explain one extraordinary feature of their philosophical language: namely, their demand for an ontology that is both idealistic and realistic. During the late 1790s and early 1800s the early romantics would often write of an "ideal-realism" or "real-idealism." This was not a deliberately paradoxical or glib turn of phrase but the expression of a very reasonable philosophical program: the call for a form of idealism that could do justice to the reality of the external world. The early romantics were convinced that there should be some middle path between a complete materialism on the one hand and a total subjective idealism on the other hand. That middle path was their objective idealism. It alone could interpret the world as a manifestation of the ideal—and so avoid materialism—but it could also allow the world to exist independent of the subject—and so escape subjective idealism.

Realizing that the early romantics are objective idealists in this sense also makes it possible to stress a side of early romanticism that has been underplayed by Frank but that has been rightly emphasized by some older commentators.[18] This is the Platonic dimension. All the early romantics—Friedrich Schlegel, Schleiermacher, Hölderlin, Novalis, and Schelling—were profoundly influenced by Plato in their youth, and this had a pervasive impact on all their thinking. Oskar Walzel was entirely correct, I believe, when he wrote, nearly a century ago, that romanticism was the greatest revival of Platonism since the Renaissance.[19] The Platonic dimension of the romantics' idealism appears in their identification of the absolute with reason or *logos* or idea. I will have to forgo here marshalling and citing all the evidence for this interpretation, a task I have executed elsewhere.[20] Assuming, however, that we adopt this Platonic interpretation, the consequences for our general interpretation of romanticism are weighty. For it means that we have to reject the pervasive and popular interpretation of romanticism as a form of irrationalism, as a rebellion against the *Aufklärung* and as a more radical form of the *Sturm und Drang*. The romantic doctrine of the primacy of aesthetic experience over the forms of discursive thinking was not meant as a rejection or limitation of reason in general but was intended to elevate intuitive forms of reason over discursive ones. It was never intended as a rejection of rationality as such.

Some object to attributing objective idealism to the romantics, and subsuming them under the Platonic tradition, on the grounds that the romantics rejected the thesis that being is completely transparent and intelligible. On this view it is necessary to distinguish between idealism and romanticism along the following lines: the idealists insist on the transparency of being while the romantics stress its opacity.[21] This seems simplistic to me, too black and white, because knowledge of being can be a matter of degree. While the romantics certainly did not hold that we can have a perfect knowledge of being, they did think that we can know it a little, through a glass darkly. The medium by which we know it would be aesthetic intuition, the vision of the forms in Plato's *Phaedrus*. In any case, objective idealism does not presuppose any doctrine about the knowledge of the ideal or intelligible. Objective idealism, on my account, is an *ontological* thesis that holds that everything is an appearance of the ideal or intelligible; but it is not an *epistemological* claim that we, as finite human beings, have complete or perfect knowledge of being itself.

This objection is partly inspired by and based on the point that the romantics were opposed to foundationalism, which was part and parcel of the idealist tradition. This is indeed one of the chief reasons for the distinction between romanticism and idealism. According to this version of the distinction, the romantics were fundamentally antifoundationalist, while the idealists were essentially foundationalist in their epistemology.[22] Fichte and the early Schelling were followers of Reinhold's foundationalist program—his *Elementarphilosophie*—which was basically a revival of the old *philosophia prima* that we find in Descartes, Spinoza, and Leibniz. While Hegel rejected the Reinholdian program, he never abandoned foundationalism but simply pursued it through other means: his famous dialectic. The early romantics were among those many philosophers in the *Jena Wunderzeit* who rejected the Reinholdian program, which was one of the starting points for their own philosophy. Frank has especially stressed the antifoundationalism of early romanticism, and his explorations and elaborations of this theme are, I believe, one of his major contributions to research on early romanticism. I agree with Frank entirely about the antifoundationalism of early romanticism, and I have, following in his footsteps, incorporated it into my own work. Here we have indeed good reason to make a distinction between early romanticism and idealism, and I do not think I have emphasized that point enough in my earlier work.

However, it is necessary to add: the antifoundationalism of early romanticism does not make it any less idealistic in the precise sense of idealism I have in mind. There is nothing in the thesis of objective idealism, as explained above, that commits its adherents to foundationalism. We can affirm that all reality is a manifestation of the ideal and deny every form of foundationalism. It is possible to hold the following position: that we perceive the ideal through intuition or feeling, through the dark glass of aesthetic experience, and to be critical of all foundationalism. That was indeed, as I see it, the romantic position.

2.3. ROMANTIC AESTHETICS AND IDEALISM

Having laid to rest, at least for now, the question of how romanticism in general relates to idealism, I want to move onto another more specific question about that relationship, namely, how romantic *aesthetics* relates to the idealist tradition. And now, for your amusement, Frank and I will exchange roles. The knights, now battered and bruised, will swap armor and horses and charge from opposing sides of the court. For now it will be Frank who stresses the importance of the idealist legacy for romanticism, and it will be I who underplays its significance. Why this strange role reversal? It has come about because Frank, in his *Einführung in die frühromantische Ästhetik*, champions the cardinal importance of Kant's Copernican Revolution for romantic aesthetics. There Frank points out a striking analogy between Kant's epistemology and romantic aesthetics: that just as the Kantian subject creates its standard of knowledge, so the romantic genius creates the standards of art. Supposedly, it was Kant's revolutionary claim that knowledge consists in the conformity of object with concept (rather than concept with object) that liberated aesthetics from the stranglehold of the classical doctrine of imitation, according to which the artist has to copy the given appearances of nature.[23] In thus stressing the affinity between Kant's Copernican Revolution and romantic aesthetics Frank follows a venerable tradition. This analogy has a long history, having had some powerful advocates besides Frank himself. One of its greatest champions was Hans Georg Gadamer, who, in *Wahrheit und Methode*, made it the basis for his charge that the romantics had undertaken a radical subjectivization of aesthetics.[24] Among its adherents were Haym, Korff, and Hartmann, those protagonists of the old theory that romanticism is simply "a poetic form of Fichte's *Wissenschaftslehre*." The tradition shows no signs of dying out, and its latest appearance is Jane Kneller's *Kant and the Power of Imagination*.[25] So I am charging my Rocinante against a formidable phalanx indeed!

Before I spur that stubborn beast, let me pause to note the curious tension in Frank's position. It is strange that he separates romanticism so firmly from idealism but then stresses the significance of the Kantian Copernican Revolution for romantic aesthetics. For if we adopt the paradigm of knowledge behind Kant's Copernican Revolution, we quickly get back into the squalid depths of subjective idealism. That paradigm states, as Kant famously formulates it in the preface to the second edition of the first *Kritik*, that we know a priori only what we create.[26] If we insist that such creativity is necessary for all knowledge, as Kant surely does, then we get caught inside the circle of our own representations. What the world would be on its own, prior to the application of our creative cognitive activity to it, turns out to be that notorious monster, the Kantian thing-in-itself.

Here something has to give because Frank cannot have it both ways. And what does give is Frank's emphasis on the Copernican Revolution. For in the course of his *Einführung* Frank finds himself retracting the importance of the analogy he first made his guiding theme. He sees, perfectly correctly, that there is something amiss with the analogy. The problem is this: when the Copernican doctrine is applied to aesthetics, it leads to the doctrine that aesthetic judgment is noncognitive. It is no accident that Kant tells us emphatically and explicitly in the first paragraph of the *Kritik der Urteilskraft* that aesthetic judgment has nothing to do with truth, that it does not refer to anything whatsoever in the object, because it concerns only the feeling of pleasure in the spectator.[27] The Kantian doctrine of the strictly subjective status of pleasure is the immediate consequence of the Copernican Revolution *because* it places the standard of beauty in the faculties of the perceiver rather than in the object itself. Kant saw the opposing doctrine—the rationalist theory that aesthetic judgment formulates an intuition of perfection in the object itself—as a relapse into the bad old ways of metaphysical dogmatism, which placed the standard of beauty in the object itself, and more specifically in its perfection or unity-in-variety. But it is precisely Kant's denial of cognitive status to aesthetic judgment that shows the profound difference between his Copernican Revolution and the romantics. For the romantics were, one and all, passionately committed to the doctrine that aesthetic perception is cognitive, that it does give us insight into truth. Frank knows this all too well, of course, and it is noteworthy that for this reason he retracts, qualifies, or fails to follow through with his analogy.[28]

As soon as we consider the consequences of Kant's Copernican Revolution for the cognitive status of aesthetic judgment, we have to acknowledge that Kant's aesthetics was more a challenge than a stimulus for romantic thinking. If we wish to trace the sources of romantic aesthetic theory, then we have to go back to classical doctrine, and more specifically Platonic doctrine. So here again I want to strum my Platonic lyre! For it was the Plato of the *Phaedrus* and *Symposium*—not the Plato of the *Republic*—who was the main inspiration for the romantics. The romantics too were Diotima's children, and the source of their aesthetic doctrine goes back to Diotima's teaching that beauty consists in the sensual perception of intellectual form. That teaching was also the heart of the rationalist tradition—the aesthetics of Wolff, Baumgarten, Gottsched, Winckelmann, and Mendelssohn—according to which beauty consists in the intuition of perfection (*intuitio perfectionis*).[29]

Now, having made some grand sweeping claims, let me make another, one more heretical than the preceding. Namely, rather than seeing romantic aesthetics as built on a Kantian foundation, we should see it as an attempt to rehabilitate rationalist aesthetics and as a reaction against Kant's Copernican Revolution. For the romantics wanted first and foremost to restore the classical doctrine of the cognitive status of aesthetic judgment against Kant's subjectivism. The very doctrine that Kant was intent on burying they were intent on reviving. The romantic emphasis on the truth behind poetry and art, and their Platonic heritage, permits no other conclusion.

There is still, of course, a great difference between the romantics and their rationalist forebears. Namely, the romantics turned the rationalist hierarchy of knowledge upside down. While the rationalists placed aesthetic experience *below* the powers of reason—here understood in the traditional sense as the powers to conceive, judge, and infer—the romantics placed it *above* them. It is in just this respect, of course, that it is fair to stress Kant's influence on the romantics, for they did accept some of his critique of traditional metaphysics. Kant's attack on the powers of discursive reason was indeed crucial for their elevation of aesthetic experience over all forms of knowledge. But this point has been taken too far, as if the break with rationalist metaphysics meant a break with its aesthetics. That too is a non sequitur.

Although there is a clear affinity between romantic aesthetics and the rationalist tradition, and although there is a clear tension between romantic aesthetics and the Kantian tradition, I am not optimistic that scholars will begin to turn their attention away from Kant and toward the rationalists. The old habits of looking at Kant as the fount of aesthetic wisdom are simply too hard to break. We romantics know what the Kantians do when the post coach from Königsberg breaks down. Rather than going without truth for weeks, they go ferreting into the more obscure recesses of the *Kritik der Urteilskraft* to find solace. They rummage through the text for every trace of evidence for the romantics' indebtedness to this *non plus ultra* of the aesthetic universe. And, sure enough, they find doctrines that seem to anticipate later romantic themes. Thus they point to Kant's concept of genius, to his idea of art as a symbol of morality, and to the paradox of purposiveness without a purpose. All of these ideas might have been indeed suggestive to the romantics. But the problem with them is that they are too hedged with regulative qualifications to support the romantic faith in the cognitive status of art. Kant never permits the artist to have insight into the ideas behind nature for the simple reason that these ideas have for him only a regulative validity. He permits us to treat nature only *as if* it were created according to ideas, but not to assume that it actually is so. The Kantian artist is still left trapped inside the circle of consciousness of subjective idealism.

Regarding these old Kantian habits, I frankly have to state my incredulity. The romantics were never fervent admirers of Kant's *Kritik der Urteilskraft*, and they never went poring over the text to find inspiration. What could one say after all about a text that made the arabesque the height of aesthetic perfection? The great admirer of the *Kritik der Urteilskraft* was Schiller, and it seems that Kant's influence on Schiller, and Schiller's influence on the romantics, licenses by transitivity Kant's influence on the romantics. But there is a great gap between Schiller's *Aesthetische Briefe* and Hölderlin's *Neue Aesthetische Briefe*. The latter work was meant to vindicate the claim to aesthetic truth undermined by the former. One reason the alleged affinity between Kant and the romantics lacks credibility is because it fails to acknowledge, and to see the consequences of, one basic but simple fact: Kant did not read Greek. Most of the young romantics were trained in that language from an early age, and it is that which gave them access to, and a deep appreciation of, Plato's *Timaeus, Symposium*, and *Phaedrus*. It was Kant's ignorance of Greek that puts a major cultural barrier between him and the romantic generation. Let us face it: the stiff and dry sage of Königsberg had no appreciation of the erotic, and so he would never have understood the soul of Diotima's teaching.

In one respect I am willing to concede that the old analogy between Kant's Copernican Revolution and romantic aesthetics contains a grain of truth. Namely, the romantics did stress the creative role of the artist, and they did not expect the artist simply to replicate the appearances of external nature. But this point leaves us with a problem, which the protagonists of this analogy do not recognize. Namely, how could the romantics stress *both* the creative role of the artist *and* the power of art to reveal the truth? It might seem that the artist's creativity simply reveals his own feelings and desires rather than anything about the world outside him. The problem here is how to bring together the romantic faith in artistic creativity with a doctrine of the imitation of nature, a doctrine the romantics never really renounced and which is even required by their ontological realism. The explanation for this apparent paradox, I would suggest here, lies in the romantics' general conception of nature, and more specifically, their conception of nature as an organism. According to that idea, the organic powers of nature reach their highest organization and development in the creativity of the subject, so that what he creates is also what nature creates through him. The artist, through his own creativity, then becomes the instrument for the self-realization and self-revelation of nature herself. The paradigmatic expression of this idea is in Schelling's *System des transcendentalen Idealismus*. If I am correct that this is the solution to the paradox, then it shows the importance of romantic *Naturphilosophie* for their aesthetics. It is only when we place romantic aesthetics in the context of their *Naturphilosophie*, their conception of nature as a whole, that the claims it makes for the cognitive powers of art begin to make sense.

And so there you have it. With that diatribe I have made my last parry in this tournament. My Rocinante is tired now, as I imagine my spectators are too. I quit the field not knowing what favors Mathilde might care to bestow upon me. Whether I or Frank deserves her blue flower I will leave the spectator to judge.

NOTES

1. Manfred Frank, *Unendliche Annäherung. Die Anfänge der philosophischen Frühromantik* (Frankfurt am Main: Suhrkamp, 1997), 27, 65–66, 663–65, 715.
2. Frederick C. Beiser, *German Idealism: The Struggle against Subjectivism, 1781–1801* (Cambridge, MA: Harvard University Press, 2002); and *The Romantic Imperative: The Concept of German Romanticism* (Cambridge, MA: Harvard University Press, 2003).
3. See Manfred Frank, *Auswege aus dem deutschen Idealismus* (Frankfurt am Main: Suhrkamp, 2007), 16–17. Elizabeth Millán-Zaibert has also taken issue with my subsumption of the romantics under idealism in her *Friedrich Schlegel and the Emergence of Romantic Philosophy* (Albany: State University of New York, 2007).
4. Arthur Lovejoy, "On the Discriminations of Romanticism," *Proceedings of the Modern Language Association* 39 (1924), 229–53. Reprinted in Lovejoy, *Essays in the History of Ideas* (New York: Capricorn, 1960), 228–53.
5. We could, of course, extend the date beyond 1801. But I will leave that aside here, for the purposes of a more precise comparison with the early romantics. By 1801 the essentials of Schelling's and Hegel's objective or absolute idealism were formed, and Schelling's and Hegel's works only expounded the main ideas in more systematic detail. I will also leave aside the problem of applying the term "idealism" solely to the period from Kant and Hegel. This is problematic because it ignores Lotze and Trendelenburg, two of the most influential thinkers of the nineteenth century in the idealist tradition.
6. Rudolf Haym, *Die romantische Schule* (Berlin: Gaertner, 1882); H. A. Korff, *Geist der Goethezeit* (Leipzig: Koehler und Amelang, 1964), III, 244–52; and Nicolai Hartmann, *Die Philosophie des deutschen Idealismus* (Berlin: de Gruyter, 1923), I, 220–33, esp. 221, 224, 226, 228.
7. Haym, *Die romantische Schule*, 332.
8. I argue for this distinction in *German Idealism*, 349–74, 379–91, 418–21, 447–51, 491–505.

9. My interpretation of Schelling's break with Fichte, which I cannot explain in any detail here, is in my *German Idealism*, 469–505.

10. See Hegel, "Vorerinnerung," *Differenz des Fichteschen und Schellingschen Systems der Philsophie*, in *Werke in zwanzig Bänden*, ed. K. Michel and E. Moldenhauer (Frankfurt am Main: Suhrkamp, 1970), II, 9–11.

11. Frank, *Unendliche Annäherung*, 27.

12. Ibid., 128, 133.

13. So I have argued in *German Idealism*, 4–6.

14. See his review of Elizabeth Millán-Zaibert's *Philosophical Foundations of Early German Romanticism* in *Notre Dame Philosophical Review*, 2004.12.09. Http://ndpr. nd.edu/news/23011-the-philosophical-foundation-of-early-german-romanticism.

15. Frank, *Auswege aus dem deutschen Idealismus*, 19–26.

16. Ibid., 19, 21.

17. See Schlegel, *Philosophische Lehrjahre*, in KA 18, 31, no. 134; 38, no. 209; 80, no. 606. Novalis held similar views. See his *Allgemeine Brouillon*, in NS 3, 382–4, no. 634; 252, no. 69; 382, no. 633; 429, no. 820, and *Fragmente und Studien*, NS 3, 671, no. 611.

18. The Platonic heritage was stressed by Oskar Walzel, *German Romanticism* (New York: Putnam, 1932) and Erwin Kirchner, *Philosophie der Romantik* (Jena: Diederichs, 1906), 8–34.

19. Walzel, *German Romanticism*, 5, 8.

20. See my essay "*Frühromantik* and the Platonic Tradition," in *Romantic Imperative*, 56–72, esp. 67–72.

21. This is the view of Millán-Zaibert, *Friedrich Schlegel and the Emergence of Romantic Philosophy*, 32, 34, 36, 38.

22. This conception of the idealist tradition goes back to a forgotten but venerable source: Jakob Friedrich Fries's *Reinhold, Fichte und Schelling* (Leipzig: Reineicke, 1803). Fries shows how Fichte and Schelling adopt the foundationalist program of Reinhold, and makes weighty objections against that program. He makes passing references to Hegel, who would soon become his nemesis.

23. Frank, *Einführung in die frühromantische Ästhetik* (Frankfurt am Main: Suhrkamp, 1989), 9–14.

24. See Hans-Georg Gadamer, *Wahrheit und Methode* (Tübingen: Mohr, 1990), 93–94. Gadamer says little about the romantics but sees them as part of Schiller's program of aesthetic education, which he thinks has subjectivized aesthetics.

25. Jane Kneller, *Kant and the Power of Imagination* (Cambridge: Cambridge University Press, 2007).

26. Kant, *Kritik der reinen Vernunft*, B xviii. Cf. B xii, xiii.

27. AA 5, 204. Cf. 214.

28. Frank, *Einführung in die frühromantische Ästhetik*, 38–39, 122–23, 129.

29. Such is the thesis of my *Diotima's Children: German Aesthetic Rationalism from Leibniz to Lessing* (Oxford: Oxford University Press, 2009).

PART TWO

History, Hermeneutics, and Sociability

3

History, Succession, and German Romanticism

KARL AMERIKS

Romantic poetry is a *progressive universal poetry*. Its aim isn't merely to reunite all the separate species of poetry and put poetry in touch with philosophy and rhetoric. It tries to and should mix and fuse poetry and prose, inspiration. and criticism.... The Romantic kind of poetry is still in the state of becoming; that, in fact, is its real essence.[1]

3.1. THREE OLD VIEWS AND A NEW ONE

Not least among the accomplishments of German romanticism[2] is its leading role in the advocacy of a major new option in the philosophical understanding of history and the related issue of a historical understanding of philosophy.[3] There are only a few basic forms in which the relationship of history to philosophy has tended to be conceived, the most familiar of which are the options of either a circular, linear, or chaotic shape.[4] The romantics deserve special credit for having made prominent a fourth basic option here, namely, that of an elliptical path.[5] The romantic notion of an elliptical path is often shorthand for the thought of history as kind of gyre, or open-ended rising spiral, such that there is directionality and progress in a multidimensional fashion, one that requires repeatedly returning to one's original place in a way that involves development through off-center movements with more than one focal point.

This pattern combines elements of circularity, linearity, and eccentricity in an original and influential way, one that begs to be elaborated in terms of the romantics' famous call, quoted in the epigraph, for "universal progressive poetry." Although this phrase is well known in literary circles, its philosophical significance still does not seem to have been fully appreciated, for its tripartite structure not only ideally fits romanticism but also appears to capture, better than the other basic options, the distinctive historical self-understanding of much of late modernity. Once it is explicated in its full meaning—which I take to be about writing in the broadest philosophical sense rather than "poetry" as a limited literary genre—the tripartite structure of its defining phrase can be argued to imply three corresponding kinds of basic advantages for the romantic view.

Although key elements of the notion of an elliptical historical pattern can be found in writings by highly influential earlier figures such as Lessing, Rousseau, Herder, and Kant, these writers do not yet conceive the pattern in the fully complex and distinctively open way featured in the best works of the romantics, especially in their reflections on the significance of their own pivotal historical era at the end of the eighteenth century. To illustrate this special kind of openness, I will conclude by discussing a way in which the notion of universal progressive poetry provides an especially appropriate rubric for appreciating a key philosophical aspect of Friedrich Hölderlin's work, and in particular the conception of history expressed in major poems such as his *Friedensfeier* (Celebration of Peace).

3.2. THE CIRCULAR VIEW: SIMPLE AND COMPLEX

According to recent studies of mythology,[6] a view characteristic of societies that derive largely from the Southern Hemisphere, in contrast to the fundamental orientation of the northern societies that have dominated "our history," is that human experience exhibits basically circular patterns, with essentially the same kinds of customs and rituals repeating themselves at the center of daily life and culture. Aspects of a kind of circular view can also be found in the North, and often the view is associated with the worldviews of what is called "the ancient world" (especially of Greece and Rome) before, or outside of, the traditions of the Abrahamic religions.[7] Nonetheless, the main works of the ancients, from Gilgamesh on, are circular in a complex rather than simple way, for they stress dramatic quest motifs, such as the founding of cities and the forward-looking project of overcoming outside challenges and philosophical quandaries—although this is still not to say that they already possess the restless Faustian dynamism of later European culture.

Leaving aside for specialists the factual question of which groups have in fact been governed by which version of the view, my initial aim here is simply to characterize, through broad conceptual contrasts, the most basic feature of what I mean by a circular view in general: Although a circular view allows accumulation of expertise over time, which can be incorporated into the evolving "second nature" of each successive generation, its defining presumption, whether simple or complex, is that there are only refinements and no absolutely fundamental historical developments in philosophical truth itself, especially with respect to the central issue of what, in the eighteenth century, was called the "vocation of humanity" (*Die Bestimmung des Menschen*).

Given this general characterization, one can regard, as a mere complex variation of the circular view, views of history that include a stress on highly dramatic quests of various far-ranging types (e.g., the *Iliad*, the *Odyssey*, the *Republic*) but that still regard progress as largely a matter of reinstating central structures of an original harmony. Such views can be found in the ancient Western societies mentioned earlier, as well as in "organic" conceptions of society and history that arise much later, such as Hegel's mature notion of "ethical life" and "reason in history." Hegel is, of course, well known for his emphasis on the feature of progress in Western civilization, not only in technological and economic-political matters but also in terms of the appreciation of the fundamental notions of philosophy itself. Hegel takes these notions to define not only the concrete processes of nature, society, and history but also the basic understandings in terms of which humanity's "absolute spirit" eventually makes explicit this full structure.[8] Nonetheless, because Hegel's ultimate position (on traditional "schoolbook" readings) is that the pure system of his "logic" and related work prefigures all the most basic forms of progress within human history, it still can be said that his view on history is a circular one, albeit of a very complex rather than simple type.[9] The "absolute knowledge" of Hegel's system can be taken, in its content, as just a reflective formulation of what is implicit from the start within reason's "Idea" of a reconciled harmony of object and subject, and so, despite the dramatic reality of an extensive sequence of quests and necessary changes within the world of appearance, there remains an underlying and unchanging philosophical order, one without any fundamental incompleteness.[10]

This is not to say that the monistic unfolding in time of what Hegel calls the "absolute," which is as much "subject" as "substance," is a matter of a merely analytic unpacking of isolated terms or entities. The main point, as Hegel insists, is that, however complex this "development"[11] appears to be, it constitutes a system of reason that is not only necessary and eventually transparent, but also, from the start, necessarily complete, and hence it has an eternal form that in essence preconditions its temporal instantiation. The transitions from era to era are, to be sure, extraordinarily complex for Hegel, and they involve a necessary dialectic of "determinate negation" that appears as an unpredictable process. But even though this process can be comprehended only in retrospect, the main point of Hegel's system is that in late modernity we finally *can* retrospectively comprehend and be satisfied by what is, in a philosophical sense, an in principle complete course of history. The dynamic complexity of lived history is thus still consistent with a basically constant and reconciling picture of humanity's overall trajectory and its underlying logic. We have moved in three steps: first, from a stage of relative immediacy, then through the dramatic appearance of a complete sequence of forms of alienation, and finally into (the beginning of) a stage of higher immediacy, with an essentially reconciling harmony of "substance" and "reflection."

3.3. THE LINEAR VIEW: SIMPLE AND COMPLEX

In contrast to the relatively self-enclosed nature of both the simple and the complex versions of the circular view of history, the linear view understands human history as an ongoing process of striking new inputs to experience that are more additive than restorative, and that essentially are generated from contingent sources *outside* of what is in our original human nature or reason. Simple versions of this kind of outward and forward-looking perspective can be found in popular early strands of Enlightenment thinking, in Comtean positivism, in the scientific pragmatism endemic to American thought, and in fully naturalistic forms of Marxism. These views typically assume, in a deeply optimistic way, that we happen to be set up in line with an encompassing outside environment that, like a benevolent wave, will carry us along inexorably, as well "cradled" natural beings heading toward a destined fulfillment of the race.[12]

A variant of this linear approach is the complex linear view of mainline versions of Abrahamic religious traditions that are defined by the confident expectation of a final phase of radical redemption that is supernaturally generated in a *unique* way.[13] The end phase that humanity moves toward on this view involves something like the complexity of Hegel's circular system insofar as it has as its crucial precondition the drama of a sequence of dialectical stages within history that are revolutionary in the limited sense of requiring a reversal of serious previous shortcomings in our basic attitudes but not a denial of an original teleological blueprint for existence on the whole. The traditional religious version of this approach is linear and complex, however, insofar as it emphasizes the nonnatural feature of absolute free choice in both human and divine agency. The goal of history is therefore neither, as with strict Hegelianism (and its complex circular view), metaphysically determined by the eternal necessities of speculative logic, nor, as with strict naturalism (and its simple linear view), is it naturally determined by givens of the external world that happen to fulfill us more and more by physical necessity. Instead, "the end of all things" is understood as a fortunate final phase that depends essentially on a complex contingent convergence of absolutely free divine and human action.[14]

The actualization of this phase is conceived as a complex absolute "Faktum," an overarching arrangement that did not absolutely have to be set up by the unique creative power or lived up to by lesser but volitionally independent created powers. Here our future is understood not primarily as a matter of simply receiving, adding, and rearranging goods (in a relatively mechanical way) through the gifts of structures that are outside us, but instead as a partly autonomous struggle that requires even more than a mere reversal of not being satisfied or good enough earlier. History on this complex linear view requires above all the thought of a *single* triumphant church marching along a strictly orthodox line into a radically new world, one grounded in part on a human nonnatural choice permanently to reverse the fact of a prior attachment to radical evil and a rejection of an originally good free creation.[15]

3.4. THE CHAOTIC VIEW: SIMPLE AND COMPLEX

The third basic conception of history is the chaotic view, which begins by taking a critical attitude toward all accepted teleologies and can also be filled out by distinguishing simple and complex variants. A simple chaotic view consists merely in holding that, considered on the whole, human existence lacks rhyme and reason. Even if this view does not necessarily go so far as to understand value claims nihilistically or as mere projections, it does deny that our history exhibits any deeply meaningful circular pattern, or any overall natural or supernatural line of ascent. On the basis of readings of figures such as Nietzsche, the later Heidegger, and Foucault, many relativist postmodernists and antitheory theorists appear to be attracted to this chaotic view, as are many nonoptimistic positivists as well.

The figures who became most famous by inspiring others to hold a simple chaotic view of history tended themselves, however, to adopt a complex chaotic position, one that eschews relativism, as well as nihilism and positivism, and that adds the wrinkle of stressing that there are key eras, or compartments of life, in which it is important to appreciate that very significant "developments" of various overlooked kinds can be, and should be, uncovered. These developments also involve decline, as in the "death" as well as "birth" of "tragedy," or the "event" of "presence" as well as of "being," or the rise of "the clinic" as well as of "the care of the self," followed by a "pandemonium" of consequences. These processes are thus taken to be limited stages that have no absolutely lasting trajectory and still fail to show that human life as a whole is heading in a particular direction with an increasingly positive (or clearly negative) value.

3.5. ROMANTICISM CONTRA CIRCULAR, LINEAR, AND CHAOTIC VIEWS

Against the background of this characterization of the three traditional options, it can be argued that the romantic view of history as universal progressive poetry offers an ideal combination of what is best in each of the three other views. First, as universal, the romantic view picks up on the attractive broad scope of the circular view, which consists in being especially open to regarding the significance of human life as not limited to the circumstance of belonging to any particular slice of space or time; wherever and whenever ordinary human beings live, they all can participate in what is said to make life most meaningful. This positive feature of open scope contrasts with both the linear view, which can make life's meaning appear to be largely an unfair accident of being exposed to a particular limited tradition (salvation through local revelation, or a fully secular but late-blossoming process), and also with the chaotic view, which, at best, is either relativism or typically limited to an episodic and elitist view of meaning. In contrast to the circular view, however, the romantic view has the further, distinctively historical advantage that for it the universal significance of human life is neither—as on the complex circular view—dependent on a highly questionable teleology rooted in speculative logic, nor—as on the simple circular view—regarded as a brute feature of nature's recurrent patterns that has nothing essentially to do with what is special about human history as a very broadly extended project.

Second, as progressive, the romantic view picks up on the attractive optimistic feature of the linear view, for it implies that not only is life meaningful, but it can also become increasingly meaningful in a fundamental way through the efforts of succeeding generations that connect with and retrospectively enhance the efforts of the past. This positive feature of dynamic value contrasts both with the circular view, which sees nothing essentially new in human life, and again with the chaotic view, which is sensitive to novelty but does not have a highly positive view of life as such. In contrast to the linear view, however, the romantic view can have the further, distinctively historical advantage of thinking neither, in a familiar simple way (as in crude versions of positivism), that history's value is an inevitable natural product of being given later bits of positive value to add on to much inferior earlier life stages, nor, in a traditional complex way, that its value depends on the millenarianism of a unique, and *evidently* supernaturally arranged, final phase.

Third, as poetry, the romantic view, with its insistence on an open and unclear future, picks up on the attractive methodological feature of the chaotic view, its critical attitude in regard to straightforward traditional claims about a fully established teleological structure to human life. The romantic view's positive feature of a stress on humanity's absolutely free[16] capacity for creating highly imaginative initiatives contrasts with the circular view, which overlooks the value of this capacity, as well as with the linear view, which ultimately understands progress in terms of externally generated and clearly conclusive forms of satisfaction and thus discounts the growing uncertainties of late modernity. That is, both the simple and complex versions of the linear view neglect the special value of humanity's ongoing struggle of unsure and unorthodox efforts toward inclusive continuity in a decentered world that is increasingly secular and splintered but not merely scientific. Finally, in contrast with the chaotic view, the romantic view has the distinctively historical advantage of holding that each generation can introduce new layers of deep genuine meaning, and that this meaning is part of a significant successive structure in human existence as a whole, albeit a whole that has no determinable final phase or even a guarantee of "approximation."

3.6. ROMANTICISM AS DISTINCTIVELY POSITIVE

This triadic comparative outline of the possible overall superiority of the romantic view has admittedly been presented in a very abbreviated way and with many controversial presumptions; it is meant more as an initial sketch of a new "system program" than as a direct argument. No doubt there may be more sophisticated versions of the three other theories, and one might also worry, as many have, that the romantic view has serious shortcomings of its own. One might argue, for example, that the values that the view appeals to are not genuine or fundamental. Or one might claim that even if the view could meet these challenges, it still could be true that its values are not most appropriate for understanding our actual history and may not even be realizable. That is, even if the romantic approach turns out to be one that introduces appealing prospects for an understanding of history's distinctive value, especially given our late modern sensibilities, it still could be true that all that we have evidence for is a much more modest conception of how history proceeds, something closer to the ever more popular chaotic view.

If this last problem is the only one that remains, however, then the romantics could still at least deserve credit for having articulated a unique and relevantly challenging positive conception of our historical situation, even if it may seem overly optimistic to most secular intellectuals in our era. As Immanuel Kant and William James argued, and as many contemporary antifoundationalists have noted,[17] there are important situations in which agents should not limit their options to what is present in the form of evidence, for such a limitation can undercut not only itself (since it is hardly clear that foundationalism's own ground, as a principle, is evident) but also the unrefuted possibility of achieving very significant goals. Moreover, because the romantics typically present their work—and especially their philosophy of history—in various "poetic" forms, it is clear from the start that they understand the argumentative uncertainty of any global view. In particular, they see the need to present any general position on history not as a demonstrated assertion but as an imperative, a call to other free individuals to join with them in seeking to make humanity's future, despite its dim record and prospects, a process that is "in the state of becoming ever more universal and progressive."[18]

3.7. CONTRA MISCONCEPTIONS OF ROMANTICISM

A different kind of worry that one can have about this presentation of the romantic view is that it still is not clear how well it fits what the romantics actually hold. To meet this worry it is impossible to provide a survey here of the entire romantic movement or even an in-depth study of one of its parts. For the most part, however, I take myself to be working in concert with a reading of the romantics that—even though it conflicts with stereotypes still present in many philosophical quarters—is largely meant to reflect ideas that by now are common currency in mainline literary interpretations.[19] My aim is simply to supplement these outstanding interpretations by articulating in the most general philosophical terms how a specific romantic strand of thought in a creative writer such as Hölderlin can help to illumine a new and significant position on one of philosophy's most difficult issues—namely, what, if anything, is the special relation between writing of philosophical significance, especially in our late modern era, and history as such, especially given what appears to be the recent wandering shape of our historical path.

First, however, it is still necessary, in a general philosophical context, to spell out some of the "common currency" of recent scholarship in order to ward off preconceptions that continue to obstruct a full appreciation of the romantic achievement. There is, for example, considerable confusion caused by the fact that a movement called romanticism continued in many other countries and in many other fields into the later nineteenth century, and that many examples of this movement, including the (very different) later writing of key figures such as Friedrich Schlegel, came be to be associated with reactionary doctrines and chaotic subjectivism.

An instructive, unfortunate, and very influential effect of this peculiar development is the fact that Nietzsche often speaks of "romanticism" as if it were just a matter of the style of this late phase and always a sign of decadence. It is important to realize that for the most part Nietzsche has later romantics and not the Early Jena circle in mind. He mysteriously never even deigns to refer to Friedrich Schlegel, despite the fact that he himself studied for a while in Bonn (where Schlegel's illustrious brother August taught) and surely must have known of Schlegel's highly original early writings on the special value of "pre-Socratic" Greek culture and of a deeply historical approach to philosophy and writing in general.[20] The main points in these early writings are in fact so close to Nietzsche's own early work on history, the Greeks, and philosophical methodology that one is forced to hypothesize special repressive forces at work in Nietzsche's lack of reference to them, forces like those that may still be at work today, keeping many readers from taking a direct and open-minded look at the romantics. In particular, the later association of Schlegel with Catholicism and related supposedly nonrigorous developments in philology probably play a large role here. This development is a reminder of the fact that, just as with the reception of Nietzsche's own work, once the suggestion arises that a position manifests reactionary thought or willful subjectivism, it is very difficult to remove the damage, no matter how unfair the accusation.

Similar points can be made about the influential tendency of strands of Hegelianism that continue Hegel's own vigorous campaign against romantic writings, as if they must be tantamount to the espousal of social chaos and evil itself. Here too, in the work of Hegel and his early followers, lingering insecure worries in Protestant Germany about a new Counter-Reformation may continue to play a significant role. Despite their prevalence, such concerns are especially out of place for the main German romantic writings around the turn of the century, and they certainly should not be directed at the work of figures such as Hölderlin, or the early work of Schelling, Schleiermacher, and Schlegel, which constantly flirts with Spinozism and explicitly distances itself from Catholic and Protestant orthodoxy.

3.8. ROMANTICISM AND RELIGION

There is a need to dwell on this issue because in the writings that define the central era of romanticism, just as in practically all radical German thought before the post-Hegelian period, some form of intense religious considerations do in fact play a central role. Here it is important to keep in mind that the term "religion" has a variety of very different senses, and in the context of advanced German thought in this era it usually has a very general and nonsectarian meaning. Thinkers in this group are generally very sympathetic with, rather than opposed to, the Enlightenment, although they are opposed to various mechanistic positions associated with the term "Enlightenment." The general tendency of the best-known Enlightenment movements in German-speaking countries, including Austria (consider Mozart as well as the early Reinhold), is to focus on reforming religion rather than (as in the radical French Enlightenment) destroying it. Philosophically, "religion" has a broad cosmic meaning here, and basically it just signifies an absolutely serious emotional as well as intellectual concern with life as a whole, in the broadest sense.[21] It is precisely in the name of religion itself that radical strands of thought—in figures such as Hegel, Schelling, Schleiermacher, and others—make reactionary religious institutions, determined by rigid authoritarian traditions, an object of attack rather than a model to follow. Hence, to appreciate writers such as Hölderlin in particular, in an honest and philosophical way, a typical contemporary reader with a highly secular orientation needs to bracket allergic reactions to the very notion of religion. One needs to be patient enough to see that concepts used in the context of explaining transitions that are often referred to in explicitly religious terms can also be employed in a broader way to help make sense of the general notion of a universally progressive sequence of historical and philosophical transitions. This point will be crucial in understanding the general significance of works such as Hölderlin's *Friedensfeier* (see below, section 12).

Precisely because it is explicitly universal and progressive, romanticism places a special emphasis on paying attention to all of our past—a past that in fact is largely a common religious heritage.[22] This special openness to the past, however, leads to another common charge against romanticism that needs to be countered, namely, that it is basically nostalgic and aims primarily to return to, or simply imitate, bygone eras rather than to face the challenge of living within the apparently irreversible structures of modern life. It is understandable that such charges arise, but they miss the special depth and complexity of the romantic revolution, and its realization that the best way to move forward effectively can lie in an innovative appropriation of the most powerful—because longest enduring—forces in our past.

Because of the earlier pathbreaking work of figures such as Rousseau and Herder, the romantics generally assume, without belaboring the point, that one need not think of prior stages in human history as normatively primitive simply because they are earlier. They also realize that one need not think—despite what naive successors of Herder believe—that therefore all stages are on a par, let alone what naive successors of Rousseau believe—that humanity's first stages are more pure, and even better, merely because of being earlier. The definitive romantic attitude is neither relativism nor primitivism but instead a realization that precisely those who are concerned with our universal progress as historical beings need to be open to taking a fresh look not only at the full spatial extent of the human race but also at its roots, its full temporal extent (hence, for example, Schlegel's early intensive study of Sanskrit). It is a basic romantic insight that it is only through appreciating how thoroughly the great works of the past have shaped us, that later writers, as "exemplary" successors of that past,[23] can create the most effective means for moving beyond imitation and toward engendering a related but significantly new culture for the future.

3.9. THE PROBLEM OF SUCCESSION

For highly gifted creative writers such as the romantics, this perspective is relatively easy to arrive at because, like all great literary minds, they appreciate the importance of ancient classical models, including scriptural writings. They feel the full "burden of the past," that is, the need constantly to read anew and incorporate the true "spirit" of the best earlier writers so that one then has enough strength to become an original successor, a model to inspire future geniuses.[24] This orientation toward the past can, of course, appear suspect to philosophers still locked into the typical premise of the early modern era (that continues into Kant's work), namely, that philosophy is basically like exact science and should build simply on the most recent findings of contemporary thought without having to be sensitive to much earlier stages—just as it is possible, for example, to learn modern geometry adequately without the labor of going through Euclid's work. This defining presumption of early modern philosophy has had a long run, from Descartes and then through Kantianism and the positivists of the mid-twentieth century, but now, just as in the romantic era, its presuppositions are being seriously questioned by all kinds of more historically sensitive philosophers. Although it is true that some types of philosophical discussion can be fruitfully carried out without direct reference to writers from another era, the fact is that, outside of purely formal subareas, most of the most interesting work in contemporary philosophy has for some time been developed by figures such as Thomas Kuhn, Michel Foucault, Bernard Williams, Richard Rorty, Michael Friedman, and Robert Brandom, as well as many others in the field of ethics alone (e.g., Rawls, MacIntyre, Schneewind, Darwall, Irwin) who have continued to carry out what can be called the phenomenon of the "historical turn."[25]

The original form of this turn has its origins in the mid-1780s, an era dominated by the conflicting accounts offered by Herder, Reinhold, and Jacobi of the interlocking trajectories of modern religion, science, and philosophy (after Kant, Hume, and Spinoza), and then the reaction to these accounts by the young seminarians of Tübingen—Hölderlin, Hegel, and Schelling—in their movement toward a "system program" that would combine a "new physics" and "new mythology" in an at once universal, progressive, and aesthetic philosophy of the future. The main immediate complication in this era, from Reinhold through Hegel, is the still influential thought that any philosophy that is genuinely modern has to be thoroughly systematic and scientific in a sense that can

supposedly correspond to and even outdo the power of the new mathematical sciences.[26] Only when the dominance of this presumption finally declines,
toward the end of the eighteenth century, and an alternative is sought for the
overambitious thought of making philosophy absolutely certain and systematic
in a quasi-mathematical sense,[27] is the way cleared for the new antifoundationalist conception of philosophy that the romantics embrace. On this conception,
philosophical writing is not antithetical to science, but it is liberated to be distinctive by being historically argumentative in form, and thereby largely interpretative and even poetic in a broad sense—although precisely not as a matter
of mere "artistic" expression or amusement.

3.10. HÖLDERLIN'S EXEMPLARY ROMANTICISM

If, in the late modern age, after the ambiguous legacy of Kant's Critical system
and the French Revolution, philosophy in general, as well as philosophy of history in particular, can no longer convincingly ground or simply model itself on
natural science, how then can it best approach the phenomenon of development in humanity's basic ideas of itself? The most interesting reaction to this
problem is, I believe, to be found in Hölderlin's writings, which are obsessed
with the phenomenon of historical transmission in culture. In *Friedensfeier*
Hölderlin introduces the thought that human beings are fundamentally partici-
pants in a successive "Gespräch" that is broadly philosophical and political as
well as religious, and that involves loss through reflection as well as sustenance
through common experiences of mourning and celebration. He sees that the
core problem here, not only of philosophy of history but also of the distinctive nature of late modern writing and philosophy in general, has become a
matter of understanding the broadly argumentative successor relation between
truly exemplary writers—writers who introduce epoch-changing philosophical
notions that cannot be literally imitated in the precise way that defines the work
of exact scientists.

Hölderlin formulates his response to this problem in exceptionally dense letters and prose reflections on the nature of writing and the course of modern
philosophy, as well as, most influentially, in numerous haunting poems with
titles such as *Dichterberuf* (The Poet's Vocation) and *Dichtermuth* (The Poet's
Courage). In its broadest terms, for anyone in Hölderlin's general spatial and
temporal position the problem of writing historically can be nothing other than
the problem of making sense of, and courageously confronting, the upcom-
ing second major transition in "our" civilization. This transition is defined by a
movement that goes not, as before, from a universe of declining imperial pagan
culture to an era of nearly universal Christian culture, but from a modern

universe of regionally divided exclusivist versions of the Abrahamic religions to a late modern multicultural era, one in which no truly contemporary society can assume the absolute dominance of any single form of religion, and thus the very notion of a unified society is replaced by the pluralistic but not necessarily chaotic thought of an "age in need."[28]

It is in this spirit that Hölderlin writes to Schelling in 1799 and speaks of a broadly religious[29] "free demand for reciprocal effectiveness and harmonious alternation," and the need for a "humanistic journal" that "would be practically poetic, then again also historically and philosophically instructive about poetry, finally historically and philosophically instructive from the viewpoint of humanity."[30] Note the systematic progression here in Hölderlin's desperate call (after he had been separated from his lover and was facing poverty, although he had already written the novel *Hyperion*, the tragedy *Empedocles*, and many significant poems) to his seminary friend for collaboration in instituting this new forum, one that would move from a seemingly merely aesthetic concern (poetry) to a philosophical (i.e., universal) concern with history, and then finally to a use of this concern for the (progressive) sake of humanity. It is as if Hölderlin cannot keep himself from explicitly reiterating the central conceptual structure of romanticism that surfaces in the three key terms of Schlegel's fragment no. 116. At this time Hölderlin is on the verge of his greatest odes and hymns, although unfortunately the prose record of his line of thought quickly becomes more and more fragmentary. Its fundamentally cosmopolitan and inclusive direction continues to reveal itself, however, in compressed form in documents such as a letter to Böhlendorff, in which Hölderlin discusses his interest in Greece and France and states that "in the progress of education (*Bildung*) the truly national [the gifts of just one people or sect] will become the ever less attractive."[31]

3.11. HÖLDERLIN'S PREDECESSORS

One surprising but highly relevant model for beginning to think about major transitions of this magnitude can be found in the extraordinary achievement of Milton's work. As recent research has shown, Milton had a considerable and long-hidden effect on Kant's thought and, at least indirectly, a significant relation to Hölderlin's as well.[32] By harmoniously appropriating pagan as well as biblical motifs, Milton's major writings seek to accomplish for the early modern Protestant realm what Dante's *Divine Comedy* aims to provide for the medieval Catholic world,[33] namely, the impression that Christianity has a relevant integrating significance for the whole course of history, that is, even before the church was founded and into all of the future. On these points there are, as Michael Hamburger pointed out years ago, many striking direct parallels between Milton and Hölderlin, such as the fact that the young Hölderlin aims to unite nonscriptural and scriptural traditions by writing on both Hesiod and the book of Proverbs, as well as (even more directly like Milton) on both Pindar and the book of Revelation.[34] These parallel interests are consistent with deep differences in content, of course, given the contrast in eras. Milton is still committed to a militant form of early modern religion, and it is no surprise that he invokes Samson as a relevant hero, whereas Hölderlin, as a late modern, feels a need to dwell on Empedocles (perhaps in part as a warning about the Jena attitude of Fichte) and philosophy, and to worry about how increasingly sophisticated abstract thought can lead to cultural dead ends. Instead of pursuing these parallels further, I will conclude by simply drawing attention to how one can use Schlegel's tripartite definition of romanticism to begin to understand works such as Hölderlin's *Friedensfeier* as figuratively addressing precisely the same kind of general philosophical-historical problem that works such as Milton's pose—namely, how, in the face of the enormous historical diversity of modern culture in general, to proceed as a contemporary exemplary writer who feels the need to unify and reform society by being all at once intensely philosophical (universal), political (progressive), and broadly religious (poetic).

3.12. PEACEFUL PROCESSION

Hölderlin's response to this challenge is to compose, on the eve of the hope of a lasting European peace in his own embattled age, a hymn to a spirit, or more precisely a procession of spirits, that may make possible true peace in general. His *Friedensfeier* (1801) goes far beyond even Kant's extraordinary vision (1795) of an eventual instauration of "perpetual peace" through a complex reform of international political structures, for Hölderlin (here and in related works such as *Brod und Wein*, *Patmos*, and *Andenken* [Remembrance]) goes so far as to display a way to tie together the whole sequence of pre-Christian gods, the era of original Christianity, and the spirit of modernity and the ages to come. His key strategy—similar to what Novalis, Schleiermacher, and others close to the Jena group also propose—is to move religious and philosophical thinking away from an insistence on celebrating ("naming") only one system, or divinity, and toward a sensitivity for the multiplicity of connected forms that the "spirit" of true peace appears to take as history proceeds. This pluralism is not a regression to paganism or relativism but an attempt to enlarge the mainstream heritage of Hölderlin's own tradition, that is, to regard the spirit of Christianity as a fruitful outgrowth of an ancient Greek setting with similar concerns (for example, in aspects of the Dionysus cult), and as something that can be replanted in new settings, albeit with increasing difficulty, in later ages.

The key to identifying the "prince" of peace, that is, the figure awaited and celebrated throughout the poem, is to avoid the exclusivist fallacy of hypothesizing that it is simply Napolean, Jupiter, Jesus, the poet himself, or some other particular figure such as Dionysus or Heracles. Instead, as Peter Szondi has pointed out, one should note that Hölderlin uses a long sequence of varied holy names, names that are not singular but rather descriptive of different aspects of what we know as best in "spirit."[35] It thus can be argued that it is the very succession of names, and naming processes, that is the subject of the "celebration" of peace, and that Hölderlin's own poem is intended, like the multiple scriptures of old, to be but one stage in this process—and a reminder of the importance of maintaining this kind of process as such.[36] The poem celebrates:

> Der Allversammelnde, wo Himmlische nicht
> Im Wunder offenbar, noch ungesehn im Wetter,
> Wo aber bei Gesang gastfreundlich untereinander
> In Chören gegenwärtig, eine heilige Zahl
> Die Seeligen in jeglicher Weise
> Beisammen sind.[37]

For Hölderlin, spirit dwells now neither in a pagan "thunderstorm" age (of mere naturalism), nor in an orthodox "miracle" age (of mere supernaturalism),[38] but in a late modern age of "hymns" and gatherings for a struggling movement toward universal progressivism. "All" are to be assembled in a celebrative process in which they understand themselves as being "present" together through writings that literally re-collect the past and help forge a "blessed" future in a creatively extended tradition.

It is up to theologians to debate whether Hölderlin is a genuinely theological writer, and if so, whether he is a heretic or a permissible member of their union. Without getting into these issues, a historian of philosophy can propose that Hölderlin's work can be read not only as a serious attempt at an all-inclusive kind of creative religious writing—like Milton's and Dante's—but also as an exhibition of a general manner of thinking that is exemplary specifically for late modern philosophy. His work provides a figurative model, in form as well as content, for fusing transitions that bridge massively different conceptual frameworks by providing an overall narrative with implicit argumentative connections that lead from the distant past into the indefinite future. The key idea in *Friedensfeier*, that we need to see ourselves as an ongoing historical "Gespräch," is the guiding "form" for Hölderlin's thought as a whole, just as it implicitly is, in a detailed argumentative mode, for all works of productive philosophical retrieval in late modern philosophy's "historical turn"—such as in MacIntyre's turn to Aristotle, or Rawls's turn to Kant. This idea is reiterated as an organizing theme in Hölderlin's many tributes to cities, rivers, and heroes as sources of our culture, and in his reference, for example, to the need to construct "lightly built bridges" in *Patmos*, or to show how "that which happened before, but hardly was felt / Only now is manifest" in... *As on a Holiday*. The guiding "content" of Hölderlin's work—which can also be found in late modern philosophies such as MacIntyre's and Rawls's, whatever their other differences—is the related thought that the very fulfillment of human nature (its "Bestimmung" or "Beruf") consists in an ongoing "homecoming," one wherein, from now on, our entire past should become a legacy increasingly "felt" in progressive forms of "holy" or celebrative activity that can be shared universally in a pluralistic future that is always "becoming." (Hegel's *Phenomenology*, read in a spirit of "nonclosure," can also be seen as in this sense a vibrant philosophical successor of Hölderlin's project—but it is not the only one.)

My own historical hypothesis is that Hölderlin was at least subliminally influenced in *Friedensfeier* by a sequence of three scriptural passages that, as a rigorously trained seminarian, he must have known are treated by Lutherans as a triad highly relevant to the implications of understanding spiritual succession after Pentecost, namely, Numbers 11: 4–6, 10–16, 24–29, Mark 9: 30, and James 5: 13–20.[39] This scriptural sequence is instructive, quite apart from whatever one's theological views may be, because it shows how one can even draw on some aspects of orthodox traditions in order to introduce the general notion of a universally progressive and poetic, that is to say, creatively open, extension of a tradition—precisely the point that is given shape (either as conceived literally as an effect of "the spirit," or just as promoting a strikingly similar message) in works such as *Friedensfeier*. The hypothesis that Hölderlin's work is motivated by the general point of such scriptural passages, which dramatically encourage openness to outsiders, is supported by his constant concern with providing reminders of biblical motifs and preserving holy words, as well as the fact that, in contexts quite apart from religion, he repeatedly focuses on the issue of a procession of genial figures who inspire us with the task of encouraging new "prophets," ones who come from "outside the tent." Hölderlin's series of striking poetic portraits of (relatively) nonreligious figures clearly has as its aim to remind us that our late modern culture must develop itself through redefining its philosophical relation to earlier innovative outsiders such as Empedocles, Kepler, and Rousseau.[40] Just as these revolutionary figures struggled to seek successors for their work, so our own age is being reminded by Hölderlin of the need to redefine itself by generating true successors of his own work, with new conceptual frameworks that can be exemplary for the future.

Hölderlin's reminder has had a delayed but considerable effect, especially at a literary level, in the work of Walter Benjamin, Paul Celan, and many others. It remains true, however, that, unlike his contemporaries Reinhold, Schlegel,

Hegel, and Schelling,[41] Hölderlin does not provide an extended prose narrative that fills out, in a broadly logical way, exactly how the spirit of universal progressivism has passed from the key philosophical conceptions of one paradigmatic perspective on to another. But he certainly leaves enough hints for more prosaic minds to continue trying to spell out the implicit argumentative details of his distinctive romantic understanding of "our" "Gespräch," and its procession of diverse writers creatively tending the "firm letter"[42] of many overlapping traditions.

NOTES

1. Friedrich Schlegel, *Athenaeum Fragments*, no. 116, in *Philosophical Fragments*, trans. Peter Firchow (Minneapolis: University of Minnesota Press, 1991), 31–32, a volume put together in Jena in 1798 as an act of "sym-philosophy" by Schlegel and Novalis (Friedrich von Hardenberg). Italics added.

2. By "romanticism" I mean the period of *early German* romanticism that blossomed primarily in Jena in the late 1790s, although this includes authors associated with "classicism" and "idealism."

3. See my *Kant and the Historical Turn: Philosophy as Critical Appropriation* (Oxford: Clarendon Press, 2006).

4. This classification contrasts somewhat with Kant's distinction of three views ("progressing," "regressing," and "standstill") on the question of whether "humankind is continually improving," in *The Contest of the Faculties* (1798) (AA 8, 81).

5. This pattern is also treated by the romantics as an "eccentric path," and as highly relevant to individual life as well as history as a whole. See Charles Larmore, "Hölderlin and Novalis," in *The Cambridge Companion to German Idealism*, ed. Karl Ameriks (Cambridge: Cambridge University Press, 2000), 141–60. It is well known that the value of focusing on elliptical patterns was an important astronomical insight of Johannes Kepler's, but it is sometimes forgotten how Kepler's general courage to "think outside the box" in this literally eccentric way made him a hero in Germany on a level with Copernicus and Galileo. Kant compared his own work to Kepler's breakthrough (AA 8, 18), and Hölderlin, who, like Kepler, studied in Tübingen, wrote a noteworthy early poem in praise of the astronomer's daring. For further philosophical implications of the notion, see my *Kant's Elliptical Path* (Oxford: Clarendon Press, 2012).

6. See the contrast between "Laurasian" and "Gondwana" mythologies in E. J. Michael Witzel, *The Origins of the World's Mythologies* (Oxford: Oxford University Press, 2012).

7. See e.g., René Girard, "A Christian conversion is never circular. It never returns to its point of origin. It is open-ended." "Conversion in Christianity and Literature" (1988), in *Mimesis & Theory: Essays on Literature and Criticism, 1953–2005*, ed. Robert Doran (Stanford: Stanford University Press, 2008), 266.

8. Hence the title of Robert Brandom's neo-Hegelian volume, *Making It Explicit: Reasoning, Representing, and Discursive Commitment* (Cambridge, MA: Harvard University Press, 1998).

9. There are, of course, more pragmatic readings of Hegel, especially by contemporary interpreters such as Robert B. Pippin and Terry Pinkard. Nonetheless, the schoolbook, or "end of history," reading that I am invoking here has had a huge influence.

10. The peculiarity of including a consideration of history in Hegel's system of philosophy as a science is noted in Eckart Förster, *Die 25 Jahre der Philosophie: Eine systematische Rekonstruktion* (Frankfurt am Main: Klostermann, 2011), chap. 12, "Hat die Philosophie eine Geschichte?"

11. In its original meaning "development" (*Entwicklung*) can signify mere conceptual elucidation, as in the context of analytic judgments. See Kant, *Jäsche Logic* (AA 9, 111 n.).

12. Here "natural" means explicable entirely by natural science in a strict sense. The image of "cradling" ("uns wiegen lassen"), albeit with a somewhat different sense, comes from Hölderlin's poem *Mnemosyne*, discussed in Alice Kuzniar, *Delayed Endings: Nonclosure in Novalis and Hölderlin* (Athens: University of Georgia Press, 1987), 133.

13. For an enlightening recent Jewish interpretation of this tradition, see Yoram Hazony, *The Philosophy of Hebrew Scripture* (Cambridge: Cambridge University Press, 2012).

14. Among the German idealists, broadly speaking, it is Kant who holds on most firmly to this libertarian aspect of traditional religion. On divine concurrence in his notion of the highest good, see e.g., notes from the lectures, "Ethic Herder" (AA 27, 16). Among the romantics, Hölderlin most fully appreciates this aspect of Kant's doctrine of freedom. See his "On the Law of Freedom" (1794) in *Friedrich Hölderlin: Essays and Letters on Theory*, ed. Thomas Pfau (Albany: State University of New York Press, 1988), 33f., and his letter to his brother, April 13, 1795, "what is most indispensable here is certainly freedom of the will," *Essays and Letters*, 127–28. Hölderlin also follows Kant, who follows Rousseau, in attributing contemporary evil primarily to our giving in to the inherited trappings of luxury and modern culture: "that which was the general reason for the decline of all peoples, namely that their originality, their own living nature succumbed to the positive forms, to the luxury which their fathers had produced, that seems to be our fate as well, only on a larger scale—" in "The Perspective from Which We Have to Look at Antiquity" (1799), *Essays and Letters*, 39.

15. One can also add, of course, an account in which our future is taken to be basically negative rather than positive (see above, note 4), but that is also a kind of "progression."

16. On Hölderlin's grasp of Kant's libertarian notion of absolute free choice, see above, note 14. See also Hölderlin's letter to Niethammer, February 24, 1796, "Philosophy is once again my almost exclusive occupation. I have taken Kant and Reinhold and hope to collect and strengthen my spirit in this element" (*Essays and Letters*, 131); and his letter to his brother, January 1, 1799, "Kant is the Moses of our nation who leads it out of Egyptian apathy into the free, solitary desert [of the moral law]" (*Essays and Letters*, 137).

17. See Alvin Plantinga and Nicholas Wolterstorff, *Faith and Rationality* (Notre Dame, IN: University of Notre Dame Press, 1983).

18. Cf. Simon Critchley, *The Faith of the Faithless: Experiments in Political Theology* (New York: Verso, 2012), 251: "what is rather being called for is a rigorous and activistic conception of faith that proclaims itself into being at each instant without guarantee or security."

19. In this essay, I directly invoke classic studies by Peter Szondi, Ernst Behler, Michael Hamburger, Dieter Henrich, Manfred Frank, Charles Larmore, and Alice Kuzniar; more recently I have also been influenced by Frederick Beiser, Richard Eldridge, Karsten Harries, Jane Kneller, Elizabeth Millán, Fred Rush, and Eric Santner. I am also indebted to very helpful comments by the editor of this volume.

20. As is recounted in Ernst Behler, *German Romantic Literary Theory* (Cambridge: Cambridge University Press, 1993), August Wilhelm Schlegel helped to make Friedrich's early views on this topic very well known throughout Germany.

21. See above note 18, and Simon Critchley's recent effort to recapture "for the left" a similar broad and somewhat romantic conception of religion for a secular generation.

22. See e.g., Reinhart Koselleck, "The Status of the Enlightenment in German History," in *The Cultural Values of Europe*, ed. Hans Joas and Klaus Wiegandt (Liverpool: Liverpool University Press, 2008), 253–64.

23. These terms come from Kant's *Critique of the Power of Judgment* (§ 49); their relevance to romanticism and contemporary philosophy in general is discussed in my *Kant's Elliptical Path*, chap. 15.

24. See Sanford Budick, *Kant and Milton* (Cambridge, MA: Harvard University Press, 2010), which picks up on themes first emphasized in W. Jackson Bate, *The Burden of the Past and the English Poet* (Cambridge, MA: Harvard University Press, 1970), and Harold Bloom, *The Anxiety of Influence* (Oxford: Oxford University Press, 1973).

25. See above, note 3.

26. See above, note 10.

27. This a point that Manfred Frank and others have documented in the wake of the results of Dieter Henrich's massive Jena research project. Manfred Frank recounts this work in his contribution to this volume, chapter 1 above.

28. "in dürftiger Zeit," from *Brod und Wein*.

29. See Hölderlin, "On Religion" (1797), which speaks of a "more than mechanical interrelation, a higher destiny," *Essays and Letters*, 90.

30. Hölderlin to Schelling, July 1799, in *Essays and Letters*, 146.

31. Hölderlin to Casimir Ulrich Böhlendorff, December 4, 1801, in *Essays and Letters*, 149.

32. Budick's *Kant and Milton* (see above, notes 23 and 24) demonstrates the many ways in which Kant's philosophy is an attempt to thematize the problem of succession as it occurs in Milton's work. One can also argue that Kant's own work, and his theory of genius in particular, is meant to exemplify an achievement of succession that can serve as a kind of model for later truly genial philosophical writers—a challenge that the romantics immediately took up. See my *Kant's Elliptical Path*, chap. 13, "On the Extension of Kant's Elliptical Path in Hölderlin and Novalis."

33. Cf. Schlegel's explicit characterization of romanticism (which enlists Goethe in the movement) as an attempt to succeed the giants of previous ages, Dante and Milton: "The Satan of the Italian and English poets may be more poetic; but the

German Satan is more satanic; and to that extent one might say that Satan is a German invention." *Athenaeum Fragments*, no. 379, 77. Understanding well his role as a major successor, it is no accident that Milton traveled to Dante's and Galileo's region of Italy—and that Dante earlier, in cantos 26 of the *Inferno* and *Purgatorio*, links himself to Virgil and Homer's Odysseus.

34. Michael Hamburger, "The Sublime Art: Notes on Milton and Hölderlin," in *Contraries: Studies in German Literature* (New York: E. P. Dutton, 1957), 46.

35. Peter Szondi, *Schriften I* (Frankfurt am Main: Suhrkamp, 1978), 332–33, notes at least ten different designations in the poem: "Jüngling," "dem Donnerer," "der Alllebendige," "der Vater," "Geist der Welt," "Herrn der Zeit," "ein Gott [anders als Sterbliche]", "der Meister," "der stille Gott der Zeit," and "Fürst des Festes."

36. In this way the poem can be read as a "Gottesdienst," a literary substitute for the career of an orthodox minister that Hölderlin felt he could not assume within the establishment of his time.

37. "The all assembling, where heavenly beings are / Not manifest in miracles, nor unseen in thunderstorms, / But where in hymns hospitably conjoined / And present in choirs, a holy number, / The blessed in every way / Meet and forgather." *Friedrich Hölderlin: Selected Poems and Fragments*, trans. Michael Hamburger (London: Penguin, 1998), 215.

38. Given his close reading of Kant, it may be no accident that Hölderlin's conceptual contrast of these two inadequate options ("thunderstorms," "miracle") echoes the contrast Kant draws between the two inadequate options of "being veiled in obscurity" (*in Dunkelheiten verhüllt*) and "being in the transcendent region" (*im Überschwänglichen*), and the fortunate alternative ("present") of what "I see before me" (*ich sehe—vor mir*); see the conclusion of the *Critique of Practical Reason*, the sentence directly after Kant's most famous phrase, concerning the "starry heavens" and "the moral law" (AA 5, 161–62).

39. The book of Numbers speaks of seventy elders who, "when the spirit rested upon them—prophesied. But they did not do so again." At this point, when two others "outside the tent," Eldad and Medad, start prophesizing and one of Moses's own chosen assistants, Joshua, pleads for Moses to stop them, Moses's reply is: "Are you jealous for my sake? Would that all the Lord's people were prophets, and that the Lord would put his spirit on them!" This point is taken to be repeated and amplified in Mark. Here, after John says to Jesus, "Teacher, we saw someone casting out demons in your name, and we tried to stop him, because he was not following us," the reply of Jesus is, "Do not stop him—whoever is not against us is for us." The general idea then appears again, in James, which stresses that "whoever brings back a sinner from wandering—will cover a multitude of sins." *New Revised Standard Version with Apocrypha*, Augsburg Fortress Press, 1992. It is striking that the passage from Mark is cited in Kant's *Religion* (AA 6, 84).

40. See above, note 33.

41. For a discussion of Schelling's views on history as a version of the romantic tradition, see my "History, Idealism, and Schelling," *Internationales Jahrbuch des Deutschen Idealismus/International Yearbook of German Idealism* 10 (forthcoming).

42. "vesten Buchstab," from *Patmos*. The mention of "tending" should not be taken to imply a merely retrospective project. The writer's vocation is to use the "letter" to lead humanity into the "Gesang" of the future, that is, a kind of poetic existence in general. (My thanks to Martin Sticker for a reminder of the importance of this point.) For a complementary theological discussion of Hölderlin's significance, see Cyril O'Regan, "Aesthetic Idealism and its relation to theological formation: reception and critique," in *The Impact of Idealism. The Legacy of Post-Kantian German Thought*, vol. 4: Religion, ed. Nicholas Adams (Cambridge: Cambridge University Press, 2013), 142–66, which draws on Jean-Luc Marion's perceptive study of Hölderlin's poetry in *The Idol and Distance: Five Studies* (New York: Fordham University Press, 2001), 298–338.

4

Romanticism and Language

MICHAEL N. FORSTER

One of the commonest misconceptions about German romanticism is that it lacked intellectual sophistication and rigor. The leading German Romantics were in fact *anything but* theoretical lightweights. One area in which this can be clearly seen is that of their views about *language*. In this article, I will try to provide a survey of those views that conveys something of their serious-ness and depth. For reasons of space, I will focus on Friedrich Schlegel and Schleiermacher, with only occasional remarks on other important figures (in particular, August Wilhelm Schlegel and Wilhelm von Humboldt, a sort of fel-low traveler of romanticism).[1]

4.1. PHILOSOPHY OF LANGUAGE

The German Romantics' philosophy of language sensu stricto is largely bor-rowed from and very similar to Herder's, but with one important exception. Friedrich Schlegel in *On the Language and Wisdom of the Indians* (1808) and Schleiermacher in his psychology lectures (1818–34) both take over the spe-cific naturalistic theory of the origin of language that Herder had developed in his *Treatise on the Origin of Language* (1772) (though Schlegel restricts it to only the most important of two broad types of languages that he distinguishes, namely "organic" languages rather than "mechanical" ones, and gives an alter-native naturalistic account of the latter).[2] Schleiermacher also takes over from Herder such important theses as that language is fundamentally social in nature and that language is not merely added on to the mental processes that human beings share with animals but instead infuses all human mental processes, lending them a distinctive character (for example, structuring human beings' sensory images in distinctive ways).

More importantly, Schlegel and Schleiermacher both take over a certain powerful theory about the nature of thought, meaning (or conceptualization), and language that Herder had developed (especially in his *Fragments on Recent German Literature* [1767–68]). His theory consisted of three main doctrines:

(1) Thought is essentially dependent on, and bounded by, language— that is, one can only think if one has a language, and one can only think what one can express linguistically.

(2) Meanings or concepts are not the sorts of things, in principle autonomous of language, with which much of the philosophical tradition has equated them, for example, the referents involved, Platonic forms, or subjective mental "ideas," but instead—*usages of words*.

(3) Conceptualization is essentially bound up with (perceptual and affective) sensation. More precisely, Herder espoused a quasi-empiricist theory of concepts according to which sensation is the source and basis of all our concepts, though we are also able to achieve something like nonempirical concepts by means of metaphorical extensions of empirical ones—so that all of our concepts ultimately depend on sensation in one way or another.

Friedrich Schlegel adopted versions of doctrines (1) and (2). For example, as early as 1798–99 he writes that "every spirit has its word, the two are inseparable";[3] in the Cologne lectures on philosophy from 1804 to 1806 he connects reason intimately with language,[4] and states that "each concept must be a word";[5] and he opens the Cologne lectures on German language and literature from 1807 by saying that language is fundamental to all human activities because "one cannot think without words."[6] Similarly, in the *Lectures on the History of Literature* (delivered in 1812, published in 1815), he says: "What is there more completely characteristic of man or of greater importance to him than language? Reason alone excepted, and even she must perforce employ the vehicle of language… Reason and language, thought and word, are… essentially one."[7] In addition, while it is less clear that Friedrich espoused a version of doctrine (3), it is at least clear that his brother August Wilhelm did. For example, August Wilhelm says that "the sense of words is determined according to the intuitions which people are in the habit of associating with them; so that we are in constant danger of ascribing to the words of the Greek poets a quite different meaning than they had for them and their audience, even when we understand them grammatically as exactly as you please."[8]

Schleiermacher espoused versions of the three doctrines as well. Thus, concerning (1), in his hermeneutics lectures (1805–33) and elsewhere he from an early period adopted a radical version of the doctrine that claimed an outright identity between thought and language.[9] And while some of the secondary literature has claimed that he eventually gave up this position, we still find him in his psychology lectures from 1830 speaking of "the activity of thought in its identity with language."[10] Concerning (2), he too adopts a view of meanings that equates them—not with such items as referents, Platonic forms, or subjective mental "ideas"—but with word-usages, or rules of word use. For example, in the hermeneutics lectures he says that "the...meaning of a term is to be derived from the unity of the word-sphere and from the rules governing the presupposition of this unity."[11] Finally, concerning (3), in his psychology lectures he argues that although thought and conceptualization are not *reducible* to sensuous images, the latter are an essential *foundation* for the former. Similarly, in his late hermeneutics lectures and elsewhere he is strongly attracted to Kant's theory of empirical schemata, according to which empirical concepts consist in unconscious rules for the generation of sensuous images, and he attempts to turn this theory into an account of the nature of *all* concepts.

Schlegel and Schleiermacher could be accused of making Herder's original theory cruder in certain ways.[12] However, they also achieve at least one very important refinement of it. This is the introduction of a form of *holism*. Like most of the Enlightenment before him, Herder had normally given the impression that languages are merely aggregates of particular words/concepts. By contrast, Schlegel in *On the Language and Wisdom of the Indians* develops a much more holistic conception of language that holds that such particular items are only possible in the context of a larger linguistic whole—a conception he expresses by characterizing languages as "organisms" or "systems."[13] In addition, he identifies as the most fundamental unifying principle of such linguistic "organisms" their *grammar*.

Following Schlegel's lead, Schleiermacher likewise adopts a holistic conception of linguistic meaning—especially in his dialectics lectures (1811–34) and in "On the Different Methods of Translation" (1813).[14] His holism has at least three distinguishable components: (*a*) Like Schlegel, he holds that a language's *grammatical* system (e.g., its system of declensions) is partly constitutive of the character of the concepts that are expressed within it. (*b*) He also holds that the nature of any particular concept is in part defined by its relations to a "system of concepts." In this connection, he emphasizes in the dialectics lectures a concept's relations as a species-concept to superordinate genus-concepts, relations as a genus-concept to subordinate species-concepts, and relations of contrast to coordinate species-concepts falling under the same genus-concepts.

However, he would probably include other types of conceptual relationships here as well (e.g., those between "to work," "worker," and "a work"). (*c*) As can be seen from a passage already quoted, he also espouses a doctrine of "the unity of the word-sphere." This doctrine in effect says that the various specific senses that a single word will typically bear, and which will be distinguished by any good dictionary entry (e.g., the different senses of "impression" in "He made an impression in the clay," "My impression is that he is reluctant," and "He made a big impression at the party"), always form a larger semantic unity to which they each essentially belong (so that any loss, addition, or alteration among them would entail an alteration in each of them, albeit perhaps a subtle one).[15]

4.2. LINGUISTICS

Friedrich Schlegel essentially founded the modern discipline of linguistics, namely in *On the Language and Wisdom of the Indians*. He did so on the basis of the central Herderian doctrines in the philosophy of language just discussed, in particular doctrines (1) and (2), together with two additional Herderian doctrines:

(4) Herder had argued that human beings exhibit profound differences in their modes of thought, concepts, and language, especially between different historical periods and cultures, but even to some extent between individuals within a single period and culture.[16]

(5) In light of doctrines (1) and (2), he had also argued that investigating the differences in the characters of people's languages can, and should, serve as a primary and reliable means for discovering the differences in their modes of thought and concepts.[17]

Schlegel takes over this whole set of Herderian doctrines in *On the Language and Wisdom of the Indians*. Concerning doctrines (1) and (2), we already saw evidence of his commitment to these in both earlier and later works. Concerning doctrine (4), he had already written in the *Philosophy of Philology* (1797) of "the immeasurable difference..., the quite distinctive nature of antiquity,"[18] and a similar insight into sharp cognitive differences remains fundamental to *On the Language and Wisdom of the Indians*. Concerning doctrine (5), this is the implicit foundation of his procedure in that work of undertaking an investigation of the Sanskrit language in the first part as a prelude to then exploring Indian thought and conceptualization in subsequent parts. Indeed, doctrine (5) constitutes the most important motive for the new science of linguistics that he begins to develop in the work: it is supposed to provide a reliable window on people's varying modes of thought and conceptualization.[19]

Schlegel's own holism concerning language, his conception that languages are "organisms," and in particular that their fundamental unifying principle is their grammar, is also fundamental to his project of founding linguistics in *On the Language and Wisdom of the Indians*.

Building on all these materials, he develops the new discipline in the work roughly as follows:

(a) Whereas the early Herder of the *Treatise on the Origin of Language* had implied at one point that grammar is inessential to language in its more original and natural forms, merely being a product of the late theoretical oversophistication of grammarians,[20] and at another point (rather inconsistently) that grammar is basically the same across all languages (with the exception of Chinese),[21] the later Herder of the *Ideas for the Philosophy of History of Humanity* (1784–91) had argued that languages differ dramatically in their grammatical structures: in addition to exhibiting rich variety in *other* ways, "in the structure [*Bau*] of language, in the relation, the ordering, and the agreement of the parts with each other, it is almost immeasurable."[22] Schlegel rejects the early Herder's position but embraces this later position of Herder's, himself arguing that grammars differ deeply in their character from one language to another, thereby constituting deep differences in particular words/concepts as well (which may also differ for more superficial reasons).[23]

(b) Schlegel consequently identifies "comparative grammar" (an expression/concept that he virtually coined in *On the Language and Wisdom of the Indians*)[24] as the primary task of an empirical investigation of languages.

(c) Besides the fundamental motive mentioned above of providing a reliable window on the different modes of thought and concepts that occur, an additional important motive behind this project of comparative grammar that Schlegel emphasizes lies in his conviction that it promises to shed more light on the genealogical relations between languages than merely lexical comparisons can.[25]

(d) Schlegel himself begins the task of actually comparing different grammars in an empirically careful way. In doing so, he introduces the following broad typology: a contrast between, on the one hand, "organic," or highly inflected, languages, of which Sanskrit is his paradigmatic example, and on the other hand, "mechanical," or uninflected, languages, of which Chinese is his main example.[26] He also demonstrates the genealogical relations between the various Sanskritic (or as we would now call them, Indo-European) languages with greater insight and accuracy than had ever been achieved before.[27]

(e) In addition (but much more questionably), he draws from this comparison of grammars certain normative conclusions about the relative merits of different languages as instruments of thought—in particular, arguing for the superiority of highly inflected languages such as Sanskrit over uninflected languages such as Chinese. His case for the superiority of the former over the latter mainly rests on a claim that inflected languages have a privileged connection with "awareness" (*Besonnenheit*), or rationality. This part of his position is much more dubious than the preceding parts, however—both factually and ethically.[28]

Friedrich Schlegel's groundbreaking work quickly inspired a great wave of important further work based on the same principles. This wave included Bopp's *On the Conjugation System of the Sanskrit Language in Comparison with That of the Greek, Latin, Persian, and Germanic Languages* (1816), which focused on the Indo-European languages and their grammars;[29] Friedrich's brother August Wilhelm's Sanskrit studies, and *Observations on Provençal Language and Literature* (1818), which focused on the Romance languages and their grammars; and Jakob Grimm's *German Grammar* (1819), which focused on the Germanic languages and their grammars. Friedrich Schlegel's principles also soon inspired the general linguistics of Wilhelm von Humboldt, which Humboldt mainly developed in a series of public addresses and unpublished manuscripts that he wrote during the 1820s and in his crowning work *On the Diversity of Human Language-Structure and Its Influence on the Mental Development of Mankind* (1836).[30]

4.3. HERMENEUTICS

Friedrich Schlegel and Schleiermacher also made vitally important contributions to the development of both hermeneutics, or the theory of interpretation, and the theory of translation.

Their theories in these areas build on ones that had already been developed by Herder. Most fundamentally, they build on Herder's doctrines (1)–(4). Doctrine (4) poses a profound challenge to both interpretation and translation, and the main task of all the theories in question is to cope with this challenge.

Schlegel's and Schleiermacher's theories also fundamentally presuppose their own new insight into the *holistic* nature of linguistic meaning, which exacerbates the sorts of cognitive differences involved in (4), and hence adds to the difficulty of interpretation and translation.

Schlegel and Schleiermacher began to develop their new theories of interpretation and translation during the late 1790s, a time when they lived and worked together in Berlin, in particular conceiving the joint project of translating and commenting on the works of Plato (a project that Schlegel eventually gave up, but which Schleiermacher largely completed). As a result it is often difficult to say which of the two men deserves the credit for specific contributions in these areas. Because Schleiermacher developed his theories of interpretation and translation in much more systematic and elaborate ways than Schlegel, he has tended to receive most of the credit. But closer inspection suggests that this is unjust to Schlegel, especially in the area of interpretation theory. In this section I shall discuss their hermeneutics, or theory of interpretation, in the next their theory of translation.

Let us begin with Schleiermacher's hermeneutics. Schleiermacher lectured on this subject frequently between 1805 and 1833. The following are some of his main principles:

(a) Hermeneutics is strictly the theory of *understanding* linguistic communication—as *contrasted*, not equated, with explicating, applying, or translating it.

(b) Hermeneutics should be a *universal* discipline—that is, one that applies equally to both sacred and secular texts, to works on all subjects matters, to oral as well as written language, to modern texts as well as ancient, to works in one's own language as well as works in foreign languages, and so forth.

(c) In particular, the interpretation of sacred texts such as the Bible falls within it—this must not rely on *special* principles, such as divine inspiration (of either the author or the interpreter).

(d) Interpretation is in one way an easier task than has sometimes been realized, in that an author's thoughts and meanings at least cannot transcend his linguistic competence (as, for example, Plato supposed). (This is an application of doctrines (1) and (2).) But in another way it is a much more difficult task than has usually been realized: contrary to a common misconception that "understanding occurs as a matter of course," "misunderstanding occurs as a matter of course, and so understanding must be willed and sought at every point." (This is a consequence of doctrine (4).)

How, then, is it to be accomplished?

(e) Before interpretation proper can even begin, the interpreter must acquire a good knowledge of the text's historical context.[31]

(f) Interpretation always has two sides: one "linguistic," the other "psychological." Linguistic interpretation's basic task (which rests on doctrine (2)) is to infer from the particular known uses of a word to the rule that governs them, that is, to its usage, and thus to its meaning. Psychological interpretation instead focuses on the author's individual psychology. Linguistic interpretation is mainly concerned with what is shared in a language; psychological interpretation with what is distinctive to a particular author.

(g) Why does the interpreter need to complement linguistic interpretation with psychological in this way? Schleiermacher implies several reasons. First, a need to do so arises from doctrine (4) as it concerns individuals: the linguistic and conceptual-intellectual distinctiveness of individuals. This leads to the problem for linguistic interpretation that the actual uses of words that are available to serve as evidence from which to infer an author's exact usages, or meanings, will generally be few in number and poor in contextual variety. An appeal to the author's psychology is supposed to help solve this problem by providing additional clues. Second, an appeal to the author's psychology is also required in order to resolve apparent ambiguities in linguistic meaning that arise in particular contexts. Third, in order fully to understand a linguistic act one needs to grasp not only its linguistic meaning but also what more recent authors would call its "illocutionary" force or intention.

(h) Interpretation also requires two different methods: a "comparative" method and a "divinatory" method. The "comparative" method is essentially a method of plain induction. The "hypothetical" method is essentially a method of tentative, fallible hypothesis based on but also going well beyond the available empirical evidence.[32] Schleiermacher sees the former method as predominating on the linguistic side of interpretation (where it takes the interpreter from the particular uses of a word that are known to the rule for use that governs them all), the latter method on the psychological side. Accordingly, in the hermeneutics lectures he writes that divination is required in order to construct "a complete image of a person from only scattered traces," noting that "we cannot be too careful in examining from every angle a picture that has been sketched in such a hypothetical fashion. We should accept it only when we find no contradictions, and even then only provisionally."[33]

(i) Interpretation should be a holistic activity. (This principle to some extent rests on Schleiermacher's *semantic* holism, but also goes far beyond it.) In particular, any given part of a text needs to be interpreted in light of the whole text to which it belongs, and both of them need to be interpreted in light of the whole language in which they are written, their historical context, a broader preexisting genre, the author's whole corpus, and the author's overall psychology.

(j) Such holism introduces a pervasive circularity into interpretation. For, ultimately, interpreting broader items of the sorts in question in its turn depends on interpreting parts of texts. This circularity might seem vicious. However, Schleiermacher denies that it is. Why? His solution is not that all of these tasks can be accomplished simultaneously, for that is beyond human cognitive capacities. Instead, it turns on the very plausible thought that understanding is not an all-or-nothing matter but instead something that comes in *degrees*, so that it is possible to make progress towards full understanding in a gradual way. For example, concerning the relation between a part of a text and the whole text to which it belongs, he recommends that one first read through and interpret each of the parts of the text in turn as well as one can in order thereby to arrive at an approximate overall interpretation of the text, and that one then apply this approximate overall interpretation in order to refine one's initial interpretations of the parts, which in turn gives one an improved overall interpretation, which can then be reapplied towards further refinement of the interpretations of the parts, and so on indefinitely.

Up to this point, Schleiermacher's theory of interpretation is almost identical to Herder's, mainly just drawing together and systematizing ideas that were already scattered through a number of Herder's works. This continuity extends well beyond doctrines (1)–(4). For example, the theory also owes to Herder its two central moves (often wrongly thought to be original with Schleiermacher) of complementing "linguistic" with "psychological" interpretation, and of identifying "divination" as the predominant method of the latter.[34] And both the theory's emphasis on the need for holism and its methodological solution to the resulting problem of circularity come from Herder as well.[35] Schleiermacher's theory does also contain a number of additional ideas that depart from Herder's in various ways. However, it is precisely here that it tends to become more problematic.[36]

Friedrich Schlegel's theory of interpretation is largely similar to Schleiermacher's, only less systematically presented. However, it may well be that he makes an even more important contribution than Schleiermacher. This is in part due to a fact that has already been noted by some of the secondary literature, namely that he largely anticipated and helped to generate Schleiermacher's theory.[37] But it is even more due to the fact that he in addition developed some vitally important ideas of his own that are not really to be found in Schleiermacher (though they had again been anticipated by Herder to a considerable extent). Let us consider five of these:

(a) The first idea—or rather, family of ideas—concerns *genre*, a crucially important subject that Schleiermacher had almost ignored. Many of the key insights in this area had already been achieved by Herder, in such works as *Shakespeare* (1773) and *This Too a Philosophy of History for the Formation of Humanity* (1774). His insights included the following: (i) The correct identification of genre plays an essential role in the interpretation of both literary and nonlinguistic art. (ii) Genres are radically mutable over the course of history. (iii) An interpreter therefore often needs to identify unfamiliar, newly invented, and sometimes even uniquely instantiated genres. (iv) He also therefore often needs to resist a strong temptation to misidentify a genre he encounters by falsely assimilating it to a superficially similar-looking genre from another time or place with which he happens already to be more familiar (e.g., to misidentify the genre of Shakespearean "tragedy" by falsely assimilating it to that of ancient Greek "tragedy"). (v) Likewise, a critic often needs to identify an unfamiliar, newly invented, or even uniquely instantiated genre if he is to judge a work of literary or nonlinguistic art in terms of the genre-purposes and genre-rules that it really aspires to realize rather than in terms of ones that it does not, and he needs to resist strong temptations to assume some more familiar genre and as a result evaluate the work in terms of genre-purposes and genre-rules that it does not even aspire to realize in the first place. (vi) The interpreter or critic consequently needs to employ a painstaking empirical approach to the identification of genres in order to identify them correctly. Friedrich Schlegel's achievement in this area largely just lay in the fact that he retained these vitally important Herderian insights in his best thinking on the subject of genre.[38] (The same was true of his brother August Wilhelm.)

But Friedrich Schlegel (followed by his brother) in addition made two very important *new applications* of these Herderian insights about genre. One of these concerned the interpretation of ancient Greek tragedy. Before Friedrich Schlegel the understanding of Greek tragedy as a genre had been dominated by Aristotle's treatment of it in the *Poetics*, which had been considered virtually sacrosanct not only by most French dramatists and critics but also by their recent German opponents Lessing and Herder. With Friedrich Schlegel, especially in *History of the Poetry of the Greeks and Romans* (1798), there emerged for the first time—in light of his Herderian awareness of the historical mutability of genres and of the dangers of assimilating one genre to another, more familiar genre, together with a more scrupulous empirical investigation of the surviving Greek tragedies themselves conducted in the spirit of Herder's methodological empiricism—a realization that Aristotle's treatment of Greek tragedy was in fact at least as much an obstacle to properly understanding it as an aid. Among other things, Friedrich Schlegel saw that Aristotle had falsely assimilated tragedy's greatest fifth-century forms to later forms of it that had become prevalent in his own day, and that largely as a result of this he had misrepresented it in important respects, for example obscuring its deeply religious-Dionysiac and civic-political nature. By breaking Aristotle's undue influence on the interpretation of Greek tragedy in this way, Friedrich Schlegel (followed by his brother) initiated a deep rethinking of its nature that subsequently continued with Nietzsche's *The Birth of Tragedy* and still continues today (e.g., in the work of Vernant, Vidal-Nacquet, Goldhill, and Winkler).[39]

Another new application of Herder's basic insights about genre concerned the very birth of romanticism itself. For when the young Friedrich Schlegel in a famous preface that he added to his *On the Study of Greek Poetry* (1795) in 1797 suddenly changed from an initial classicism concerning the distinction between "classical" and "interesting" (or "romantic") poetry towards a recognition of the equal legitimacy and value of the latter, thereby giving birth to his romanticism, this change was largely the result of a sudden recognition on his part that the historical shift from the former type of poetry to the latter was basically an example of the sort of historical shift between different but equally well-defined and legitimate genres that Herder had already discussed, and that this precluded any simple valorization of the one at the expense of the other, in particular any negative assessment of the one in terms of the standards of the other (he had just reviewed a discussion of these very issues in Herder's *Letters for the Advancement of Humanity* in a review article from 1796).[40]

Finally, Friedrich Schlegel also made two further significant contributions concerning genre. First, again in continuity with Herder but more emphatically, he recognized that genres (e.g., tragedy) give birth to what theorists would today call genre-modes (e.g., "tragic"), which may then qualify works in other genres (for instance, one could plausibly characterize Thomas Hardy's novels as "tragic novels"). Second, he recognized that genres are sometimes systematically interdependent and interdefined. This sort of situation is fairly obvious in certain cases, such as the case of parody. But, as Friedrich Schlegel (and his brother) showed, there are also less obvious, more interesting cases— for instance, ancient tragedy and comedy, which (unlike their modern counterparts) are partly defined by their sharp exclusion of each other.

(b) A second important idea concerning interpretation that Schlegel developed is the idea that texts sometimes express meanings and thoughts, not explicitly in any of their parts, but instead implicitly through their parts and the way in which these are put together to form a whole. Thus he writes in *Athenaeum Fragments* (1798–1800), no. 111: "The teachings that a novel hopes to instill must be of the sort that can be communicated only as wholes, not demonstrated singly and not subject to exhaustive analysis." He applies this point not only to novels (e.g., to Goethe's *Wilhelm Meisters Lehrjahre* in *On Goethe's Meister* [1798]), but also to the philosophical texts of Spinoza and Fichte (in *On Lessing* [1797/1801]), and to ancient literature. In the last of these connections, he writes at *Athenaeum Fragments*, no. 325 (echoing a famous fragment of Heraclitus): "But Apollo, who neither speaks nor keeps silent but intimates, no longer is worshipped, and wherever a Muse shows herself, people immediately want to carry her off to be cross-examined."

(c) A third important contribution Schlegel made to hermeneutics concerns the role of *unconscious* meanings and thoughts in texts, and hence in their proper interpretation. The general idea that unconscious mental processes occur already had a long history in German philosophy by Schlegel's day, and had indeed already been discussed in connection with questions of authorship and interpretation by Herder in *On the Cognition and Sensation of the Human Soul* (1778). However, it was above all Schlegel who developed this idea into a principle that the interpreter must penetrate beyond an author's conscious meanings and thoughts to discover his unconscious ones as well. Thus he writes in *On Goethe's Meister* that "every excellent work... aims at more than it knows"; and in *Athenaeum Fragments*, no. 401 that "in order to understand someone who only partially understands himself, you first have to understand him completely and better than he himself does."

(d) A fourth important contribution Schlegel made to hermeneutics concerns the presence of inconsistency and confusion in texts. The important hermeneutic theorist Ernesti had already encouraged the interpreter to attribute inconsistencies and other forms of confusion to profane texts when appropriate, and Herder had extended that principle to sacred texts as well. Schlegel accepts Herder's broader version of the principle. But he also places even more emphasis on it and develops it further, not only insisting that confusion is a common feature of texts and should be recognized when it occurs, but also arguing that in such cases the interpreter needs to seek to *understand and explain* it. Thus he already writes in a note from 1797: "In order to understand someone, one must first of all be cleverer than he, then just as clever, and then also just as stupid. It is not enough that one understand the actual sense of a confused work better than the author understood it. One must also oneself be able to know, to *characterize*, and even *construe* the confusion even down to its very principles."[41]

(e) A fifth important contribution Schlegel made to hermeneutics concerns the interpretation of nonlinguistic (or perhaps: "nonlinguistic") art—that is, painting, sculpture, architecture, instrumental music, and so on. Herder had begun his career arguing in the early parts of the *Critical Forests* (1769) that nonlinguistic art does not express meanings or thoughts at all but is instead merely sensuous in nature. On such a view, the question of *interpreting* it would not even arise. But Herder had subsequently changed his mind about this, instead coming to recognize that nonlinguistic art often *does* express meanings and thoughts, namely (in order to stay consistent with doctrines (1) and (2)) ones that are implicitly grounded in the artist's language, and that it therefore does need to be interpreted. This later position of Herder's is far more plausible. Schleiermacher is usually retrograde on this issue, and therefore restricts hermeneutics to texts and discourse. But Schlegel deserves great credit for taking over Herder's later position and developing it in some very insightful ways. In particular, he develops a rich set of hermeneutic principles to guide the interpretation of nonlinguistic art. Some of these principles are similar to the ones that he espouses for interpreting linguistic texts, but others are distinctive to the interpretation of nonlinguistic art, in particular principles concerning a certain sort of *symbolism* through which it conveys meanings and thoughts.[42]

After Schlegel and Schleiermacher, the latter's pupil August Boeckh, an eminent classical philologist, recast Schleiermacher's hermeneutics in an even more systematic and elaborate form in lectures that were eventually published posthumously under the title *Encyclopedia and Methodology of the Philological*

Sciences (1877). In the course of doing so he laudably restored genre to the central place that it had received in the hermeneutics of Herder and Schlegel. The combined influence of Herder's, Schlegel's, Schleiermacher's, and Boeckh's treatments of hermeneutics secured for this tradition of hermeneutics something very much like the status of the official interpretive methodology of nineteenth-century Germany across such fields of research as biblical scholarship, classical philology, history, and history of philosophy. The extraordinary quality of that research constitutes eloquent testimony to its value.

4.4. THEORY OF TRANSLATION

Especially in the *Fragments on Recent German Literature*, Herder had developed a powerful new methodology of translation based on his doctrines (1)–(4). He had recognized that doctrine (4) entails that when translation takes place there will often be a deep gulf between the resources of the source language and those of the target language. He had seen that this causes serious problems for achieving semantic faithfulness and (in the case of poetry) musical faithfulness, even to the point of making this strictly impossible and forcing the translator to be satisfied with mere approximation. He had noted that because of the gulf in question translation needs to compromise in one direction or the other, either sacrificing the preexisting character of the source language or that of the target language. He had argued the translator should err in the latter direction rather than the former, first and foremost because this is necessary in order to maximize semantic-musical faithfulness, but also because it promises to create new semantic-musical resources in the target language. And he had advocated two more specific techniques in such a spirit: first, "bending" preexisting word-usages in the target language in order to approximate the word-usages, and therefore the meanings, in the source language as closely as possible (this technique rested on doctrine (2)); and second, striving to reproduce the musical features of the source language as accurately as possible in the target language (not only for musical reasons but also for semantic ones, the latter deriving in part from doctrine (3)). This whole Herderian methodology of translation was subsequently taken over and developed by Friedrich Schlegel (along with his brother August Wilhelm) and Schleiermacher. Let us consider each of their versions of it in turn.

As has already been mentioned, when Schlegel moved to Berlin in 1797 and befriended Schleiermacher there, they developed an ambitious joint project of translating the works of Plato. Accordingly, some of Schlegel's writings from around this period are concerned with the theory of translation—especially, his *Philosophy of Philology* (1797) and fragments from the late 1790s.[43] In addition, his Cologne lectures on German language and literature from 1807 contain comments about meter and its reproduction in another language, while shortly afterwards *On the Language and Wisdom of the Indians* likewise contains a little theorizing about translation as well as some actual translations of Sanskrit texts. From these materials it is possible to reconstruct the main lines of his early theory of translation. It includes the following principles:

(a) A modern translator typically confronts the problem that an intellectual gulf divides himself and his culture from an ancient author and his: "the immeasurable difference…, the quite distinctive nature of antiquity," "the *absolute* difference between the ancient and the modern."[44] This gulf consists first and foremost in conceptual incommensurability, but also in a sharp divergence of metrical principles.[45]

(b) This makes translation extremely difficult, even to the point of being strictly speaking impossible: "Whether translations are *possible* is a question no one has worried about."[46]

(c) However, the proper response to this situation is not to despair, but instead to regard the task of translation as one of endless approximation: "Every translation is an indeterminate, infinite task."[47]

(d) The translator who confronts an intellectual gulf of this sort faces a choice between either attempting to reproduce the original meaning and music of the source text faithfully or undertaking to transform them: "Every translation is a transplanting or a transforming or both."[48]

But how can translation of the former type be achieved?

(e) This requires that the translator possess hermeneutic (or "philological") expertise: "Translation is obviously something [philological];"[49] "Translation belongs entirely to philology, is a thoroughly philological art."[50] Especially on the musical side, it also requires that the translator be artistic.[51]

(f) In terms of specific approach, it requires that he modify the word-usages and the music features of the target language in order to approximate those of the source language as closely as possible. Thus Schlegel already remarks in the *Philosophy of Philology* that "one should translate in order to mold the modern languages classically."[52] And in *On the Language and Wisdom of the Indians* he argues that in translations of Sanskrit texts into German the German should "mold

itself" (*sich anschmiegen*) to the original Sanskrit and should attempt
to reproduce the meters found in the Sanskrit texts.[53]

(g) In addition to its primary virtue of reproducing the original text as
accurately as possible, this approach also has the virtue of enriching
the target language both conceptually and musically. Schlegel already
implies this when he says that "one should translate in order to mold
the modern languages classically." He also makes the point in a more
general form: "Each translation is actually language-creation."[54]

(h) This sort of translation elevates the translator to the rank of an
artist: "Only the translator is a linguistic artist."[55]

Schleiermacher went on to develop a very similar theory of translation,
but much more elaborately. Schleiermacher was a masterful translator, whose
translations of Plato into German are still widely used and admired today, two
centuries after they were first done. His views about translation therefore come
with great prima facie authority. He explains his theory of translation mainly in
the classic essay *On the Different Methods of Translation* (1813). The following
are his most important theses:

(a) Translation proper (as opposed to mere imitation) is an extremely
difficult task. For it faces a number of serious challenges that
only admit of partial solution. The primary task of translation is
to reproduce the original meaning accurately, and this is itself a
huge challenge. But there are also additional tasks that compound
the difficulty. For one thing, at least in the case of poetry it is
necessary to reproduce not only semantic but also musical features
of the original, such as meter and rhyme. This is not only an
aesthetic desideratum over and above translation's primary task of
reproducing meaning, but also an essential *part* of the latter, both
because meters bear their own meanings (Schleiermacher's friend
August Wilhelm Schlegel had especially emphasized this point) and
because the musical features of poetry serve as essential vehicles for
the precise expression of affective sensations and hence of meanings
(Herder had anticipated this point, which rested on a version of his
doctrine (3)). For another thing, in addition to reproducing a work's
meaning, a translation should also convey where its author was being
conceptually conventional and where, by contrast, conceptually
original—a task that can at least be accomplished to a certain extent
by using older vocabulary from the target language in the former
cases and newer vocabulary from the target language in the latter
cases. In addition to being intrinsically difficult, both of these

secondary tasks will often stand in deep tension with the primary task of finding the closest semantic fit, as well as with each other. For example, it will often turn out that the target-word that would best reproduce a rhyme or best reflect a concept's vintage is not the one that is closest in meaning to the source-word.

(b) The central challenge for translation, though, lies in its primary task of reproducing meaning accurately, and arises from the fact that translation typically faces a conceptual gulf between the source language and the target language (as they already exist). (This point is an application of Herder's doctrine (4).)

(c) Schleiermacher in particular notes the following complication that arises here (one might call this *the paradox of paraphrase*): if, faced with the task of translating an alien concept, a translator attempts to reproduce its *in*tension by reproducing its *ex*tension by means of an elaborate paraphrase in his own language, he will generally find that, as he gets closer to the original extension, he undermines the original intension in *other* ways.

How, therefore, should translation proceed? The following points constitute the core of Schleiermacher's answer:

(d) Because of such challenges the translator needs to have real interpretive-hermeneutic expertise and to be an "artist" if he is to cope with the task of translation at all adequately.

(e) The conceptual gulf that poses the central challenge here might in principle be tackled in one of two ways: either by bringing the author's linguistic-conceptual world closer to that of the reader of the translation or by bringing the reader's closer to the author's. The former approach had often been advocated and practiced (e.g., by Luther, who called it *Verdeutschung*). However, Schleiermacher finds it unacceptable, above all because it distorts the author's meaning. He therefore champions the alternative approach of bringing the reader towards the linguistic-conceptual world of the author as the only acceptable approach.

But how can that possibly be accomplished?

(f) The key, according to Schleiermacher, lies in the *plasticity* of language. Thanks to this plasticity, even if the usages of words, and hence the concepts, expressed by the target language *as it already exists* are incommensurable with the author's, the translator can "bend the language of the translation as far possible towards that of the original in order to communicate as far as possible an impression of the system of concepts developed in it."[56] (This solution presupposes doctrine (2).)

(g) This approach requires that a particular word from the source language normally be translated in a uniform way throughout the translation instead of by switching back and forth between two or more different ways of translating it in different contexts, as is usually done.

(h) It also inevitably results in translations that are less easy to read than those that can be achieved by the competing approach because of oddities that result. However, this is an acceptable price to pay given that the only alternative is a failure to convey the author's meaning at all accurately. Moreover, the oddities in question actually have a positive value, in that they constantly remind the reader of the conceptual unfamiliarity of the material being translated and of the "bending" approach being employed.

(i) In order to work effectively this approach needs to be applied consistently to large amounts of material, both so that the reader becomes accustomed to it in a general way and so that he acquires enough examples of a particular word's unfamiliar usage in enough different contexts to enable him to infer the unfamiliar rule for its use that is involved.

(j) Even this optimal approach has severe limitations, though. In particular, it will often be impossible to reproduce the *holistic* aspects of meaning—the several related usages of a given word, the system of related words/concepts to which it belongs, and the distinctive grammar of the language. And because these holistic features are internal to a word's meaning, that will entail a shortfall in the communication of its meaning by the translation. For this reason— together with such additional reasons as those mentioned in (a)— even this optimal sort of translation is bound to remain imperfect, only a poor second best to reading the originals.

(k) It remains justified and important, however. This is true not only for the obvious reason that people who cannot read the original languages need translations, but also for the less obvious reason that this optimal sort of translation through its "bending" approach and its reproduction of musical features enriches both the conceptual and the musical resources of the target language. Schleiermacher's picture of translation (as indeed of interpretation) is therefore that it is ultimately a matter of striving for an ideal that is never fully attainable, but striving for which nonetheless remains important and valuable. (This is also a characteristically Romantic model of the human condition more generally.)

(l) Nor (Schleiermacher adds in answer to a worry that Herder had raised in the *Fragments*) need it be feared that this enrichment will deprive the target language of its authentic nature. For one thing, it will often be confined to the sphere of translations. For another thing, when it is not so confined and really conflicts with the nature of the target language, the enrichments involved will soon wither from the language.

As in the case of Schleiermacher's theory of interpretation, not only doctrines (1)–(4), but *most* of these doctrines about translation come from Herder (especially from the *Fragments*). However, whereas, as we noted, Schleiermacher's theory of interpretation tends to worsen Herder's, his theory of translation tends to refine Herder's in some significant ways. Among the positions listed above, examples of this occur in (a), where the ideal of making clear in a translation at which points an author is being conceptually conventional and at which points conceptually original, and the strategy for achieving this, are new; (c), where the paradox of paraphrase is original; (h), where the point that the discomfort that the "bending" approach causes readers actually serves positive functions is novel; (i), where the point that this approach needs to be implemented on a large scale is new; (j), where the point that semantic holism inevitably limits the success of such translations is original; and (l), which plausibly contradicts Herder.[57]

The radical new methodology of translation developed by Herder, Friedrich Schlegel, Schleiermacher, and others in their circle quickly became the predominant methodology of translation in Germany, exercising an enormous and beneficial influence there on both the theory and the practice of translation, an influence that it continued to exercise well into the twentieth century (e.g., in Benjamin, Buber, and Rosenzweig). Nor is its influence by any means confined to the past or to Germany. For example, it remains the predominant influence on the work of the two most important recent theorists of translation, Antoine Berman in France and Lawrence Venuti in the United States, both of whom continue its "foreignizing" approach.[58]

NOTES

1. For a more detailed treatment of some of the topics that follow, see my *After Herder: Philosophy of Language in the German Tradition* (Oxford: Oxford University Press, 2010) and *German Philosophy of Language: From Schlegel to Hegel and Beyond* (Oxford: Oxford University Press, 2011).

2. Schlegel's *On the Language and Wisdom of the Indians* can be found in KA 8. Schleiermacher's psychology lectures can be found in FSSW 3/6.

3. KA 18, 289.

4. *Friedrich Schlegels philosophische Vorlesungen aus den Jahren 1804 bis 1806*, ed. C. J. H. Windischmann (Bonn: Eduard Weber, 1846), 2:28–29, 223.

5. Ibid., 2:83.

6. KA 15, 2–3.

7. Friedrich Schlegel, *Lectures on the History of Literature* (London: Bell and Daldy, 1873), 6–7.

8. See A. Huyssen, *Die frühromantische Konzeption von Übersetzung und Aneignung* (Zurich: Atlantis, 1969), 89. Cf. 69ff. on August Wilhelm's closely connected appropriation of Herder's interpretive method of *Einfühlung*.

9. There are two main editions of the hermeneutics lectures, both of which are available in English: *Hermeneutics and Criticism*, ed. A. Bowie (Cambridge: Cambridge University Press, 1998) and *Hermeneutics: The Handwritten Manuscripts*, ed. J. Duke and J. Forstman (Atlanta: Scholars Press, 1986).

10. FSSW 3/6, 263.

11. *Hermeneutics: The Handwritten Manuscripts*, 50.

12. For example, whereas Herder's version of doctrine (1) restricts itself to a claim that thought is essentially dependent on and bounded by linguistic competence, Schleiermacher turns this into a principle of the outright *identity* of thought with language, or with inner language. But such strong versions of the doctrine turn out to be philosophically untenable—vulnerable to counterexamples in which thought occurs without any corresponding (inner) language use, and vice versa. Again, Schleiermacher's late attraction to Kant's theory of empirical schematism turns out to be problematic. For Kant's theory implied a sharp dualism between concepts or meanings (conceived as purely psychological) and word-usages, so that Schleiermacher's espousal of it implies the same, and hence conflicts with his commitment to doctrine (2).

13. Strictly speaking, he restricts this new conception to "organic," i.e., inflected, languages, as opposed to "mechanical" ones.

14. A decent English translation of this essay by A. Lefevere from which I shall quote in this article can be found in *German Romantic Criticism*, ed. A. L. Wilson (New York: Continuum, 1982). However, it should be noted that the translation is not *completely* reliable, in particular because it omits an important long footnote concerned with the translation of poetry.

15. Wilhelm von Humboldt is another figure, closely related to and strongly influenced by the Romantics, who took over Herder's philosophy of language and developed it in the direction of holism. As we shall see, he was also a fellow traveler of the Romantics in the areas of linguistics, hermeneutics, and translation theory.

16. See, for example, "Von der Veränderung des Geschmacks" (*On the Change of Taste*) (1766) in HW 1 and "Auch eine Philosophie der Geschichte zur Bildung der Menschheit" (*This Too a Philosophy of History for the Formation of Humanity*) (1774) in HW 4.

17. For example, he writes in *Ideen zur Philosophie der Geschichte der Menschheit* (*Ideas for the Philosophy of History of Humanity*) (1784–91): "The finest essay on the

history and the diverse character of the human understanding and heart…would be a *philosophical comparison of languages*: for a people's understanding and character is imprinted in each of them" (HW 6, 353).

18. F. Schlegel, *Philosophie der Philologie* (*Philosophy of Philology*), in "Friedrich Schlegels 'Philosophie der Philologie' mit einer Einleitung herausgegeben von Josef Körner," *Logos* 17 (1928), 16. Cf. 54: "absolute difference."

19. As E. Fiesel points out—*Die Sprachphilosophie der deutschen Romantik* (Tübingen: J.C.B. Mohr, 1927), 215–24—this sort of rationale for the new discipline, though predominant in Herder, Schlegel, and Humboldt, tended to recede from nineteenth-century versions of the discipline after Humboldt (arguably to the discipline's great detriment).

20. HW 1, 762.

21. HW 1, 803.

22. HW 6, 353.

23. Schlegel's emphasis on the striking differences between languages in fact includes not only deep grammatical differences and more superficial verbal/conceptual differences but also such intermediate differences as, for instance, the fact that the Manchou language relies much more heavily on onomatopoeia than other languages (KA 8, 167).

24. Strictly speaking, it had already been used by his brother August Wilhelm in a review article from 1803.

25. Schlegel had some forerunners in this idea. See H. Gipper and P. Schmitter, *Sprachwissenschaft und Sprachphilosophie im Zeitalter der Romantik* (Tübingen: Gunter Narr, 1985), 22–26.

26. Concerning the latter type, Schlegel also cites Alexander von Humboldt's collection of Native American grammars and Wilhelm von Humboldt's already ongoing work on the Basque language (KA 8, 153–55).

27. In doing so, he builds on, and also credits, the work of Sir William Jones. Cf. Gipper and Schmitter, *Sprachwissenschaft und Sprachphilosophie*, 47–48.

28. It should be noted, though, that Schlegel was himself innocent of ethnocentric motives here (his own ethical orientation was decidedly cosmopolitan; indeed, one of the main purposes of his book was to show that Europe and Asia are "one large family," as he actually put it), and that he took considerable pains to try to forestall any inference from his normative ranking of languages to an invidious ranking of peoples.

29. Bopp's work follows Schlegel's *On the Language and Wisdom of the Indians* closely not only in its contents but even in its form (e.g., like Schlegel's work concluding with a set of translations).

30. Concerning this subsequent history, see also J. Trabant, *Apeliotes oder der Sinn der Sprache. Wilhelm von Humboldts Sprachbild* (Berlin: Akademie Verlag, 1986), 163; Gipper and Schmitter, *Sprachwissenschaft und Sprachphilosophie* (as well as other works by Gipper); H. Nüsse's introduction to KA 8; and Fiesel, *Die Sprachphilosophie der deutschen Romantik*, 110ff.

31. The suggestion in some of the secondary literature that Schleiermacher thinks such knowledge *irrelevant* to interpretation is absurd.

32. The widespread conception in the secondary literature (e.g., Dilthey and Gadamer) that for Schleiermacher "divination" is a process of psychological self-projection into texts is basically mistaken. Like Herder before him, because of principle (4), he is rather concerned to *discourage* interpreters from assimilating the outlooks of people they interpret to their own. For example, he writes in the hermeneutics lectures: "Misunderstanding is either a consequence of hastiness or of prejudice. The former is an isolated moment. The latter is a mistake which lies deeper. It is the one-sided preference for what is close to an individual's circle of ideas and the rejection of what lies outside it. In this way one explains in or explains out what is not present in the author [*sic*]" (*Hermeneutics and Criticism*, 23).

33. *Hermeneutics: The Handwritten Manuscripts*, 207.

34. See especially Herder's "Über Thomas Abbts Schriften" (*On Thomas Abbt's Writings*) (1768) in HW 2 and "Vom Erkennen und Empfinden der menschlichen Seele" (*On the Cognition and Sensation of the Human Soul*) (1778) in HW 4.

35. See especially Herder's "Die Kritischen Wälder zur Ästhetik" (*Critical Forests*) (1769) and *This Too a Philosophy of History*. (Note that holism as a method of discovering meaning is quite different from holism as a thesis about the very nature of meaning, i.e., the thesis that the Romantics were the first to introduce. The former might indeed be based on the latter, at least in part, but it need not be and was not yet in Herder. It is plausible, however, to hypothesize that earlier commitments to the former by Herder and others made a significant contribution to the eventual development of the latter by the Romantics. Incidentally, a similar transformation of a merely epistemological thesis into a stronger ontological one had already occurred previously concerning the connection between meaning and word-use: Ernesti had merely held that investigating word-usage was the right way to discover meaning, but Herder had then strengthened that position into a doctrine that meaning *was* word-usage.)

36. Two examples of this have already been mentioned in a previous note and concern Schleiermacher's specific formulations of doctrines (1) and (2), namely his outright equation of thought with language and his adoption of Kant's theory of schematism. But there are further examples as well. One is the fact that whereas for Herder principle (4) is only an *empirically* established *rule of thumb*, Schleiermacher purports to give an *a priori proof* that conceptual-intellectual and linguistic diversity occurs even at the level of individual people *universally*—a proof that is not only very dubious in itself (both in its a priori status and in its specific details), but also has the highly counterintuitive consequence (often explicitly asserted by Schleiermacher) that, strictly speaking, no one *ever* fully understands another person. Again, unlike Herder, Schleiermacher specifies psychological interpretation more closely as a process of identifying, and tracing the necessary development of, a single "seminal decision" (*Keimentschluß*) in the author that was the source of his work and unfolded itself as the work in a necessary fashion. But this too seems an unhelpful move. For how many works are actually composed, and hence properly interpretable, in such a way (rather than, say, involving a whole series of decisions, perhaps together with some serendipity along the way)? Again, whereas Herder includes among the evidence relevant to psychological interpretation both an author's linguistic behavior and his nonlinguistic behavior, Schleiermacher normally insists

on a restriction to the former. But this seems misguided (e.g., the Marquis de Sade's recorded *acts* of cruelty are surely no less relevant to establishing the sadistic side of his psychology than his cruel *statements*). Again, whereas Herder rightly emphasizes that the correct identification of *genre* plays an essential role in interpretation, and that this is often extremely difficult due to variations in genres that occur between historical periods, cultures, individuals, and sometimes even different works by the same individual, Schleiermacher pays little attention to this. Again, unlike Herder, who normally considers interpretation and natural science to be similar activities, Schleiermacher regards the central role that "divination," or hypothesis, plays in interpretation as a ground for sharply *distinguishing* interpretation from natural science, and hence for classifying it as an art rather than a science. However, he should instead have seen it as one good ground for judging them *similar*. (His mistake here was caused by a false assumption that natural science works by plain induction rather than by hypothesis.)

37. Josef Körner and Hermann Patsch have both made cases for Schlegel's importance for hermeneutics on these grounds. Their cases differ in details but both essentially take the form of arguing—largely on the basis of the evidence supplied by Schlegel's *Philosophy of Philology* from 1797, a set of notes that roughly coincided with the beginning of his relationship with Schleiermacher in Berlin—that Schlegel anticipated and influenced key moves in Schleiermacher's hermeneutics lectures (which Schleiermacher subsequently began to deliver in 1805). There is much truth in this argument. Schleiermacher clearly looked up to Schlegel at this early period. And while it is often difficult to ascertain intellectual priority between them with any certainty given the meagerness of the available evidence and the fact that they cooperated in a spirit of "together-philosophy" (*Symphilosophie*), several of the doctrines in Schleiermacher's hermeneutics that Körner credits to Schlegel really do seem to have been more originally Schlegel's: in particular, the doctrines that the interpreter needs to understand an author better than he understood himself; that it is important for the interpreter to identify an author's psychological development; that the interpreter should interpret the parts of a text in light of the *whole* text; and that the interpreter should reject *philologia sacra*. Moreover, the same is true of several further doctrines that Patsch credits to Schlegel: in particular, the doctrines that philology/hermeneutics is not merely a science but an art; that hermeneutics and criticism are interdependent; and that *divination* plays an essential role in criticism/hermeneutics. Indeed, the same seems to me true of several additional doctrines as well: in particular, the doctrines that interpretation often faces the problem of a deep intellectual difference dividing the interpreter and his age from the author interpreted and his; that in interpretation misunderstanding, rather than being the exception, is the rule; and that, beyond the generic principle of identifying an author's psychological development, the interpreter of a text needs to identify, and trace the unfolding of, an author's "seminal decision" (*Keimentschluß*) (in Schleiermacher's terminology).

38. However, it should be noted here that there are also some contrary strands in Friedrich Schlegel's thinking about genre. These have been well explained, but with misguided enthusiasm, by Peter Szondi.

39. For a fuller treatment of this subject, see my "Friedrich Schlegel's Hermeneutics," in *German Philosophy of Language*, and especially my "The German Romantic Re-thinking of Ancient Tragedy" (forthcoming).
40. For more on this subject, see my "Friedrich Schlegel" and "Friedrich Schlegel's Hermeneutics," in *German Philosophy of Language*, and especially my "Herders Beitrag zur Entstehung der Idee *romantisch*," in *Die Aktualität der Romantik*, ed. M. N. Forster and K. Vieweg (Berlin: LIT, 2012).
41. KA 18, 63. Cf. *On Incomprehensibility* (1800).
42. For Schlegel's espousal and development of Herder's later position, see especially *Athenaeum Fragments*, no. 444; KA 4 (on painting), passim; *Friedrich Schlegel's Vorlesungen aus den Jahren 1804 bis 1806*, 2:244–45; *Lectures on the History of Literature*, 190–91. For a more detailed discussion of this topic, see my "Friedrich Schlegel's Hermeneutics."
43. The latter can be found in KA 18.
44. *Philosophy of Philology*, 16, 28.
45. Concerning the latter, see the Cologne lectures on German language and literature from 1807, at KA 15/2, 94–99.
46. *Philosophy of Philology*, 42.
47. Ibid.
48. KA 18, 204.
49. Ibid.
50. *Philosophy of Philology*, 47.
51. KA 18, 71.
52. *Philosophy of Philology*, 50.
53. KA 8, 324–25.
54. KA 18, 71.
55. Ibid. Cf. the *Dialogue on Poetry* (1800): "The translation of poets…has become an art."
56. *On the Different Methods of Translation*, 25.
57. Besides Herder, Friedrich Schlegel, and Boeckh, another important figure from this period who was in broad agreement with Schleiermacher's theories of interpretation and translation is Wilhelm von Humboldt. For example, concerning interpretation, like Schleiermacher, Humboldt argues in his Kawi introduction of 1836 that not only nations but also individuals within nations are always deeply different linguistically and conceptually-intellectually so that "all understanding is always at the same time a misunderstanding." And concerning translation, he argues in the introduction to his translation of Aeschylus's *Agamemnon* (1816) for an approach to translation that is virtually identical to Schleiermacher's.
58. See esp. A. Berman, *L'épreuve de l'étranger* (Paris: Gallimard, 1984) and L. Venuti, *The Translator's Invisibility: A History of Translation* (London: Routledge, 1995).

5
_____

Hermeneutics, Individuality, and Tradition

*Schleiermacher's Idea of **Bildung** in the Landscape of Hegelian Thought*

KRISTIN GJESDAL

It is a widespread assumption that early nineteenth-century philosophy bifur-cates into a romantic and a Hegelian camp. One the one hand, we have a roman-tic turn to individuality, feeling, and immediacy, on the other Hegel's focus on *Bildung*, historicity, and the sociality of reason. Countering Hegel's hyperbolic worries about romanticism, defenders of this paradigm often proceed by call-ing for a reevaluation of individuality, aesthetics, and feeling—and, by impli-cation, art and literature, the domains where these aspects of subjectivity are expressed and sheltered—and not by asking if this is what romantic philosophy is all about in the first place.[1]

It is the aim of this paper to shed critical light on the notion that there is a sharp, unbridgeable division between the romantics and Hegel or, more precisely, between the emphasis on individuality and the commitment to philosophy of *Bildung*, that is, education in and through culture. My point of departure—my test case, as it were—is Friedrich Schleiermacher's theory of interpretation, a model that is often viewed as a proto-example of aesthetic-romantic attitudes, be it taken as a point of criticism (Hegel and Gadamer) or as an occasion for praise and laudation (Szondi, Ricoeur, Frank). In my view, Schleiermacher's hermeneutics is not about aesthetic feeling or a celebration of style. His is a model that addresses meaning and thought as expressed in the communal medium of language and thus views *Bildung* and understanding as two sides of the same coin.[2]

For Schleiermacher, language is always marked by individuality as well as the cultural and symbolic resources of a given, historical era. Yet the living individuality of a text and its insights tends to be stifled as it is integrated into the dominant patterns of understanding. Schleiermacher's hermeneutics seeks to shake up such hardened patterns of understanding. As such, it finds its form as a critical theory of interpretation. Further, this critical theory is motivated by a wish to keep tradition alive and dynamic—a self-renewing source of education and *Bildung*.

From this point of view, the chief difference between Hegel and the romantics is not that Hegel has a notion of *Bildung* and the romantics do not. In early nineteenth-century philosophy, we do not encounter positions *for* or *against Bildung*. Instead we face a set of alternative conceptions of *Bildung*, be it, with Hegel, along the lines of a rational, continuous tradition, or, with Schleiermacher, with the awareness that tradition carries with it the risk of turning into a stifling interpretative scheme and is thus in need of revitalization from the point of view of critical engagement with concrete, symbolic expressions. This latter notion of *Bildung* complements Hegel's model, and is, as such, deserving of rehabilitation—be it within the field of interpretation studies or within the larger, philosophical discourse of *Bildung*.

5.1. THE UNIVERSALITY OF HERMENEUTICS

Schleiermacher taught hermeneutics in the years between 1805 and 1833. Yet he never produced a book-length study in this area. The available material consists in part of lecture notes and student annotations. This has given rise to extensive discussion of the chronology of the texts as well as their thematic organization.[3] Interesting as it is, this debate must be put aside in order to allow for a brief overview of Schleiermacher's place within the hermeneutic tradition.[4] What is the chief concern of Schleiermacher's theory of interpretation? How is his contribution different from those of his predecessors? And why is his work ascribed such an important role within the history of hermeneutics? The initial answer to these questions is simple enough. Schleiermacher's main idea, and the source of his historical influence, is his universalization of hermeneutics. What is implied by this formulation is less straightforward. There are at least two aspects of Schleiermacher's universalization-thesis: The first (a) relates to the self-understanding of the humanities. The second (b) concerns the emphasis on individuality. Each of these points must be spelled out in more detail.

(a) It is helpful to keep in mind that before Schleiermacher, philologically minded theoreticians such as Friederich Ast, Johann August Ernesti, and Friedrich August Wolf had seen hermeneutics as a tool for the study of certain academic areas, in particular the study of temporally or culturally distant texts (the Bible and texts from classical antiquity being two examples).[5] Schleiermacher, by contrast, insists that hermeneutics not only concerns the untangling of old, knotty, or incomplete texts, but also deals with language use across the board: past as well as present, culturally distant as well as near. In his words, hermeneutics is "the art of understanding particularly the written discourse of another person correctly" (HC 3).[6]

The significance of this turn should not be underestimated. With Schleiermacher's universalization thesis, hermeneutics is no longer viewed as an aid to specific groups of scholars engaging in specific kinds of textual explanation or exegesis (theology and classical studies).[7] Hermeneutics now emerges as a discourse of the epistemic conditions for reflected and academically adequate interpretation as such. In this form, it shelters the systematic self-reflection of the humanities, the domain of research in which the scholar encounters the symbolic self-presentation of subjectivity in and through history and culture. It is with reference to hermeneutics that the human sciences justify and realize their scientific status.[8]

However, if hermeneutics is viewed as the epistemic self-reflection of the human sciences (as anchored in the human capacity for symbolic expression), only one humanistic discipline can outline its nature and principles, namely philosophy. Other human sciences are limited to the study of specific areas of symbol production and the application of interpretation theory within these areas. Philosophy, by contrast, maps the conditions of possibility for understanding as such. Hence, with Schleiermacher, hermeneutics is established as the general methodology of the humanities, as an intellectual domain deserving of study in its own right, *and* as an area to which philosophy has privileged access. Needless to say, this move has gained approval in the philosophical camps. Even Hans-Georg Gadamer, who often comes across as Schleiermacher's harshest critic, welcomes this maneuver by quoting, as the epigram to the third part of *Truth and Method*, Schleiermacher's claim that "everything presupposed in hermeneutics is but language."[9]

(b) According to Schleiermacher, the universality of hermeneutics must be led back to the fact that all language use, all symbolic expression, is marked by a dimension of individuality. As he puts it, "Every person is on the one hand a location in which a given language forms itself in an individual manner, on the other their discourse can only be understood via the totality of language" (HC 8). Hence, the force of Schleiermacher's universality claim ultimately rests with the plausibility of his turn to individuality. In this context, three further points will need to be made.

With regard to Schleiermacher's notion of individuality, the first thing that must be noted is that it does not, within the context of his hermeneutics, refer to the feelings or inner life of a particular person. It refers to a given use of language, an aspect of our symbolic-expressive capacity (HC 10). As such, individuality serves as a generic concept that covers all aspects of language use that cannot be understood solely with reference to a universal genre, rule, concept, or grammatical grid. The literature of a certain period can emerge as individual. The same applies to a constellation of writers that work together or are being exposed to the same source of influence and thus share a certain literary orientation. Further, a given language-user might be characterized by reference to an individual style, gesture, or use of language that differs from that of his or her peers. But there might also be differences within his or her language-use that make it plausible to speak, in the case of a literary expression, about a given author's early as opposed to his or her late work. In this way, individuality functions as an interpretative lens with different scopes and adjustments.[10]

The second point that must be emphasized is that there is no opposition in Schleiermacher's model between creative-individual and ordinary or communal uses of language. Individual use of language is not understood in contrast to but as enabled by *and* enriching the shared symbolic resources of a given language area. Individual language-use concerns the way that, at any point in time, a given speaker, author, or group of such shapes the available linguistic resources—how these resources are realized only from within or with reference to a given point of view, a given outlook on the world, that is, from within the perspective of a particular, human being (or group of such) with a particular history, cultural context, and set of experiences (HC 91). For Schleiermacher, every individual is unique and irreducible. Yet all symbolic expressions voice a shared world of experience, events, and entities.

Third, Schleiermacher's notion of individuality shows how thought is always articulated by a concrete individual. Every person represents, potentially, a unique point of view, a particular perspective on the world. In some kinds of discourse, Schleiermacher suggests, this uniqueness plays a comparatively insignificant role. Scientific texts make up one such example. In other cases, such as modern poetry, individuality is played up (HC 19, 64). Most discourse finds itself situated somewhere in the middle. In engaging the infinite spectrum of human expressivity, the reader, if attentive to the uniqueness of the author's point of view, may expand her horizon by, so to speak, allowing her imagination to go visiting the outlook of another. For Schleiermacher, there is an epistemic aspect of this expansion of one's own horizon, though in his early work it is ultimately pitched as an ethical enterprise, one that is related to the very constitution of the self through the interplay between self and other.

5.2. INDIVIDUALITY RECONSIDERED

Schleiermacher's notion of individuality, as discussed above, is not opposed to the idea of a shared linguistic community but targets the way that language takes form when concretely applied. How, then, should the critical interpreter proceed in order to get a grasp on the individual-universal aspect of a given text or utterance? And, further, what exactly is gained or understood in the act of understanding? Schleiermacher answers these questions by (a) outlining his thoughts on the hermeneutic procedure and (b) discussing what kind of meaning the interpreter is focusing on.

(a) Schleiermacher's guidelines for interpretative work are obscured by his use of technical terms and a somewhat inconsistent application of his chosen vocabulary. He speaks about the need to proceed through a combination of grammatical interpretation, geared towards the universal linguistic resources available to the given language-user and his peers, and technical interpretation, geared towards the individual application of the shared resources (HC 94). However, sometimes Schleiermacher also talks about psychological interpretation. Even though Schleiermacher wavers between these two terms, it is fair to say that both designate the concrete use, and thus the realization, of communal symbolic resources (and not an inner individual realm of intentionality, emotions, and feelings).

These two aspects of understanding, grammatical and technical interpretation, highlight different aspects of the text (the author as being shaped by his or her culture and the author as he or she shapes her culture). Yet they serve as general guidelines only. In encountering a given utterance, the interpreter cannot a priori know whether the text in question requires an emphasis on grammatical or technical interpretation. This is a matter that begs a certain *Gefühl*, sensitivity, or hypothesis-making on the part of the interpreter. Schleiermacher terms this hypothesis-making "divination" (HC 92–93). In a typical scenario, the interpreter will have to start out, on the basis of the available text, with an interpretative hypothesis, measure it against the available historical material (other texts by the same author, texts by his or her peers, the larger cultural horizon), and then, if needed, revise her initial hypothesis. Schleiermacher's hermeneutics thus includes a reference to the interplay between divination, intuitive hypothesis-making, and comparison, that is, historical-philological work (HC 93, see also HC 100). Just like technical and grammatical interpretation, divination and comparison are mutually constituting aspects of hermeneutics. Under ideal circumstances each should yield the same result as the other. Yet the world of the interpreter is real, not ideal, and the interpreter must move between hypothesis-formation (divination) and the support or rejection of this hypothesis by reference to other works by the same author, works written by his or her contemporaries, and other historical circumstances (comparison).[11] Schleiermacher views this as an infinite process (HC 23). To grasp once and for all the one and only correct and irrefutable meaning will always be beyond the reach of a finite, individual interpreter (HC 88).

Does that, then, mean that Schleiermacher ditches the idea of correct interpretation? Not necessarily. For Schleiermacher—and here he clearly distinguishes himself from hermeneuticians of a more Heideggerian persuasion—interpretations vary by degree of adequacy and correctness. The meaning of the text does not, as in the case of Gadamer, rest with its being applied in ever new contexts of understanding.[12] Interpretations are not simply different, they are also more or less plausible when assessed in light of their purported claim to validity. The idea of correct interpretation serves as a point of orientation, a regulative idea, lending the interpreter purpose, direction, and motivation.[13] A correct interpretation would be one in which the historical situatedness of the interpreter is quelled, suspended, or otherwise put out of play. However, in Schleiermacher's understanding, the interpreter is always already individualized and situated in history. A neutral interpretative "point of nowhere" is not within reach. Interpretation is, by definition, fallible and subject to constant revision. Precisely because interpretation is fallible and subject to constant revision, is it crucial that the interpreter distinguish between the activity of understanding, on the one hand, and the application of the insights she arrives at, on the other. If the distinction between interpretation and application of the meaning (truth or insight) of the text collapses, there would be no way that the interpreter could make the encounter with a text from a culturally or temporally distant context challenge her own prejudices and beliefs.[14]

In my view, this is one of the most important insights of Schleiermacher's hermeneutics. Only by acknowledging how the interpreter challenges her outlook through the encounter with the points of view of an other can we see how Schleiermacher's hermeneutics, while clearly responding to an epistemological problem, is also driven by a strong and underlying ethical motivation circling around the notion of mutual recognition. This is a point that, in equal measures, has been overlooked by Schleiermacher's critics (who accuse him of centering in on an aesthetic notion of individuality) and his defenders (to the extent that they celebrate his notion of style for its own sake). So much about Schleiermacher's procedure or method of interpretation.

(b) What, then, is understood in and through a successful interpretation (an interpretation that strikes the right balance between technical and grammatical analysis)? This question has received little attention in the scholarship. Again, this may be due to the relative consensus about Schleiermacher's interest in style.[15] Another reason may be that Schleiermacher's hermeneutics has been read as a transcendentally oriented theory, that is, a contribution that brings to light the enabling conditions for understanding and thus conducts, as it were, a Copernican turn away from the textual material to the methodological tools or procedures of the interpreter. However, the question of *how* understanding is possible is not, in Schleiermacher's work, detached from the question of *what* is understood. Quite to the contrary, the two are closely related. Schleiermacher's reflection on the object of understanding—what the interpreter is getting at, the meaning of the text—is rather abstract in nature (as it has to be, given his wish to cover symbolic expression and understanding across cultures, ages, and subjective dispositions). In this context, two aspects of Schleiermacher's theory of meaning must be singled out for further discussion: first, his insistence on the intersubjective dimension of meaning, and, second, his analysis of the distinction between primary and secondary thoughts.

First, Schleiermacher claims that understanding presupposes the interpreter's familiarity with the subject matter discussed in the text. In the context of reconceptualizing Schleiermacher's notion of individuality, this point is significant. In the hermeneutic process, the interpreter, taking into account the perspectives of technical and grammatical analysis, is not intentionally directed towards the feelings of another or the style of the text, but towards the issue, topic, problem, or subject matter addressed. As he aspires to clarify the conditions of possibility for validity in understanding (overlapping, in his view, with the conditions of possibility for understanding as such), Schleiermacher centers on the kind of interpretation that is directed towards thought, as it is given shape by and expressed through language. By definition, language is ascribed an intersubjective dimension. According to Schleiermacher, "Speech is the mediation of the communal nature of thought" (HC 7). Hermeneutics is thus made possible by a shared orientation towards a given idea or subject matter and seeks to bring this to the level of full, reflective awareness. As Schleiermacher elaborates, "Every act of understanding is the inversion of a speech-act, during which the thought which was the basis of the speech must become conscious" (HC 7). If understanding presupposes a shared orientation towards that which is understood, the reflective interpreter seeks to grasp how a given expression, being shaped by its time and culture, sheds light on a particular problem or subject matter.[16] At stake is an orientation towards a mutual understanding of a given subject matter, problem, or issue as seen or experienced by another concrete, historical human being.

Second, Schleiermacher elaborates this point by introducing a distinction between primary and secondary thoughts (thoughts that are crucial and thoughts that are merely facilitating the exposition of the main arguments, ideas, or intuitions). This distinction is needed to help the interpreter hone in on central claims or ideas and bracket that which is peripheral. In his account, the distinction between primary and secondary thoughts sometimes requires a laborious and cognitively uncertain process of interpretation. Neither in relating to a text from a geographically or temporally distant culture, nor in relating to language use that is closer to the interpreter's own symbolic practice, does there exist an absolutely certain way to determine whether or not the interpreter has arrived at the central thoughts of a given text.

Whether a text is close to or distant from the horizon of the interpreter, there is always a risk that the interpreter hypostatizes thoughts that are peripheral to the concerns of the author (and possibly more congenial to the interpreter's horizon of interpretation), and, as a consequence, allows the interpretation to be colored by prejudices. By referring to historical context or other works by the same author, the interpreter can support his or her interpretation or point out how a given reading of a text misrepresents its meaning or is lacking in justification. A positive and concluding justification of a given account of the relationship between primary and secondary thoughts cannot, however, be provided. As such, these terms do not present a methodological device that guarantees the successful outcome of interpretation, but, again, only a heuristic guideline that grants direction to the process of understanding.[17]

Summing up the discussion so far, it is clear that Schleiermacher's hermeneutics does not represent a hypostatization of aesthetic individuality, but is built on the notion of language as historical and concretely used (this was the point made in section 1 above). Further, hermeneutic activity, in his work, is not geared towards feeling, intention, or psychology, but towards the thought-content of the utterance (as argued in section 2). Together, these points indicate how Schleiermacher's orientation towards individuality transcends the scope of a merely literary or broader stylistic analysis and that it, as such, can, in principle, contribute to a theory of *Bildung*.

5.3. CRITIQUE AND TRADITION

The purpose of my reinterpretation of Schleiermacher's hermeneutics is not simply to avoid an aestheticizing reading of the romantic theory of interpretation, but also to enable a reading of Schleiermacher's hermeneutics that situates it within his larger turn to *Bildung*. In my view, it is unfortunate that Schleiermacher's hermeneutics is often read in isolation, and that, to the extent that it is discussed in the context of his broader philosophical engagement, it is usually his *Dialectics* that is brought in.[18] Schleiermacher's work in dialectics is no doubt important.[19] However, a one-sided emphasis on his dialectics may easily lead to a bias in favor of the epistemological aspects of hermeneutics and, as a consequence, an overlooking of the social and ethical motivation that drives his philosophy as a whole.

I have already mentioned that present readers of Schleiermacher only have access to a fragmented version of his hermeneutic lectures. In the existing editions of the text, Schleiermacher lays out the basic principles of hermeneutics, but he does not say much about why it matters so much that we understand other human beings or the texts of the past. It is an open question whether or not such reflections—reflections on the relevance of hermeneutics—were ever included in the lectures. In the existing version of the lectures, Schleiermacher focuses more on the principles of hermeneutics (*What* does it mean to say that I understand a text or spoken language? *What* do I understand when I understand a text?) than the question of its relevance and motivation (*Why* is it worthwhile engaging in hermeneutic activity in the first place?). Thus, in order to address the relevance of hermeneutics, we need to move from Schleiermacher's reflections on interpretation proper to the broader context of his work. Only in this way is it possible to see how Schleiermacher's philosophy can help us overcome the notion of the opposing paradigms of Hegel and romantic thought. Two points prove central in this context: (a) Schleiermacher's critique of tradition and (b) his understanding of the self and its interpreting relationship to others.

(a) In the secondary literature, little attention has been paid to Schleiermacher's notion of tradition. One reason for this oversight might be that his reflection on tradition emerges out of his early theological writings, which, in turn, have often been isolated from his more technical hermeneutical work. Particularly important in this context is *On Religion*, a work in which Schleiermacher discusses the challenges of a tradition that no longer appears alive and worthy of real, intellectual engagement.[20]

Schleiermacher addresses his fellow philosophers' denouncement of religion, that is, their self-proclaimed status as "cultured despisers" of religion (thus *On Religion* is significantly subtitled *Speeches to its Cultural Despisers*).[21] With their knowledge of the tradition and its canonical texts, the cultured despisers believe that they are familiar with the Christian scriptures and, by implication, know exactly what they are rejecting when rejecting Christian faith and practice. Schleiermacher, by contrast, argues that the central texts of the Christian religion have been caught in a deadlock of interpretative stagnation. Generations of readers abide by the predominant doctrines of understanding. Generations of readers *think* they know what these texts are about. A consensus of interpretation is gradually brought about, the consensus hardens, and eventually it is virtually impossible to read the texts of tradition independently of the lens provided by the established paradigm. In this way, religion is subject to a barren uniformity (OR 108). We face dead letters (OR 108, see also OR 85 and 91), not a disclosure of philosophical, theological, or existential meaning. Interpretation is reduced to a scholastic quibbling, a hermeneutic lethargy that Schleiermacher deems the sign of a new barbarism (OR 151). Schleiermacher draws from this that what the despisers of religion really despise, though they themselves may not know it, is the passive mediation of older texts. The despisers of religion conflate the meaning that a dominant interpretative tradition has ascribed to a given text with the meaning of the text as such.

In *On Religion*, Schleiermacher stages a contrast between stifling textual exegesis and true religious feeling, which is expressed in the intuition of the universe as a whole.[22] In the hermeneutics lectures, by contrast, he asks how the meaning of ancient texts, including the cornerstones of the Christian religion, can be resuscitated by hermeneutic work.[23] The assumed presumption is, again, that the philosopher, theologian, or humanist starts out with a text or body of texts whose meaning has been handed down through generations and centuries of scholarship that, eventually, turns into prejudice and dead doctrines. Schleiermacher encourages us not to take for granted the traditional interpretation of these texts. We *think* we understand, but the challenge for the hermeneutician is critically and reflectively to ask whether his or her presumed understanding is adequate or merely prejudicial. On passively assuming familiarity with a given text or body of literature, the interpreter risks confirming and cementing misunderstanding rather than avoiding it. In Schleiermacher's view, this is why we need a critical and reflective hermeneutics; this is why we, for all its technical and scholastic distinctions, need a standard or checklist with reference to which we can assess and reflect on the validity of our interpretative endeavors.

(b) In the hermeneutics lectures, Schleiermacher draws attention to this point when he discusses the special cases of ancient scientific and ethical texts (which also exemplifies his point about primary and secondary thought). Given his background in classical Greek philosophy, Schleiermacher is concerned with the difficulties that potentially arise when the interpreter deals with texts from a scientific or ethical paradigm other than her own. As Schleiermacher puts it, "Revolutions in the area of natural science and ethics have produced new systems and rejected old ones" (HC 65). As a consequence of this, the interpreter, when dealing with older texts, cannot appeal to the criteria or guidelines of contemporary science, ethics, or models of thought. Schleiermacher begs caution when moving between the paradigm or mindset of the present period and that of the text. He advises that in such an interpretative situation it is easy to mistake key thoughts and ideas (primary thoughts) for peripheral ones (secondary thoughts) and vice versa. Schleiermacher further counsels that it would be a mistake at this point to try "immediately to compare details in the new system with details in the preceding system" (HC 65), that is, to read old texts in light of or as providing answers to contemporary concerns and questions. The relationship between the whole and the parts, between primary and secondary thought, "is different in every whole" (HC 65). Through the circular movement between a hypothesis about the meaning of the text as a whole and a reading of the whole in light of its various parts, argumentative steps, and supporting material (from a larger textual corpus, to chapters, sections, and down to the level of the single sentence, the smallest hermeneutic unit), the interpreter must attempt to ferret out the intrinsic structure and organization of the individual expression at stake. It is within this wider hermeneutic context—that of facing a tradition we think we know, but which may prove to be the results of prejudice and doctrine—that Schleiermacher's concrete guidelines for interpretation finds philosophical meaning.

In focusing on ancient scientific and ethical texts, Schleiermacher's point is not to argue that these texts constitute a special hermeneutic subgroup. The particular cases of old scientific and ethical texts are expressive of a global risk, namely that the interpreter allows her present-day views, her prejudices or horizon of understanding, to skew her reading. Thus Schleiermacher's hermeneutics draws a distinction between, on the one hand, the tacit everyday understanding that serves as a basis for the interpreter and his or her prereflected relation to tradition and, on the other, a critical understanding that seeks systematically to question the legitimacy of existing patterns of interpretation. The real hermeneutic problem typically occurs when the interpreter is confident that he or she understands and thus fails to question the limits of his or her preconceptions. The allure of prejudices is not only that they thematically guide the interpreter's reading of a given text, but also that they have him or her look for confirmation of his or her own interpretative hypothesis rather than critically reflecting on its validity. As finite beings, we tend to reconstruct meaning in light of what appears plausible from our own point of view, rather than questioning whether our own point of view is adequate or hermeneutically helpful. An obvious example, taken from Schleiermacher's own time, is the way that Winckelmann, Hegel, and a whole generation of German philosophers of art would follow their predecessors in emphasizing the whiteness of ancient Greek sculpture, claiming that the remaining traces of paint were the result of medieval vandalism (thus barring the possibility that the marble had been painted from the very beginning).

Facing this predicament, as it is baked into the dialectics of tradition itself, Schleiermacher's point is not that we should carry with us a whole arsenal of hermeneutic doctrines in order to make sense of everyday utterances in our own language. What he suggests, rather, is that the critical hermeneutician, when striving to avoid misunderstanding, must anchor her interpretative hypothesis in a reflected point of view, a point of view that can be discursively accounted for and justified.[24] In order to do so, the interpreter needs a theory, a set of directions and guidelines by reference to which it is possible for him or her to reflect on and critique his or her preconception of a given text, utterance, or subject area. To provide such directions and guidelines is the mission of Schleiermacher's hermeneutics.

5.4. SELFHOOD AND SOCIALITY

Why, then, does it matter that the interpreter reaches a more adequate understanding of the text, that he or she is able, critically and reflectively, to break through petrified patterns of understanding? Again this question must be answered with reference to Schleiermacher's broader philosophical program. His notion of selfhood is particularly important in this context. For if we are to argue, as I wish to do in this article, that Schleiermacher's hermeneutics, with its critical turn to tradition, can serve to undermine the perceived dichotomy between romanticism and philosophy of *Bildung*, it needs to be shown that understanding, by his lights, is not simply a matter of getting an objectivized tradition "right," but that the interpreter's being situated in history and tradition interferes, at a much deeper level, with his or her self-understanding.

As far as his theological writings go, Schleiermacher's philosophy of selfhood (and, ultimately, self-understanding) has been read in light of his notion of absolute dependency.[25] Against the Fichtean turn to an I that, at a transcendental level, posits itself as absolutely self-positing, thus ensuring the noumenal freedom of subjectivity, Schleiermacher, in *The Christian Faith* (1830–31), argues that the I, though furnished with a capacity for freedom, is not responsible for or the author of its own being (as free). That is, the I must understand itself as both constitut*ed* and constitut*ing*, both dependent and free.[26] The freedom of subjectivity is expressed through the structuring capacity of discursive reasoning. The feeling I, however, experiences itself as dependent on a nonsubjective world, a dimension of being that enables the exercise of spontaneity and the capacity to create the order and structure that experience presupposes.

However, Schleiermacher's notion of absolute dependency and his idea of the linguistic mediation of thought is balanced by an account of how the self—finite and dependent—realizes itself in free interaction with other selves. There are traces of this kind of thinking in Schleiermacher's *Dialectics*, in which the contemplation of another individual's point of view is ascribed a fundamental epistemic importance. Yet this aspect of his theory is most clearly laid out in an earlier, unfinished text, *Essay on a Theory of Social Behavior*, from 1799 (that is, the same year as the publication of *On Religion*).

Articulating the dos and don'ts of a free social life, Schleiermacher's *Essay on a Theory of Social Behavior* has been read as a philosophical defense of the romantic salon.[27] Schleiermacher, indeed, was a regular in the Berlin salons at the time and was seen, even by his contemporaries, as the philosopher who had theorized its dynamic of free sociality.[28] However, Schleiermacher's text is not simply a historical documentation of the spirit of the salon, but also a complex philosophical contribution to a debate initiated by another aspect of Fichte's philosophy, namely his theory of intersubjective recognition.[29]

The individual, for Schleiermacher, is determined as unique and representing an irreducible point of view, a particular realization of humanity. In Schleiermacher's own words: "As a finite being, every individual has his or her definitive sphere in which he or she alone can think and act and thus also impart him or herself" (ESB 160). Hence Schleiermacher calls for a sociality that is not based on abstract identification, but on a kind of community that allows individuals to encounter each other freely, a sociality that is not justified with reference to external, unifying aims but is a goal in itself (ESB 154, 157). Such a sociality is based on reciprocal contribution and respect for difference. It is based, in short, on individual diversity, on identity *in* difference and not *in spite of* it. This is a sociality that encourages a free play of feeling and thought *in* the individual, but also a free interaction *among* individuals (ESB 158–59).[30] Showing off or underplaying one's own individuality threatens such sociality (ESB 158). Schleiermacher's idealized notion of enlightened sociality aims to create relationships based on mutual respect and acknowledgment. As a regulative ideal, as a goal towards which we ought to strive, such a sociality would involve nothing less than an ongoing education in humanity (ESB 154). As Schleiermacher puts it, all manifestations of humanity will become known, one after the other (ESB 154).

Now, if the manifestations of humanity, understood as the maximum of possible outlooks or viewpoints on the world, are gradually to be revealed, the capacity to understand—and the quest for self-critique and reflection on limiting prejudices—moves to the very center of philosophy. It is at one and the same time expressive of an epistemological commitment that has to do with a finite being's ability to expand its own horizon of understanding and knowledge, *and* an ethical commitment having to do with the fact that such understanding is based on a will to recognize the other as a somebody whose perspective might be as valid as my own. Disagreement is only possible to the extent that the interlocutor is recognized as a rational agent and as defending a position worth taking seriously. Only through such recognition, ethical and epistemological, can the individual gain education in culture, that is, *Bildung*.

Understood in this way, Schleiermacher's hermeneutics is not, as his critics as well as his defenders have often suggested, a theory of aesthetic individuality or style. It is, rather, a theory that reflects the finality of reason in the sense that each individual, in his or her epistemic endeavors and ethical orientations, is situated in a given historical culture. One way that the individual, as a finite historical being, can reflect on this culture and try to keep it alive and expanding, is by encountering symbolic expressions from temporally or culturally distant contexts of origins. But in facilitating such encounters, the interpreter needs, as a regulative ideal or a practical-hermeneutic maxim, a normative set of guide-lines in light of which he or she can reflect on and critique his or her prejudices so as to allow the other to speak as a possible other and thus as somebody who can, potentially, challenge the outlook or view of the interpreter him- or herself. Schleiermacher's hermeneutics is an effort to discuss and take seriously the idea of such a critical-dialogical interaction.

5.5. CONCLUSION

Against the background of such a reading, the notion of a bifurcation of nineteenth-century thought into the clearly marked-off constellations of the romantics and Hegel will have to be questioned. As represented by Schleiermacher's hermeneutics, the romantic project does itself entail a notion of tradition and the individual's formation in and through engagement with the past.[31] This, however, does not imply that Schleiermacher (or, for that sake, romanticism more broadly) and Hegel represent the same view. What it does imply, though, is that rather than pitching Hegel's relation to the romantics in light of a contrast between aesthetic individuality and *Bildung*, we should take these models to represent two different responses to one and the same prob-lem: the interrelation between selfhood and historicity, criticism and prejudice in tradition, that is captured in the nineteenth-century turn to *Bildung* in the first place. When viewed in this light, the contrast between the romantics and Hegel is not a matter of being for or against *Bildung*, historicity, or a notion of the self as intersubjectively meditated. From Schleiermacher's point of view, such a contrast would make no sense: as a meaning-producing agent, the self is always already situated within a context of tradition—that is, a shared space of action and meaning. Hence the problem—ethically as well as epistemologi-cally speaking—is how to keep tradition, as a space of understanding, open, dynamic, and achieving a balanced relationship between preservation and criti-cism. Understood in this way, Hegel and Schleiermacher present two different ways of thinking about *Bildung*: on the one hand, an emphasis on the continu-ity and intrinsic rationality of tradition (as a space of possible meaning), on the other, a stressing of the constitutive importance of a plurality of different historical and individual perspectives that constantly transcend and challenge the synthesis of tradition.

As such, Schleiermacher's understanding of *Bildung* deserves to be revis-ited. His is a theory that seeks to unify a notion of *Bildung* with a hermeneutic model that is committed to the diversity of individual outlooks. Further, it is Schleiermacher's achievement to show that the commitment to a reflective standard or method in interpretation is not opposed to a turn to *Bildung*, but, rather, a condition of possibility for it. Only when the interpreter critically and reflectively evaluates his or her own prejudices, only when a given historical expression is situated within its own horizon of meaning, can it challenge, and possibly also expand, the horizon of the interpreter. Finally, Schleiermacher does not take as his point of departure the notion of a unifying and total-izing tradition. For Schleiermacher, tradition is a condition of possibil-ity for understanding. However, tradition is also a field in which prejudices and systematically distorted beliefs can be bolstered and handed down. For him, hermeneutics is committed to a consideration of individual points of view, an acknowledgment of the diversity of standpoints and the need for a gradually expanding understanding of the world. This is in my view where Schleiermacher's philosophy should be located—in the very intersection between nineteenth-century philosophy of *Bildung* and interpretation theory more broadly conceived.

NOTES

1. For Hegel's criticism, see for instance Hegel, *Lectures on the History of Philosophy*, vol. 3, *Medieval and Modern Philosophy*, trans. E. S. Haldane and Frances H. Simson (Lincoln: University of Nebraska Press, 1995), 506–10. For a study of the complex-ity of Hegel's relationship to romanticism, see Otto Pöggeler, *Hegels Kritik der Romantik* (Bonn: Friedrich Wilhelms-Universität, 1956 [dissertation]).

2. This is an aspect of Schleiermacher's philosophy that is left out in Manfred Frank's study. While Frank gets beyond Szondi's efforts to read Schleiermacher as a modernist philosopher *avant la lettre*, his chief motivation is to show that Schleiermacher's work anticipates insights later to be associated with what he terms existential-ontological and semological-structuralistic approaches to literature. See Peter Szondi, "Schleiermacher's Hermeneutics Today," *On Textual Understanding and Other Essays*, trans. Harvey Mendelsohn (Minneapolis: University of Minnesota Press, 1986), 97. For Frank's reading, see *Das individuelle Allgemeine. Textstrukturierung und Textinterpretation nach Schleiermacher* (Frankfurt am Main: Suhrkamp, 1977), 13 and 23.

3. See Wolfgang Virmond, "Neue Textgrundlagen zu Schleiermachers früher Hermeneutik. Prolegomena zur kritischen Edition." In Kurt-Victor Selge et. al. eds., *Schleiermacher-Archiv*, vol. 1, part 2, Internationaler Schleiermacherkongreß 1984 (Berlin: Walter de Gruyter, 1985), 575–590.

4. For a more detailed discussion of Schleiermacher's hermeneutics (and its recep-tion), see my *Gadamer and the Legacy of German Idealism* (Cambridge: Cambridge University Press, 2009), 155–219.

5. Friedrich Schleiermacher, *Hermeneutics and Criticism*, trans. and ed. Andrew Bowie (Cambridge: Cambridge University Press, 1998), 4. Further references to this work will be abbreviated HC, followed by page number. See also Joachim Wach, *Das Verstehen. Gründzüge einer Geschichte der hermeneutischen Theorie im 19. Jahrhundert*, 3 vols., vol. 1 (Tübingen: J. C. B. Mohr, 1926–33), 31–82 and Peter Szondi, *Introduction to Literary Hermeneutics*, trans. Martha Woodmansee (Cambridge: Cambridge University Press, 1995), 94–109.

6. It should be added that Schleiermacher's claim that he is the first to articulate a universal hermeneutics is exaggerated and betrays either a lack of knowledge of the hermeneutic tradition or a wish to stand forth as original in this respect. For a discussion of this point, see Werner Alexander, *Hermeneutica Generalis. Zur Konzeption und Entwicklung der allgemeinen Verstehenslehre im 17. und 18. Jahrhundert* (Stuttgart: M&P, Verlag für Wissenschaft und Forschung, 1993), 3–5.

7. Paul Ricoeur emphasizes this dimension of Schleiermacher's notion of universal hermeneutics in "Schleiermacher's Hermeneutics," *The Monist* 60, no. 2 (1977), 183–84.

8. Dilthey, in particular, views this as the main achievement of Schleiermacher's hermeneutics. See Wilhelm Dilthey, *Schleiermacher's Hermeneutical System in Relation to Earlier Protestant Hermeneutics*, trans. Theodore Nordenhaug, in *Selected Works*, vol. 4, *Hermeneutics and the Study of History*, ed. Rudolf A. Makkreel and Frithjof Rodi (Princeton: Princeton University Press, 1996), 132–229.

9. Hans-Georg Gadamer, *Wahrheit und Methode*, trans. Joel Weinsheimer and Donald G. Marshall (New York: Continuum, 2003), 381.

10. Thus Schleiermacher even sees language, as originating in speech-acts, as "an individual in relation to others" (HC 10).

11. Thus Schleiermacher also contrasts divination to a historical method (HC 23).

12. See *Truth and Method*, 307–11.

13. As Schleiermacher puts it, "nobody can be satisfied with simple non-understanding" (HC 29).

14. Whereas Gadamer views interpretation and application as two sides of the same coin, Schleiermacher insists that the hermeneutician may encounter texts that can be understood (i.e., they can be seen as coherent, meaningful, and a rational response to a given problem), yet their meaning cannot be applied (if, say, the problem to which the text responds is no longer recognized as relevant). Further, he keeps open the possibility that a text, in its approach to a given subject matter, problem, or issue, can put into perspective, possibly also question, the way in which a problem or issue is typically addressed within the culture of the interpreter. Again this requires, for Schleiermacher, a distinction between interpretation (addressing the meaning of the text) and application (addressing the question how it can help the interpreter better understand a given subject matter).

15. Yet "style" in his work is defined as "individuality of presentation" (HC 95), thus implying that something is presented in the first place.

16. Thought, however, is not reduced to propositional content, but includes the free play of poetry (HC 64).

17. This mirrors the limits of grammatical and technical interpretation. As Schleiermacher puts it, both grammatical and technical interpretation "can only be reached by approximation" (HC 96).

18. This is particularly clear in the work of Manfred Frank. Not only does Frank draw on Schleiermacher's dialectics in *Das individuelle Allgemeine*, but he also published a version of Schleiermacher's hermeneutics that is supported with excerpts from the dialectic lectures as well as his late ethics. Friedrich Schleiermacher, *Hermeneutik und Kritik*, ed. Manfred Frank (Frankfurt am Main: Suhrkamp,

1977). Two exceptions to this tendency are Christian Berner, *La philosophie de Schleiermacher. Herméneutique. Dialectique. Ethique* (Paris: Les Éditions du Cerf, 1995) and Gunter Scholtz, *Ethik und Hermeneutik. Schleiermachers Grundlegung der Geisteswissenschaften* (Frankfurt am Main: Suhrkamp, 1995).

19. Schleiermacher makes this point himself when he argues for "The dependence of both [hermeneutics and rhetoric] on dialectics" (HC 7).

20. As already Dilthey makes clear, this is in line with the broader orientation of Lutherian theology.

21. Friedrich Schleiermacher, *On Religion: Speeches to its Cultured Despisers*, trans. Richard Crouter (Cambridge: Cambridge University Press, 1988). Further references to this work will be abbreviated OR, followed by page number.

22. Indeed, in Schleiermacher's judgment, this puts hermeneutics on a par with philosophy: "If you put yourself on the highest standpoint of metaphysics and morals, you will find that both have the same object as religion, namely, the universe and the relationship of humanity to it" (OR 97).

23. Thus, in the hermeneutics lectures, no other text gets more attention than the Bible and the question as to how the Bible can and should best be understood. These discussions are ample; for an example, see HC 15–20.

24. Gadamer is in other words wrong in viewing Schleiermacher's hermeneutics as a universalization of misunderstanding (*Truth and Method*, 179–80, 184–85, 190–91). Schleiermacher does not claim that misunderstanding, de facto, is universal, but that no utterance, in principle, is safe from misunderstanding. Hence critical hermeneutics must approach all utterances in the same, reflected way. As he puts it, "The business of hermeneutics should not only begin where understanding is uncertain, but with the first beginning of the enterprise of wanting to understand an utterance" (HC 228).

25. See for example Frank's reading in *Das individuelle Allgemeine*, 91–94.

26. As Schleiermacher puts it, "In every self-consciousness there are two elements, which we might call respectively a self-caused element (*ein Sichselbstsetzen*) and a non-self-caused element (*ein Sichselbstnichtsogesetzthaben*)." Friedrich Schleiermacher, *The Christian Faith*, ed. H. R. Mackintosh and J. S. Stewart, trans. D. M. Baille et al. (London: T&T Clark, 1999), 13.

27. Friedrich Schleiermacher, *Essay on a Theory of Social Behavior*, trans. Peter Foley in Peter Foley, *Friedrich Schleiermacher's "Essay on a Theory of Social Behavior" (1799)* (Lewinston, NY: Edwin Mellen Press, 2006), 153–76. Further references to this work will be abbreviated ESB, followed by page number.

28. See Hannah Arendt, "Berlin Salon," in *Essays in Understanding 1930-1954* (New York: Harcourt Brace, 1994), 57–66.

29. For a discussion of this point, see Andreas Arndt, "Geselligkeit und Gesellschaft. Die Geburt der Dialektik aus dem Geist der Konversation in Schleiermachers 'Versuch einer Theorie des geselligen Betragens,'" in *Salons der Romantik. Beiträge eines Wiepersdorfer Kolloquiums zu Theorie und Geschichte des Salons*, ed. Hartwig Schultz (Berlin: Walter de Gruyter, 1997), 45–61.

30. At this point, Schleiermacher goes beyond Schiller, whose 1795 letters on aesthetic education address the free play between the different aspects of humanity, but not the interplay between different individuals.

31. My focus on Schleiermacher should not be taken to indicate that he is the only romantic philosopher contributing to the area of hermeneutics. For a study of romantic hermeneutics more broadly speaking, see Reinhold Rieger, *Interpretation und Wissen. Zur philosophischen Begründung der Hermeneutik bei Friedrich Schleiermacher und ihrem geschichtlichen Hintergrund*, Schleiermacher-Archiv, vol. 6 (Berlin: Walter de Gruyter, 1988).

6

Sociability and the Conduct of Philosophy

What We Can Learn from Early German Romanticism

JANE KNELLER

At the end of the "Critique of Aesthetic Judgment" Kant gestures towards the possibility of a society that creatively engages intellectual, moral ideas with natural human feeling to construct a truly human sociability. He defines "humanity" as the combination of two universal capacities, namely "the *feeling of participation*, and the ability to *communicate* universally one's inmost self," and goes on to say that the realization of these capacities "constitutes the sociability that befits our humanity." Such a society would develop the "art of reciprocal communication" that would discover "the mean between higher culture and an undemanding nature," fully developing taste into "the universal human sense" (AA 5, 355–56). This possibility is merely suggested by Kant here, but the gesture is important for expressing Kant's recognition that the capacity that underlies what the eighteenth century called "taste," namely, aesthetic reflective judgment, is a cognitive condition of social communication necessary for the construction of a higher form of human sociability. This "social" sociability, deliberately and progressively constructed, stands in sharp contrast to Kant's hypothetical "unsocial" sociability that drives humanity to better its own condition without regard to (and often in spite of) individual human choices.[1]

In what follows I will argue that the early German romantics took up the project of deliberately constructing this sort of social sociability by experimenting with and theorizing new forms of social discourse that balanced expressions of high culture on the one hand, and the unpretentious originality of ordinary human nature on the other. That is to say, using Kant's idiom, the early German romantic movement aimed to create new modes of participatory feeling and self-expression that pushed the art of reciprocal philosophical communication to new, higher levels. This essay will examine the methods of philosophizing undertaken by the early German romantics in the 1790s, concluding with an examination of Friedrich Schleiermacher's attempt to summarize and generalize romantic philosophical practice into a "theory of human sociable conduct."

6.1. SOCIABILITY IN EARLY GERMAN ROMANTICISM

It is perhaps the *collective* character of this early manifestation of Romanticism in Germany which most conspicuously distinguishes it from all other Romantic movements in Europe.[2]

[The ideal of the seminar] was reflected quite clearly... in certain of the literary works that emerged at Jena just at that time [in 1798]... it was precisely the coincidence of the rudimentary form of the seminar, the familiar model of the Platonic dialogue, and the lively exchange of the social setting that contributed in a typically Romantic interaction to the first true realization of the academic seminar.[3]

In his work on the institutions of German romanticism, Theodore Ziolkowski stresses the importance of what he calls "the educational ideal" and the "ideal of the seminar" in the writings of the early romantics in Jena and Berlin. He describes this ideal as it developed at the University of Jena between 1785 and 1795, out of the context of poor state funding, a rough and rebellious student body, and, in the early 1790s in Jena, a chaotic period in the aftermath of the French Revolution during which students clashed often and violently with government militias. Low faculty salaries and a reputation for an uncouth and demanding student body made recruitment and retention of prestigious faculty difficult, forcing administrative authorities to recruit younger, cheaper faculty, and to put up with their new ideas in order to retain them. Hiring the likes of Friedrich Schiller (who taught history there) and then Johann Gottlieb Fichte brought drama and moral zeal to the lecture halls of Jena, and, Ziolkowski argues, Jena became a magnet for young intellectuals attracted by the opportunity to remake the university into a "locus for the intellectual excitement of the era."[4] Kantianism had already taken firm hold in Jena by the 1790s thanks to K. L. Reinhold's impassioned and extremely popular lectures. Schiller's first lectures in 1789 at Jena were blockbusters, beginning with a call to students to study world history disinterestedly, not for professional gain but for the sake of knowledge itself. Fichte's public lectures on the ethics of the scholar also elevated the calling of the academic to a moral as well as an intellectual one, arguing that the role of student-scholar required recognition that their academic abilities and privileged situation within the university brings with it greater social responsibility. As Ziolkowski puts it:

> This was a heady message for the students of Jena, who saw themselves challenged by the compelling moral presence of the age not merely to lift themselves out of the mire of brutishness that had hitherto characterized their university but also to prepare themselves to be the teachers, the educators, and even the priests of mankind.[5]

What Ziolkowski calls the "Jena mode of discourse" that took hold among the circle of romantic philosopher poets in the 1790s was indebted, he argues, to this new "discourse of the academy" in a historical moment of genuine scholarly communication led by a succession of gifted professors at the University of Jena:[6] Early German romanticism is thus to be distinguished from other "romanticisms" by its use of academic genres such as the lecture, the persuasive public speech, and the dialogue: "In sum, the modes of discourse preferred by the Jena Romantics show the pronounced influence of the lecture hall and the seminar room—places ideally suited to the kind of *Symphilosophieren* of which Friedrich Schlegel, Novalis, and their contemporaries so often spoke."[7]

Given the sense that attaches to the term "academic" in our own time, it may seem very odd to suggest that the early German romantic style, which is anything but dry and pedantic, was an emulation of academic discourse. The point, however, is that these academic forms were being reinvented during the 1790s in Jena. The "heady" messages of these enthusiastic academic voices turned dusty intellectual discourse into a bright, impassioned call for social and moral progress. In the crucible of the French revolutionary era the creativity and moral enthusiasm of "academics" like Schiller and Fichte in Jena transformed the old institutions. Kant's call for a new form of reciprocal communication was already being put into practice at the time Kant wrote it, and indeed by some of the most gifted minds of the time. When in their lectures, seminars, and speeches Schiller and Fichte urged their students to become a *part* of their academic discourse, and when they expressed to their students their own view that individuals shared universal interests in the continuing progress of history, these new academics were in effect carrying out Kant's call for the construction of a reciprocal communication based on feelings of participation and the universalization of the individual's innermost self.

It is no wonder that their students—the next generation of poets, critics, and philosophers—were fired up and inspired to carry this transformation even further, into critical, poetic, and philosophical masterpieces. What is remarkable about the early romantics' embrace of academic social responsibility was that they held sociable conduct up as a model also for their criticism, poetry, and philosophy. Sociability was woven into the very practice and processes of their scholarly and artistic disciplines: They managed, for a brief time at least, to turn what had traditionally been solitary academic tasks into a shared social project. Ernst Behler sums it up well: the early German romanticism that manifested itself in Jena was distinguished first and foremost by its "*collective* character." Their greatest contributions were written in and through the attempt to construct in their midst a version of the sociability that Kant had said "befits our humanity."

6.2. SCHLEGEL AND NOVALIS: SYMPHILOSOPHY

In a remarkable experiment in what Friedrich Schlegel and Novalis, referring to their own collaboration, called "symphilosophizing," early German romanticism practiced the "art of reciprocal communication" among a group that for that historical period in Europe was surprisingly diverse in class, ethnicity, and gender. In the salons of Berlin attended by Friedrich Schlegel and Friedrich Schleiermacher, Dorothea Veit, and Ludwig Tieck, among others, as well as in meetings in the home of August and Carolina Schlegel (Friedrich's brother and sister-in-law) in Jena, the sort of intimate and sympathetic philosophical conversation Kant hoped for in the critique of aesthetic reflective judgment actually took place.[8]

From the very start the early German romantics were captivated by the problems and promise of aesthetic reflective dialogue. Touched by social changes in their midst and abroad, and challenged to shoulder their share of social responsibility and carry it into the dawn of a new century, their project was social to the core. Like Kant they saw the need to include the cultural and aesthetic claims of individuals from different social and historical backgrounds, but for the early German romantics this variety of perspectives became the very form and substance of their entire enterprise: In full recognition of the problem of the incommensurability of subjects' positions, they nevertheless enthusiastically embraced the project of giving voice to a chorus, and a chaos, of multiple perspectives. Their writings and discourses aimed at maximizing mutual understanding without minimizing discordant notes, and even provoked them (e.g., Schlegel's exquisitely ironic "On Incomprehensibility"). They addressed the problem of how subjective experience and the inner life of the individual can ever "get outside itself" (e.g., Novalis' Fichte and Kant studies and his *Novices of Sais*), and they returned again and again to the larger issue of how a society or social group with members from different vocations, religious backgrounds, and genders can find common ground through self-expression (Schlegel's *Dialogue on Poetry*, Schleiermacher's *Speeches* on religion and his *Theory of Sociable Conduct*).

To see this, a brief discussion of some of these exemplary pieces written during the pinnacle of the early German romantics' creative productivity (1798–99)
is in order. The kernel of many of the texts of the Jena circle was contained in
the journal published between 1798 and 1800 by Friedrich and August Wilhelm
Schlegel, the *Athenäum*. This journal was truly "the axis of Romantic aesthetics," containing much, if not "almost everything" that was central to the early
German romantic movement.[9] It was also novel in its inclusion of a variety of
literary forms including reviews, short essays, speeches, and poetry, and most
notably, collections of fragments—a literary form brought to new heights by
Friedrich Schlegel. The final volume closed with an essay addressing a frequent
criticism of the *Athenäum* aimed especially at the fragments, namely the charge
of incomprehensibility. Schlegel's reply, "On Incomprehensibility," is a model of
romantic irony that circles around and plays with the problem of communication between reader and writer. Playful and sarcastic, by turns self-effacing and
self-aggrandizing, at once jocular and serious, Schlegel challenges his critics to
get off their high horse and take themselves less seriously, in part by modeling
how that is done in the essay itself. But it is also a deadly serious argumentative
performance illustrating his conviction that art and philosophy must begin and
end where we find ourselves, in medias res, together with his view, famously
articulated in an early fragment in the *Athenäum*, that romantic poetry is philosophic, sociable, and aims to make society more "poetic" in this sense as well:

> Romantic poetry is a progressive universal poetry. Its aim isn't merely to
> reunite all the separate species of poetry and put poetry in touch with phi-
> losophy and rhetoric. It tries to and should mix and fuse poetry and prose,
> inspiration and criticism, the poetry of art and the poetry of nature; and
> make poetry lively and sociable, and life and society poetical; poeticize
> with and fill and saturate the forms of art with the pulsations of humor. It
> embraces everything that is purely poetic, from the greatest systems of art,
> containing within themselves still further systems, to the sigh, the kiss that
> the poetizing child breathes forth in artless song.... The romantic kind of
> poetry is still in the state of becoming; that in fact is its real essence: that it
> should forever be becoming and never be perfected... in a certain sense all
> poetry is or should be romantic. (KA 2, 182–83)[10]

Poetry (*Poesie*) is universal because it aims at an ideal that is itself never
fully articulable and thus "incomprehensible." It is progressive because it never
gives up *attempting* to comprehend and be comprehensible, that is, it aims constantly to better communicate itself to others, both present and future. Schlegel
describes how in response to the charge of incomprehensibility he had initially
resolved to

have a talk about this matter with my reader, and then create before his eyes—in spite of him as it were—another new reader to my own liking: yes, even to deduce him if need be. I meant it quite seriously… I wanted for once to be really thorough and go through the whole series of my essays, admit their frequent lack of success with complete frankness, and so gradually lead the reader to being similarly frank and straightforward with himself. (KA 2, 363–64; Firchow, 260)

Schlegel continues describing how he had hoped to show the reader, in the clearest terms, how incomprehension is "relative" to each individual and that the highest form of incomprehension occurs precisely in the arts and sciences, where the aim is total clarity of comprehension. But this confession artfully shades off into a mock encomium to the recent discovery (by Kant) of a "real language" and to the "critical age" he lives in, in which "everything is going to be criticized except the age itself" and in which, in the newly dawning millennium "humanity will at last rise up in a mass and learn to read." Elizabeth Millán Zaibert sums up the piece, and Schlegel's use of irony, nicely:

Irony is a sort of play that reveals the limitations of a view of reality that presumed to have the last word. With the use of romantic irony, Schlegel showed that there was no last word. And once we give up a last word, aesthetic methods become sensible alternatives to the methods of mathematics and the natural sciences.[11]

One of the aesthetic methods prized by the early romantics was the dialogue form, and here again Schlegel provides a model of the romantic mode of discourse that fused philosophy and poetry in an attempt to make them "lively and sociable" and to make "life and society poetical." In his introduction to the *Dialogue on Poetry*, modeled upon the many actual conversations of the early romantics, Schlegel insists upon the social nature of poetry: it "befriends and binds with unseverable ties the hearts of all those who love it" no matter how much at odds they otherwise may be "in their own lives" (KA 2, 284–87).[12] Poetry is expansive by nature and true poetry exists when one seeks to expand one's poetry to increasingly incorporate the work of others. Aware that one will always return to oneself, poetry requires "reaching out time and again beyond oneself to find the complement of one's innermost being in the depths of another": "The play of communication and approaching [others] is the business and the force of life: absolute perfection exists only in death." What constitutes progress in Schlegel's expansive "poetry" is not its becoming more and more true, or "real" but rather when it tries to connect its own particularity to all other poetry by finding "the center point, through communication with those who have found their [poetry] from a different side, in a different way." Schlegel asserts that the poet is "a sociable being" and then leads into the *Dialogue* with the promise to present a "many-sided" conversation that is intended to set against one another quite divergent opinions, each of them capable of shedding new light upon the infinite spirit of poetry from an individual standpoint, each of them striving to penetrate from a different angle into the real heart of the matter (KA 2, 286; Behler and Struc, 55).

The fact that the "real heart of the matter" is no more comprehensible than a "real language" in no way hinders, and in fact is precisely what drives, the romantic project to *attempt* to get to it. The goal is the striving—that is, the striving for an increasingly expansive poetry that "approximates the loftiest possibility of [poetry] on earth" through reciprocal communication leading to the discovery of multiple views to be incorporated into one's own.

Before turning to Friedrich Schleiermacher's contribution to a romantic theory of sociable conduct, it is important to briefly mention the contribution that Novalis (Friedrich von Hardenberg) made to this core element of early German romanticism. Novalis's close friendship with Friedrich Schlegel and their commitment to "fuse" their accounts of poetry and philosophy in the process of *Symphilosophieren* makes it difficult to separate their views. But Novalis's extensive notes and comments upon Fichte's early lectures at Jena, as well as notes and comments on Kant's *Critique of Pure Reason*, lend his account of sociability a decidedly metaphysical aspect that is not nearly as prominent in Friedrich Schlegel's work from this period. His keen interest in Fichte's work attests to Novalis's fascination with the nature of the self, or the "inner world" of the "I." His collected notes on Fichte focus largely on the question of self-cognition and self-awareness and do not deal much with social communication, but the philosophical underpinnings of his views on sociability are clear in passages that echo and improvise upon Fichtean themes: For instance, that philosophy begins with the "I" of self-awareness ("Philosophy is limited strictly to the determinate modification of consciousness"), but that self-consciousness itself requires an "other" ("The *human being* is as much Not-I as I") (NS 2, 268, nos. 559, 561, 562).[13] He notes that modern philosophers "have limited [philosophy] to the thinking of a ground of *representations* and sensations, in short to the alteration of the subject," but ends his massive study of Fichte with the enigmatic blurring of the individual/species distinction (NS 2, 272, no. 567; Kneller, 169):

> On humanity. Its pure complete development must first be in the art of the individual—and only then pass over to the great masses of people and then the species. To what extent is the species an individual? (NS 2, 271, no. 567; 296, no. 667; Kneller, 169; 194)

This fundamental interplay of the inner self with the outer world—especially with other "selves"—becomes a trope in Novalis's maturing philosophical and literary work. In his studies of Kant he muses that philosophy includes treating the sciences (*die Wissenschaften*) both scientifically and *poetically*, and raises the question whether the poetic is not perhaps identical to the practical, in the sense of being a specification of it. He worries about whether there are means other than mere sense perception for "getting outside ourselves and reaching other beings" (NS 2, 390). One of his last literary efforts, the *Novices of Sais*, makes clear that for Novalis, the answer to these metaphysical questions about the nature of the subject is that it is essentially social, and specifically it is most itself when it is "in love" with other human beings. The work depicts many "interpersonal" exchanges with nonsubject selves (plants, rocks, the ocean) in which "both types of perception [feeling and thinking] gain: the outer world becomes transparent and the inner world becomes varied and meaningful" (NS 1, 71–109).[14] But a crucial "fairy tale" told by one of the novices underscores Novalis's commitment to the primacy of the social: a young man journeys to the veiled statue of a woman said to be "the mother of things," but the story ends not, as in Schiller's poem, with the death of the seeker from despair induced by what he had unveiled, but with the young seeker of knowledge lifting the veil to discover once again the lover, and eventually the family, friends, and community he had earlier spurned in his quest for knowledge. This extraordinary little story of the fantastic journey culminating in everyday life is typically early romantic, and in its portrayal of fundamental human wisdom as rooted in community with others, it encapsulates a fundamental principle of early romanticism.

6.3. SCHLEIERMACHER: TOWARDS A THEORY OF SOCIABLE CONDUCT

The most direct record of the romantic social-dialogic experiment, however, is Friedrich Schleiermacher's attempt to theorize a romantic ideal of sociable conduct in ordinary (nonacademic) discourse. This work on sociability represents the social cooperative turn of early romanticism at its most intense, and is very closely tied to the views of both Novalis and Friedrich Schlegel. What follows is a sketch of this unfinished essay by Schleiermacher during the period of his life and work in which he was most closely tied to the Jena romantics.

In January and February of 1799 the first two installments of Schleiermacher's *Essay on a Theory of Sociable Behavior* were published anonymously in the *Berlin Archive of the Age and its Taste* (*Berlinisches Archiv der Zeit und ihres Geschmackes*). The final installments were never finished,[15] but the first sections yield a fascinating glimpse into the world of the Berlin salons of which he and his close friend Friedrich Schlegel were both active. The *Essay* illustrates the centrality of the very idea of social reflective activity for early romantic philosophy, picking up the thread of Kant's comment at the end of the "Critique of Aesthetic Judgment" about the need for developing a "sociability that befits our humanity." Schleiermacher begins with the claim that free sociability is a "higher goal of humanity": "free sociability, neither fettered nor determined by any external end, is demanded vociferously by all educated people as one of their primary and most cherished needs" (KGA 165; Foley, 153).

He elaborates by pointing out that people's jobs (their "civil life") and their home life take up so much time and energy, that their sphere of "mental activity" is increasingly narrowed and their perspectives and activities become increasingly one-sided. Thus he says, the higher aim of free and unfettered conversation with others is to expose us to the widest possible variety of perspectives:

> There must be a state that... enables an individual's sphere to be intersected as variously as possible so that each of one's own points of limitation will afford a view into a different and strange world. In such a manner, all manifestations of humanity will become known, one after the other, and the most alien temperaments and relationships can also become familiar and similarly intimate to that individual. This objective is realized by rational people engaging in mutual self-education when they *freely* keep company. (KGA 165; Foley, 153)

Schleiermacher, echoing Kant's language of a kingdom of ends, continues by characterizing *free sociability* as a moral end "realized by rational people" when they set aside self-interested ends and transport themselves into an intellectual world in which they act as a member:

> Only here, owing to the inherent lack of civil authority, everyone must be their own legislator and must see to it that the common good sustains no damage. All improvement must proceed from this principle and can only really be brought about by every individual adjusting his or her behavior in accordance with that common goal. (KGA 166; Foley, 154)

There is an important difference, however: This romantic society is real and its members are there not only intellectually but in the flesh. They conduct themselves freely with an eye to the good of the society *and also* "in accordance with [their] inclinations" (KGA 165; Foley, 154). Both individuality and pleasure in the activity of social reflection are a part of this embodied, aesthetic realm of ends. Because these societies are made of real people, Schleiermacher is acutely aware of the difficulties of setting up and sustaining them. Still, his own experiences in the salons of Berlin convinced him that, if only he can root this account solidly within common human nature, some systematic account of how they must be formed and conducted is possible. Thus he describes the free society as a construct for which guidelines may be set out in theory, beginning with the "view that free sociability [is] a natural tendency that cannot be circumvented" and "the point of departure will be merely the initial concept of sociability that is available of its own accord in every person" (KGA 168; Foley, 156). Since free sociability is naturally sought for its own sake, the continuous and uninterrupted free activity of all the individuals involved in forming and maintaining these societies is also desirable in itself. Furthermore, "If we analyze the concept of free sociability of society in its truest sense," Schleiermacher says, then "we find that several people should affect each other and that this affecting is by no means permitted to be one-sided" (KGA 169; Foley, 157–58). To this end the distinctive character of such societies is one of reciprocity, that is, the free and equal participation of each member aimed at "nothing but the free play of thoughts and feelings by means of which all members excite and animate one another" (KGA 170; Foley, 159).

Because societies are made up of participating individuals they will each have their own special character, and yet certain rules apply to them all. First, all communication must be reciprocal (form) and second, what is communicated should be an expression from and about each individual.[16] Since individuals are of a variety of types unique to every group, Schleiermacher says, "Each society has its own outline and profile: whosoever fails to contribute to creating this; or whosoever does not know how to remain within the confines of this, is as good as not there for this society" (KGA 170; Foley, 159). Hence a third rule applies, namely that individual members must limit their activity to what will not undermine the society as a whole. To avoid the formation of exclusionary groups, "Nothing should be evoked that does not belong to the communal sphere of all" (KGA 171; Foley, 160). This creates another problem, namely that for the individual to limit herself is to fail to express her unique individual self to the society. Societies are easily destroyed by self-centered members, but self-deprecating team players are just as destructive because they do not contribute their own, *unique* share. Alternating between the two types of contribution (of self-aggrandizing and self-effacing) is no solution, Schleiermacher says: "the one-sidedness is not avoided by doubling it" (KGA 172–73; Foley, 61–63). Thus a major problem for free sociability is that of figuring out how to contribute one's individuality completely and at the same time to fully participate in the character of the society.

Schleiermacher's proposed solution is to resolve the tension by recognizing two senses in which my individuality can be limited: in "manner" and in what he calls "tone," that is, subject matter. My manner (how I handle and convey the subject matter) is my own and can be freely expressed without destroying the character of the society, whereas the character of the society is set by its subject matter ("tone"), which *ought* to be limited. Schleiermacher also gives guidelines for delineating the subject matter: It is to be determined by a kind of sensitive, reflective equilibriation on the part of all the members, between the poles of each individual's own interests and the intersection of those interests that are common to all. Beginning from each side and reflectively balancing our concerns, we "seek to determine the sphere of the society between the given limits with ever increasing precision," he says. Ideally then, every contribution of every individual fully establishes the society's tone and character while at the same time allowing each participant to express him- or herself fully in a unique individual manner. Schleiermacher does not worry about a domineering person or subgroup hijacking the conversation: "To hold one's disagreeable qualities within bounds is the task of the others, and they will surely attend to that" (KGA 175; Foley, 165).

On Schleiermacher's final analysis, in the freely sociable society, "All social statements must consequently have a double tendency, a double meaning as it were":

> This meaning should be one that I should like to call the common denominator and is related directly to maintenance [of the society's character]... and another, as it were, a higher one that is thrown out with some uncertainty to see if someone will pick up on it and pursue the intimations it contains. (KGA 181; Foley, 165)

The ways in which this can be carried out, he says, are practically uncountable, and the doubling of purpose in every individual's statements lends itself to insinuation, banter, irony, and parody, all of which, so long as they are not directed against another individual absent or present, are fine ways of moving the social interactions to a high point. The *Essay* ends with a caution: "it is in the nature of a theory and does not really require explicit evincing that the ideas presented here are ideals that practice is only meant to approach" (KGA 181–82; Foley, 173).

Two comments on this theory should be stressed. First, the final description clearly owes much not only to the actual sociability of the meetings of the Berlin salons and the Jena sessions that Schlegel and Novalis dubbed "symphilosophizing," but it also portrays the romantic program defined by Novalis, namely that of romanticizing, carrying an activity in two directions at once, elevating and lowering, making the ordinary extraordinary and the extraordinary common (NS 2, 545, no. 105). By placing this poetic demand in the setting of a social gathering of individuals, Schleiermacher personalizes Novalis's definition and brings into relief the element most commonly associated with this movement, namely the importance of human social intimacy, not merely abstracted but also realized.

Second, although there are elements of Schiller, of Fichte, and of other influences at work in the *Essay*,[17] there is also clearly much of Kant in this account, and not simply in the use of Kantian ethical conceptions. Whether intended or not, the *Essay* is redolent of Kant's aesthetics. In fact, it is in many respects no more or less than a detailed, social instantiation of Kant's views of the free play that takes place in judgments of taste. I want to conclude by pressing this point a bit further, turning to one particularly interesting connection between Schleiermacher's notion of free sociable reflection and a key notion in Kant's account of artistic genius, namely, the aesthetic idea.

6.4. SOCIALIZING GENIUS IN EARLY GERMAN ROMANTICISM

In making this connection I am not arguing that Schleiermacher's project is intended as a response to Kant's aesthetics, although there can be no doubt that he is using Kant's moral theory with explicit intent when he employs the language of maxims of action and the ethical commonwealth model in the *Essay*.[18]

Still, even at the height of their antiestablishment moods, the revolutionary young romantics could never dismiss Kant. Novalis is clear that Kant's Copernican turn is simply to be taken as a given, and in the Berlin lectures A. W. Schlegel is at pains to comment upon and criticize Kant's theory of imagination and genius. His Vienna lectures of 1808 mention Kant's aesthetics in a recommendation to Schlegel's "brilliant audience of both sexes" to read Kant's section on the sublime for a nearly perfect account of the philosophical underpinnings of tragedy (nearly perfect because, he says, Kant appears to have lacked much acquaintance with ancient tragedy). In truth, no account of the development of romantic aesthetics could entirely ignore Kant's views on this subject.

Schleiermacher, who was working on a review of Kant's *Anthropology* at the same time he worked on the *Essay*, would thus not have ignored Kant's aesthetics entirely. Kant's *Anthropology* contains a few sections of distilled lecture material on genius, which ends with the famous three maxims of judgment including the command that in communication with others, one should put oneself in their place, like the "liberals" who "accommodate themselves to the concepts of others" (AA 7, sec. 59, 228). Moreover, the fact that Schleiermacher describes his theoretical project in the *Essay* as aiming "to construct sociable life as a work of art" and not just a "beautiful fantasy" suggests Kant's distinction between art objects, which have a final purpose or intent, and the free beauty of nature, whose purposiveness is always merely a regulative background assumption.

Perhaps most striking, however, is the parallel between Schleiermacher's account of a sociable society and Kant's notion of genius, laid out in much greater detail in the third *Critique* in terms of a newly introduced notion of aesthetic ideas. Kant's analysis in section 49, "On the powers of the mind that constitute genius," begins with a discussion of particular interest in this context, of what he calls "spirit [*Geist*] in an aesthetic sense":

> Of certain products that are expected to reveal themselves at least in part to be fine art, we say that they have no *spirit*, even though we find nothing to censure in them as far as taste is concerned. A poem may be quite nice and elegant and yet have no spirit. A story may be precise and orderly and yet have no spirit. An oration may be both thorough and graceful and yet have no spirit. Many conversations are entertaining, but they have no spirit. Even about some woman we will say that she is pretty, communicative, and polite, but that she has no spirit. (AA 5, 313)

Schleiermacher aims this same criticism at social discourse that stifles individual contributions. He worries about the conversational "emptiness" and "paltry insipidness" of societies that require the individual to stifle contributions that might in any way rock the conversational boat. By adopting a maxim that sets decorum above all else, they hold that "Whatever meets the eye beyond this middle average is unseemly and would require sanding down like rough edges" and hence,

> All idiosyncrasies would have to be suppressed.... This [false] maxim [to avoid saying anything outside common limits] completely suspends the final goal of society and strives toward that emptiness that is complained about the most frequently in the highest and the finest circles. (KGA 173; Foley, 162)

In Kant's terms, what such conversations lack is aesthetic spirit, where "spirit" is defined as "the animating principle in the mind" (AA 5, 313).

Kant immediately delves into a deeper cognitive analysis of what is going on in the most elevated and 'spirited" minds, namely that in the mind of the genius. "Spirit" or this "animating principle is nothing but the ability to exhibit aesthetic ideas,"

> and by an *aesthetic idea* I mean a presentation of the imagination which prompts much thought, but to which no determinate thought whatsoever,

i.e., no determinate concept, can be adequate, so that no language can express it completely and allow us to grasp it. (AA 5, 313)

So the animating principle, or "spirit" in the mind that constitutes genius, is identified with creative imagination, which takes a given concept and freely connects it

> with such a multiplicity of partial presentations that no expression that stands for a determinate concept can be found for it. Hence [the resulting aesthetic idea] is a presentation that makes us add to a concept the thoughts of much that is ineffable, but the feeling of which quickens our cognitive powers and connects language, which otherwise would be mere letters, with spirit. (AA 5, 316)

Genius then, is the ability to discover and express aesthetic ideas, and Schleiermacher's theory of sociable conduct is the functional, intersubjective equivalent of Kant's "inner" subjective account of genius. For Schleiermacher, Kant's account of the inner state of the subject—the mind of the genius—is writ large in the sociable (romantic) "society," that is, an assemblage of individuals whose sole purpose in gathering is to discover their social capacity (their humanity) and to further it in free, reciprocal dialogue. Their only purpose is the regulative one of creating a society that is an expression of the union of their multiple individualities and their shared social community. Each member expresses her views in her own "manner," leaving her professional standing, her class and family standing, and so on, aside (except to the extent that it will manifest itself in the manner of her expression). In Kant's terms, her expressions together with all the others, serve to constitute a "multiplicity of partial presentations," and these serve to enlarge but not determine the "given concept." In Schleiermacher's terms, her contributions along with the others serve to maintain and entertain (*unterhalten*) the whole group and at the same time to elevate the subject of the conversation, and human sociability itself.

Put another way, on Schleiermacher's social model the partial representations in the mind of Kant's genius become the individual members' contributions to the conversation. It is as if he took the complexities of the Kantian notion of imaginative creative functioning and instantiated them in a network of individual thinking, sensing, and feeling human beings who are drawn together by a natural urge to communicate ever more intimately. Because they are undertaking conversation for the sake of communication itself, such conversations never end with a "determinate" concept. No final answer to a problem, and no definitive, final explanation of an issue, will be uncovered or constructed by it. But that is of course not the point, any more than it is the job of artistic genius to categorize objects or determine their goodness. The point is rather to discover and express new ideas. It is the expansion of its own abilities and the enlargement of given concepts that is at issue for genius on Kant's account and so too for Schleiermacher's social model. To be sure, the point of the romantic society is free play and the disinterested pleasure that this freedom brings its members, but this social reflective freedom also serves a larger purpose insofar as it discovers and creates enlarged philosophical perspectives and new ways of looking at old concepts.

In his interpretive account of the *Essay*, Peter Foley argues that the role of the salons in Berlin was extremely important in shaping Schleiermacher's model of sociability: the Berlin salons of Henrietta Herz, Rahel Levin, and other were diverse not only in gender and religious ethnicity but also in professional occupations and in degree and kind of education. At their best they were largely successful experiments in cross-cultural understanding and intellectual discovery. Schleiermacher is quite clear that a multiplicity of such societies is possible and desirable, and that each must formulate its own tone, and find its own equilibrium. Like Kant's genius, the successful sociable society cannot formulate the rules by which it operates in such a way that others can clone that success simply by following these rules. Creative free societies can serve as *exemplars* for other would-be societies, just as genius can give examples to other budding genius. Genius must create itself from its own inner resources, just as a successful society must create itself through the particular individuals that constitute it. In short, based on his own experience in the romantic mode of discourse, Schleiermacher was able to sketch in some detail an ideal of an egalitarian society that values individual difference—indeed, *requires* it—in the process of constructing a unique discursive community.

In sum, Schleiermacher and his romantic cohort provided working models of a kind of intellectual sociability that is relevant even now. Insofar as Kant's aesthetic theory provided a cognitive model for imaginative creativity, he did more than merely hint at the possibility of a new form of aesthetic reflective sociability—he laid the groundwork for it. But it took a generation of bold academics who were willing to publicly call for academic social and moral responsibility to inspire their "freely sociable" young followers to experiment with and socialize genius in art and philosophy. As an intellectual movement, the early German romantics were remarkable for letting these sociable discursive practices drive their literary, critical, and philosophical endeavors. Contemporary academics should recognize and applaud the role that the literary and philosophical figures of the 1790s in Jena played in sparking this movement. However brief this historical moment, it deserves our attention and respect, and should challenge us to recreate the pluralistic academic and social discursive practices of early

German romanticism in an even more expansive and inclusive way appropriate to our time.

NOTES

1. Kant introduces this hypothesis in his "Idea for a Universal History from a Cosmopolitan Point of View" published in 1784. AA 8, 15–31.
2. Ernst Behler and Roman Struc, introduction to their edition of *Friedrich Schlegel: Dialogue on Poetry and Literary Aphorisms* (hereafter Behler and Struc) (University Park: Pennsylvania State University Press, 1968), 4.
3. Theodore Ziolkowski, *German Romanticism and Its Institutions* (Princeton: Princeton University Press, 1990), 267–68.
4. Ibid., 237.
5. Ibid., 245.
6. Ibid., 254.
7. Ibid., 255–56.
8. For an extended discussion of the philosophically substantial role played by the women in the circle, see my contribution titled "Feminism" in the *Oxford Handbook to German Idealism*, ed. Michael Forster and Kristin Gjesdal (Oxford: Oxford University Press, forthcoming).
9. Behler, introduction to *Friedrich Schlegel*, 4. Behler claims that it contained "almost everything of importance written in those years by the earlier German Romanticists."
10. For English translation, see *Friedrich Schlegel's "Lucinde" and the* Fragments, trans. Peter Firchow (hereafter Firchow) (Minneapolis: University of Minnesota Press, 1971), 31–32.
11. Elizabeth Millán-Zaibert, *Friedrich Schlegel and the Emergence of Romantic Philosophy* (Albany: State University of New York Press, 2007), 168. Her summary of this essay is an insightful and useful account of Schlegel's underlying, antidogmatic philosophical commitments.
12. Friedrich Schlegel, "Gespräch über die Poesie"; for the English translation, see Behler and Struc, 53–55.
13. Novalis, *Fichte-Studien*; for the English translation, see Novalis, *Fichte Studies*, ed. Jane Kneller (hereafter Kneller) (Cambridge: Cambridge University Press, 2002), 166.
14. *Die Lehrlinge zu Saïs*; for the English translation, see *The Novices of Sais*, trans. Ralph Manheim, with sixty drawings by Paul Klee (New York: Curt Valentin, 1949), 77.
15. The *Essay's* authorship was only determined in the early twentieth century. The reasons for its being abandoned include the fact that Schleiermacher found himself finishing it in social isolation, and that he was working on several other projects at the time. See Peter Foley's *Friedrich Schleiermacher's "Essay on a Theory of Sociable Behavior" (1799): A Contextual Interpretation* (Lewiston: Edwin Mellon Press, 2006), 125ff. References to Schleiermacher's *Essay* in what follows are to KGA volume 12, followed by the pagination in Peter Foley's translation (hereafter Foley), included in his book.
16. Schleiermacher refers to it as "communicating what is mine" (KGA 170; Foley, 15).

17. See Foley's commentary, 1–151.
18. In general, although Kant's influence on the romantics was clearly important to their ethical and political philosophical development, it is less clear that his aesthetic theory had much of a direct influence, and such influence as it did have appears to have been largely negative. (See Richard Crouter's introduction to Friedrich Schleiermacher, *On Religion: Speeches to Its Cultured Despisers*, edited by Richard Crouter [Cambridge: Cambridge University Press, 1996], xix, n 26). A. W. Schlegel criticizes it in his lectures on literature and art in Berlin 1801–2. His brother Friedrich, as Ernst Behler points out, "settled his differences with Kant" primarily by ignoring him and developing his own views on art and imagination (Ernst Behler, *German Romantic Literary Theory* [Cambridge: Cambridge University Press, 1993], 77). Novalis studied Kant again, after his intense engagement with Fichte's philosophy in 1795, but his study seems to have been limited to the first and second *Critiques*. Crouter points out that Schleiermacher is said to have owned a copy of the *Critique of Judgment*, but argues that he seemed not to have read it, based on a dismissive remark he made that Kant's third *Critique* contained only "incidental" mention of art. See Günter Meckenstock, ed., *Schleiermachers Bibliothek* (Berlin: de Gruyter, 1993), 210. (Given the romantic's central focus on art, however, this doesn't strike me as proof that Schleiermacher never read it. It could be exactly what Schleiermacher thought, having skimmed or even read the book cover to cover, since by the romantic's standards, there was much less time devoted to discussions of art than they would have liked to see.)

PART THREE

Literature, Art, and Mythology

"Doch sehnend stehst/Am Ufer du" ("But Longing You Stand On the Shore")

Hölderlin, Philosophy, Subjectivity, and Finitude

RICHARD ELDRIDGE

7.1.

As the name of the discipline implies, philosophy is centrally concerned not simply with knowledge alone, but with wisdom or with the problem of orientation or with the achievement of a life of felt and reasonable meaningfulness. In strongly traditional societies, this problem may not arise, or solutions to it may be held in place as what is simply to be done, without diverse paths or possibilities of reflection on them significantly presenting themselves. Within modern social economies, marked in contrast by technological development and strongly divided labor, things are much less settled, in ways that can provoke both anxiety and reflection. But how is reflection then to develop fruitfully? If it is significantly abstract overall, then it threatens both to lose touch with concrete life practices and in doing so to turn either emptily escapist or dogmatically tyrannical. Yet if it lingers entirely in the concrete, then it threatens to fail to resolve anxieties and to challenge social and practical fractures that are already in place. In the face of this dilemma, reflection seems both impossible and necessary.

Writing roughly between 1795 and 1815 in the wake of emerging secularization and showing a strong consciousness of social life as both fractured

and unavoidable, a number of writers whom we now class as Romantic—
pre-eminently Hölderlin and Wordsworth, Goethe in his lyric poetry, and Blake
and Coleridge—developed a kind of practice of philosophy by other means.
Swerving between abstract reflection and concrete description and between
rationalism and empiricism, they developed strong senses of human subjects as
bound to a temporality that is not discernibly plotted and yet with which one
can (so they suggested) at times come to terms. They accept neither human fat-
edness to life within unintelligible and impersonal processes alone nor fantasies
of either escape or full control of the conditions of life, so that "romanticism"
becomes a name for philosophy done, the problem of orientation addressed,
otherwise than only in abstract distantiation from the ordinary. Its images of
coming to maturity, even if imperfectly and without dogmatism and final closure, stand as models that are distinctly relevant to our thinking about maturity
and orientation in life, given a modern social economy that we significantly
share with them.[1] Attention to their strongly temporalized thought and writing
can help alert us both to how philosophy and poetry may be entangled with
one another in relation to certain central problems of modern human life and
to possibilities of maturity that we might otherwise fail to notice or articulate.

7.2.

It is well known that Hölderlin's mature poetry is significantly motivated by
his sense, developing out of his criticism of Fichte, of the self-occlusion of the
Absolute. As in German idealism generally, "the Absolute" names that which is
not dependent on anything else and simply is—a self-determining whole that
includes all of nature and human life. Contra Fichte, Hölderlin argues, "If I say: 'I
am I, [then] the subject ("I") and the object ("I") are *not* united in such a way that
no separation could be performed without violating the essence of what is to
be separated; on the contrary, the I is only possible by means of this separation
of the I from the I."[2] Ignoring the mistaken treatment of the *is* of identity as the
is of predication, the argument is straightforward and compelling. Being a subject—that which we primarily refer to by means of "I"—implies apperceptive
unity; that is, it implies at least the possibility of coming to be explicitly aware of
the contents of one's consciousness *as* the contents of one's consciousness. Any
thing that lacked this capacity could not properly be called a subject. But this
capacity in turns implies the ability, as it were, to separate oneself from oneself,
in particular to focus on the contents of one's consciousness as *not* essential to
what one is. I am thinking of a dog, say, but I could be thinking instead (and
sometimes do think instead) of a cup of coffee. Hence neither of these contents
is itself essential to my identity as a subject. But for the Absolute, in contrast,
everything is essential. That is, it is not subject-like. And hence, further, we, as

finite subjects are separated, cast out, from this original, all-embracing unity of Being as such. Insofar as we do possess a consciousness that is both apperceptively unified and discursive (such that we are able to form judgments), we are "outside" a more original, inclusive unity, able to attend to this or that, but never simply bound within the flow of the whole. Our status as subjects is marked, as Hölderlin puts it, by an "arche-separation," an *Ur-theilung*.[3] Both reflection and we as subjects capable of reflection are somehow within the Absolute, but also separated from *its* continuous self-development, not essential to it.

It is not immediately clear how much of this argument is sound or what its implications are. It might well be conceded that the Absolute—supposing to begin with that we find much use for a concept of the whole of Being—is not itself subject-like or reflective or apperceptively unified in the way that we are as finite subjects. But why should that thought imply the further thought that we, as finite subjects, are somehow exterior to it, separated or cast out from it?

Here Hölderlin is best taken as registering an *experienced* sense of exteriority, of absence of orientation, and of the capacity for reflection as a set of undischarged burdens that have roots that are all at once religious, biographical, sociohistorical, and anthropologico-developmental. In religious terms, an understanding of the Absolute as non-subject-like and self-enclosed already registers a sense of the collapse or unavailability of any narrative of God's providence. In his 1785 *Briefe über die Lehre Spinozas* that initiated the Pantheism Controversy, Jacobi had already associated Spinozism with materialism and atheism, and this association was well known to Hölderlin and his Tübingen circle during his student years. A Spinozist Absolute is, therefore, marked as a nonprovidential, non-Christian Absolute for Hölderlin.

Biographically, Hölderlin experienced a continuing series of failures to settle into a permanent position. From 1793, when he left Tübingen, to 1802, he held a series of tutorships in private families at Waltershausen, Frankfurt, Hauptwil (Switzerland), and Bordeaux (France), retaining only one of them for more than four months. The exception—January 1796 to September 1798 in the household of the Gontards in Frankfurt—was marked by an intense and disastrous love affair with Suzette Gontard, the much younger wife of his banker employer. Following his dismissal from this post, Hölderlin managed a number of clandestine meetings with Suzette up until her death in June 1802. After 1802, following his return from Bordeaux in a precarious mental condition, Hölderlin lived primarily in Homburg with an official salary as court librarian, but no real duties, until his removal to a Tübingen asylum in 1806 and final years in the care of Ernst Zimmer from 1807 to 1843. This unstable itinerary shows a marked lack of any unifying narrative or sense of continuing orientation. Improvised arrangements are made hurriedly, and they do not last long. Sociohistorically, Hölderlin's career is marked by his refusal to take up the post of a village pastor for which he had been trained at Tübingen. Not much else was open to him other than a position as a private tutor. Hölderlin was neither noble nor rich enough to enter court life, nor was either the university or the market economy yet fully open to an ambitious young man with primarily theological training. Hence Hölderlin's drift, though exacerbated by his mental instability, is not untypical of the rootlessness of a young male member of an emerging humanistically educated class who lacked definite social prospects. Finally, anthropologico-developmentally, it is, after all, a mystery how anyone comes to be a subject with discursively structured consciousness. This development into a life of explicit claim-making, norm-mongering, and reflectiveness does not happen with other animals. How, then, do we move from the dependent infants we initially are into being the active makers of judgments we come to be? Surely training, initiation into language, and the attentions of others play important roles in this development, but how, and to what purpose? A sense of rootlessness or undirectedness might well arise for anyone in light of this course of development, and on Hölderlin's part this sense can only have been exacerbated by his religious, biographical, and modern sociohistorical experiences.

Independent of argument, then, about exclusion from a Spinozist Absolute, Hölderlin's sense of exteriority to Being as such is, to put it mildly, overdetermined. Whether or not there is a proof of the exteriority of reflective consciousness to being, Hölderlin nonetheless powerfully thematizes an experience of exteriority and difficulty of orientation. Or, as he puts it, there is "a universal contradiction within man… between the striving for the absolute and the striving for restriction."[4] We seek, that is, to achieve mastery or appropriate orientation by means of philosophical knowledge of the whole of Being and our place in it, and we also find ourselves driven to throw off the burden of reflective consciousness and to accept limitation and naturalness. As Terry Pinkard usefully explicates the point, the founding thought of both German idealism and German romanticism, initiated by Hölderlin, is that "it is the way in which we hold such oppositions together that characterizes our agency…. We always begin with a 'certainty' about where we are––with a practical, pre-reflective implicit grasp of what counts as vouching for our judgments, our practices, our valuations… and we then come to ask whether that 'certainty' has any 'truth' in light of the kinds of skepticism that open up as that form of 'certainty' subjects itself to its own internal tests."[5] Hegel's wager is that this prereflective "certainty" is already implicitly conceptual and that that conceptual commitment can be made explicit, tested, and revised until we arrive at stable enough orientation. Hölderlin's particular honesty and courage—his openness to continuing skepticism—is instead to hold that both striving for a reflective understanding of appropriate orientation *and* openness to sudden, abrupt, uncontrolled limitation (whether via reversal or via the absorptive sweep of love, beauty, and passion) persist always in tension with one another, with no standing resolution and only moments of relative balance.[6]

The result in Hölderlin's writing, both theoretical and poetic, that enacts this tension is a kind of back-and-forth movement between distantiated, abstract theorizing and immersive, absorptive dwelling in perception and feeling as given. In the mode of abstract theorizing, he seeks the "true profundity" of "complete knowledge of the parts that we must found and combine into one, and deep knowledge of that which founds and comprehends, piercing to the farthest end of knowledge."[7] Without fundamental knowledge of one's place in the whole, there is neither dignity nor actively maintained orientation. In more optimistic Fichtean moments, Hölderlin suggests that "he who truly acts according to the whole is by himself thereby more consecrated to peace and more disposed to esteem the individual."[8] This implies that action according to the whole is possible and hence that the wages of reflection on the whole that issues in appropriate action need not be only distantiation and alienation. Likewise, in a 1797 letter to Schiller, Hölderlin argues that abstract reflection, shying from life into thought, while difficult, is also both natural and fruitful.

I now regard the metaphysical mood as a kind of virginity of spirit, and I believe that shyness in the face of the material, however unnatural it is in itself, is nonetheless very natural at a certain period of life, and that it is for a time beneficial, just as all flights out of determinate relations are, since they check the power in oneself and make the spendthrift youthful life thrifty, for just so long, until its now ripe exuberance drives it to divide and distribute itself [sich zu theilen] in relation to manifold objects... I believe also... that the Idea is prior to the Concept, just as the tendency is prior to the (determinate, regular) act. I regard Reason [die Vernunft] as the beginning of the understanding [der Verstand], and if the good will hesitates and has to exert itself in order to form a useful intention, so do I find this just as characteristic for human nature in general as it is characteristic for Hamlet, for whom it is so difficult to do something for the sake of the single end of avenging his father.[9]

Here, however, the optimism, while present, is substantially more moderated. Instead of giving up philosophy as fruitless, as Schiller had urged him to do, Hölderlin defends metaphysics and abstract reflection as appropriate for a certain period of time at a certain stage of life. It as it were helps us to gather and collect our powers, thence to use them appropriately, rather than wasting them in heapish series of unreflective, ill-considered actions. But as the concluding reference to Hamlet suggests, it may nonetheless be far from straightforward to translate the fruits of reason into specific action.

In recoil, then, from a life of abstract reflection that produces as much continuing anxiety as direction, Hölderlin also celebrates the fact that the "airy spirits [*Luftgeister*] with metaphysical wings"[10] have left him, thus enabling greater peace in freedom from reflection. Persistent thinking about orientation, without fixed and stable results, yields only restlessness; without receptivity, there is no composure. Something must come from without, in order to inform and give content to thinking. Thought alone is unable to generate determinate objects. "When I think an object as possible, then I only repeat the previously existent consciousness by means of which it is actual. There is for us no thinkable possibility that was not at one time actuality."[11] As Violetta Waibel usefully comments, "Hölderlin seems not simply to negate principles and a priori moments of thinking, but rather to regard them as forms of abstraction that are not thinkable independently and without being bound to concrete states of affairs."[12] Broadly speaking, as Waibel also notes, a suspicion of abstract thinking on Hölderlin's part is a continuing point of contact between his poetological writings and the skepticism of Jacobi. Both Jacobi and Hölderlin, as Waibel puts it, give primacy to "existential orientation in the world [*Befindlichkeit in der Welt*]" and so "assign to anthropology... a precedence over a philosophical mode of explanation that threatens to become an intellectual end in itself."[13] This suspicion of abstract thinking is further reinforced by Hölderlin's reading of Plato, especially of the *Symposium*, where love (eros) is presented as a force of attraction to concrete things that is co-primordial with the emergence of consciousness itself. Or in Hölderlin's own formulation:

As our original infinite essence became suffering for the first time and as our free, full power felt its first limits, as poverty mated with exuberance, then there was love. Ask yourself: when was that? Plato says: on the day that Aphrodite was born. Thus just then, when the beautiful world began for us, when we came to consciousness, then we became finite.[14]

This condensed parable of the emergence of finite consciousness shows it as always already marked by concrete attraction to finite, beautiful, given objects of attention. Hölderlin's sense that human consciousness is always so marked leads him, as Thomas Pfau puts it, to develop a "neo-Platonist project of overcoming the sensible/intelligible dualism without relegating the concrete, individual intuition to a mere ancillary *function*."[15] Moreover, as Pfau goes on, "Hölderlin does not simply stabilize this convergence of intuition and the intelligible in an ontological sense either; for its occurrence, linked to the creative imagination, is 'accidental,' that is, cannot be freely grounded as a necessity."[16] That is to say, while developmentally discursive consciousness begins as always already bound up with experiences of intense felt attractions to natural, more or less maternal, presences, the recurrence of such intensities of attraction at later stages is hostage to fortune. Within the orbit of this Neoplatonic anthropology that sees thought as bound up with eros, Hölderlin in contrast to idealism shifts, as Pfau puts it, "from a notion of intuition as *Anschauung* to intuition as analeptic *Ahndung*."[17] ("*Ahndung*" is Hölderlin's archaic Swabian spelling of *Ahnung*—presentiment, foreshadowing, or intuitiveness. "Analeptic" indicates that such a presentiment is animating or restorative.) That is to say, orientation in life is achieved, if it is achieved at all, only through an unpredictable, restorative moment of receptivity that furnishes content to a desire that aims to reachieve the intensities of attraction characteristic of early childhood. That such experiences of animated receptivity are essentially occasioned and accidental thus calls into question the very possibility of getting a grip on one's life according to abstract principles generated in reflection. In Pfau's formulation, "it poses a serious challenge to the possibility of an integral subjectivity, that is, to the continuity of a 'self' as such."[18]

And yet Hölderlin does not quite abandon reason and reflection altogether. He continues to see the pursuit of autonomy and self-command, grounded in rational reflection and expressed in adherence to principles, as also part of man's higher than merely animal nature. Unlike other animals, we are, as both burdened and gifted with reflection, anticipation, and memory, open to "infinite satisfaction,... provided that [man's] activity is of the right kind, is not too far-reaching for him, for his strength and skill, that he is not too restless, too undetermined nor, on the other hand, too anxious, too restricted, too controlled."[19] As the unresolved two directions of mutual qualification in this passage show—we must be determined, resolute, in charge of what we do, but not too much; and we must be receptive, open, and ready to accept what happens but not too much[20] ––Hölderlin develops a philosophical anthropology that combines elements from Kant, empiricism, and what would become Hegelianism, but that also differs strikingly from each of them. As in Kant, the exercise of reason and reflection to generate a moral law matters as a fundamental aspect of our dignity, but in contrast with Kant this exercise cannot take place on its own, apart from intense experiences of attraction. As in empiricism, receptive sense-experience is an essential source of content for orientation in life, but in contrast with empiricism sense-experience is not simply dispositive, and it is available not continuously, but only intermittently, in moments of intense attraction to a concrete object, person, or scene. As in Hegel, there is prereflective orientation to the world that can be to some extent articulated, but in contrast with Hegel the relevant articulation that yields orientation is itself temporary, strongly temporalized, and bound up more with erotic attractions, embodiment, and openness to natural beauty than with participation in public life.

Given, then, Hölderlin's continuing intense and intensely ambivalent, competing attractions to both active, reflective, abstract theorizing and immersive, absorptive dwelling in perceptions and relationships, it is no surprise that he is unable to follow Schiller's (all too autobiographical) advice to him that he should "flee philosophical material wherever possible; it is the most thankless of all, and the best powers are often consumed in fruitless wrestling with it. Remain closer to the world of the senses so that you will be less in danger either of losing sobriety [Nüchternhheit] in rapture [Begeisterung] or of straying into a contrived [gekünstelt] expression."[21] For Schiller, philosophy and abstract reflection could and should be left behind, as Schiller indeed abandoned them and returned to drama after the period of his intense absorption in Kantianism from 1793 to 1795. In contrast, instead of turning away from philosophy and to poetry as a separate and distinct practice, Hölderlin takes up the task of incorporating alternations between moments of abstract reflection and moments of intense absorption into a self-developing poetic whole. As he comments in a 1799 letter to his brother,

> Poetry unites men not, I say, in the manner of play; it unites them, namely, when it is genuine and functions [wirkt] genuinely—with all the manifold suffering, happiness, striving, hoping and fearing, with all the opinions and errors, all the virtues and ideas, with everything great and small, that is among them—as a living, thousandfold divided [gegliedert] heartfelt [innig] whole.[22]

The consequence in the poetry of the bearing of this task is that poetry remains internally related to philosophy, as it is oriented around what Hölderlin calls transitions (Wechsel) in mood, where the transitions themselves are marked by the same sort of difficulty and abruptness that mark their occurrence in daily life. Or as Hölderlin puts it to his brother, "I cannot easily find my way out of reasoning [Raisonnement] and into poetry, and vice versa.... Perhaps only a few people will have as much difficulty with the transition [Übergang] from one mood to another as I do."[23]

The result is a difficult poetry more continuously of open, even abrupt, transition than of completed doctrinal closure. As Waibel usefully puts it, Hölderlin's concept—decisive for his poetry—of reciprocal determination (Wechselbestimmung) of moods must be understood in the framework of a theory of drives. One concept at the same time determines its opposite, so that both stand in a relation of reciprocal determination. Something must stand opposed to the I that is infinite in itself—either an object or alternatively a world of objectivity—in order for it to feel and cognize. In the same way, a striving toward the infinite, that is, a striving to realize ideas, is also unthinkable,

without a simultaneous striving toward limitation, that is, toward an actual recognition of the conditioned character of existence.[24]

Neither drive—neither the drive toward selfhood and fully autonomous
activity in self-sustaining abstract thinking, nor the drive toward receptivity to
and absorption in the finite—can properly be denied, abandoned, or avoided.
Or as Hölderlin puts it in a prose fragment of the metrical version of *Hyperion*,
"we cannot deny the drive to free ourselves, to ennoble ourselves, to progress
into the infinite. That would be animalistic. But we can also not deny the drive
to be determined, to be receptive; that would not be human."[25] Since both drives
remain present and undeniable, with neither being sacrificed to the other and
with no possibility of their stable integration, the result, as Waibel puts it, of
"the thought-figure of reciprocal determination" is "a metaphysics of the finite"
that continuously accepts and embraces "the possibility of reversal."[26]

Within the poetry that enacts this sense of the subject always open to the possibility of reversal, it is necessary, always, "to bear the momentarily incomplete."[27]
"Real effectiveness" requires neither too much mingling of self-determining,
ennobling, reflective activity with sensuousness, receptivity, and the ordinary
nor too much isolation from them.[28] Instead of simply reaching a doctrinal
conclusion, and instead of maintaining itself either in the sphere of pure reflective activity or in the sphere of the registering of the sensuously given, the successful poem must instead *work through* reflective-rational activity in relation
to experience of a sensuously given object. The proper thematic subject matter
of poetry in general is thus, one might say, not a given object, but rather an
object   as-it-is-experienced-by-a-subject-prompted-to-feeling-and-reflection
in relation to it. In close proximity to the Wordsworthian thought that it is "the
feeling [and associated reflection] therein developed [that] gives importance
to the [given] action and situation, and not the action and situation to the feeling,"[29] self-recognition is possible only by attending to and working through
relations between subject activity and determinate objects. As Waibel summarizes the point, for Hölderlin

> Self-knowledge can only grasp the determinations of human existence when
> it reaches out beyond a merely formal self-relation. This self-knowledge
> must withdraw itself from the aporias of either taking itself to be completely
> graspable through its own activity—which would produce only a completely
> reflective but thereby dead unity—or preserving an original liveliness [of
> experience], but thereby being unable to grasp completely either the determi-
> nation of humanity or the determination of poetic composition [*Dichtung*].
> Self-knowledge arises in a living manner, according to Hölderlin, when the
> subject freely chooses an object through which it recognizes itself.[30]

Self-knowledge is achieved, therefore, through an essentially temporal course of development of modulated thoughts and feelings in relation to a given object of experience. A narration of the course of its achievement—the only way to render its content—will consist essentially of four successive stages or registers of experience that are reflected in the poem:

(1) An initiating, felt, unarticulated total impression of an object, scene, or incident
(2) The weakening of this initial receptive impression through reflection and the division of the objects presented in the total impression into opposed yet interrelated parts
(3) The maintaining of the identity of the subject as a locus of active attentiveness in relation to the development of the poetic material in moving from 1 to 2
(4) The achievement in writing of complete internal relatedness of 1, 2, and 3 in a constructed sequence of modulations from beginning (initial total receptiveness--1) to middle (conditioned but active subject activity--2 and 3) to end (modulated expressiveness of the good-enough stability of the subject thus achieved across varying moments of thought and receptivity—4).[31]

The successful poem that begins in 1, moves through 2 and 3, and completes itself constructively in 4 is thus itself an achievement of a good-enough self-unity despite the omnipresent fact of reversals of subject activity by sensuous givenness and of sensuous givenness by subject activity. Hence the underlying thought that is embodied in successful Hölderlinian lyric poetry is that "Es war doch so schön"[32] --it was all so beautiful anyway. In its registering, expressing, and enacting of the play of opposed drives, the successful lyric poem is an acknowledgment of the fundamental circumstances of human life as a life of conditioned subject activity open to reversals. It is, hence, not the abandonment of philosophy and reflective activity in favor of poetry, but instead their situation as conditioned within the context of ongoing human life.

7.3.

Thematically and formally, Hölderlin's poetic practice that situates philosophical reflection within the course of life develops out of a number of earlier experimentations in theme and form. His earliest poems, such as his early Tübingen hymns, alternate between sentimental expressiveness of a subjective mood in the style of Klopstock (as in "The Oaks" and "To the Aether") and a more objectively celebratory mode derived from Schiller (as in "Hymn to the Goddess of

Harmony" and "Hymn to Immortality"). Significantly, however, already these early hymns display a certain awkwardness in stance, as though the standpoint for what is either to be worshipped or objectively celebrated were not entirely secure.[33] During his Frankfurt period from January 1796 to September 1798, Hölderlin produced a number of Diotima poems, inspired by Suzette Gontard, as well as nature poems and shorter, epigrammatic odes.[34] A sharper sense of the difficulties of maintaining an enthusiastic or a celebratory stance and voice, a sense that is evident also in the contemporary correspondence and theoretical writings, then seems to develop during the composition of *Hyperion* in the period from 1794 to 1797, perhaps influenced by the difficulties of his clandestine relations with Suzette/Diotima. As Hölderlin famously writes in the preface to the penultimate version of the novel,

> We all run through an eccentric path [*eine exzentrische Bahn*], and there is no other way possible from childhood to completion [*Vollendung*].
>
> Blissful unity, Being in the unique sense of the word, is lost for us and we had to lose it if we are to strive after it and achieve it.
>
> …We have fallen out with nature, and what was once (as we believe) One is now in conflict with itself, and mastery and servitude alternate on both sides. It often seems to us as if the world were everything and we nothing, but often too as if we were everything and the world nothing.
>
> …But neither our knowledge nor our action can attain in any period of our existence to that point at which all conflict ceases, where All is one; the determinate line can be united with the indeterminate only through an infinite approximation [*in unendlicher Annäherung*].[35]

Here the subject position is markedly and unresolvedly unstable. Conflict is endemic between the human subject standing out from blissful immersion in the whole and the whole within which that subject's activity should be but cannot be harmoniously resolved. As a result, nothing can be simply and unreservedly praised or celebrated; no doctrine is available to stabilize and justify the stance of the subject who would praise, but who remains caught within alternations between excess, merely subjective enthusiasm ("as if we were everything and the world nothing") and quiescent, merely passive absorption ("as if the world were everything and we nothing").

The result of this sense of the subject position as always already bound up in conflict is a poetry of loss and finitude that tracks and expresses this plight of the subject without resolving it. It narrates arcs of motion through moments of absorption in the given that are always liable to be ruptured by reflection and moments of reflection, power, and insight that are always liable to be ruptured by a returning, attractive but recalcitrant given. Rather than announcing a doctrine achieved, whether conciliatory or despairing, it moves in fits and starts, halted by this moment of perception, then regaining an energy of compositional onwardness in registering it, then faltering again as the energy cannot be sustained in any single continuing direction. That is, the major poetry enacts an effort together with its foundering. It tracks and locates the place of the human subject as a being capable of self-initiated attention, reflection, and thought within a whole that it should know, but cannot, and within which it should be at peace, but cannot be. It is neither within philosophy nor outside it, but is rather marked internally by both philosophy and its foundering, just as we live neither continuously within reflectiveness nor altogether outside it, neither altogether at home nor altogether as nomads.

7.4.

Among Hölderlin's major poems, the substantial but still incomplete "Rousseau" (1800) is especially clear thematically in illustrating Hölderlin's mature sense of the problem for the human subject of living simultaneously within the necessity of reflection and the impossibility of completing it. It is in part a reworking into an alcaic ode of the slightly earlier asclepic ode "To the Germans." (Its opening line is line 1 of strophe 11 of "To the Germans.") Its general project is simultaneously to praise Rousseau's exemplary achieved subjectivity while also describing its limitations, thus avoiding any triumphalist doctrinalism. Rousseau, as Hölderlin sees him, bears up, one might say, under the burden of a subjectivity given over both to visionary reflection on new possibilities of more meaningful human life and to their standing incompleteness. Hölderlin had read Rousseau's *The Social Contract* in 1791. As one of the so-called uncouth Jacobins, Hölderlin planted a Liberty Tree in a meadow near the Tübingen seminary on Bastille Day, 1793, an act that provoked Duke Karl Eugen to place the group under surveillance. While in Jena in September 1795, Hölderlin planned to draft a new educational program modeled on Rousseau's *Emile* and *Julie, ou la nouvelle Héloïse*.[36] Noting that Rousseau's name is the first name of a modern writer that appears on a list of writers on whom Hölderlin planned to write for his projected journal *Iduna*, Stanley Corngold remarks that Rousseau "represents Hölderlin's first leap of thought to modern writing; he constitutes Hölderlin's frame for his grasp of literary modernity."[37] Commenting on the appearances of Rousseau in "The Rhine" (1801), Paul de Man notes that Rousseau is, for Hölderlin, paradigmatically the one who exercises the distinctive powers of a human subject in using language: "Rousseau, as in the ode that bears his name, appears above all as the man of language: he listens (l. 143) he speaks (l. 144), he gives language (l. 146), and song (l. 165)."[38] Richard Unger describes Rousseau as functioning as a precursor figure and uncanny double for Hölderlin himself. "Rousseau's "strangeness" for Hölderlin is…the uncanniness a poet must experience in another man who ultimately projects his own destiny. Paradoxically, Hölderlin views Rousseau, a writer of prose, as the man who most clearly anticipates the poetic fulfillment he himself desires."[39]

Both the destiny of the modern human subject as the bearer of language and reflectiveness and the sort of qualified poetic fulfillment that is possible for such a subject are then projected onto Rousseau in the poem "Rousseau," and the itinerary of the bearing of that destiny and of the achievement of that qualified fulfillment is tracked narratively. The poem consists of ten strophes, with the first four in strict alcaic metric patterns (lines of 11, 11, 9, and 10 beats with a regular pattern of stresses) and the last six in uncompleted approximations to the alcaic. The first line of the seventh strophe includes an unfilled in past participle prefix ("ge"), marking it as uncompleted. The last line of the tenth and final strophe is a nonstandard, more abrupt seven-beat line that lends an air of conclusion to the fragment, despite its ending as a fragment with a comma rather than a full stop. First in German and then in Nick Hoff's English translation, it reads as follows:

ROUSSEAU

Wie eng begränzt ist unsere Tageszeit.
    Du warst und sahst und stauntest, schon Abend ists.
       Nun schlafe, wo unendlich ferne
          Ziehen vorüber die Völkerjahre.

Und mancher sieht über die eigene Zeit
    Ihm zeigt ein Gott ins Freie, doch sehnend stehst
       Am Ufer du, ein Aergerniß den
          Deinen, ein Schatten, und liebst sie nimmer.

Und jene, die du nennst, die Verheißenen,
    Wo sind die Neuen, daß du an Freundeshand
       Erwarmst, wo nahn sie, daß du einmal
          Einsame Rede, vernehmlich seiest?

Klanglos ist, armer Mann, in der Halle dir,
    Und gleich den Unbegrabenen, irrest du
       Unstät und suchest Ruh und niemand
          Weiß den beschiedenen Weg zu weisen.

Sei denn zufrieden! der Baum entwächst
    Dem heimathlichen Boden, aber es sinken ihm
       Die liebenden, die jugendlichen
          Arme, und trauernd neigt er sein Haupt.

Des Lebens Überfluß, das Unendliche,
    Das um ihn und dämmert, er faßt es nie.
        Doch lebts in ihm und gegenwärtig,
            Wärmend und wirkend, die Frucht entquillt ihm.

Du hast gelebt! ge auch dir, auch dir
    Erfreut die ferne Sonne dein Haupt,
        Und Stralen aus der schönen Zeit, es
            Habe die Boten dein Herz gefunden.

Vernommen hast du sie verstanden die Sprache der Fremdlinge,
    Gedeutet ihre Seele! Dem Sehnenden war
        Genug der Wink, und Winke sind
            Von Alters her die Sprache der Götter.

Und wunderbar, als hätte von Anbeginn
    Des Menschen Geist, das Werden und Wirken all,
        Des Lebens alte Weise schon erfahren

Kennt er im ersten Zeichen Vollendetes schon,
    Und fliegt, der kühne Geist, wie Adler den
        Gewittern, weissagend seinen
            Kommenden Göttern, voraus.

How limited the time of our day.
    You were and saw and marveled, it's evening already.
        So sleep now, where infinitely far
            The years of the nations drift overhead.

And some see past their own time,
    A god has shown them the open, but longing
        You stand on the shore, a scandal to your kin,
            A shade, and you no longer love them,

And those you name, the new and inspired ones,
    Where are they to warm you with their
        Friendly hands, and where do they approach so that you,
            Lonely speech, might one day be heard?

The halls, poor man, give no echo,
    And like the unburied dead you wander
        Unsettled and look for rest, and no one can
            Show you the determined path.

So content yourself with this! the tree outgrows
    Its native soil, but its loving
        Youthful boughs droop down,
            And it bows its crown in mourning.

The overflow of life, the infinite,
    That around him, dawning, he never grasps it.
        Yet it lives in him, and, all the while,
            Warming and effective, the fruit springs forth from him.

You have lived! The distant sun ed you too
    And gladdens too your head,
        And rays from a better time,
            The messengers have found your heart.

You perceived, you understood the language of strangers,
    Interpreted their soul! The hint sufficed
        The longing one, and hints have long
            Been the language of the gods.

And wondrous, as if from the outset the human spirit
Had experienced all that would be born and made manifest,
    The ancient way of life

In the first signs he sees their completion
    And, emboldened with this insight, flying like an eagle
        Ahead of the storm, he prophesies
            The coming of his gods.[40]

The plot of the fragment divides into roughly three parts. Strophes 1–4 describe Rousseau's alienation from and outsiderliness to his contemporaries and his failure to win an audience for his writing. Strophes 2–8.2 describe a kind of consolation available to Rousseau in having lived and produced something anyway. Strophes 8.2–10 offer generalizations about the stance of anyone who might be moved to flights of vision and composition.

Part I begins with a generalization that emphasizes the general fact of human finitude, without specific reference to Rousseau. Rousseau then appears as the second-person, past-tense addressee in line 2, where he is described as having been, having seen, and having been astounded by things. But that time of vision is past. The years pass by, as though their passing were the natural course of things, without occasioning any particular pain. In the second strophe, however, Rousseau is particularly marked as someone who stands out against his time, on the shores of something different, an annoyance or scandal to his kin and a shadow who is unable to love them. The third and fourth strophes then reinforce and deepen this outsiderliness, as those to whom he has called do not appear, so that Rousseau himself, metonymized as "lonely speech" (*Einsame Rede*), stands alone, without being heard, without echo or reception, hence unreceived, like the unburied, and given over to inconstancy, restlessness, and errancy, without any allotted path to follow. Far from treating Rousseau as a successful and confident prophet, the master thought in these first four strophes is of Rousseau in his reflective visionariness and hopes for more meaningful life as inherently outside the common and barred from any terms of reception.

The main pivot of the poem then comes in the first line of strophe 5, as the speaker offers Rousseau a kind of consolation or at least a command to be satisfied anyway, inasmuch as the tree that outgrows its ground nonetheless remains connected to it, casting its branches downward. So too might Rousseau, mourning, remain in contact with the people who fail to receive him. And so too, though he is unable successfully to grasp or understand it in order to master it, might there remain a life or power in him that produces something, as the tree produces its fruit unknowingly. One who accepts this consolation will then have lived and written anyway and so stood within a movement of life that nonetheless cannot be understood and mastered. Thus in writing Rousseau will have written for those who are yet to come, even if this writing remains less the purveying of a doctrine than a felt interpretation of the soul or life energy that they are to actualize expressively in a new life of autonomy blended with love. Rousseau himself then remains in the position of the one who is longing ("dem Sehnenden"), not the one who confidently knows and guides.

What Rousseau has then achieved—a felt, expressive, but indeterminate response in words to a difficult, fragmented condition coupled with a visionary but indeterminate hope for a better one—is then generalized as characteristic of anyone who is longing for life otherwise. Such a one may be responsive to hints ("Winke"), as if, subjunctively ("hätte") the ground plot and purpose of human life were determinately available to reflection and poetic vision, even though they are not or not fully. What remains as possible is then to fly over the land and life of the people, discerning signs and anticipating their fulfillment, but still only prophesying what remains yet to come.

And this very movement that is ascribed to Rousseau—a movement from problematic, visionary outsider, to locus of the expression of life and power that are not discursively grasped, to a renewed, qualified ability to live and move anyway—this movement is itself completed in the poem, as Hölderlin / the speaker moves from awed captivation with Rousseau's visionary strangeness and untimeliness to a larger sense that strangeness and uncanniness as such may be both aspects of and expressible within a wider movement of life itself. Reflection and speech are, therefore, possible for a finite, human subject within life, even when the terms of that life are not open to full, discursive, philosophical understanding. Sustaining and developing this thought through the course of the poem composed in relation to Rousseau as an object of both absorption and reflection amounts, then, to a kind of temporalized self-knowledge, or a kind of Romantic philosophy in the absence of systematic philosophy, that takes both human powers of reflection and human finitude seriously.

NOTES

1. For an extended argument in support of this characterization of romanticism, see Richard Eldridge, *The Persistence of Romanticism* (Cambridge: Cambridge University Press, 2001), esp. 1–28, 102–23, and 229–45.
2. Friedrich Hölderlin, "Judgment and Being," in Hölderlin, *Essays and Letters on Theory*, trans. and ed. Thomas Pfau (Albany: State University of New York Press, 1988), 37–38; emphasis added.
3. Ibid., 37, where "arche-separation" translates "Urtheilung"; HSW 4/1, 216.
4. Hölderlin, "Letter no. 121, To his Brother," June 2, 1796, in HSW 4/1, 133.
5. Terry Pinkard, "Subjects, Objects, and Normativity: What Is It Like to *Be* an Agent?" *Internationales Jahrbuch des Deutschen Idealismus / International Yearbook of German Idealism* 1 (2003): 201–219; here: 202, 206.
6. This is a master theme of Dieter Henrich's epochal work on Hölderlin, as in Henrich's observation that for Hölderlin "Conscious life is at once *shaped and unbalanced* by the basic conflicting tendencies orienting it. And the formative process of life aims at finding a balance and harmony amidst this strife, in which no one tendency is entirely suppressed or denied in its own right." Dieter Henrich, "Hölderlin in Jena," in *The Course of Remembrance and Other Essays on Hölderlin*, trans. Taylor Carman, ed. Eckart Förster (Stanford: Stanford University Press, 1997), 112; emphasis added. For a reading of Hölderlin in relation to the persisting "truth of skepticism" (as characterized by Stanley Cavell) and focusing on Hölderlin's deliberately ambiguous, formal poetic response to this situation, see Eldridge, "Cavell and Hölderlin on Human Immigrancy," in *The Persistence of Romanticism*, 229–45. For a masterful reading of how this sense of tension inhabits Hölderlin's theoretical texts, especially his essay "On the Operations of the Poetic Spirit," followed by a reading of Hölderlin's "The Ages of Life" ("Lebensalter"), see Hannah Vandegrift Eldridge, "The Influence of Anxiety: Poetology as Symptom," *German Quarterly* 86, no. 4 (Fall 2013): 443–62.
7. Hölderlin, "Letter no. 121, To his Brother," in *Essays and Letters on Theory*, 133.
8. Hölderlin, "Letter no. 219, To his Brother," HSW 4/1, 419; my translation.
9. Hölderlin, "Letter no. 144, To Schiller," HSW 4/1, 249; my translation.
10. Hölderlin, "Letter no. 128, To Hegel," HSW 4/1, 222; my translation.
11. Hölderlin, "Urtheil und Sein," in HSW 4/1, 216; my translation.
12. Violetta Waibel, *Hölderlin und Fichte, 1794–1800* (Paderborn: Schöningh, 2000), 102; my translation.
13. Ibid., 104.
14. Hölderlin, *Hyperion: Die metrische Fassung*, HSW 3, 192; my translation.
15. Thomas Pfau, "Critical Introduction," in Hölderlin, *Essays and Letters on Theory*, 9.
16. Ibid., 16.
17. Ibid., 28.
18. Ibid., 18.
19. Hölderlin, "On Religion," in *Essays and Letters on Theory*, 90.
20. See Hannah Vandegrift Eldridge's remarks about a similar ambivalence and structure of unresolved qualification in Hölderlin's Essay "On the Operations of the Poetic Spirit," in "The Influence of Anxiety."
21. Friedrich Schiller, "Letter no. 28, To Hölderlin," in HSW 7/1, 46; my translation.

22. Hölderlin, "Letter no. 172, To his Brother," in HSW 4/1, 306; my translation.

23. Ibid. 305; my translation.

24. Waibel, *Hölderlin und Fichte*, 132; my translation.

25. Hölderlin, *Hyperion: Die metrische Fassung*, in HSW 3, 194; my translation.

26. Waibel, *Hölderlin und Fichte*, 196; my translation.

27. Hölderlin, "Reflection," in *Essays and Letters on Theory*, 46.

28. Ibid., 48.

29. Wordsworth, *"Preface* to Lyrical Ballads," in Wordsworth, *Selected Poems and Prefaces*, ed. Jack Stillinger (Boston: Houghton Mifflin, 1965), 448.

30. Waibel, *Hölderlin und Fichte*, 294; my translation.

31. Compare ibid., 349.

32. This line, appearing in both the Song of the Tower Warden in Goethe's *Faust* and as the last line of Wedekind's *Pandora's Box*, is taken by Herbert Marcuse as the formula, as it were, of successful art, art that achieves "the reconciliation which...catharsis offers [that] also preserves the irreconcileable." Marcuse, *The Aesthetic Dimension*, trans. Herbert Marcuse and Erica Sherover (Boston: Beacon Press, 1977), 59.

33. See Richard Unger's summary of the earliest work in *Hölderlin's Major Poetry: The Dialectics of Unity* (Bloomington: Indiana University Press, 1975), 11–20.

34. Ibid., 29.

35. Hölderlin, *Hyperion: Die vorletzte Fassung*, in HSW 3, 326; trans. Richard Unger in ibid., 22–23, 25, supplemented by my translation.

36. The biographical information in this paragraph about Hölderlin's relations to Rousseau comes from David Constantine, *Hölderlin* (Oxford: Oxford University Press, 1988), 20, 397; Eric Santner, "Chronology," in Hölderlin, *Hyperion and Selected Poems* (New York: Continuum, 2002), xi, and Scott J. Thompson, "Friedrich Hölderlin: A Chronology of His Life," http://www.wbenjamin.org/hoelderlin_chron.html.

37. Stanley Corngold, "Implications of an Influence: On Hölderlin's Reception of Rousseau," in *Romantic Poetry*, vol. 7, ed. Angela Esterhammer (Amsterdam: John Benjamins, 2002), 474.

38. Paul de Man, "The Image of Rousseau in the Poetry of Hölderlin," in de Man, *The Rhetoric of Romanticism* (New York: Columbia University Press, 1984), 40.

39. Unger, *Holderlin's Major Poetry*, 138.

40. HSW 2/1, 12–13; Hölderlin, *Odes and Elegies*, trans. Nick Hoff (Middletown, CT: Wesleyan University Press, 2008), 89, 91.

8

On the Defense of Literary Value

From Early German Romanticism to Analytic Philosophy of Literature

BRADY BOWMAN

8.1. THE CRISIS OF LITERARY VALUE AND ITS ORIGINS

The value of what we have come to call *literature* has, in one way or another, always been in question. Plato's criticism of poetry as a morally dubious and metaphysically derivative representation of reality introduced a suspicion that continues to haunt our relationship to literature today: the suspicion that a mode of representation that is paradigmatically fictional cannot in principle convey knowledge, reveal truth, and hence cannot be taken with the full measure of seriousness.[1] Although Plato's suspicion has hardly impeded the production and appreciation of literature during the intervening millennia, defenders of literary value would be overly sanguine to conclude that it is powerless to influence the cultural and institutional fate of literature. Since the inception of literary studies as an academic discipline in the nineteenth century, the maintenance of the literary heritage in scholarly editions, the cultivation of literary sensibility in the next generation of readers and writers, even the transmission of practical know-how and the support of literary artists have increasingly been entrusted to our university systems—despite some authors' scorn for academia and the "academic poetry" created there. As we know, these institutions are sensitive to a variety of political, social, and economic pressures. In this context, the humanities generally and literary studies in particular are vulnerable.

The notion of *modern*, as opposed to classical or biblical, philology is a child of romanticism, as is the Humboldtian conception of the modern research university. Roughly contemporaneous with the creation of modern literary scholarship as an academic discipline, however, occurs the integration of the exact sciences into the regular university curriculum, and it is these fields that today have achieved ascendency as the *paradigmatically scientific* disciplines. (Notably, the term "scientist" was coined, at the instigation of Samuel Taylor Coleridge, by William Whewell, the man who proposed and oversaw the introduction of the Natural Sciences Tripos at Cambridge; it replaced the older term "natural philosopher," which until then had enjoyed exclusive currency.)[2] It is here that Plato's charge against poetry reveals its abiding power, dramatic shifts in modern metaphysics notwithstanding: For despite the pretensions of mid-twentieth-century structuralism, *the study of literature is clearly not a science*. Its subject is not a natural kind marked out by intrinsic properties;[3] it possesses no uncontested methods of research; it uncovers no laws; it contributes in no way to humanity's technological empowerment; and it produces no demonstrably objective results.[4] The legacy of Plato's charge that poetry is constitutionally incapable of transmitting knowledge makes contemporary literary studies especially vulnerable in the setting of the modern, technologically driven university.

This child of German romanticism thus exists today both as a key institution in the production and reception of literature and in a state of more or less permanent crisis.[5] That this should be so is partly the consequence of the ambivalent fortunes of romanticism itself. Jena romanticism was a remarkably unified movement in literature, philosophy, and—importantly—in the post-Newtonian natural sciences of chemistry and electromagnetism that held out prospects of bridging the gap between physics and organic life and even the life of the mind.[6] It sought to go beyond the mechanistic paradigm of scientific explanation that rendered both the natural existence of freedom and the phenomenon of life—the two most intimate components of human self-understanding—virtually inexplicable, drawing a veil between our lived experience and its ultimate grounding in the real. Romantic science and philosophy of nature strove to establish a new paradigm of understanding that could unify the basic forces of matter with the fact of organic life and the existence of an autonomous human mind, whose highest expressions are to be found in religion, philosophy, and art. Thus Schelling's *Darstellung meines Systems* (1801) concludes with the promise to continue, in a future installment, with the "construction of the ideal series" of the intellectual faculties and their categories from organic nature, all the way to the "construction of the absolute center of gravity in which, as the two highest expressions of indifference, *truth* and *beauty*, coincide" (HKA 1/10, 211).[7]

Art in general and poetry in particular were thus accorded supreme status in the romantic hierarchy of human cognition.[8] Recall Schelling's famous remarks at the close of his *System of Transcendental Idealism* (1800):

> For the philosopher... art is supreme, for it opens to him the holiest of holies, where that which is separated in nature and history, and which can never be united either in life and action or in thought, burns as though in a single flame in eternal and primordial unity.... Just as in the childhood of the sciences philosophy was born of poetry and nurtured by it, so too, when these are brought to perfection, they will all flow back like diverse rivers into the single ocean of poetry from which they first arose. (HKA 1/3, 628–29)[9]

I will soon return to this quintessentially romantic motif of poetry's status as both origin and consummation of science. And as I will point out, the romantic legacy has never ceased to exercise its influence on philosophy throughout the twentieth century and into the present. Yet despite its far-reaching cultural ramifications and its role in shaping the modern university, we must also concede that the romantic revolution achieved at best only partial success. Neither the structures of organic life nor those of self-consciousness have come to supplant inorganic forces as the paradigmatic objects of science: contemporary debates on the very coherence of nonreductive physicalism in the philosophy of mind show the extent to which the romantic revolution *failed* to transform the common sense of the scientific community.[10] In its contemporary form, the question of the value of literature, literary experience, and literary criticism is at least in part a symptom of this broader failure of the romantic revolution.

Nevertheless, the *Frühromantik* continues to offer resources for addressing this ongoing crisis in literary studies. Romanticism offers a powerful and unified vision of literature as an unceasing and open-ended project of cultural formation, of *Kulturschaffen* in the literal sense of *creating the site of human meaning, the place of authentic human reconciliation with the world.*[11] This project requires that we rethink literature as situated at a level both prior to the (recurring) genesis of individual sciences and higher than what those sciences, left purely to themselves, could ever tell us about the nature of the world they serve to reveal. As an integral dimension of this project, however, philosophical romanticism requires that we narrow the scope of what truth and knowledge, as such, may legitimately claim to offer, while broadening our understanding of cognitive value to include modes of understanding irreducible to the propositional variety in which the sciences, as we now understand them, exclusively trade. These resources, properly understood, continue to offer efficacious and philosophically responsible means for addressing the value crisis in literary studies.[12]

8.2. THE LEVELING OF THE DISTINCTION BETWEEN
LITERATURE AND TRUTH-SEEKING DISCOURSE, OR HOW
NOT TO SAVE LITERATURE

Talk of "narrowing the scope of what truth and knowledge may claim to offer" requires further specification, particularly in the context of Jena romanticism and its relation to philosophy and the sciences. For there is more than one way of giving a critical romanticist account of the nature and scope of discursive, propositional knowledge and of literature's role in relation to it. Let me begin discussion with what I consider to be a less felicitous appropriation of early romanticism. It has been most visible in the tradition of a certain *skepticism* regarding philosophical foundations, rational closure, and reason's ability to liberate humanity from the alienated and existentially precarious situation into which our technologically oriented culture has plunged us. Kierkegaard, Schopenhauer, and Nietzsche, with their profound distrust of reason and the value of truth, inaugurate this strain of romanticism, developing it with unrivaled virtuosity. Heidegger's critique of metaphysics and the vision of egocentric sovereignty inherent in the metaphysics of subjectivity can be seen to have been anticipated by the insights of Fichte and Hölderlin.[13] Poststructuralist critiques of the subject, systematic closure, and the self-transparency of reason clearly have important sources in romanticism, partly by way of Heidegger's seminal thought. Adorno's critique of the "logic of identity" and his alternative conception of a "logic of disintegration" also stand in this tradition.[14] The early Wittgenstein, too, whose admiration for Schopenhauer and Goethe is well known, is rehearsing a romantic gesture when in the *Tractatus* he concludes "that even if *all possible* scientific questions be answered, the problems of life have still not been touched at all."[15]

The methodological assumptions and critical strategies underlying this tradition of romantic skepticism can to some extent be traced back to Friedrich Schlegel. His cultivation of the fragment, his emphasis on the open-ended unfolding of thought over against the search for first principles and systematic completeness, his celebration of the irony inscribed in (necessarily antinomial) attempts to give propositional expression to the absolute—these are the most conspicuous features of a sublime defeatism that has worked irresistible charms time and again over the course of the last century. Simon Critchley exemplifies this view when he writes, "Jena Romanticism is rooted in the acute self-consciousness of its unworking or failure, the exploration of the lack of final synthesis in a continual process of self-creation and destruction and the quasi dialectics of wit and irony."[16]

From Schlegel through Kierkegaard and Nietzsche to Heidegger, Adorno, and Derrida, there has existed a strain of thinkers who have both practiced and preached *the unity of philosophy and literature* first declared by the early romantics.[17] As Nietzsche famously argues in *Truth and Lie in a Non-moral Sense*, truth itself is a poetic fiction—"a mobile army of metaphors, metonyms, and anthropomorphisms."[18] If this is so, then literature is an achievement situated along the same continuum as mathematics, physics, and philosophy; indeed, in its open and exuberant *fabrication* of worlds, literature is situated closer to the origin of "truth" than either science or philosophy, since these falsely lay claim to a special epistemic dignity merely by virtue of their resting on metaphors so entrenched as to appear to be unalterable features of reality.[19] Thus does the Platonic charge dissolve into air: *There are no truths but those the poet wittingly or unwittingly fabricates and philosophy itself is a branch of imaginative fiction.* Plato's charge, viewed thus, is at once accurate and empty.

Nietzsche's claim, as put into practice by poststructuralist theoreticians, provoked sharp reactions from those who sought to defend the specific nature and status of truth-seeking discourse like philosophy and the sciences, polarizing debate throughout the 1980s and 1990s. In my view, the most tenable position is that taken by those who, like Manfred Frank and Gottfried Gabriel, have argued that intensely poetic and rigorously discursive uses of language play mutually irreducible and complementary roles in grounding and guiding our cognitive access to the world.[20] Moreover, no favor has been done to literature and literary studies by urging the identity of poetry with philosophy and the sciences. For as others have pointed out, that position seeks to rebut Plato's charge not by promoting literature to the status of the truth-seeking disciplines, but by demoting the latter to the status of "mere" fictions.[21] This is no more than a *tu quoque* argument, and to the extent that it succeeds at all, it hardly shows why human resources should be devoted either to *literary* fictions or to *philosophical* "fictions" if neither has real cognitive value.

The aestheticist-constructivest legacy of Jena romanticism therefore appears counterproductive when it comes to giving positive arguments for the value of literature. However, there are other streams within early romanticism more broadly construed and these hold resources for making a stronger case for the cognitive value of literature.

8.3. COMPLEMENTARITY, PRIORITY, FULFILLMENT: A COMPETING ROMANTIC VIEW OF THE RELATION BETWEEN POETRY AND SCIENCE

Manfred Frank and Gottfried Gabriel have argued that literature and truth-seeking practices like philosophy and the sciences are irreducibly complementary to each other (the *complementarity thesis*).[22] Both Frank and John

Gibson have furthermore argued that nondiscursive forms are in important ways more basic and hence prior to discursive thought (the *priority thesis*).[23] And Gibson further suggests that literary cognition is in fact *the proper fulfillment* of discursive knowledge (the *fulfillment thesis*). In this section I will argue, first, that the best defense of the complementarity thesis must be mounted by way of the much stronger priority and fulfillment theses. My second point is that the strong claims of priority and fulfillment put forward in recent analytic philosophy of literature have an important source in Jena romanticism and that renewed consideration of romantic thought can help in formulating a contemporary philosophy of cultural value along the lines of the fulfillment thesis.

A striking feature of Jena romanticism is its aesthetic and literary cognitivism. One need only recall Schiller's *Letters on the Aesthetic Education of Man*, Hölderlin's late hymns, or the idea of a "new mythology of reason" in the so-called *ältestes Systemprogramm des deutschen Idealismus*.[24] What I want to underscore, however, is a conception of art and poetry as *complementary* to the discursively oriented endeavors of philosophy and science. Schelling's notion of art as the "organon" of philosophy provides the most striking instance of this: He does not intend an instrumental relation in which art would subserve the discursive formulation of truths it can only suggest; on the contrary, art bears immediate and certain witness to a unity that cannot in principle be formulated discursively, yet which forms the content and orienting goal of philosophic and scientific inquiry.[25]

Such a notion of complementarity between the aesthetic and the discursive can help orient debates about the relation of literature and philosophy. As Manfred Frank writes, an important function of literary art is to open what he calls a "space of intelligibility... that must be there already in order that propositions can take their place within it."[26] Hence, as he argues against Habermas, it would be misguided to argue against the poststructuralist leveling of the distinction between literature and philosophy by insisting on an unbridgeable gulf between "world-disclosure" on the one hand and "truth-committed argumentation" on the other.[27]

This same point has recently been pressed by philosophers in the analytic tradition. In his 2007 book *Fiction and the Weave of Life*, John Gibson argues that the activity of literature "enjoys a certain priority to the search for truth and knowledge, at least, and perhaps only, in this respect: before we can query the truth of a vision of our way in the world, we must first have the vision itself. That is, what makes possible the search for truth is a prior cultural accomplishment: the construction of varying ways of taking our world to be."[28]

Gibson makes no explicit reference to romanticism. However, two philosophers upon whose work he bases his argument provide the missing link to romantic thought: Ludwig Wittgenstein and Stanley Cavell.[29] I mentioned

Wittgenstein's well-known admiration for Schopenhauer and Goethe above; Manfred Frank has pointed out affinities between Wittgenstein's early philosophy and the thought of Novalis, while Jonas Maatsch has traced Novalis's encyclopedism and Wittgenstein's conception of an *übersichtliche Darstellung* to Goethe as the common methodological source.[30] In the case of Stanley Cavell, there is an openly avowed line of influence linking his thought back through Emerson and Coleridge to Kant and the early romantics.[31] Thus it is hardly a coincidence that specifically romantic doctrines resurface in Gibson's thought.

Cavell broadens the conception of cognition to include, in addition to knowledge in the strict sense of justified true belief, what he calls *acknowledgment*.[32] This concept of acknowledgment as the *fulfillment* of knowledge may be the most important contemporary development of the romantic legacy. Without this differentiation within the broader sphere of cognition, the complementarity thesis can neither be rigorously formulated nor combined with the idea that aesthetic experience *positively completes* the work of the sciences—a thesis close to the heart of Jena romanticism.

Why is Cavell's concept of acknowledgment so crucial to a rigorous formulation of the complementarity thesis? If we grasp aesthetic experience as providing a certain kind of *knowledge*, then we immediately face unanswerable objections: For one, literature engages in none of the practices of argument, research, experimentation, weighing of counterexamples, and so on, that constitute the truth-seeking disciplines; nor is literature sensitive to contradictions among the visions presented in various works of literature: we are not constrained to *choose* between *Pride and Prejudice* and *Naked Lunch* as we are constrained to choose between, say, Galen and Harvey on the circulation of blood.[33] Rather, literary works assume that their readers *already know* about what is being presented between their covers, discounting the odd fact that could as easily be gleaned from standard works of reference: If you do not already know guilt, remorse, and repentance before you crack the first page of *Crime and Punishment*, you will hardly understand the book's central themes, much less make your first acquaintance with them there, for such acquaintance is a presupposition of identifying those very themes.[34] And this remains true even in those cases in which the psychological, ethical, and cultural content of the work is bound up with a way of life and thereby a set of concepts that the reader may not possess. As Cora Diamond has argued, the conceptual losses we may suffer as a culture can render us speechless in regard to our interests and experiences, and thus alienate us from them, preventing us from being able to acknowledge how it is with us; but such losses "have not actually changed us into human beings limited to the interests and experiences and moral possibilities we can express in our depleted vocabulary."[35] What, therefore, literature can make available for expression and thus for acknowledgment is not a new fact or experience, but a conceptual space that we already inhabit yet without having an explicit consciousness and mastery of the concepts proper to it.[36] But if this is right, then to assume that literature seeks to convey knowledge and that it is such *knowledge* that is complementary to that of more overtly truth-seeking disciplines, is to be confronted with the apparent cognitive triviality of literature.[37]

Following Gibson, we can see how Cavell's concept of acknowledgment allows us to understand literature as a form of cognitive access to the world that is both intimately related to and at once distinct from knowledge—a form of access that is, in Cavell's words, *more than mere knowledge*.[38] The concept broadens the cognitive space to include something beyond truth and knowledge, namely our understanding of the ways that truths themselves matter, how they cohere within the tightly woven yet open texture of human forms of life and locate them within a world that, in the exclusively truth-seeking perspective, we are constantly on the verge of losing. Literature is complementary to philosophy and the sciences precisely to the extent that literature and the imaginative achievement for which it stands are both prior to discursive knowledge and its fulfillment.

Once this difference is formulated in terms that do not confuse the complementary natures of their respective cognitive contributions, the cultural *Vollendungscharakter* of the aesthetico-literary emerges. Not only is literature prior to knowing; it also marks the cultural achievement of (re)integrating knowledge into the life of culture and thus *perfecting that knowledge in the only sense in which the essentially infinite task of modern science ever can be perfected*: in *beauty*.[39] Thus, just as there must be a sense in which the conceptual spaces in which we act and carry out our world-directed inquiries must precede, shape, and be already implicit in our actions and inquiries, so too is there a sense in which those same conceptual spaces can be explicitly displayed to us through works of literary imagination. To quote Gibson once again, "literature records not [only] the first but *the final word* in our culture's awareness of its world, the word that *effectively concludes the story* we have to offer of the nature of our world as we experience it and find ourselves within it."[40]

A statement like that is about as close as a twenty-first-century analytic philosopher is likely to get to Schiller's and Schelling's celebration of poetry as the alpha and omega of human knowledge—and it is very close indeed. The finality of the aesthetic is of course not a temporal finality. We can usefully contrast it with the project of scientific knowing that is incapable in principle of completion: the best a scientific theory can reasonably hope for is to pave the way toward deeper insights into nature that, eventually, will render the earlier theory obsolete. Whatever value such a theory may have, it is inseparable from reference to further work to come.[41] By contrast, art facilitates an experience of beauty and, as such, an experience of perfection. The work of art is therefore essentially complete; it gives all in all wherever it is present in the least.[42] The finality of art is therefore not an object of anticipation, nor does it imply closure in a fixed and obligatory canon of works. As Schopenhauer says: "Art is every-where at its goal."[43]

8.4. CONCLUSION: ROMANTIC UNITY—HOPELESS NOSTALGIA OR PRESENT TASK?

So what have I tried to show? For one, the early romantic legacy is ambivalent. Neither romantic irony (in its more extreme forms) nor the identification of philosophy with literature exhausts the possibilities of romantic thought, and neither offers resources for defending the value of literature. Even supposing that our truth-seeking practices may be permanently compromised by our lim-ited points of view, the contingent nature of discovery, and even by features of reality that necessarily elude human comprehension, so that the intelligibility we manage to produce is, finally, just that—our product, our *fiction*—this "fact" (if it can be called that) still would not warrant the leveling of the distinction between our truth-seeking practices and the practice of literature.[44] For pre-cisely this reason, however, we must recognize both that literature does not impart knowledge and that knowledge is not the only cognitive game in town. Yet in arguing for the *complementarity* of literature and philosophy, we are also constrained to argue that literature's imaginative achievement is both *prior to* and the *fulfillment of* discursive knowledge.

Second, I have insisted that this idea, too, is part of the romantic legacy, and that we find it explicitly stated by romantic thinkers in a manner that is thor-oughly compatible with scientific realism. This strain of romantic thought offers important resources for defending the value of literature and literary studies in the context of the post-Humboldtian university. Early romanticism brought modern literary scholarship to the academy and it still harbors powerful argu-ments for why it should remain there.

Third, I have tried to show how the two different strains of romantic philoso-phy of literature have shaped twentieth-century thought, and that the comple-mentarist strain in particular is re-emerging in some contemporary analytic philosophy of literature. The sphere of cognition is not defined solely by truth, nor is rational discourse confined to the propositionally "sayable"—this insight is accessible from either side of the analytic-continental split; to explore its ram-ifications is the privilege of neither.

Literature is the ongoing creation of a universal yet multiple imagination of our single world. There is, of course, a romantic spirit of alienation that holds

such unity to be illusory and its evocation to be nostalgia. Schiller's bitter laudation of the gods of Greece is of that spirit, as are some of Hölderlin's odes.[45]
However, the greatest of Hölderlin's mature poems (for example, late odes such
as *Dichtermut* and *Blödigkeit* or the elegy *Brot und Wein*) go beyond resignation
and nostalgia; they evince a faith in the power of the literary imagination to
reveal, transfigure, and create an authentic second nature in which the human
can after all be at home. It is the same faith evinced in the passage from Schelling
quoted above, where he says that, in art, "that which is separated in nature and
history... burns as though in a single flame in eternal and primordial unity." The
absence of such unity in our primary experience of nature—and the alienation,
skepticism, and nihilism that form our response to that absence—do not tell
against its reality. Rather, it is the imperative of culture to create a second nature
in which the human is at home in a more than human world. And that, as the
romantics teach us, is the work of poetry.

NOTES
1. It might be objected that in the case of ancient Greece, the status of literature especially as embodied in Homer was authoritative, and that the case of Greece may
   not be singular: So the value of literature would *not* always have been in question.
   Indeed, in its strongest form, the "priority thesis" I will argue for below states that
   art, science, and religion all originally spring from literature ("poetry") as their
   source. This again implies a state of affairs in which the value of literature would
   not have been in question. We ought, however, to distinguish between what *we
   have come to call literature* and the related practices and institutions prior to the
   acceleration of cultural differentiation that renders religion, art, science, and poetry
   into distinct realms of cultural endeavor. Socratic philosophy represents a crucial
   moment in the history of this process of differentiation in the West, and it is no
   coincidence that a fundamental critique of the authority and value of poetry is its
   concomitant. I acknowledge, however, that Plato's accomplishments as a writer
   indicate that his attitude toward literature must surely have been more complex
   than his explicit critique of poetry would seem to allow.
2. On Whewell's relationship to English romanticism and on his philosophy of science
   more generally, see Richard R. Yeo, *Defining Science: William Whewell, Natural
   Knowledge, and Public Debate in Early Victorian Britain* (New York: Cambridge
   University Press, 1993).
3. See Arthur C. Danto, *The Transfiguration of the Commonplace: A Philosophy of Art*
   (Cambridge, MA: Harvard University Press 1981), chap. 1; "Philosophy as/and/of
   Literature," in *The Philosophical Disenfranchisement of Art* (New York: Columbia
   University Press 1984), 135–62.
4. Insistence on the nonscientific character of literary studies does not entail commitment to the dichotomy of "two cultures"—one scientific, one humanistic—whose
   basic incompatibility is ensured by the psychological distinction of two opposed
   modes of cognition, *Erklären* versus *Verstehen*.

5. For the formation of German philology and literary scholarship as an academic discipline in Germany, see Jürgen Fohrmann and Wilhelm Voßkamp, eds., *Wissenschaft und Nation. Studien zur Entstehungsgeschichte der deutschen Literaturwissenschaft* (Munich: Fink 1991), as well as their book *Wissenschaftsgeschichte der Germanistik im 19. Jahrhundert* (Stuttgart: Metzler 1994). Michael J. Hofstetter investigates the influence of German romanticism on the British university in *The Romantic Idea of a University: England and Germany 1770-1850* (New York: St. Martin's Press 2001). For the (slightly later) American scene, see Gerald Graff, *Professing Literature: An Institutional History* (Chicago: University of Chicago Press 1989). Eloquent testimony to the crisis of value that has taken hold of modern literary studies is borne by a recent issue of the PMLA (117, no. 3 [2002]: 487–521), in which numerous representatives of the field show themselves flummoxed by the question, "*Why major in Literature? What we say to our students.*" For a critical response to that discussion see Gregory Jusdanis ("Two Cheers for Aesthetic Autonomy," in *Cultural Critique* 61 [2005]: 22–54), who situates the present crisis in an "anti-aesthetic" strand of twentieth-century literary theory and seeks remedies in renewed engagement with the German romantic theory of aesthetic autonomy.

6. For a recent discussion of romantic *Naturphilosophie* and its seminal role in the early scientific investigation of electrochemistry and electromagnetism and its influence on the work Ørsted and others, see Michael Friedman, "Kant—Naturphilosophie—Electromagnetism," in *Hans Christian Ørsted and the Romantic Legacy in Science: Ideas, Disciplines, Practices*, ed. Robert Brian, Robert Cohen, and Ole Knudsen (Dordrecht: Springer 2007), 135–58.

7. Schelling follows up on his promise in the dialogue *Bruno oder über das göttliche und natürliche Princip der Dinge* (HKA 1/11) and in his 1802/3 lectures on the philosophy of art (HKA 2/6) (thanks to Dalia Nassar for pointing this out). Cf. Hölderlin's letter no. 179 to his brother (June 4, 1799), in HSW 6, 329. On the character of romantic science and its institutional framework in Jena see Paul Ziche and Olaf Breidbach, eds., *Naturwissenschaften um 1800. Wissenschaftskultur in Jena-Weimar* (Weimar: Hermann Böhlaus Nachfolger 2001); see also Ziche "Naturforschung in Jena zur Zeit Hegels. Materialien zum Hintergrund der spekulativen Naturphilosophie," *Hegel-Studien* 32 (1997): 9–40, and Ziche, "Gehört das Ich zur Natur? Geistige und organische Natur in Schellings Naturphilosophie," *Philosophisches Jahrbuch* 108 (2001): 41–57.

8. In this paper I do not distinguish systematically between the terms "poetry" and "literature." The romantics themselves preferred to speak of "poetry" (*Dichtung, Poesie*) and would presumably have balked at identifying it with the broader category of *Literatur* (or *Litteratur*, as it was then commonly spelled) encompassing the totality of published writing. But "poetry" in contemporary English is more narrowly and thus misleadingly associated with verse than the romantics' term *Dichtung* or *Poesie*, and in the present context my use of "literature" to cover roughly the same range of phenomena seems unlikely to cause confusion or prompt unwanted associations with other uses of the term, e.g., as used when speaking of "the literature" on a given subject.

9. Unless otherwise indicated, here and in the following all translations from German editions are my own. Schelling's words obviously echo Schiller's philosophical ode,

Die Künstler (1789), which makes similar claims for the *prior role* of art and poetry in the *generation of the sciences* and for poetry's role as the *culminating point of unity* of completed science. See *Schillers Werke. Nationalausgabe* (Weimar: Hermann Böhlaus Nachfolger, 1943ff.), vol. 1, 201–14, especially the concluding strophe and its image of differentiation and reintegration: "Wie sich in sieben milden Strahlen / Der weiße Schimmer lieblich bricht, / Wie sieben Regenbogenstrahlen / Zerrinnen in das weiße Licht…so fließt in *einen* Bund der Wahrheit / In *einen* Strom des Lichts zurück! [As into seven gentle rays / the white luster gently breaks, / as seven rainbow beams dissolve / returning into lustrous white…, so too shall you flow back into a *single* bond of truth / a *single* stream of light]." These same lines are echoed by Hölderlin in *Hyperion*, see HSW 3, 81.

10. Perhaps the decisive word in these debates has been spoken by Jaegwon Kim, who contests the very coherence of nonreductive physicalism as an explanatory project: see his *Mind in a Physical World: An Essay on the Mind-Body Problem and Mental Causation* (Cambridge: MIT Press, 2000), esp. 89–121. See also his earlier paper "Multiple Realization and the Metaphysics of Reduction," *Philosophy and Phenomenological Research* 52 (1992): 1–26, reprinted in Kim, *Supervenience and Mind: Selected Philosophical Essays* (New York: Cambridge University Press, 1993). The biological paradigm has come to guide teleo-functional approaches in the philosophy of mind (see especially Ruth Millikan, *Language, Thought, and other Biological Categories* [Cambridge, MA: MIT Press, 1984] and *Language: A Biological Model* [Oxford: Oxford University Press, 2005]), but the basic philosophical case for organic life being a necessary condition of mindedness has not yet been convincingly made (pace John S. Searle, *The Rediscovery of the Mind* [Cambridge, MA: MIT Press, 1992]).

11. Cf. Charles Larmore, *The Romantic Legacy* (New York: Columbia University Press, 1996), 7–21, 84–97.

12. The central concern of this paper thus converges with recent discussions in epistemology about the value of knowledge, particularly with a position such as the one taken by Jonathan Kvanvig, who argues that epistemic value does not reside in truth per se (though truth remains a necessary condition of knowledge), but in understanding; see *The Value of Knowledge and the Pursuit of Understanding* (Cambridge: Cambridge University Press, 2003). I suggest that in its most comprehensive form, such understanding is the work of literature.

13. See for example Martin Heidegger, "Überwindung der Metaphysik," in *Vorträge und Aufsätze*, 10th ed. (Stuttgart: Klett-Cotta, 2004), 67–96. Manfred Frank argues that Heidegger's critique of subjectivity is based on a misperception of Fichte's understanding of what he calls "the I" (with reference to Dieter Henrich, *Fichtes ursprüngliche Einsicht* [Frankfurt am Main: Klostermann, 1967] and "Hölderlin über Urteil und Seyn: Eine Studie zur Entstehungsgeschichte des Idealismus," *Hölderlin-Jahrbuch* 14 [1965–66], 73–96). See *Was ist Neostrukturalismus?* (Frankfurt am Main: Suhrkamp, 1984), 248–56. An inverse point is made by Eckart Förster, who notes critically that Heidegger borrowed from Fichte "the insight that the proposition 'I am' expresses an utterly different kind of being than any existential proposition about a thing or state of affairs," but that Heidegger fails to acknowledge the source. See *The Twenty-Five Years of Philosophy* (Cambridge, MA: Harvard University Press, 2012), 163.

14. Cf. Theodor W. Adorno, *Negative Dialektik* (Frankfurt am Main: Suhrkamp 1975), 148ff.. Adorno's concept of negative dialectics can itself be construed as a radicalization of the romantic dialectics we find in F. Schlegel and the early Schleiermacher, as Andreas Arndt has pointed out (*Dialektik und Reflexion. Zur Rekonstruktion des Vernunftbegriffs* [Hamburg: Meiner, 1994], 269ff.) Strictly speaking, it is Sartre's conception of dialectics that Arndt identifies as a radicalization of elements from romantic dialectics, but it is clear that when he turns on the same page to a discussion of Adorno, describing his negative dialectics as a "*Freisetzung*" of the Sartrean conception, he is attributing the same lineage to Adorno's thought. Adorno's poetico-methodological homage to Hölderlin in the essay *Parataxis* (in *Noten zur Literatur* [Frankfurt am Main: Suhrkamp, 1981], 447–94) is also significant in the way it places "das Moment des Zerfallenden [the moment of disintegration]" in Hölderlin's language in relation to what Adorno sees as the "romantic" aspect of Hölderlin's poetry, its "objectivism" (478).

15. Ludwig Wittgenstein, *Tractatus Logico-Philosophicus* (London: Routledge, 2001), 6.52; cf. 6.522.

16. Simon Critchley, "Cavell's 'Romanticism' and Cavell's Romanticism," in Russell B. Goodman, ed., *Contending with Stanley Cavell* (Oxford: Oxford University Press, 2005), 37–54, here 42. Charles Larmore addresses the excesses both of a one-sidedly aestheticist interpretation of *Frühromantik* and of a defeatist, Schopenhauerian understanding of its restlessness as *Weltschmerz*, and construes romantic irony instead as delicately poised between these extremes (cf. Larmore, *Romantic Legacy*, 76–83).

17. Cf. for example Novalis: "The perfected form of the sciences must be poetic" (NS 2, 527, no. 17); "Every science becomes poetry [*Poesie*]—after becoming philosophy" (NS 3, 396, no. 684; cf. the letter to A. W. Schlegel from Dec. 12, 1794, NS 4, 252). We find similar dicta in the *Athenaeum*: "The highest philosophy...would become poetry [*Poesie*] again" (KA 2, 216, no. 304). The intimate proximity of literature and philosophy is manifest in the case of Kierkegaard and Nietzsche. On Wittgenstein's conception of the unity of philosophy and poetry, see Manfred Frank, "Wittgensteins Gang in die Dichtung," in *Wittgenstein. Literat und Philosoph* (Pfullingen: Neske, 1989), esp. 60ff. Derrida's texts *Glas* (1974) and *The Post Card: From Socrates to Freud and Beyond* (1980) are the most sustained instances of his synthesis of literary and philosophical language. The cases of Adorno and (late) Heidegger are complex. On the one hand, both emphasize the specific difference and complementarity of literature and philosophy (cf. Adorno, *Ästhetische Theorie* [Frankfurt am Main: Suhrkamp, 1973], 191, 197, 392, 519; Heidegger, "Was heißt Denken?" in *Vorträge und Aufsätze*, 132). On the other hand, both also explicitly break with discursive forms of language and develop their thoughts in close dialogue with works of poetry and art: as Heidegger says about his interpretation of Hölderlin: "In thinking, it is almost as though one were participating in the creation of the poem [*Das Denken ist fast wie ein Mitdichten*]" ("Hölderlins Hymne 'Andenken,'" in Martin Heidegger, *Gesamtausgabe* 2/52 [Frankfurt am Main: Klostermann, 1982], 55). Adorno describes the compositional idea according to which his (unfinished) *Aesthetic Theory* was to be organized in terms close to those he uses in his interpretation of Hölderlin; he contrasts it with the linearity of argumentation from premises (cf. *Ästhetische Theorie*, 541); on

the literary form of Adorno's philosophical writing see Gerhard Richter, "Aesthetic Theory and Nonpropositional Content in Adorno," *New German Critique* 97 (Winter 2006): 119–35; for a comparison of Adorno and Wittgenstein, also see Gottfried Gabriel, *Zwischen Logik und Literatur. Erkenntnisformen von Dichtung, Philosophie und Wissenschaft* (Stuttgart: Metzler, 1991), esp. 47ff.

18. Friedrich Nietzsche, "Über Wahrheit und Lüge im außermoralischen Sinn," in *Kritische Gesamtausgabe*, ed. G. Colli and M. Montinari (Berlin: Walter de Gruyter, 1975), vol. 1, 880.

19. Derrida offers a sustained treatment of this idea in "White Mythology: Metaphor in the Text of Philosophy," in *Margins of Philosophy*, trans. Alan Bass (Chicago: University of Chicago Press 1985), 207–72.

20. Though they start from diverse standpoints, both Manfred Frank (*Stil in der Philosophie* [Stuttgart: Reclam, 1992]) and Gottfried Gabriel ("Literarische Form und nicht-Propositionale Erkenntnis in der Philosophie," in Gottfried Gabriel and Christiane Schildknecht, *Literarische Formen der Philosophie* [Stuttgart: Metzler, 1990], 1–25) arrive at similar conclusions regarding the complementary relation between philosophy and literature.

21. Cf. Arthur C. Danto, "Philosophizing Literature," in *The Philosophical Disenfranchisement of Art* (New York: Columbia University Press, 1984), 167–69; cf. John Gibson, *Fiction and the Weave of Life* (Oxford: Oxford University Press 2007), 39–49.

22. Cf. Frank, *Stil in der Philosophie* and Gabriel, *Zwischen Logik und Literatur*.

23. See also Christiane Schildknecht, *Sense and Self. Perspectives on Nonpropositionality* (Paderborn: Mentis Verlag, 2002); cf. her article "'Ein seltsam wunderbarer Anstrich'? Nichtpropositionale Erkenntnis und ihre Darstellungsformen," in Brady Bowman, ed., *Darstellung und Erkenntnis: Beiträge zur Rolle nichtpropositionaler Erkenntnisformen in der deutschen Philosophie und Literatur nach Kant* (Paderborn: Mentis-Verlag, 2007), 31–43.

24. On Hölderlin see especially Helmut Hühn, "Bilder des Lebendigen. Zur Erkenntnisfunktion der dichterischen 'Mythe' im Werk Hölderlins," in Bowman, *Darstellung und Erkenntnis*, 117–133. See also Dieter Henrich, *Der Grund im Bewußtsein. Untersuchungen zu Hölderlins Denken* (Stuttgart: Klett-Cotta, 1992). Schelling, Hölderlin, and Hegel have each variously been claimed as the true author of the fragment that has come to be known as "the oldest system program of German idealism." The only undisputed fact is that it is in Hegel's handwriting. The fragment itself and a number of influential articles on its authorship and significance are to be found in Christoph Jamme and Hans Schneider, eds., *Mythologie der Vernunft. Hegels ältestes Systemprogramm des deutschen Idealismus* (Frankfurt am Main: Suhrkamp, 1988). For a critical discussion of the scholarship on the fragment see Frank-Peter Hansen, *Das älteste Systemprogramm des deutschen Idealismus. Rezeptionsgeschichte und Interpretation* (Berlin: de Gruyter, 1989). For a more recent overview with further bibliographical references see Walter Jaeschke, *Hegel-Handbuch* (Stuttgart: Metzler, 2003), 76–80.

25. This conception of art and poetry as bearing essentially upon the same objects and concerns as science (and philosophy) is a constant in early romantic thought that is still discernible in Hegel's later lectures on aesthetics. Adorno's thesis that art both

supersedes the "logic of identity" and demands philosophical interpretation in the discursive medium constituted by that very logic is an equally obvious scion of romanticism (cf. *Aesthetische Theorie*, 193ff.).

26. Frank, *Stil in der Philosophie*, 72.
27. Cf. Frank, *Stil in der Philosophie*, 84.
28. *Fiction and the Weave of Life*, 144. See also the essays in John Gibson, Wolfgang Huemer, and Luca Pocci, eds., *A Sense of the World: Essays on Fiction, Narrative, and Knowledge* (New York: Routledge, 2007).
29. Cf. Gibson, *Fiction and the Weave of Life*, chapters 2.2 and 3.3.
30. See Hans-Johann Glock, "Schopenhauer and Wittgenstein," in Christopher Janaway, ed., *The Cambridge Companion to Schopenhauer* (New York: Cambridge University Press, 2000), 422–58. Frank's extensive discussion of Wittgenstein's affinities with the thinkers of early romanticism is contained in Manfred Frank and Gianfranco Soldati, *Wittgenstein. Literat und Philosoph* (Pfullingen: Neske Verlag, 1989), 7–72; cf. *Stil in der Philosophie*, 86–115. On the methodological tradition linking Goethe, Novalis, and Wittgenstein see Jonas Maatsch, *"Naturgeschichte der Philosopheme." Frühromantische Wissensordnungen im Kontext* (Heidelberg: Winter Verlag, 2007).
31. Cavell's engagement with the romantic tradition is of course most obvious in the book *In Quest of the Ordinary: Lines of Skepticism and Romanticism* (Chicago: University of Chicago Press, 1988), but it is present in his other work as well. The legacy of romanticism is also present indirectly by way of Cavell's formative engagement with Wittgenstein. For a recent discussion see Simon Critchley, "Cavell's Romanticism and Cavell's 'Romanticism.'" See also Keren Gorodeisky's contribution to this volume, chapter 9 below.
32. See (among other texts) Stanley Cavell, "Knowing and Acknowledging," in *Must We Mean What We Say?* (Cambridge, MA: Harvard University Press, 2002), 238–66.
33. These points are made forcefully (though somewhat simplistically) by Jerome Stolnitz, "On the Cognitive Triviality of Art," *British Journal of Aesthetics* 32, no. 3 (1992): 191–200. A more balanced argument for rejecting the notion that it is constitutive of literature to produce and transmit knowledge is provided by Peter Lamarque, "Learning from Literature," in Gibson et al., *A Sense of the World*, 13–23.
34. Cf. Gibson, *Fiction and the Weave of Life*, 81–99.
35. Cora Diamond, "Losing Your Concepts," *Ethics* 98, no. 2 (1988): 255–77, here: 263.
36. Tyler Burge has suggested that Frege makes room for a distinction between the *sense* of an expression and a subject's conscious grasp of that sense ("Frege on Sense and Linguistic Meaning," in *Truth, Thought, Reason: Essays on Frege* [New York: Oxford University Press, 2005], 242–69, esp. 252–57): the full and precise sense of an expression may transcend the subject's actual, conscious grasp of that sense in any number of ways, even though the sense contributes to the structure and individuality of the subject's mind. So even the most competent speakers of a language, those who grasp the linguistic meaning of the expressions in their language most thoroughly, may fail to understand the deeper rationale that underlies their deployment of a concept. I have something similar in mind here, although in the present context I would like to de-emphasize the more austerely rationalist and Platonist elements of the Frege-Burge conception and emphasize rather the notion of historically emergent conceptual

spaces that shape how we think and speak without wholly coinciding with the actual thought and speech of individuals. (A detailed attempt to extend Burge's account beyond formal sciences such as logic and mathematics has been undertaken by James Higginbotham, "Conceptual Competence," *Philosophical Issues* 9 [1998]: 149–62.) Although Burge himself plausibly charges ordinary language philosophy with blindness toward the relevant distinction in Frege ("Frege on Sense and Linguistic Meaning," 269), it seems to me that Cavell's richer understanding of ordinary language philosophy gets some purchase on the same territory that Burge is interested in. In asking *"what we should say when,"* we are not merely clarifying— on dubious authority— linguistic meaning, but a structure of reality itself that cuts across the fact-value distinction: cf. Cavell, "Must We Mean What We Say?" in *Must We Mean What We Say? Updated Edition* [Cambridge: Cambridge University Press, 2002], 1–43, esp. 18–22; cf. Burge, "Frege on Sense and Linguistic Meaning," 258, 261). The upshot is that we can and in fact often do inhabit a conceptual space that is constitutive of our actual thoughts without our for that reason necessarily counting as possessing a mastery of the relevant concepts.

37. This observation requires a certain disambiguation of the complementarist view as espoused by Gottfried Gabriel. Gabriel understands literature as a nonpropositional mode of *Erkenntnis* that complements the propositional mode of *Erkenntnis* exemplified by scientific knowledge. Everything depends here on how we understand *Erkenntnis*: Are we to take it in its rather more processual meaning as the activity of cognition? If so, then cognition taken thus is sufficiently distinct from knowledge and belief (since belief plays a role in, but does not exhaust the nature of, cognition) that we may safely extricate such nonpropositional cognition from the threat of triviality. However, if we understand *Erkenntnis* to mean *knowledge*, the implication either of triviality or of a lack of cognitive seriousness becomes ineluctable.

38. Cavell, *Must We Mean What We Say?* 192.

39. Truth, then (*pace* Keats), is not beauty, but neither is it more than beauty in the emphatic sense I'm using the term here. As Kant was the first to recognize, beauty is the *immediate* experience of that space of intelligibility in which science arises and which it strives—infinitely—to fill out with a system of truths.

40. Gibson, *Fiction and the Weave of Life*, 120.

41. On the infinity of the scientific task and the impossibility of individual human satisfaction that implies, see Max Weber, "Science as a Vocation," in *The Vocation Lectures* (Indianapolis: Hackett, 2004), 1–31.

42. I am here postulating an inner connection between art, beauty, and perfection that is sure to be controversial, though it is essentially a restatement of the classical conception of beauty as inhering in the harmony of the parts and the whole to which they belong. The limited space of the present essay does not allow for adequate discussion.

43. Arthur Schopenhauer, *Die Welt als Wille und Vorstellung*, in *Werke in fünf Bänden*, ed. Ludger Lütkehaus (Zurich: Haffmans, 2006), vol. 1, 252.

44. For a convincing discussion of this point see Gibson, *Fiction and the Weave of Life*, 147–57.

45. Cf. for example *An die Natur* (1795), in Friedrich Hölderlin, HSW 1, 198–200.

"No Poetry, No Reality"

Schlegel, Wittgenstein, Fiction, and Reality

KEREN GORODEISKY

[Criticism] exhibit[s] the relations of literature—not to "life," as something contrasted to literature, but to all other activities, which together with literature, are the components of life.

—T. S. ELIOT, *The Sacred Wood*

9.1. INTRODUCTION

Friedrich Schlegel's remarks about poetry and reality are notoriously baffling:

No poetry, no reality.... There is, despite all the senses, no external world without imagination... all things disclose themselves to the magic wand of feeling alone.[1]

Whoever conceives of poetry or philosophy as individuals has a feeling for them.[2]

In [romantic poetry] there is no regard for the difference between appearance [*Schein*] and truth [*Wahrheit*].[3]

Everything that rests on the opposition between appearance and reality... is not purely poetic.[4]

What should one say about these observations? Perhaps that they are outlandish and eccentric? "Who in his right mind would argue publicly that *reality* rests on poetry, on a mere fiction? The speaker must be a madman, one who has lost all sense for the difference between what is *real* and what is *merely* a figment of the imagination." Or one might say that, rather than philosophical observations, Schlegel's remarks are merely "poetically exaggerated" reflections.[5]

Yet another person might claim that these observations manifest a lack of mastery of our language. "The concept "poetry" and the concept "reality," this respondent may say, "have precise semantics, and very clear criteria of application. Schlegel has clearly not mastered those concepts."

I take all these responses to be mistaken. Schlegel's remarks about poetry and reality are not merely outlandish or eccentric, but deeply revealing about a prevalent confusion in theoretical approaches to the distinction between fiction and reality.[6] Rather than mere poetic exaggerations, I believe that Schlegel's pronouncements are philosophical observations that respond to a genuine confusion, a confusion that led him to express, time and again, what initially looks like eccentric views about poetry and reality.[7] The confusion at stake is expressed by the last envisioned response to his remarks. The response of the so-called semanticist presupposes mistakenly that the distinction between "fiction" and "reality" is fixed "once and for all" by a criterion, which is determined prior to any application of those concepts. Our imagined semanticist, and, I think, some contemporary philosophers of art, assume that the distinction between fiction and reality *is* and *must be* fixed independently of the ordinary practices of using the terms "fiction" and "reality" to mean something in specific situations.

I argue that we should understand Schlegel's knotty remarks about poetry and reality as addressing this assumption. I propose that we think of them as forming a kind of "transcendental criticism," to borrow Kant's label for his *diagnosis* of, and *challenge* to, what he takes to be a "natural and inevitable illusion" of the human mind.[8] Since the assumption I just mentioned shapes a line of thought in contemporary aesthetics, Schlegel's concern with this illusion is as relevant today as it was in his day.

We can begin to see the depth of Schlegel's concern by first tracing some affinities between his thought and Ludwig Wittgenstein's later philosophy. This should not be too surprising. The surface similarities between Wittgenstein's remarks in *Philosophical Investigations* and in the aphorisms collected in *Culture and Value*, and the pronouncements in Schlegel's writings are nothing short of remarkable. Here is a very limited sample:

1. One should really do philosophy only as poetry.[9]
   Poetry and philosophy should be united.[10]

2. Philosophy simply puts everything before us, and neither explains nor deduces anything.—Since everything lies open to view there is nothing to explain.[11]

The main thing [in philosophy] is to know something and to say it. The attempt to prove or even to explain it is quite superfluous in most cases.... There is doubtless more difficulty in stating something than in explaining it.[12]

3. The work of the philosopher consists in assembling reminders.///[13]The aspects of things that are most important for us are hidden because of their simplicity and familiarity.... We fail to be struck by what, once seen, is most striking and most powerful.[14]

Whoever knows this cannot be reminded often enough that he knows it. All of the highest truths of every kind are altogether trivial; and for this very reason nothing is more necessary than to express them ever anew... so that it will not be forgotten that they are still there.[15]

4. One might also give the name "philosophy" to what is possible *before* all new discoveries and inventions. /// If one tried to advance *theses* in philosophy, it would never be possible to debate them, because everyone would agree to them.[16]

To those who knew it already, philosophy of course brings nothing new; but only through it does it become knowledge and thereby assume a new form.[17]

I quote Stanley Cavell's description of his pairings of quotes as a commentary on my own pairings: "In each case the first member of the pair is from Wittgenstein, the second is…either from Friedrich or from August Wilhelm Schlegel.…That these figures take the preoccupations of Wittgenstein's sensibility deep into…German Romanticism fits my sense of his continuing the Romantic's response to the psychic threat of skepticism."[18] Although a handful of scholars pointed to certain parallels between the German romantics and Wittgenstein's late philosophy,[19] Cavell is probably the only one[20] to have acknowledged the *depth* of the legacy of the early German romantics in Wittgenstein, or the Wittgensteinian spirit of the early German romantics.[21]

The task of this paper is to advance what Cavell has only started on this front, with the aim of shedding light on Schlegel's response to skepticism and to traditional philosophy, on his concept "wit," and, above all, on the way we should, following him, approach a family of concepts—"poetry" or "fiction," "reality," and "feeling." For that purpose, section 2 explores the affinities between the Schlegelian spirit and the Wittgensteinian spirit, and section 3 explains how these commonalities, when applied to a confusion about poetry and reality, shed light on the remarks that open the paper.

9.2. THE SCHLEGELEAN AND THE WITTGENSTEINIAN SPIRIT

In addition to affinities between the content and the form of Schlegel's mature project and Wittgenstein's later philosophy, their respective philosophical methods reveal a related "spirit."

Wittgenstein described the methods of his late philosophical writings as closely related to methods in aesthetics.[22] That Schlegel's methods are analogous to methods in aesthetics is not news. I am convinced that those methods also resemble Wittgenstein's methods in some important respects, and that they are so similar because both Wittgenstein and Schlegel understand traditional philosophy and skepticism in a closely related manner.[23]

Why should philosophy proceed, as it were, "aesthetically"? Here is how G. E. Moore remembers Wittgenstein's reflection on that matter:

> *Reasons*, he said, in Aesthetics, are "of the nature of further descriptions": e.g., you can make a person see what Brahms was driving at by showing him lots of different pieces by Brahms, or by comparing him with a contemporary author; and all that Aesthetics does is "to draw your attention to a thing," to "place things side by side."... And he said that the same sort of "reasons" were given not only in Ethics, but also in Philosophy.[24]

Schlegel and Wittgenstein belong to a tradition, which suspects that the identification of aesthetic reasons and general rules is unfaithful to the practice of aesthetic appreciation.[25] For aesthetic communication does not aim to achieve agreement in *opinions* or *beliefs* about the work at stake,[26] but at allowing another to share the critic's love for (or dissatisfaction with) the work for being beautiful (or ugly) in this or that particular way. But to permit another to share the critic's vision, appreciation, and love for *this* particular work, the critic must allow her interlocutor to see the particular aspects that make it powerful *in the way* that they do. The critic must enable her interlocutor to stand to the work in a relation that allows her to see in it what the critic sees in it, and to feel for it what the critic feels for it.

Wittgenstein suggests that this aim requires that we align the work we love with other works that are similar to it, and dissimilar from it in revealing ways: works by the same artist, works belonging to the same genre, or to the same historical period.[27] Schlegel seems to agree. We should not expect philosophy, he argues, to give us an absolute, a priori definition of art, but we can, and perhaps should expect it to help us "order the given artistic experiences and the existing artistic principles... and raise the appreciation of art, extend it with the help of a thoroughly learned history of art."[28] Nor can we answer "the simplest and most immediate questions... without the deepest consideration and the most erudite history of art."[29] You understand "Sapphic poems" only when you compare them with Petrarch's and with Horatian poems.[30] And the comparison of different works, particularly a historical comparison, is, for Schlegel, the essence of criticism.[31]

Wittgenstein takes a similar method of comparison to be necessary in philosophy too. "It is not our aim to refine or complete the system of rules for the use of our words."[32] Instead, the ordinary uses of words ("language-games") that he invites us to observe and imagine are "set up as *objects of comparison* which are meant to throw light on the facts of our language by way not only of similarities, but also of dissimilarities."[33]

It is all too tempting to misinterpret Wittgenstein on this point. One might think that he pursues philosophy by comparing different ways we use words because he believes that "meaning is use," a slogan often associated with *PI* §43. This may well be true, *depending* on how we read §43. I read this passage as suggesting neither that understanding the meaning of a word or a sentence requires a pragmatic analysis over and above a semantics and syntax,[34] nor that the meaning of a word is determined simply by a certain context.[35] Rather, according to Wittgenstein, we cannot understand the meaning of a word or a sentence in isolation from the particular way(s) the word or the sentence can be used *to mean* something specific on a *particular* occasion. In order to grasp the meaning of a word we need to remind ourselves, to imagine or observe, how it can be used by *someone* to mean *something specific*.

What motivates Wittgenstein to align meaning and use in this way is not a wish to guide our understanding, but a concern about a prevalent confusion about meaning, which Cavell calls "an illusion of meaning." A person is under this illusion when he "imagines himself to be saying something when he is not, to have discovered something, when he has not."[36] What happens when a person "hallucinates what he or she means;"[37] What happens when, as Wittgenstein puts it, she uses her words "outside of a language-game?"

Usually, when a person is under this illusion she fails to use the words in a way that grants them their necessary connections to some other words and human practices. I might speak outside of a language-game if, for instance, I say, "*Only I* know my feelings" in a way that is detached from any specific situation in which it can make sense (independently, for example, of any anger I might feel toward someone, perhaps my therapist, or my mother, for ascribing to me certain feelings that I either don't believe I have, or am not willing or capable of ascribing to myself). I use this sentence outside of a language-game if, detached from any such practice in which it naturally makes sense, I use it to mean (I imagine that it means) that the feelings of another are accessible to *no one* other than the feeling person.

We might also speak outside of a language-game if we try to use words to mean both what they ordinarily mean, and something "special," "unordinary." This double use is characteristic of the skeptic's talk—both the skeptic who doubts the existence of the external world, and the skeptic who doubts our knowledge of other minds.[38] The plight of the skeptic is this: her *inability* to mean what she says is *internal* to her way of using the words she is using.[39] The success of the skeptic[40] *depends* on her using words *both* in the ordinary way and in a technical way. On the one hand, the skeptic *must* use her words in a "special" way if her words are to gain the kind of generality she needs. Only if the expression, "Only I know what I feel" is severed from any specific ordinary context of uttering it to express anger about some infringement of privacy, about an imposition of feelings that we are unwilling to accept, and so on, can the skeptic claim that it has a "general reach," or that it implies a theory about the metaphysical nature of all feelings ("private"), and about the epistemic impossibility (of *any* person) to know other minds. On the other hand, the skeptic must also insist that she uses her words in the way in which they are ordinarily used, if she is to be justified in claiming that what she has "discovered" (the nature of feelings and of knowledge) "conflicts" with our everyday understanding of feelings and knowledge. Otherwise, the skeptic cannot achieve her aim of pulling the rug out from under what we usually say and believe. Properly responding to the skeptic requires that we enable her to see that putting the question the way she does—as both ordinary and special—puts her own question into question.

So Wittgenstein uses "an aesthetic method" in philosophy—he reminds us of what we ordinarily say and do, by way of aligning different uses as "objects of comparison"—because he believes that, especially as philosophers, we are prone to be subject to an illusion about the way we use our words, and about the meaning of our words.[41] The illusions and misunderstandings that Wittgenstein is concerned with cannot be refuted by a counterargument, or by a proof or a rule that shows the necessary, systematic, and fixed nature of language and meaning. "The confusions which occupy us arise when language is like an engine idling, not when it is doing work."[42] This kind of confusion can be resolved only by reminding the speakers who use language indolently how language actually works, how it must work if it is to do any work.[43]

Such a work of reminders has to be of a special kind because of the great "urge to misunderstand," because of the tendency to be bewitched by the workings of our language, and because "the aspects of things that are most important for us," particularly, those that allow words to mean, "are hidden because of their simplicity and familiarity.... The real foundations of his enquiry do not strike man at all. Unless *that* fact has at some time struck him.—And this means: we fail to be struck by what, once seen, is most striking and most powerful."[44]

One way of allowing the most familiar to be striking is to compare a certain use of words with other imagined and real uses until it attains "complete clarity."[45] But once this complete clarity is achieved, "philosophical problems should *completely* disappear. The real discovery is the one...that gives philosophy peace, so that it is no longer tormented by questions which bring *itself* into question."[46] The only resolution of skepticism is its dissolution by means of disillusionment.[47]

You may think that Schlegel can in no way be viewed as *responding* to the skeptic, either in a "Wittgensteinian" or in any other way. And you might think so because you believe that Schlegel himself is a skeptic. Schlegel undoubtedly doubts the possibility of absolute foundations[48]—in a spirit similar to Wittgenstein's doubt about the existence of an absolute, fixed system of rules as the foundation of language. And he questions the possibility of an absolute comprehension of the world—just as Wittgenstein believes that explanations "come to an end."[49]

But in spite of these "doubts," neither Wittgenstein nor Schlegel is a (traditional) *skeptic*, surely not a skeptic about the traditional objects of skepticism. Both of them take skepticism very seriously, but take it seriously because they view it as confused in ways that represent some of the prevalent confusions of traditional philosophy itself. Schlegel's understanding of skepticism resembles Wittgenstein's: he also recognizes the power of a certain philosophical use of words to lead us astray,[50] and holds that a "corrupt manner in which language is used" can easily lead to mistaken systematizing enterprises.[51] And Schlegel seems also to share Wittgenstein's understanding of our great urge to misunderstand the workings of language:

> I wanted to point out that *words often understand themselves better than do those who use them*, wanted to draw attention to the fact that *there must be secret societies among philosophical words, words that, like a host of spirits sprung forth too early, confuse everything, and exert invisible force of the world spirit even on those who do not wish to acknowledge them....* I had to think in terms of a popular medium, in order to bond chemically this holy, delicate, fleeting, airy, fragrant, and as it were imponderable thought. Otherwise, *how severely might this thought have been misunderstood, since it is only through its well-understood use an end could be put to all the understandable misunderstanding?*[52]

That Schlegel is not a skeptic, but a subtle critic of skepticism who challenges it by employing some of Wittgenstein's later terms of criticism is supported by his following observations: "Eclecticism and Skepticism lead to Mysticism, the *abyss* into which everything sinks."[53] But abyssal as skepticism may be, no

counterargument can silence it. Properly responding to the skeptic requires
that we allow her to see the incoherence internal to her own position:

> The three positions [eclecticism, skepticism, and mysticism] not only mutu-
> ally reciprocally annihilate each other, but each also destroys itself. It is a
> foregone conclusion that the consistent skeptic must end in remaining silent
> and ceasing to think, and thus finally equals zero. He would also have to
> cease refuting because he refutes himself, or else he would have to realize
> that he can only refute what is refutable.[54]

This self-contradiction is not externally imposed on the skeptical position,
but generated by the position's internal instability: "The mystic is freer than the
skeptic and the empiricist; he begets his contradiction. The others allow their
contradictions to be *dictated* to them."[55] And the source of this instability lies
in the skeptic's use of words—her use of a "special language," which she tries
to (indeed, must) deny if skepticism is to get off the ground: "All three—the
skeptics, the empiricists, and the mystics—have their own languages and yet all
three protest against jargon."[56]

You might think that even if this is a plausible reconstruction of Schlegel's
approach to skepticism, this is only another indication that he *is* nonetheless a
kind of skeptic—the kind of skeptic who doubts the representational power of
philosophical language. Azade Seyhan writes: "For Friedrich Schlegel...irony
points to the failure of philosophy to represent the infinite adequately."[57] This is
undoubtedly true. But the literature that emphasizes the romantic ironic recognition of the limitations of philosophical language tends to undermine important nuances. Schlegel repudiates neither reason nor philosophical language *as
such*. Nor does he merely remind philosophers of the limitations of this language *as philosophical language*. Alert as he is to different uses of language,
Schlegel calls on us to be cautious about a *certain* use of philosophical language,
governed by an illusory picture of language, philosophy, and rationality (i.e.,
the picture of these three as grounded in absolute foundations, or as unlimited
manners of cognizing and articulating the Absolute).[58] Though suspicious and
critical of *this* use (or misuse) of philosophical language, he also reminds us
that we can do philosophy in a different spirit, positively, not only negatively by
pointing to philosophy's limitations: "Wouldn't it be worthwhile trying now to
introduce the concept of the positive into philosophy as well?"[59]

As tempting as the picture of philosophy that often drives us to transcend the
limitation of language and reason may be, we can avoid its pitfalls, while still
using philosophical language. For, though limited, philosophical language also
has an inherent potential, a potential embodied in its necessary reliance on the
ordinary use of language. Since language as we ordinarily use it is teeming with

(positive) possibilities that philosophy can legitimately and correctly use for achieving its (philosophy's) own aims, the first task we must undertake, if we are to direct philosophy back from its illusory path to a meaningful pursuit, is to remind ourselves of our ordinary use of words.

Schlegel's antidote to the illusory use of language is reflected by his style of writing. Not unlike Wittgenstein, Schlegel chooses a dialogical and conversational style (he writes fragments that communicate with fragments written by others, fragments that embody the voice of an opposing interlocutor, and a dialogue).[60] Like Wittgenstein's dialogical voice, Schlegel's approach allows him to respond to a host of confused interlocutors. He claims that when philosophy is done properly it is done as "symphilosophy" between two interlocutory voices, and that symphilosophy is, fundamentally, intrapersonal—a recasting of two voices internal to the self:

> If in communicating a thought, one fluctuates between absolute comprehension and absolute incomprehension, then this process might already be termed a philosophical friendship. For it's no different with ourselves. Is the life of a thinking human being anything else than a continuous inner symphilosophy?[61]

Both Schlegel and Wittgenstein suggest that the "urge to misunderstand," and misuse words is neither rare, nor exclusive to the skeptic. A skeptical voice, "the skeptic in oneself,"[62] inheres in all of us. We are all prone to certain confusions and illusions that affect our use of words. The "voice of temptation" is as much a part of each self as the "voice of correction."[63]

Wittgenstein aims to "correct" the part of us that gave in to temptation by inviting us to observe and imagine how we ordinarily use words. Schlegel uses a related philosophical approach. He also invites us, I think, to observe and imagine how we use certain words, and make certain distinctions, and how those distinctions express what we can and cannot do with those words. For example, he calls on us to resist the attempt to define art *überhaupt*, but instead to reconstruct it before our eyes through a detailed analysis and comparison of works.[64] Instead of talking about writing as such, or about *the* writer, we should distinguish between different kinds of writers, for example, between the analytic writer and the synthetic writer.[65] To understand suicide, we need to remind ourselves in what circumstances we call it an action, and in what circumstances we call it an accident, and what we must mean when we say that it is wrong.[66] Reminding ourselves of the distinction between folly and madness has both philosophical and political consequences.[67] And to understand the novel, the best we can do is to compare Shakespeare with Boccaccio, the two of them with Cervantes, and all of them with a detailed reading of Goethe. Above all, in a Wittgensteinian spirit,

Schlegel claims that philosophy can teach us nothing new. And yet only through philosophy do we come to know, to be reminded of and become familiar with, what it teaches us—what we have always already "known."[68]

Schlegel takes up this "work of reminders" also, I believe, by reviving the power of wit, a power that he regards as profoundly philosophical: "Even philosophy has blossoms. That is, its thoughts; but one can never decide if one should call them witty or beautiful."[69] Wit does not have the special power of reminding us of what we are already familiar with but for the most part fail to notice simply because, as a matter of fact, it is a figure of speech that is used in ordinary conversation. Wit's special force lies in its characteristic way of behaving. For it is wit that, through humor and surprise, often startles us, challenges what we take for granted, and, by so doing, allows us to look at our life and words from a fresh perspective, and thus to see, as if for the first time, what we are already familiar with.[70] The meaning of "a witty idea which is enigmatic to the point of needing to be solved should be immediately and completely clear as soon as it's been hit upon."[71] Once achieving complete clarity, Schlegelian wit dissolves (rather than directly solves) the problem it was meant to address. For like philosophy, wit "brings us nothing new"—it only puts us in touch with what we are already familiar with by showing it in a new light. Through the surprising power of wit, the ordinary becomes for the first time an object of awareness and knowledge.[72] And so, "imagination and wit are everything to you!"[73]

Schlegel's witty remarks function similarly to Wittgenstein's grammatical remarks. And their success is gauged in similar ways. A grammatical investigation is successful if an interlocutor can use the philosopher's reminding summons to test herself, if the interlocutor can accept the invitation to share words and world.[74] For Schlegel too, the mark of a good, successful philosophical approach, "the criterion of authentic philosophy," is not its "applicability," but "*communicability*."[75] One of the "universally valid and fundamental laws of written communication" is that "one should really be able to communicate it and share it with somebody, not simply express oneself. Otherwise it would be wiser to keep silent."[76] Wittgenstein's and Schlegel's ways of comparing different circumstances in which we ordinarily use the words that the philosopher also aims to use is not a way to defend common sense in an antiskeptical way, or to refute traditional philosophy. Their appeal to the ordinary is a solicitation of agreement, an invitation to share their world.

9.3. POETRY AND REALITY

The remarks at the opening of this chapter should also be read as what I call "witty" or "grammatical" remarks.[77] They are meant to remind us of the ways in which we ordinarily approach the distinction between reality and fiction, and what we say when we ordinarily speak about our feelings for fictional works and for "real" situations and people.[78] I suspect that Schlegel uses those reflections on poetry, reality, and feeling as reminders of that sort because he recognizes a few related tendencies in theoretical considerations of (1) the distinction between poetry and reality, and (2) the distinction between our feelings for poetic works (and the fictional characters in them), and our feelings for our fellow human beings, and "real life" circumstances.

Different as these two distinctions are, Schlegel's remarks suggest that the prevalent theoretical approaches to both of these distinctions are based on a shared confused picture: Schlegel points to a tendency, manifest primarily in philosophy and literary criticism, to think that poetry and reality, as well as our feelings for the former and our feelings for the latter, are distinguished once and for all by a fixed criterion, which is determined independently of our life with these terms.

I take this prevalent approach to the distinction between the real and the fictional to be *structurally analogous* (but by no means identical) to the skeptic's approach that I described above. And for that reason, I regard both of them as calling for a similar response. This is what I mean: The skeptical doubt about the existence of the external world, on the one hand, and the confusion about reality and fiction, on the other, are *not* similar in content. I do *not* claim that the latter raises a question about our epistemic capacity to tell reality from fiction, or that it challenges our capacity to ever know that what we experience is real rather than fictional. Nor do I claim that the philosophers whose views are shaped by this confusion are searching, like the external world skeptic, for some *experiential* "marks and features"[79] to distinguish reality from fiction. But the assumption that governs their confusion is analogous to the one that governs the skeptical confusion, and the source of the two is a misunderstanding about meaning.

The confusion at stake in this paper is guided by the mistaken belief that every judgment in which we apply certain concepts is essentially underdetermined *if* the judgment is not grounded in a stable determination of these concepts prior to their applications. In short, this picture is based on a misunderstanding of the way language works. One might be prone to this confusion because of an inclination to think that language is based on an absolute foundation. But Schlegel suggests that viewing language in this manner expresses "a fad for the absolute [*die Liebhaberei fürs Absolute*]," from which we must find "a way out,"[80] just as we must overcome the urge to ground philosophy in absolute foundations.[81] Because this approach to fiction and reality is grounded in a misunderstanding of the meanings of words, and their necessary relation to ordinary language, the proper response to it is not a refutation, but the response that I take Schlegel to offer—a response that allows his interlocutor to recognize for herself how words acquire their meanings when we use them ordinarily.

It seems that Schlegel found a variant of this attitude towards poetry and reality to be the picture that *he himself*, the early Schlegel, had been captive by a few years before he wrote the statements that open this chapter. The remarks about poetry and reality, from his so-called mid to late period, starting approximately in 1797,[82] may be designed to challenge the picture that had shaped the early Schlegel's faith in the absolute distinction between reality and poetry. They challenge, particularly, his early belief that, in its perfected mode (exhibited in the works of antiquity), poetry is "an utterly peculiar activity of the human mind; it is distinguished from every other activity by *eternal boundaries* [because it is the expression of] an eternal human objective... that is only indirectly connected to man."[83] Schlegel uses the remarks quoted at the opening of this chapter in part to take issue with the faith in the possibility of an objective science that could irrevocably distinguish the "real"—the everyday life of ordinary men and women who live in actual, empirical surroundings—from the absolutely objective, pure, and self-sufficient realm of poetry and art, the embodiment of the "ideal." Proclaiming that without poetry there is no reality, that the distinction between reality and appearance is not poetical, and that "life and society should become poetic"[84] may be a way of raising a question about the assumption that "there [is] more than one world"[85]—the real world and the world presented by the art of fiction—a self-sufficient, "isolated," ideal world, which is only "indirectly [*mittelbar*] related to man."

Perhaps surprisingly, the picture of poetry and reality that I take Schlegel's remarks to address does not shape only his early view, but also a contemporary debate in aesthetics: the debate about whether the emotions we feel for fictions are real and rational. Before I introduce this debate, two qualifications are in order. First, I do not claim that Schlegel had in mind this contemporary debate in aesthetics. And yet, I suspect, both that he was responding to a related illusory picture, the one that shaped his early thought, and that his reflections on poetry and reality include resources for clearing away the confusion in the contemporary literature about fiction. Due to limitations of space, in this paper I merely *gesture* towards the way in which these resources can address the contemporary discussion. Second, I do not argue that the parties to this debate presuppose, like the early Schlegel, that "poetry" and "reality" (in their terms, "fiction" and "reality") are two distinct "domains" or "worlds." But I do think that a central line in this debate presupposes that our emotional responses to fiction and our emotional responses to "real" situations and individuals *are* distinguished by means of a single criterion, which is determined in isolation from the ways in which we ordinarily engage with fictions and with "real life," and from the criteria that these engagements give rise to. Although this confusion and the confusion of the early Schlegel are distinct, I think that they share an understanding (well, a misunderstanding) of the meaning of words as determined a priori, all by itself, independently of what we do and mean when we use language.

How does this confusion enter into the contemporary literature? In taking for granted that an emotion can be "real" only if it involves a belief in the existence of its object,[86] some parties to this debate assume that what is "real" and what is "fictional" (what is merely part of a game of make-believe, to use the terms that Kendall Walton contributed to this debate) is already determined, independently of what we actually do and say when we are engaged with "real" people, and with fictions, and the criteria we use when engaged in such ways.[87] For example, Walton holds that we do not "really" feel, say, pity and pain for Anna Karenina, but feel them only as part of a "make-believe" game because "real" emotions always require a belief in the existence of the objects of those emotions.[88] Walton thus assumes that the distinction between "real" and "fictional" emotions *is* set independently of any language-game.[89]

In contrast to this line of thought, Schlegel's reflections on poetry and reality in his mid to late period suggest that the distinction between poetry and reality should not be regarded as obvious. There are reasons not to take it for granted, but to explore its nature, just as there are reasons to explore and question the "Greek separation of all things into the divine and the human…the Roman dualism of At Home and At War. And the modern [distinction between] the world of the present and the world of the hereafter, as if there were more than one world."[90]

Why is it not to be taken for granted? For one, poetry and reality do not seem to be distinguished in the same way that ordinary objects, like tables, trees, or birds, are distinguished. If someone says, "This is a goldfinch," it is reasonable in certain circumstances to ask him how he knows that it is a goldfinch and not a goldcrest. If such a doubt arises, the speaker, if he knows what he is talking about, can easily pacify the doubt. "I know that it is a goldfinch because, though goldfinches and goldcrests both have a red head, there are no goldcrests in those areas," or "Goldcrests have pinkish-red head, but goldfinches have wine-red heads." No matter how "alike" goldfinches and goldcrests are, there are clear "marks and features" that distinguish the one from the other, marks and features that we can come to know if we receive the right kind of training, and if we are situated properly. It is questionable whether there are similar marks and features to distinguish the fictional from the real, if any doubt arises. What can I possibly answer Betsy, my neighbor, if she asks me how I know that the neighborhood we live in is real, rather than the setting of a novel? For her to ask that question would bespeak a misunderstanding of the nature of the distinction.

As much as it differs from the distinction between goldfinches and goldcrests, the distinction between fiction and reality also importantly differs from the distinction between *mere* appearance and reality, between what is *not real* and what is *real*, or between a real goldfinch and a decoy[91] (as well as between dreaming and waking life, the distinction that interests the external world skeptic). For what is fictional, poetry, is (or should be) at least as real as our "real life": "Works whose ideal doesn't have as much living reality and, as it were, personality for the artist as does his mistress or his friend are best left unwritten. At any rate, they do not become works of art."[92] Schlegel also reminds us that our "real," everyday life often presents itself to us as a work of fiction: "Even in life...the common often makes a very romantic and pleasant appearance."[93] And poetry itself, he claims, functions more often then not *in* nothing other than our everyday reality: "It is a permanent feature of the highest poetry to appear in holy wrath and express its full power even in the strangest material, that is, everyday reality."[94]

By making these and other remarks, Schlegel suggests that whether what we do, undergo, or encounter is real or fictional can be determined only in light of our language-games with fiction—only in light of what we ordinarily do or don't do when we are engaged with fictions, for those language-games alone embody the criteria of what can and cannot count as either fiction or reality. Schlegel proposes that any effort to use the terms "real" and "fictional"[95] as if their meaning is determined in isolation from the particular practices in which specific speakers use them could only result in our failing to mean what we say. Just as the activity of modern poetry lacks "a firm basis,"[96] but depends instead on the activity of each individual poet, so too what counts as "poetry" and what counts as "reality" lacks a "firm basis," but depends instead on particular uses of the terms.

But this does not imply that the meaning of our concepts is arbitrary, subjectivist or even merely conventional. Schlegel claims that even though modern poetry has no "firm basis" other than the creative talent of individual poets, it is not merely arbitrary, or "idealist"—it is not the expression only of the ideals, or the mind, of the particular poets who create it, as contrasted with reality. Rather, modern poetry does not only facilitate genuine realism, a true expression of the reality in which modern poets live, but it also constitutes "the harmony of the ideal and the real."[97] Similarly, even though meaning is not determined once and for all, independently of what we mean when we use words in particular situations, it is *not* arbitrary, subjectivist, or conventional. Cavell writes, "I am trying to bring out...that any form of life and every concept integral to it has an indefinite number of instances and directions of projection; and that this variation is not arbitrary. *Both* the 'outer' variance and the 'inner' constancy are necessary if a concept is to accomplish its tasks."[98] Even if our concepts and words are infinitely open to revision, even if they are so plastic as to allow infinite yet unidentified instances to fall under them, what would fall under any concept is not arbitrary or subjective. Unless a certain object or context *invites* the application of an existing concept, which has not yet been applied to this object or context, the application would not be legitimate. Properly using our words requires that we be attuned to those contexts that allow them to be projected onto and those that do not. Being ungrounded in any list of necessary and sufficient rules or conditions, and being, *essentially*, an intersubjective activity of particular speakers does not prevent language, *our* language, from being normatively grounded rather than arbitrary.

Notice that Schlegel's remarks about poetry and reality are not to be read as a refutation of the philosopher who is subject to the confused picture about fiction and reality that I am attempting to flesh out in this section. Instead, he invites his interlocutor to share his own world, a world that is made perspicuous, is animated and maintained by the fictional works we are engaged with as much as it is animated and maintained by the "real" people we interact with.[99] And he invites the interlocutor (and us, his readers) to do so by reminding us that seeing how the words "poetry," "reality," and "feeling" acquire their meaning, and recognize the criteria for applying them in different situations only requires that we observe the ordinary practices of reading and appreciating, of meeting friends to engage in a "lively discussion about a new play"[100] and so on.

Instead of offering a counterargument, Schlegel wishes to remind anyone who is prone to the confusion about poetry and reality how people use, in ordinary circumstances, the terms, which the philosopher also attempts to use. This is what I take Schlegel to be doing when he asks, "Is there an art worthy of the name if it does not have the power to bind the spirit of love with its magic word, to make the spirit of love follow and obey it?"[101] The question whether the emotions we feel for fictional characters and narrative are "real" seems to lose its hold on us when we remind ourselves that we hardly ever call a work an *art*work, let alone a great work of art, if we do not take it to inspire "the spirit of love," if we do not take it both to be capable of moving its audience, and to merit the audience's love and admiration. What sense does it make to insist that whatever we feel for fictional characters cannot be "real" but a "quasi-emotion" because we believe that those characters do not "really" exist, if one of the primary ways we have for determining what counts as fictional works is to gauge whether they merit feelings of sympathy, love or admiration?

Schlegel writes, "The first principle in love is to have a sense for one another, and the highest principle, faith in each other."[102] Rather than a belief in the existence of the beloved—the requirement of *real* feelings for anything according to the contemporary aestheticians I mentioned above—the requirement for *real* love is a sense for, and faith in the other. *That is* what we seem to demand of *real* love, and perhaps other emotions, at least in many circumstances. The sorrow I feel for Anna, then, might not be real *if*, for example, I think that she deserves her dismal end, or if I think that she brought it on herself. My sorrow is not real, in other words, if I have no faith in her decisions and actions. This means that there *are* criteria for distinguishing "real" emotions from "unreal" ones (where the latter refers to faked or insincere emotions). But these criteria are part of the ordinary grammar of the concepts of these emotions, part of the life surrounding our emotional lives. They are not determined independently of the ways in which we usually respond to, behave around, and talk about our emotional lives, and they suggest that our emotions for fictions often count as real. Assuming that whether our emotions for fictions are "real" depends solely on whether they involve a belief in the existence of their objects ignores the variety of criteria that we ordinarily use to determine whether an emotion is real. Indeed, *sometimes* we must conclude that an appearance of emotion is not real, but only a *mere* appearance, *because* it does not involve such a belief. But Walton's assumption ignores the fact that, *for the most part*, whether or not a seeming emotion is real, apparent, or only a part of a make-believe game does not depend on the existence of such a belief, but on a host of other criteria.[103]

When the declaration "no poetry, nor reality" opens a remark about the necessity of feeling for properly responding to actual individual human beings and to the world as such, it cannot mean that there is no difference between poetry and reality.[104] Instead of reading this passage as obliterating the distinction, or as suggesting that there is no way out of poetic and linguistic constructions, it would be more natural to read it as proposing that we learn how to properly respond to our fellow human beings (and to the "external world" of which we are a part), when we become attuned to poetry, and, at the same time, we learn how to properly respond to poetry, when we learn how to be responsive to our fellow human beings, and to the world as such. "Whoever conceives of poetry or philosophy as individuals has a feeling for them."[105]

Writing about poetry or fiction philosophically, which drives us to draw absolute boundaries between art, as belonging to an "ideal" world, and life as belonging to the "real" world, or to ask whether the sorrow and pity we feel for, say, Anna Karenina is real, often leads us astray from, and renders us oblivious to, the way we ordinarily use these words. The way we use these words philosophically is often entangled with a fantasy that they are independent of what *we* say and mean when we utter them. This is why leading these "words back from their metaphysical to their everyday use [*auf ihre alltägliche Verwendung*]" is not an easy task.[106] Acknowledging the "highest truths," the most basic and ordinary structures of care and concern, which allow our words to have the meanings they have, not independently of us, but insofar as we mean them in the ways that we do, is particularly exacting when we do philosophy. But as exacting as it may be, the grammatical or witty investigation of words is worth the effort. For it not only brings out the emptiness of so much of our philosophical use of words, but also our investments in the practices to which our words belong, and the different concerns, cares, and commitments embodied in our ordinary use of them. As J. L. Austin puts it, "Our common stock of words embodies all the distinctions men have found worth drawing, and the connections they have found worth making."[107] Rather than wishing to obliterate the distinction between poetry and reality, or to suggest that "art...does not need to point beyond itself,"[108] when making the remarks that open the paper, and many others that relate to them, Schlegel meant to remind us of how intimate we are with the fictions we read (and hear, and behold, and experience) on an everyday basis, and to invite us to feel this intimacy for ourselves.

NOTES

1. *Athenaeum Fragments* in KA 2, 227, no. 350.
2. *Athenaeum Fragments*, KA 2, 24, no. 414.
3. *Dialogue on Poetry*, KA 2, 334.
4. *Fragments on Literature and Poetry*, KA 16, 97, no. 146.
5. This is a paraphrase of the epithet that Rudolph Haym ascribed to Novalis, when he called him a "poetically exaggerated Fichte." See, *Die romantische Schule* (Berlin: Gaertner, 1882), 332.
6. Schlegel, of course, speaks about "poetry" and "reality," never about "fiction" and "reality." However, I think that in those specific remarks about poetry and *reality*, he uses "poetry" to refer to what we today call "fictional"—that which is constructed by the creative imagination; that which belongs to, occurs in, or is a feature of a work of fiction. Therefore, I take it to be legitimate to regard those remarks as concerning a confusion in the way we think about the distinction between what we today would call, not "reality" and "poetry," but "reality" and "fiction." Accordingly, when I speak of this confusion in sections 1 and 3, I will interchangeably speak about it as a confusion about "reality," and "poetry" and as a confusion about "reality" and "fiction."
7. In an earlier paper, I argued that Schlegel's romantic imperative, the demand to treat ordinary life and philosophy as if they were art, is *not* the result of any alleged form of poetic enthusiasm. Schlegel urges us to live and pursue philosophy aesthetically, in a manner that is isomorphic to the way we appreciate and pursue the arts, because he believes that this is the only way we could properly respond to another form of confusion that troubled him: the form of skepticism he found in Jacobi's nihilism. See Keren Gorodeisky, "(Re)encountering Individuality: Schlegel's Romantic Imperative as a Response to Nihilism," *Inquiry* 54, no. 6 (2011): 567–90.
8. Immanuel Kant, *Critique of Pure Reason*, A297/B353.
9. Ludwig Wittgenstein, *Culture and Value*, ed. G. H. von Wright in collaboration with Heikki Nyman, trans. Peter Winch (Chicago: University of Chicago Press, 1980). Hereafter *CV*.
10. *Critical Fragments*, KA 2, 161, no. 115. Hereafter, *CF*.
11. Ludwig Wittgenstein, *Philosophical Investigations*, 2nd ed., trans. G. E. M. Anscombe (Oxford: Blackwell, 1997), §126. Hereafter *PI*.

12. *Athenaeum Fragments*, KA 2, 177, no. 82.

13. This symbol stands for Wittgenstein's differently numbered remarks.

14. *PI*, §127 and §129 respectively.

15. *On Incomprehensibility*, KA 2, 366.

16. *PI*, §§126–28.

17. *Athenaeum Fragments*, KA 2, 207–8, no. 252. Compare also Wittgenstein, *PI* §132 with *Athenaeum Fragments* KA 2, 177, no. 82, and the introduction to *Dialogue on Poetry; CV*, 36 and *Athenaeum Fragments*, KA 2, 208–9, no. 255.

18. Stanley Cavell, "The *Investigations*' Everyday Aesthetics of Itself," in *The Literary Wittgenstein*, ed. John Gibson and Wolfgang Huemer (London: Routledge, 2004), 31.

19. Fredrick Beiser, for instance, points to the commitments to antifoundationalism, historicity, and hermeneutics, as shared by the German romantics and Wittgenstein. See *The Romantic Imperative: The Concept of Early German Romanticism* (Cambridge, MA: Harvard University Press, 2003), 3.

20. Richard Eldridge's work is a valuable exception to this rule. In his different writings, Eldridge pursues and develops the romantic legacy in Wittgenstein's thought. However, Eldridge focuses on Hölderlin and Wordsworth. See mainly, *Leading a Human Life: Wittgenstein, Intentionality, and Romanticism* (Chicago: University of Chicago Press, 1997), and *The Persistence of Romanticism: Essays in Philosophy and Literature* (Cambridge: Cambridge University Press, 2001). See also his contribution to this volume, chapter 7.

21. By no means do I want to claim that Schlegel was motivated by the *same* kind of considerations that motivated the late Wittgenstein, or that they understood traditional philosophy in exactly the same way. Nor do I claim that Schlegel anticipated Wittgenstein. I argue only that reading Schlegel with Wittgenstein in mind, as approaching certain philosophical tendencies in a similar spirit, can help to explain much that is obscure in Schlegel's writings.

22. Stanley Cavell, *Must We Mean What We Say?* (Cambridge: Cambridge University Press, 1969).

23. Again, by no means do I argue that Schlegel's and Wittgenstein's approaches are similar in every respect. There are obviously important differences between their projects. However, due to a lack of space, I will not discuss either the differences or their implications in this paper.

24. G. E. Moore, *Philosophical Papers* (London: Allen and Unwin; New York: Macmillan, 1959), 315.

25. E.g., "The critics are always talking about *rules*, but where are the rules that are really poetic and applicable for all works of art and not merely grammatical, metrical, logical?" (Schlegel, *Fragments on Literature and Poetry*, KA 16, 108, no. 286).

26. Cf. The aim of interpreting a rule and of understanding the meaning of a word is, according to Wittgenstein, "not an agreement in opinions but in form of life" (*PI*, §241).

27. Cf. Stanley Cavell, "Austin at Criticism," in *Must We Mean What We Say*, 104.

28. *CF*, KA 2, 163, no. 123.

29. *CF*, KA 2, 149, no. 21.

30. *CF*, KA 2, 162, no. 119.

31. Schlegel speaks here about a comparison of works that could "reconstruct [a work's] course and its structure [as well as] its inner history" ("The Essence of Criticism," in *Lessing's Thoughts and Opinions*, KA 3, 60).

32. *PI*, §133.

33. *PI*, §130.

34. On that, see James Conant, "Stanley Cavell's Wittgenstein," *Harvard Review of Philosophy* 13, no. 1 (2005), 51-65.

35. Often, the context of an utterance can be determined only by understanding the meaning of the words uttered. See Timothy Gould, *Hearing Things: Voice and Method in the Writing of Stanley Cavell* (Chicago: University of Chicago Press, 1998).

36. Cavell, *Claim of Reason: Wittgenstein, Skepticism, Morality, and Tragedy* (Oxford: Oxford University Press, 1979), 221.

37. Ibid. See mainly in the *Claim of Reason*, Part I, chap. 8, 191–243.

38. Here I follow Cavell's revealing diagnosis in "The Availability of Wittgenstein's Later Philosophy," in *Must We Mean What We Say?* 60–61.

39. It is part, you may also say, of her confusion about the way language works.

40. This is equally true of the success of her traditional opponent, the antiskeptic, or as Cavell calls him following Kant, the dogmatist. See, Cavell, *Claim of Reason*, 46, and Kant, *Critique of Pure Reason,* A viii.

41. "Our investigation is therefore a grammatical one. Such an investigation sheds light on our problem by clearing misunderstanding away. Misunderstandings concerning the use of words" (*PI*, §90); "A main source of our failure to understand is that we do not command *a clear view* of the use of our words" (*PI*, §122).

42. *PI*, §132.

43. "[Philosophical problems] are solved, rather, by looking into the workings of our language…in such a way as to make us recognize those workings; *in despite of* an urge to misunderstand them….Philosophy is a battle against the bewitchment of our intelligence by means of our language" (*PI*, §109).

44. *PI*, §129.

45. Another way (or perhaps the same way, or at least a way that is structurally akin to the first) is to read literature, fiction, to engage with the practice that has long been associated with the capacity to defamiliarize the familiar.

46. *PI*, §133

47. What I am trying to suggest here, following Cavell, is that Wittgenstein's later philosophy is animated by the threat of skepticism (and related confusions). Nevertheless, his late work cannot be taken as a direct response to the skeptic—a response that elicits the kind of criteria that are supposed to establish the existence of objects, or the knowledge of other minds with certainty. Rather, Wittgenstein's appeal to the ordinary is meant as an invitation, a summons, addressed to the interlocutor, to share with him the ordinary world we all inhabit.

48. See mainly, *Concerning the Theory of Scientific Knowledge*, KA 16, 3–14, nos. 1–125; *The Spirit of the Science of Knowledge* (1797–98), KA 13, 31–39, nos. 126–227; and Beilage I and Beilage II, KA 18, 505–16, 517–21. For detailed discussions of Schlegel's criticism of absolute foundations, see Manfred Frank, *Unendliche Annäherung. Die Anfänge der philosophischen Frühromantik* (Frankfurt am Main: Suhrkamp, 1997), Beiser, *The Romantic Imperative*, and Beiser, *German Idealism: The Struggle against Subjectivism, 1781-1801* (Cambridge, MA: Harvard University Press, 2002).

49. *PI* §1. In addition to questioning the role of general rules and principles in art criticism, Schlegel writes, "Principles are to life what instructions written by the cabinet are for the general in battle" (*Athenaeum Fragments*, KA 2, 178, no. 85). And he famously claims, in a fragment that echoes one of Wittgenstein later remarks, "it is equally fatal for the mind to have a system and not to have one. It must therefore have to decide to unite the two" (*Athenaeum Fragments*, KA 2, 173, no. 53). Cf. "Above all, someone attempting the description lacks any system. The systems that occur to him are inadequate, and he seems suddenly to himself in a wilderness instead of the well laid out garden that he knew so well" (Wittgenstein, *Remarks on the Philosophy of Psychology*, ed. G. E. M. Anscombe and G. H. von Wright [Oxford: Blackwell, 1980], vol. 1, §557).

50. *On Incomprehensibility*, KA 2, 364.

51. *Athenaeum Fragments*, KA 2, 175, no. 74.

52. *On Incomprehensibility*, KA 2, 364 [my italics].

53. *Philosophical Fragments*, KA 18, 3, no. 4.

54. *Philosophical Fragments*, KA 18, 4, no. 6. Cf. "The self-destruction of the three logical maladies must be seen in relation to their self-creation" (KA 18, 4, no. 7).

55. *Philosophical Fragments*, KA 18, 5, no. 13.

56. *Philosophical Fragments*, KA 18, 5, no. 15. Notice too that Schlegel, like Cavell, does not regard skepticism as opposed to dogmatism. Skepticism and dogmatism are two sides of the same coin—two philosophical moods that are grounded in the same confused picture: "As opposed to criticism, the three positions may be called *dogmatism*" (KA 18, 5, no. 10; cf. no. 83. Cf. Cavell, *Claim of Reason*, 46).

57. Azade Seyhan, "What Is Romanticism, and Where Did It Come From?" in *Cambridge Companion to German Romanticism* ed. Nicholas Saul (Cambridge: Cambridge University Press, 2009), 17.

58. E.g., *Blüthenstaub*, KA 2, 164, no. 3, *Concerning the Theory of Scientific Knowledge*, KA, 18, 3–14 nos. 1–125; *The Spirit of the Science of Knowledge* (1797–98), KA 13, 31–39, nos. 126–227; and Beilage I and Beilage II, KA 18, 505–16, 517–21. Schlegel argues that experience in general must be constrained by some "limit" in *Concerning the Theory of Scientific Knowledge*.

59. *Athenaeum Fragments*, KA 2, 166, no. 3.

60. "The present dialogue...is intended to set against one another quite divergent opinions, each of them capable of shedding new light upon the infinite spirit of poetry from an individual standpoint, each of them striving to penetrate from a different angle into the real heart of the matter. It was my interest in this many-sidedness that made me resolve to communicate publicly things that I had observed in a circle of friends" (*Dialogue on Poetry*, KA 2, 286).

61. *Blüthenstaub*, KA 2, 164, no. 2.

62. Cavell, *Claim of Reason*, 47.

63. Cavell, "Availability of Wittgenstein's Later Philosophy," in *Must We Mean What We Say?* 71.

64. Eg., *CF*, KA 2, 162, no. 121, and 163, no. 123.

65. *CF*, KA 2, 161, no. 112.

66. *Athenaeum Fragments*, KA 2, 167, no. 15.

67. *Athenaeum Fragments*, KA 2, 176, no. 79.

68. *Athenaeum Fragments*, KA 2, 207, no. 252.

69. *Blüthenstaub*, KA 2, 164, no. 1.

70. *CF*, KA 2, 150, no. 34, and *A* KA 2, 171, no. 37.

71. *Athenaeum Fragments*, KA 2, 179, no. 96.

72. Cf. "It was wit, not logic, that was the 'highest principle of knowledge,' and the 'principle scientific inventiveness', since Schlegel took it to be a mode through which flashes of insight are communicated" (Hans Eichner, *Friedrich Schlegel* [New York: Twayne Publishers, 1970]), p. 47.

73. *Ideas*, KA 2, 9, no. 9.

74. What I mean to stress is that Wittgenstein's grammatical method and Schlegel's "witty" approach are *not* gauged by means of what we *actually* say and do. When the so-called ordinary language philosopher says, "We say XXX," he does not invite his skeptical interlocutor to test this claim in light of what we *actually, empirically* say, so that if one of us says something different, the claim is invalid, or lacking in force. Neither the methods of the late Wittgenstein, nor Schlegel's methods are *empiricist*, as Cavell emphasizes, above all at the end of "Aesthetic Problems," and as Schlegel stresses in his criticism of empiricism in *Philosophical Fragments*. They are tested instead by their capacity to bring about agreement.

75. *Philosophical Fragments*, KA 18, 9, no. 54.

76. *CF*, KA 2, 158, no. 98.

77. Even though I read those remarks in a Wittgensteinian spirit, I will not introduce Wittgenstein's own treatment of the distinction between fiction and reality, nor compare it with Schlegel's. For an instructive treatment of Wittgenstein on this topic, see David Schalkwyk, "Fiction as 'Grammatical' Investigation: A Wittgensteinian Account," *Journal of Aesthetics and Art Criticism* 53, no. 3 (1995): 287–98; and his *Literature and the Touch of the Real* (Newark: University of Delaware Press, 2004).

78. See note 6 for the justification for my use of "poetry" and "fiction" interchangeably in this section.

79. I borrow this expression from Thompson Clarke's magisterial treatment of skepticism in his "The Legacy of Skepticism," *Journal of Philosophy* 69, no. 20 (1972): 754–69, esp. 768.

80. *Blüthenstaub*, KA 2, 164, no. 2.

81. This picture of the relation between fiction and reality might also be motivated by some kind of fear—we might worry that everything we know to be real will turn out to be "unreal" in some way, if reality is not absolutely distinguished from what is "merely fictional," an invented "figment of the imagination." We seem to worry that if the real and the fictional are not irrevocably distinguished and separated as two independent and self-sufficient realms, we might not be real to ourselves, we might not *be*.

82. For this distinction of Schlegel's career into different periods, see, for example, Arthur Lovejoy, "Schiller and the Genesis of German Romanticism," in *Essays in the History of Ideas* (New York: Putnam, 1963): 207–27; Eichner, *Friedrich Schlegel*; Dieter Henrich, *Konstellationen: Probleme und Debatten am Ursprung der idealistischen Philosophie (1789–1795)* (Stuttgart: Klett-Cotta, 1991); Frank, *Unendliche Annäherung*; and Beiser, "Friedrich Schlegel: The Mysterious Romantic," in *The Romantic Imperative*.

83. *On the Study of Greek Poetry*, KA 1, 266–67.

84. *Athenaeum Fragments*, KA 2, 182, no. 116.

85. *Athenaeum Fragments*, KA 2, 173, no. 55.

86. E.g., "Pity, worry about, hate, and envy are such that one cannot have them without believing that their objects exist, just as one cannot fear something without believing that it threatens them" (Kendall Walton, "Fearing Fictions," *Journal of Philosophy* 75 [1978]: 21 n. 15).

87. Walton's other two relevant texts on the topic are *Mimesis as Make-Believe: On the Foundations of the Representational Arts* (Cambridge, MA: Harvard University Press, 1990), and "Spelunking, Simulation, and Slime: On Being Moved by Fiction," in *Emotion and the Arts*, ed. Mette Hjort and Sue Laver (New York: Oxford University Press, 1997), 37–49. For other philosophers, who, like Walton, adopt what is known in the literature as the "Pretense Theory" (the theory that holds that we have "quasi-emotional" responses to fiction), see, for example, Susan Feagin, "Imagining Emotions and Appreciating Fiction," in *Emotion and the Arts*, ed. Mette Hjort and Save Laver (New York: Oxford University Press, 1997), 50–62, and Gregory Currie, *The Nature of Fiction* (Cambridge: Cambridge University Press, 1990). Richard Moran has articulated one of the best criticisms of this line of thought to date in his "The Expression of Feeling in Imagination," *Philosophical Review* 103, no. 1 (1994): 75–106.

88. Walton does not deny that we *do* feel something for fictional characters. But he denies that what we feel is of the same kind as "real" emotions—what we feel for real people (for example, *Mimesis as Make-Believe*, 247, and "Spelunking, Simulation, and Slime," 38).

89. The plight of this line of thought is analogous to the plight of the skeptic as I discussed it above. In order for their argument to get off the ground, the philosophers I just described must use the terms "fictional" and "real" both in the way we ordinarily use them, and in a special, "unordinary" way. For example, if Walton's argument is to work, if it is to conflict with what we ordinarily think and say about whatever we feel when we read a novel, or watch a film—as Walton suggests that it does—Walton must use the term "real" as we ordinarily use it. Otherwise, there would not be any conflict between what Walton claims to discover about our emotions, and the way most of us think and speak about our emotions. However, in order to establish the claim that *no one ever* feels "real" feelings for fictions, as Walton holds, he must also use the term "real" in a special, nonordinary way. For Walton holds that what is "real" is determined once and for all, as if "by language itself," independently of what *we* mean by the term when we use language, and that what he has discovered holds for *every* and *any* feeling we might have for fiction. *None* of those feelings, on Walton's view, *can* be real. This use of the terms departs from our ordinary use of it. And so, in order for the argument to work, Walton has to use those terms in two conflicting ways.

90. *Athenaeum Fragments*, KA 2, 173, no. 55.

91. For Cavell's instructive discussion of this distinction, and his claim that there are no criteria for distinguishing the real from the unreal, see *The Claim of Reason*, 49–64.

92. *Athenaeum Fragments*, KA 2, 183, no. 117.

93. *Dialogue on Poetry*, KA 2, 288–89.

94. *Dialogue on Poetry*, KA 2, 291.

95. Again, by "fictional" I do not mean "fictitious," or "unreal," but that which belongs to, occurs in, or is a feature of a work of fiction.

96. *Dialogue on Poetry*, KA 2, 312.

97. Ibid., 315. In the same work, Schlegel also suggests that confessions—the expression of a subject—can be more "realistic" than the novels, for example, of Richardson, which are standardly considered to be quintessentially realistic because of their attention to, and description of details of everyday experience (KA 2, 337–38).

98. Cavell, *Claim of Reason*, 185.

99. This animation might rest on the work of the imagination, as a (cognitive) capacity that reveals reality, not simply fantasy. More would have to say about this capacity in an elaboration on this paper.

100. Schlegel, *Dialogue on Poetry*, KA 2, 287.

101. *Dialogue on Poetry*, KA 2, 312.

102. *Athenaeum Fragments*, KA 2, 178, no. 87.

103. Compare with the different though related idea that Moran uses to challenge Walton's view: "It is unlikely that the various responses we classify with the emotions form anything like a natural-kind.... For this reason it is unlikely that there could even in principle be a *general* problem of fictional emotions" ("Expression of Feeling in Imagination," 81).

104. This is the full fragment: "No poetry, no reality. Just as there is, despite all the senses, no external world without imagination, so too there is no spiritual world without feeling, no matter how much sense there is. Whoever only has sense can perceive no human being, but only what is human: all things disclose themselves to the magic wand of feeling alone. It fixes people and seizes them; like the eye, it looks on without being conscious of its own mathematical operation."

105. *Athenaeum Fragments*, KA 2, 24, no. 414.

106. *PI*, §116. On that, compare also Schlegel, *On Incomprehensibility*, KA 2, 366; compare with *PI*, §89.

107. J. L. Austin, "A Plea for Excuses," in *Philosophical Papers*, ed. J. O. Urmson and G. J. Warnock (Oxford: Oxford University Press, 1979), 182–83.

108. Andrew Bowie, *Aesthetics and Subjectivity from Kant to Hegel* (Manchester: Manchester University Press, 2003), 53.

The Simplicity of the Sublime

A New Picturing of Nature in Caspar David Friedrich

LAURE CAHEN-MAUREL

> I take my inheritance to be Caspar David Friedrich—you know, that kind of Romantic tradition of the sublime and deep space that is a moment of wonder.
>
> —ANISH KAPOOR[1]

10.1. INTRODUCTION

It has been almost forty years since the art historian Robert Rosenblum in his book *Modern Painting and the Northern Romantic Tradition: Friedrich to Rothko* traced the origin of abstract expressionism in post–World War II America to the vast and barren seascape of Caspar David Friedrich's *Monk by the Sea* (1810).[2] Indeed, according to Rosenblum, it is simply a matter of removing the figure of the monk from Friedrich's painting to arrive at the colored rectangles of Rothko's *Green on Blue* (1956), which hover above one another on a monochrome background.[3] Thus, Friedrich's treatment of pictorial space may be seen as an early formulation of what the artist Barnett Newman would later consider to be the newfound dominance of the United States over Europe in art, and which subsequently became known as the "American sublime." More recently, in the early twenty-first century, and with a keen awareness of history, the British sculptor Anish Kapoor has attempted to restore a metaphysical function to art with his explorations of space at the intersection of painting, sculpture, and architecture. As we shall see, Kapoor directly situates his work in the artistic tradition of Caspar David Friedrich, reimagining the latter's *Sea of Ice* (1824) in a monumental installation entitled *Svayambh* (2007). In short, from the formal standpoint of art history and artistic creation there is not only a sublime grandeur but something progressive and even visionary about this landscape painting that makes Friedrich one of the most celebrated and studied artists of romantic art today.

From the more philosophical point of view of the content, many commentators think that the romantic sublime is above all embodied in Friedrich's painting *Wanderer above the Sea of Fog* (1818). Here a solitary figure, painted with his back to us, stands on a rocky elevation, contemplating a grandiose high mountain landscape extending into the distance. Yet it might be objected that the wanderer's somewhat artificial and theatrical pose should be labeled more "kitsch" than sublime, and served an overtly political agenda. Accordingly, instead of conveying a visionary sublimity Friedrich's art would then partake in the regressive idea of landscape painting as an expression of the "German soul," which pertains to a darker form of patriotic and nationalistic kitsch. Furthermore, the philosophical analysis of his paintings still has not been able to provide a convincing answer to the question whether one can conceptually apply the Kantian distinction between the beautiful and the sublime to Friedrich's landscapes, as well as reconciling the experience of the sublime with the religious vocation of his art. In this regard a number of commentators of Friedrich maintain that the category of the sublime has no relevance at all for his Weltanschauung.[4]

The purpose of this paper is threefold. It proposes to answer this latter theoretical question by reconstructing the painter's own views on the sublime as found in his principal text. Next, it intends to explore the figurative means that enabled Friedrich to produce the sublime in his paintings. After this attempt at a conceptual and pictorial understanding, conclusions will then be drawn regarding the relevance of Friedrich's artistic practice for contemporary art. I argue that the sublime has a special and critical role for Friedrich, that it cannot be equated with Kant's concept of the sublime, and that its originality is best understood in conjunction with Novalis's definition of "romanticizing."

10.2. A CONTROVERSIAL QUESTION

German romanticism is traditionally considered as providing an "artistic" continuation of the problem of the sublime that had been philosophically elaborated by Kant with regard to the aesthetic experience of nature. Even more than the ugly, and far from simply being its superlative, the sublime according to Kant is conceptually opposed to the beautiful; and strictly speaking it is not objectively in nature itself. As analyzed in the *Critique of the Power of Judgment* (1790), the sublime brings to light a limit that is both "mathematical" and "dynamic," that is, theoretical and practical, concerning the capacity of the human being to directly access whatever surpasses the sensible world. More specifically, the Kantian sublime is the designation for that experience of attaining a limit when the imagination as a power of intuitive presentation is confronted with the supersensible or metaphysical—the realm par excellence of reason and the unlimited. Thus, in the aesthetic experience of nature, nature as the idea of the absolute whole surpasses the limits of our degree of comprehension in one intuition, and this surpassing of the idea of the world with respect to the power of representation causes us initially some distress, a feeling of displeasure on account of the inhibition of our vital forces. This conflicting relationship between reason and imagination is what radically separates (in essence and not in degree) the sublime and the beautiful. For the latter is only the source of a feeling of pleasure due to a harmonious accord between the imagination and the understanding when contemplating the sensible forms of nature. If Kant considers the feeling of the sublime negatively from the point of view of sensibility, then its specific positivity (that would make it the dominant category of philosophical aesthetics up until Hegel) is to be found in the fact that the emotion of the sublime enlarges our manner of thinking from sensibility to the ideas of reason. It opens up (aesthetically, i.e., subjectively) the human mind to a consciousness of itself and accustoms us to think our rational nature and moral determination. We perhaps find ourselves thinking the latter even more in the "dynamic sublime," which is defined by Kant as the experience of our physical finitude when faced with the fury of nature as pure force.

Even though the romantic sublime is not a new subject for research, the debate over the sublime in the philosophical reception of Caspar David Friedrich is still far from settled. The controversy about the applicability of the concept of the sublime to his paintings cannot be ignored, since it raises a substantial question of principle. Three main interpretative tendencies may be singled out.

1. First, it is the notion of *infinity* that seems fundamental to many
   commentators: Friedrich's art of painting visually gives the
   spectator the impression of this "absolutely large" that constitutes
   the "mathematical sublime" in Kant and highlights by contrast the
   smallness of all aesthetic comprehension and (in a more "dynamic"
   regard) our own existential smallness.[5] An often-cited example here
   is the *Monk by the Sea*, in which the sky occupies three-quarters of
   the composition and where the absence of elements framing the

perspective gives in addition the impression of a lateral infinite extension such as that found in a panoramic view. Moreover, the figure of the monk himself is much smaller and virtually vanishes in this space compared to the relatively imposing figure of the wanderer in the foreground of the *Wanderer above the Sea of Fog*. Along with this infinity of space Friedrich's paintings exhibit emptiness, that is the surpassing of the form, the *formlessness* of the absolutely large, as opposed to formal perfection in the case of the beautiful. According to these commentators, over and beyond the disappearance of all representation the art of Friedrich also shows the *inadequacy* of all representation, for it has the formal peculiarity of creating some kind of perceptual inconsistency within the representation itself.[6] This internal distortion underlines the limits of the imagination in its attempt to reabsorb the world into an image, and thus is supposed to illustrate the Kantian thesis that the absolute whole as an idea of reason is unpresentable in intuition.

2. To respond to these arguments, a second camp of interpreters points out that one can only speak of the sublime in the Kantian sense provided that there is a reference to *morality*.[7] A feeling or an intuition that implies the idea of the infinite is not in itself sublime. There has to be the thought of my own rationality that overcomes my natural determination. But this rational attitude in the horizon of a social and political community tends to disappear as soon as we enter the religious world of Friedrich's art. For the second camp, the sublime therefore disappears from Friedrich's paintings to become the beautiful. In philosophical terms this is not the Kantian concept of the beautiful but the Platonic or Neoplatonic idea of beauty, that is, a mathematical or geometrical beauty in which the sensible forms take part in the ideality of the pure forms transcending being.

3. Besides this antinomy between the Kantian sublime and Platonic or Neoplatonic beauty dominating the literature, certain specialists of philosophical romanticism have attempted to follow a third interpretative path. Briefly put, this view employs the concept of chaos in the sense of Friedrich Schlegel and Schelling to propose an immanently romantic reading of the sublime in Caspar David Friedrich.[8]

Manfred Frank's work on German romantic philosophy does not specifically address the question of the sublime. Recently, however, Frank published a text on Caspar David Friedrich entitled " 'Religionslose Kathedralen im ewigen Winter'—Der Moderne Caspar David Friedrich im frühromantischen

Kontext."[9] Although he does not explicitly examine the artist's conception of the sublime, Frank outlines a continuity between Friedrich's *Sea of Ice* and the series of vast empty evening skies among his paintings and the skepticism of the early German romantics. Accordingly, Frank argues that Friedrich's works convey a loss of the sacred and ultimately underscore the failure of the *Frühromantik* project of a new mythology. If we extend this thesis to the more specific question of the sublime, Frank's interpretation of Friedrich's intentions as skeptical with regard to the reconciliation of art and religion in real history renders the sublime in Friedrich nothing more than the Kantian *negative Darstellung*, that is, the presentation *ex negativo* of the absolute in its transcendence—in an abstract empty sky. Here the presentation of the metaphysical always starts from the infinite gap between the finite and the infinite. In the same vein, and using the language of J.-F. Lyotard, one could say that not only is there disenchantment and loss of belief in Friedrich, but also *nostalgia* or *melancholy*, which bears the weight of the sublime insofar as the artist takes a certain pleasure in the loss and in the absence.[10]

I believe that Manfred Frank is correct in stressing the modernity of Friedrich's art, and his thesis stands in sharp contrast to Reinhard Brandt's interpretation of it in terms of a Neoplatonic anagogy (the extraction of our souls as spectators from this world and their guidance into the next).[11] But the debate will not be able to be settled unless one broadens the discussion beyond the confines of a strictly Kantian reading to consider other interpretative possibilities. Moreover, all the above interpretations either fail to take into account the actual writings and views of Caspar David Friedrich, or if they do take them into account, they do not really take them seriously. In contrast, I maintain that a careful examination of Friedrich's texts can be especially fruitful for the question of the sublime, for the simple reason that they articulate its status and significance for the romantic painter himself.

10.3. THE DIVINE, NATURAL, AND ARTISTIC SUBLIME

In this section I will principally appeal to Friedrich's main manuscript: *Äußerungen bei Betrachtung einer Sammlung von Gemählden von größtentheils noch lebenden und unlängst verstorbenen Künstlern* [Considerations while contemplating a collection of paintings by artists who are for most part still living or recently deceased].[12] The work is similar to an art salon review insofar as it is a critical report on an exhibition of contemporary artists from the Dresden *Kunstverein* (the Dresden art association). Friedrich wrote the *Considerations* around 1830, but it was only published in its entirety posthumously, with minor selections from it already appearing one year after his death

in 1840. In it Friedrich revealed his own views on the art of the younger generation of German painters. This was the period of the Nazarenes—a group of
artists gathered in Rome—who sought their inspiration in early Renaissance
styles and religious subject matters. It was also the time when the colorists of
the Düsseldorf school of landscape painting were just starting to emerge, who
painted nature or reality devoid of all idealization. Friedrich's *Considerations* is
a collection of fragments of one hundred pages in length; if one wanted to draw
parallels, its form is similar to Caroline and August Wilhelm Schlegel's dialogue
from 1799 *Die Gemählde* [The Paintings], which describes and comments on
a number of paintings at the Dresden Art Gallery, or the 1810 *Empfindungen*
[Sensations] of Clemens Brentano and Achim von Arnim, a text that imagines
the impressions of different spectators passing before Friedrich's own *Monk by
the Sea*.

Although the *Considerations* does not provide a systematic exposition of the
sublime—the artist was not a theorist—we nevertheless find a brief but key discussion of its specific character. It is found in a passage where Friedrich seeks
to partly discredit art critics who demand that true artists should choose "significant" topics. In the context of this reflection, Friedrich asks of a particular
artist: "Surely he does not lack a feeling for the sublime in nature?"[13] This question is followed by a definition of what is called the sublime (*das Erhabene*),
and where Friedrich states that the traditionally preferred examples of the sublime—on which the Kantian interpretation especially draws—are not the only
possible examples:

> Because surely we mean [by "sublime"] that the choice of the subject mat-
> ter has the ability to more deeply and intimately seize (*ergreifen*) and capti-
> vate (*fesseln*) the spectator. Of course, everything in nature is significant and
> grand, beautiful and noble, but some of it is more significant, appropriate,
> and evocative for presenting in a picture than others. For depicting the most
> beautiful and the highest and what seizes us the most would obviously be the
> task of the true artist. And I do not necessarily mean here towering moun-
> tains or endless abysses.[14]

First, far from conveying the notorious philosophical aesthetics of the sublime as opposed to the beautiful in the tradition of Burke and Kant, the term
"sublime" in this passage amounts to an appreciative hyperbole, that is, to a
superlative of the beautiful. It is also clear from this passage that Friedrich
understands the artistic sublime in terms of its aesthetic (pathetic or emotive)
impact: the artistic sublime is what produces the most powerful effect. One
could call this an extremely banal and limited notion of the sublime, for to
produce an effect is of course the goal of all art. However, as we shall see, it is

precisely this accentuation of the effect that constitutes a true aesthetics here, and *not just* a hyperbolic appreciation. In the academic neoclassical tradition, represented notably by Goethe, the highest aesthetic scope or impact of a work of art depends on the intrinsic dignity of its subject matter. Natural objects do not contain any idea or ideal. Ordinary everyday objects are generally only viewed according to their physical or visual aspect, and occasionally perhaps as objects capable of stimulating an emotion in us, but one that is itself ordinary. In order to become a significant element and to develop the greatest possible aesthetic range (or the highest affective power), the object of an artistic representation must be an ideal object that the artist cannot merely find given in experience.[15]

For Friedrich, in contrast, *all* reality is significant a priori. In his writings the term "significant" (*bedeutsam*) should indeed be taken literally, that is, in its primary meaning as signification (*Bedeutung*): it designates something that is "a sign for something else," something that refers to another thing that is exterior to itself; in other words, something transcending it. Thus, a thing becomes a sign by having a *relation* to another thing. In metaphysical painting, a concrete and ordinary object of the sensible world may become significant, evocative, or important as soon as it is understood or put into relation with something abstract, invisible, and immaterial—in short, with something *spiritual*. This is the core of Friedrich's religious conception of the world: the incarnation, the word made flesh, or the New Testament as the epoch of sensible mediation. It should not be forgotten that the romantic painter was brought up in the pietistic faith and imagination; he believed in the Incarnation of God in the body of the Son and in the sacrament of the Eucharist. It is precisely this union of the divine logos and sensible flesh in the incarnation that the *Tetschen Altarpiece* (1808) celebrates, a landmark painting considered to be a manifesto of his pictorial conception.

Therefore, in Friedrich's view of landscape painting—as the artistic representation of nature as divine creation—it does not matter if the represented object is an "elevated" or "trivial" object. This hierarchy does not hold anymore. What is critical, however, concerns the human relationship to divine creation in the sense where the human being is no longer in a direct relation to the latter and has moved away from the original fullness of its meaning. In Friedrich's eyes this is where art comes into play, for art is entrusted with the possibility of retrieving the original meaning by furnishing the necessary mediation between man and that transcendent object surpassing man: the natural sublime—the natural world as an infinite cosmic order (e.g., the sky, the sea, and the shore, which in the *Monk by the Sea* cannot be contemplated as totalities)—or, what amounts to the same thing, the divine sublime, because the world is viewed from the perspective of divine creation.

"Art serves as a mediator between nature and man. The archetype (*Urbild*) is too large and too sublime to be grasped by the masses. Its reflection (*Abbild*)—the work of man—is much more accessible to the weak."[16]

Consequently, the artistic sublime is a means for this stated goal of art. Its concrete description in the earlier passage indicates that the artistic sublime is the concept that most directly deals with the *interiority* of the subject. It is not a question of any kind of pathos or sentimentality but of the spiritual strength of the affect that is able to move the soul powerfully, "deeply," and "intimately." That is to say, the artistic sublime pertains to art's active virtue of strengthening the relation between the created and the Creator by means of a more direct feeling, experienced in the interiority as the meeting point of two worlds, the corporal and the spiritual, the sensible and the intelligible. In other words, in the strict sense Friedrich conceives the artistic sublime as the religious *efficacy* of art.

10.4. SCALE, OPACITY, TRANSPARENCY: THE SUBLIME IN CASPAR DAVID FRIEDRICH'S PAINTINGS

Let us now look at the figurative treatment of this rather uncomplicated notion of the sublime. So far we have seen that sublime grandeur is not related to the status of the subjects but to the intensity of effect attached to the subject, and that the intense effect of the painting does not merely rely upon visually impressive hyperbolic grandeur. Indeed, the point that Caspar David Friedrich most emphasizes is the figurative *simplicity* of the sublime: "And I do not necessarily mean here towering mountains or endless abysses"; and a little later in the same text: "This does not imply at all that it must necessarily be some kind of special region, e.g., a large Swiss mountain or the boundless sea; but a simple wheat field would suffice, or even a simpler object, but one that is still dignified."[17] Hence, in painting his metaphysical landscapes Friedrich accepts the risk of appearing rudimentary. Trees, rocks, deserted seashores, a "simple wheat field," "or even a simpler object," such as the sandbanks of the Elbe riverbed northwest of Dresden under evening skies as illustrated in the *Large Enclosure* (1832)—all of these are signifiers available to the artist for a new picturing of nature, and he is humble enough to be content with them.

However, what exactly determines the greater or lesser strength of these paintings? The purely quantitative and geometrical components of the image (that is to say, the spatial structures of size, scale, and plans) cannot be the sole vehicle of the sublime. If the sublime is understood as what pathetically reinforces the significant beauty of nature and makes us become aware of it, then the figuration or image requires an additional qualitative element. This is its

perceptual dimension that is related to both visibility and time. In order to create an ever deeper intensity of feeling in the intimate sphere of the subject (its
interiority) and not solely at the physical level of sensation, Friedrich employs
two main devices (among others): a sublime of scale where scale is not merely
a quantitative estimation of magnitude; and a sublime that plays on the double
modality of visibility—either transparency or opacity. For it should be noted
that the topic of vision is twofold in Friedrich: it is outer and inner vision.

First, and although it is initially a quantitative component, it is clear that scale
is crucial for landscape painting, for it has to re-establish the original distance
between things, the proportion between the infinite and the finite, the large and
the small, the divine and the human. But true grandeur, in Friedrich's eyes, is not
modeled on the character of bodies that can be quantitatively measured. Nor is it a
question of perspectival order, that is, of a physical-optical translation of the world
onto the canvas. True grandeur resides rather in a certain emotional upswing
or uplift of a mind that is troubled by perceptual confinement and hence seeks
to enlarge its horizon. Far from consigning landscape painting to the reproduction of a given space, Friedrich defines it as the *creation of space* in a work. In his
Considerations the romantic painter criticizes contemporary naturalistic landscape
painting precisely because of its tendency to compress space onto the canvas. This
manner of painting fails to grasp the cosmic scale of the world (its infinite space),
with the result that one of the greatest examples of the sublime—the unlimited and
unbounded sea—becomes distorted and turned into its opposite:

> What modern landscape painters have seen in an arc of 100 degrees in
> nature, they pitilessly compress together into an angle of 45 degrees. Hence,
> what was separated in nature in large spatial intervals becomes presented
> here in compact spaces; the eye is overcrowded and oversaturated, and it
> makes an adverse and alarming impression on the spectator. And it is always
> the element of water that loses out—the sea becomes a puddle.[18]

In contrast, the successful artist gives us the impression of unlimited space
within the limited surface of the canvas:

> This painting is large; and yet we wish it were larger still. For the sublimity
> in the conception of the subject matter has been experienced in all its great-
> ness and requires an even larger extension in space. Therefore, it is always
> praiseworthy for a painting to say we wish it were even larger.[19]

Thus, Friedrich's use of the sublime of scale as creation of space on the canvas breaks with the oversaturation of the gaze caused by naturalistic landscapes. It seeks to *liberate both space and the gaze* of the spectator to allow her

to *experience the distance* between things. This explains the dilation and the emptiness in many of Friedrich's landscapes, which were rarely painted in large formats.

The second method is more concerned with the two modalities of visibility: transparency and opacity. A number of the romantic artist's paintings admit us into the presence of an inner, spiritual, and dreamlike vision—one could say, into the transparency of the sublime. We immediately enter into the fictive space of the image, for it creates an effect of direct confrontation with nature by suspending the illusion of distance found in classical forms of representation due to an unobstructed foreground. Nevertheless, opacity still remains the general rule of the sublime, and this is necessary for it to play the full role assigned to it, that is, to capture our attention and penetrate ever deeper into the living sphere of our interiority. There are numerous modalities of this opacity for outer physical sight in Friedrich's paintings. But the most sublime of all these deployments of opacity is the veiling principle of mist or fog. Let us quote again the words of the romantic painter in his *Considerations*:

> When a region is covered with fog it seems larger and more sublime; like the appearance of a young woman covered with a veil, it heightens the imagination and raises expectations. The eye and the imagination are more attracted by misty distances than by what is closely and clearly seen.[20]

These lines might be read in light of the problem of the veiling and unveiling of nature. From antiquity up to the Enlightenment, Mother Nature was frequently personified under the guise of the goddess Isis-Artemis. Allegorically represented as hidden behind a veil covering her face, she was inaccessible to the gaze of mere mortals. In Kant's *Critique of the Power of Judgment*, the image of the veiled Isis goes hand in hand with a respect for the mysteries of nature, inspired by that "most sublime" inscription on the goddess's temple prohibiting the lifting of her veil.[21] In *The Disciples of Sais*, the romantic poet Novalis also prefers the Orphic poet's respectful attitude towards nature over the Promethean attitude of modern science, yet advocates surmounting the interdiction on lifting her veil. One can only do this by going beyond the limits set by Kantian criticism, that is to say, by overcoming the limits of human finitude: "According to that inscription, if it is true that no mortal has lifted the veil, then we will just have to try to become immortal. Whoever does not wish to lift it, is no true disciple of Sais."[22] In the paintings of Friedrich, fog is a natural or material veil that is no longer merely an allegory of the secrets of nature and their inaccessibility to mortals. Fog, moreover, does not simply impede our sight and generate respect that keeps us at a distance from nature. It *attracts* our sight. In the same way as the veiled body of a woman might excite the desire to see it unveiled, fog stirs our imagination and the wish to see more by penetrating the opacity.

Friedrich's painting entitled *Fog* (1807) perfectly illustrates this point: in its extreme figurative simplicity it awakens our desire to see the fog-enshrouded three-masted sailboat that is behind the rowing boat in the foreground, then to see the distant shore behind the sailboat, and then again perhaps to glimpse the horizon behind the distant shore. Of course, this desire is not awakened in "those whose imagination is too poor to see in fog anything other than gray."[23] This accentuation of desire defines the Friedrichian sublime; it requires a certain attitude or state of mind on the part of the spectator, and stimulates an inner dynamic response to the painting. Here Friedrich is strongly opposed to an art of illusion, because the latter merely passively dazzles the viewer, and precludes her from actively exercising this intimate activity or appropriation of what the painting shows.

10.5. ANISH KAPOOR: DOING AWAY WITH THE MEDIATION IN THE FRIEDRICHIAN SUBLIME?

In this concluding section I would like to draw attention to Anish Kapoor's reinterpretation of Friedrich's *Sea of Ice* (1824), which, along with the *Monk by the Sea* and the *Wanderer above the Sea of Fog*, is considered by commentators to be one of the best examples of the sublime in Friedrich. The Kantian concept of a "dynamic" and terrifying sublime is frequently applied to the *Sea of Ice*, though it is precisely this painting that provides the clearest illustration of what makes Friedrich's art of the sublime radically different from the Kantian analysis.

At first glance this painting, also known as *The Wreck of Hope*, seems to be a narrative motif—a shipwreck—inspired by a real-life expedition to the North Pole in 1819–1820. Yet an image emerges here in which the sublime experience no longer resides in the tension of Kant's "dynamic sublime" that is characteristic of catastrophe paintings. From a Kantian perspective the resolution of this tension involves human practical rationality. In contrast to this, Friedrich's painting carries out a kind of refocusing on nature. Swallowed by ice, the ship itself is barely visible, whereas the stacked blocks of ice physically dominate the center of the composition. Or more precisely, the image shows the fragmentation of a ship whose debris mingles with natural forms. But this painting is even more unique and troubling if one recalls that all human landmarks do not in fact entirely disappear. The work involves the presence of a perceptive subject, yet one that is not depicted. The image unfolds under this gaze and gives it a more intimate nuance. For what strikes one above all in this painting is the impression of silence and stillness—it almost emanates a sense of tranquility. The sublime experience resides in a quiet and oneiric vision of a natural time, a cosmic and archaic time that is opposed to the time of history and action, a natural time in its fundamental processes: the solidification of water into ice, or the petrifaction of the ice in the foreground that gradually takes on the color of stone. This elementary matter is marked and borne by the temporality of its becoming. Yet it is a slow, infinitesimal movement that borders upon immobility, if not upon eternity—the movement of a sea of ice.

Anish Kapoor has perceptively grasped all of this. The British sculptor freely admits that his work draws its fundamental inspiration from the intrinsic aspect of a dreamlike sublime in the landscape paintings of Caspar David Friedrich. Kapoor declares he is "a painter working as a sculptor." For he creates "mental sculptures" that are no longer simply the embodiment of a real, tangible space, but presuppose and demand an act of inhabiting a space through one's viewing, similar to Friedrich's sublime of scale as a magnified space. Kapoor has made architectural scale into a principle of his sculptures, often creating site-specific work that acquires its own dimensions by developing in the site. This is the case of the gigantic installation *Svayambh*, first conceived for the Musée des Beaux-Arts of Nantes in France in 2007, and then exhibited at Munich's Haus der Kunst, which is in part a reinterpretation of the sublime vision of an archaic nature in Friedrich's *Sea of Ice. Svayambh*—a Sanskrit word meaning "born by itself"—is a massive block of red wax moving almost imperceptibly on hidden rails through the museum building along its west-east axis. The coming and going of the block with the slowness of an infinitesimal movement that is almost reduced to immobility, like the movement of a sea of ice, generates an impression of primal and potentially infinite extension. The matter of the sculpture is shaped through infinite duration and space itself; the original object is seemingly endlessly reworked, carved, planed down by passing through the arched door frames, leaving red traces on their immaculate white color as if the block were slightly larger than the frames—or, as if the building were, so to speak, swallowing the block. Viewed as a self-generating system, as an uncreated or autonomous form that creates itself and whose origin is immemorial, it is no longer historical.

Kapoor's work, however, gives a different treatment of the sublime: "I think the real subject for me, if there is one, is the sublime. . . . It's this whole notion of somehow trying to shorten the distance of sublime experience. . . . If one is looking at a Friedrich painting of a figure looking at the sunset, then one is having one's reverie in terms of their experience. . . . It is my wish to make that distance shorter so that the reverie is direct. You're not watching someone else do it; you're compelled to do it yourself."[24] That is to say, Kapoor aims at doing away with one of the very emblems of Caspar David Friedrich's art: the *Rückenfigur*— the figure with its back turned to the viewer—like in the *Wanderer above the Sea of Fog*.

It is important to understand that this specific motif, which is stereotypically associated with romanticism, and even with kitsch, is itself related to the figurative treatment of the sublime in Friedrich. On the one hand, the immobile *Rückenfigur* highlights an attitude of contemplation. But on the other hand, it is just one more mode of opacity, in addition to fog and other techniques that we have already listed above. For not only is the figure of the wanderer preventing us as spectators from seeing a part of the landscape, but he is also anonymous: the *Rückenfigur* does away with the face. As for its effect, the *Rückenfigur* is therefore disconcerting. But it is precisely through this effect that the figure deploys its positive function. It institutes a form of reflexivity in which we oscillate between two modes of contemplation, between the outer eye and the inner eye. We are forced to "go back" in ourselves, to use our "inner eye" to imagine the entire landscape that we wish we could see, because we are unable to externally project ourselves into the view.

Thus, when Kapoor intends to "shorten the distance of sublime experience" "so that the reverie is direct" and "you're compelled to do it yourself," he is perhaps unaware that Friedrich has constructed this mediation precisely to compel us to do it ourselves. For the natural (or divine) sublime is what we absolutely cannot experience without an artistic mediation. Or to put it in Novalis's words: the Friedrichian sublime resides in a "qualitative potentialization,"[25] in which our sight is elevated to an inner vision, a vision of the purely spiritual and transcendent principle of nature. And in line with Novalis's definition of romanticism, the "qualitative potentialization" of sight by means of a veiling principle may also be inverted. Here the mystical becomes known through a process of lowering or "logarhythmizing," and the imagination concentrates on the finite or the ordinary, such as a "simple wheat field." For Friedrich and the romantics at least, this is the only possible way to "shorten the distance of sublime experience."[26]

10.6. CONCLUSION

As we have seen, there is a threefold sublime in Caspar David Friedrich: a divine, natural, and artistic sublime. To be sure, his art of landscape painting strives to make the excess of the cosmic and divine sublime become perceptible within the framed space of a canvas. And certainly, it aims at uplifting the spirit of the spectator. But if one remains at an interpretation of Friedrich's painting in terms of the Kantian sublime, one fails to understand how his view of the sublime cannot be reduced to one of hyperbolic grandeur exceeding the form. Furthermore, if one only emphasizes the transcendence, the distance and incommensurability between the divine cosmic order and the human order, one overlooks the goal of the artistic sublime. The latter seeks to stir the spectator's emotive and imaginative participation and to reduce the distance between these two orders. While the Kantian sublime expresses a radical dualism and tension between the sensible and the intelligible, in the religious perspective of Friedrich's art the material and the spiritual differ but are not opposed. They are complementary rather than antagonistic, and the whole point of his painting is to make us associate and not separate them. Hence, claims that the experience of the sublime cannot be reconciled with the religious vocation of Friedrich's paintings, or that only the beautiful is at stake in his work, fail to grasp that their religious vocation actually depends on the sublime.

Why should we care about Friedrich's views? It might be argued that an art that addresses the soul and aims at a recognition of the sacred is now histori- cally dated. But without seeking to abolish the historical distance between his epoch and ours, Friedrich's views offer artistic perspectives that are still relevant for contemporary artists and theoreticians of art: a use of scale to liberate space, perceptual opacity to stimulate both our outer and inner sight, and, above all, as Anish Kapoor has attempted to do in the wake of minimalism, a simplification of the work of art. All of which constitutes the simplicity of the sublime in the works of that "metaphysician with the brush,"[27] Caspar David Friedrich.

NOTES
1. Anish Kapoor, "'I Don't Know Where I'm Going,'" interview with Alastair Sooke, *The Telegraph*, September 26, 2006, online: http://www.telegraph.co.uk/culture/ art/3655568/I-dont-know-where-Im-going.html.
2. I am grateful to Dalia Nassar for her helpful comments on an earlier version of this text.
3. See Robert Rosenblum, *Modern Painting and the Northern Romantic Tradition: Friedrich to Rothko* (New York: Harper & Row, 1975), 10f.
4. See especially Werner Busch, *Caspar David Friedrich. Ästhetik und Religion* (Munich: C. H. Beck, 2003), 64f. Busch dismisses all interpretation of Friedrich's paintings as being in line with an aesthetics of the sublime by proclaiming the sub- lime as "postreligious." See too Johannes Grave, *Caspar David Friedrich und die Theorie des Erhabenen* (Weimar: VDG-Verlag, 2001); Grave focuses his analysis on the *Sea of Ice* and maintains that in this painting Friedrich is ironically work- ing against the philosophical conception of the sublime elaborated by Kant and Schiller.
5. See among others Hilmar Frank, *Aussichten ins Unermessliche* (Berlin: Akademie Verlag, 2004), 99–100; Eliane Escoubas, "La tragédie du paysage: Caspar David Friedrich," in *L'espace pictural* (Paris: Les Belles Lettres, 2011, 1st ed. 1995), 69–90. Elsewhere Escoubas has argued for the "simplicity" of the Kantian sublime, draw- ing on a quotation from the "General Remark" to § 29 of the *Critique of the Power of Judgment* where Kant writes "Simplicity (purposiveness without art) is so to speak the style of nature in the sublime," meaning that the context of the sublime is nature in its primitive purity devoid of all artifice. See Eliane Escoubas, "Kant or the Simplicity of the Sublime," in *Of the Sublime: Presence in Question*, ed. Jean-François

Courtine, trans. Jeffrey S. Librett (Albany: State University of New York Press, 1993), 55–70. Here I will try to show that the notion of "simplicity" is even more present in the Friedrichian sublime.

6. See for example Brad Prager, "Kant in Caspar David Friedrich's Frames," *Art History* 25 (2002): 68–86.

7. See in particular Reinhard Brandt, "Zur Metamorphose der Kantischen Philosophie in der Romantik. Rhapsodische Anmerkungen," in *Kunst und Wissen. Beziehungen zwischen Ästhetik und Erkenntnistheorie im 18. und 19. Jahrhundert*, ed. Astrid Bauereisen, Stephan Pabst, and Achim Vesper (Würzburg: Königshausen & Neumann, 2009), 85–101; and "Caspar David Friedrich. Landschaftsmalerei als Seelenführung," in *Kunst und Religion. Ein kontroverses Verhältnis*, ed. Markus Kleinert (Mainz: Chorus, 2010), 31–55.

8. See for example Olivier Schefer, *Résonances du romantisme* (Brussels: La Lettre volée, 2005), 74f.

9. Manfred Frank, " 'Religionslose Kathedralen im ewigen Winter'—Der Moderne Caspar David Friedrich im frühromantischen Kontext," in *Szenen des Heiligen*, ed. Cai Werntgen (Berlin: Insel Verlag, 2011), 112–60. I am thankful to Manfred Frank for providing me with a manuscript version of his talk prior to its publication.

10. Cf. Judith Norman, "The Work of Art in German Romanticism," in *Internationales Jahrbuch des Deutschen Idealismus/International Yearbook of German Idealism* 6 (2008): 72.

11. See note 6 above.

12. Caspar David Friedrich, "Äußerungen bei Betrachtung einer Sammlung von Gemählden von größtentheils noch lebenden und unlängst verstorbenen Künstlern," *Kritische Edition der Schriften des Künstlers und seiner Zeitzeugen*, ed. Gerhard Eimer in collaboration with Günther Rath (Frankfurt am Main: Kunstgeschichtliches Institut der Johann Wolfgang Goethe-Universität, 1999).

13. Friedrich, *Äußerungen*, 53. In the original German: "Ein Gefühl für das Erhabene in der Natur fehlt es ihm doch wohl gewiß nicht?"

14. Friedrich, *Äußerungen*, 54.

15. Cf. Goethe, *Über die Gegenstände der bildenden Kunst* (Zurich: Artemis Verlag, 1961–66), vol. 13, 122–25. According to Goethe, the inherent dignity of the subject matter is what we absolutely cannot know without the artistic idealization that reveals it or brings it to light. This dignity relates to the timeless essence of the object, an idea that the artist forms through an intimate knowledge of nature. He should not regress into the fantastic, but move beyond the given sensible phenomena to the timeless idea.

16. Friedrich, *Äußerungen*, 32.

17. Friedrich, *Äußerungen*, 79.

18. Friedrich, *Äußerungen*, 70.

19. Friedrich, *Äußerungen*, 47.

20. Friedrich, *Äußerungen*, 126.

21. Kant, *Critique of the Power of Judgment*, § 49, trans. Paul Guyer and Eric Matthews (Cambridge: Cambridge University Press, 2000), 194.

22. Novalis, *Die Lehrlinge zu Sais*, NS 1, 82.

23. Friedrich, *Äußerungen*, 126.

24. Rainer Crone and Alexandra Von Stosch, *Anish Kapoor* (London: Prestel, 2008), 27–28.

25. Novalis, *Vorarbeiten* (1798), NS 2, 545.

26. For a more detailed analysis of the romantic notion of potentialization and the relationship between Caspar David Friedrich and Novalis, see my *L'art de romantiser le monde. Caspar David Friedrich et la philosophie romantique*, PhD thesis, Universität München/Université Paris IV, October 2013.

27. According to an expression of Per Daniel Atterbom, in *Reisebilder aus dem romantischen Deutschland. Jugenderinnerungen eines romantischen Dichters und Kunstgelehrten aus den Jahren 1817 bis 1819* (Berlin, 1867; reprint Stuttgart: Steingrüben, 1970), 102.

11

The New Mythology

Romanticism between Religion and Humanism

BRUCE MATTHEWS

Romanticism sought to create a new mythology capable of transforming the fragmented echoes of the Enlightenment into a symphonic age of scientific knowledge, *Bildung*, and political freedom. Uniting the discordant notes of reason and sensuous nature into a symbolic narrative of hope, this new mythology would beget a "new religion" that, unlike its predecessors, would be one that joins hands with humanism to create ideas whose aesthetic power would sanction the new normative values of this coming age. Such was the intoxicating vision advanced in the inadequately named, but perfectly mystifying "Oldest System Program of German Idealism." As Frederick Beiser concludes in *The Romantic Imperative*, due to the fact that this proposed marriage of religion's divine necessities and the freedoms of humanism was never consummated, "the problems that so troubled the romantics...are still with us."[1] Perhaps the most serious of these problems is that of our relationship to the natural world—a problem whose consequences are far from academic. As Manfred Frank has repeatedly warned, to surrender our subjectivity and free will to the deterministic vocabulary of the natural sciences will not only undermine the personal accountability that supports moral action, but it will also lead to a "political fatalism" that will destroy the legitimacy of society's defining institutions.[2]

But nowhere is the problem of our inability to create new values more real than in a problem the romantics also found so troubling, namely the damage and destruction we are doing to nature. No one saw this inevitable crisis more clearly than the young Schelling, who warned in 1804 that the course of modern philosophy, left to its own inner logic would lead to "the annihilation of nature" (SW 1/5, 274).

Accepting this warning as collateral, I would like us to extend to Schelling's thought a line of credit to support a brief examination of how he diagnoses and treats this now most threatening pathology of modern consciousness. For as I hope to show, the organic form of philosophy offered us by this most enigmatic member of the Jena Circle not only dissolves what Beiser calls "the paradox of romantic metaphysics," but the resources he prescribes also suggest a new mythology of nature whose utopian potential may, both in formal and substantive terms, provide the emancipatory power capable of liberating an engaged hope from its bondage to the ideology of irony that currently emasculates transformative political action.

In *The Romantic Imperative*, Beiser examines how the romantic thinkers grappled with the unavoidable difficulties generated by their attempts to integrate the dissonant dualities of discursivity, be they of idealism and realism, freedom and necessity, criticism and dogmatism, or, more succinctly, Fichte and Spinoza. His penetrating account of how Herder's organic framework was effectively used to negotiate this integration of opposing forces succeeds in achieving his own stated goal of restoring "the organic...to its rightful place...in romantic thinking" (*RI* 133). Herder rejects a mechanistic nature in favor of an organic nature characterized by interactive creative forces, in which humans play the essential role of seeking purpose and creating meaning. In his seminal *Ideas for a Philosophy of the History of Mankind*, Herder argues that the developmental dynamic of organic processes more adequately accounts for the order of both the natural world and human experience, be it of the individual or of long-standing cultural traditions. The principles of his philosophy are thus the "organic forces" that animate the physical and spiritual, making themselves manifest in the latter through the currents of "tradition" (HW 6, 180). In a deft move of intellectual judo, Herder explained these organic forces as grounding the oppositional centrifugal and centripetal forces of Newton's theory of gravity. Thus Newton's ideas become proof not of a mechanistic universe, but rather of a cosmos fundamentally betraying the self-organizing logic of living order; after all, what other example do we have in nature of a system capable of generating movement through the integration of active and passive forces? As such, these organic forces emerge as the DNA of an autogenetic ratio, whose interaction drives the development of nature and history, while preserving nature's necessity and history's freedom. Herder achieves this integration through the use of the concept of reciprocal causation, which, its proponents claimed, best articulated the systematic integration of opposition demonstrated by an organism's capacity to be both cause and effect of itself. Herder captures this self-organizing dynamic in humanity through Leibniz's *apperceptio*, translating this term as "recognition" (*Anerkennung*), which he posits as humanity's power for free self-determination: "No longer an infallible machine in the hands of nature, he becomes himself the purpose and aim of the work" (HW 1, 110). This intentional iteration of the forces of self-organization creates the social being of humanity engaged in the ongoing process of creating our own unique meanings as well as our communities' cultures and traditions. The telos of life is not to sate our appetites but to achieve self-realization. The resulting organic universe is thus fundamentally monistic, in that any dualism we throw at it can be transformed into a continuum of degrees of self-organization. Thus do the laws of material nature and customs of human traditions become two quantitatively different manifestations of the "organic forces" that animate our world. Schelling, who cites Herder repeatedly in his *Magistar* of 1792, captures this monistic continuum of self-organization when he writes that inanimate matter is but unconscious mind, whereas mind is matter that has become conscious of itself (HKA 1/1, 183). Betraying his Platonic roots, Herder's philosophy bets that the *unity* of experience trumps the Cartesian fixation on certainty in supplying the most comprehensive, and thus truest, starting point for making sense of our existence. Taking aim at his former mentor Kant, Herder counters his Cartesian insistence that duality is the condition of all metaphysics, since, according to Kant, only the noetic realm of *res cogitans* and its certain knowledge can supply the universality and necessity of truth required by philosophy. For Herder, however, if our world of nature and human history is at the end of the day one world, there can be no such unbridgeable divide between the noumenal and the concrete firstness of sensual nature. Rather, these two fields of our existence stand in reciprocal interaction, as mutually dependent members of this self-organizing unity we call our world. As is evident in the phenomenon of global warming, the realm of nature and human activity form an indissoluble and inescapable unity. And just as we are free to continue living in denial of the consequences of these actions, we are not free from suffering the inevitable consequences of our actions. Within a unified world such as Herder's, freedom itself appears only when accompanied by the necessities of our existence.

It is on this very point of integrating freedom and necessity that Beiser contends that the romantics' use of Herder's strategy fails to successfully overcome the paradox of romantic metaphysics, since the romantics' allegiance to Spinoza's naturalism necessitates their abandonment of Fichte's "radical freedom," and with this, the surrender of autonomous political engagement to the heterogeneous forces of traditional religion. This follows as a consequence of Fichte's understanding of radical freedom as spontaneity (*Selbsttätigkeit*) and self-positing that "excludes determination by natural causes" of the material world, and thus "presupposes the noumenal-phenomenal dualism" (*RI* 151).

According to Beiser, Fichte's account of freedom is radical on two counts. First, because it advances a self whose only essence is to create itself through the freedom of self-positing. Second, due to its total freedom from the material world, it has the power to transform that material world into a "completely rational world through infinite striving" (*RI* 171). Given this power of the self over the not-self of nature, the self does not need to break out of its subjective confines to integrate with the objective world, since its imperative is to remake the objective world so that it conforms to the rational order of the subject. Of course, "the romantics reject" this account of the self and the purpose of its radical freedom (*RI* 151). Due to their allegiance to Spinoza's naturalism, they hold that since "everything is simply a mode of God," and "God acts from the necessity of his nature," then human agency is actually divine agency, thereby undercutting any claim to autonomous action (*RI* 185). The degree to which the romantics abandon freedom falls short of Spinoza's fatalism, but only barely, since it is the optimistic form of fatalism—quietism—that is Beiser's concluding characterization of the romantics' position (*RI* 151), a position, it must be added, that he, following Heine and Marx, equates with a "reactionary" and thus conservative religion that is directly at odds with the "progressive and liberal" humanism that Fichte's radical freedom supports (*RI* 174). And it is precisely this problem of the irreconcilable demands of religion and humanism that so troubles Beiser, since we are far from achieving a successful integration of these opposing forces, so that the challenges presented by the paradox of romantic metaphysics "are still with us" (*RI* 151).

Schelling, I submit, might not recognize his philosophy in Beiser's portrayal of romantic metaphysics. While he would certainly applaud the rehabilitation of an organic way of thinking and of Herder's thought in general, Schelling might find it odd that Beiser never quotes his words—or any of the other romantics—when presenting his account of their attempted synthesis of Spinoza and Fichte via Herder, and when he does cite Schelling, he refers to "early notebooks and fragments" in which one finds the "the romantic project for such a synthesis" (*RI* 177). Yet far from a fragment or notebook, the work cited in a footnote is Schelling's symphonic *System of Transcendental Idealism* (1800), in which he argues precisely the opposite of the position attributed to him by Beiser. Far from contending that God's nature determines humanity's actions, Schelling argues here for an organic, reciprocal relationship between God and humanity, in which both are "co-poets" (*Mitdichter*) of our history (SW 1/3, 602). In fact, both parties are so necessary to this collaborative process that if "our own freedom" in creating our part were denied, "even... [God] himself would not be" (SW 1/3, 602). Far from being a puppet of a deity, the existence of the divine himself somehow depends on humanity's freedom as we actively participate in composing the poem of our history. In Schelling's words here, it seems humans are indeed determined by God's nature, but this nature is to live, create, and be free. Thus when it is suggested that for the romantics "everything is simply a mode of God," and that "God acts from the necessity of his nature," and if this divine nature is to be alive and thus free, then far from undercutting autonomous action, both God and humanity act from the necessity of their nature as *free* beings (*RI* 185). Torturing Sartre's words, we might say that according to Schelling, as a mode of a living God, we are by this very *necessity* of God's nature *condemned* to be free. Beiser's misreading of Schelling is all too common, due to the almost default allegiance to a Kantian and Fichtean idea of radical freedom that, in its Cartesian insistence on an almost gnostic-like detachment from the natural world, reveals itself to be in fact the very antithesis of Schelling's conception of an organic freedom that, embedded in the fabric of nature itself, frames his programmatic claim made in his *Naturrecht* (1796) that *life itself is the schema of freedom* (SW 1/1, 249).

This claim demonstrates the degree to which Schelling invested our embodied world with what he considered to be the divine presence of freedom. Consistent with the philosophical theology of his upbringing, he maintained that our conscious life is best understood through the same dynamic of self-manifestation as that of God. Just after leaving the *Stift*, he asks in 1797 if he may borrow his father's dissertation on Leibniz's theory of monads, written when Schelling Sr. was a student in Tübingen under the supervision of Gottfried Ploucquet (1716–1790), who, besides Wolff, was one of the most influential interpreters of Leibniz's philosophy, as well as a highly original thinker in his own right.[3] In this dissertation, with which the young Schelling was obviously quite familiar, Schelling Sr. engaged Ploucquet's own theory of monads, wherein the "*Ich (egoitas)*" is a "self-manifestation (*manifestatio sui*)," which arises out of the "reciprocal community (*commercium*)" of the *Ich* and the "*Nicht-Ichheit*" ("Non-egoitas").[4] The significant dynamic at work here is that of our living self-consciousness as the activity of a *commercium*, of a *Wechselwirkung* of an *Ich* and a *nicht-Ich*, which in its incessant activity betrays the generative forces offered through Ploucquet's idea of the divine self-manifestation.[5] And it is precisely this integrative dynamic that Schelling uses in the *Naturrecht* to argue that the moral law and its "causality of freedom reveals itself through physical causality" of living, self-conscious beings. The young Schelling pulls this off employing Kant's own categories more consistently than their author, exploiting Kant's use of the same relational category and its logical form of disjunction to resolve the antinomy of freedom and the reciprocal interaction that drives organic life. Setting the noumenal and phenomenal into the same type of interdependent feedback loop as that of an organic system's part to whole, Schelling takes as his starting point the only organic system where we are identical with the thing in itself, namely the self as a living being, which, as the point of union between the intelligible and the sensual, "must unite within itself autonomy and heteronomy" (SW 1/1, 248). That is, there must be a form of causality that unites both of these in a phenomenon that is both relative and absolute, obeys the laws of nature, and yet is also in principle, because of its autonomous power, incapable of ever being exhaustively accounted for. Schelling's position here is clear: "This causality is *life*.—Life is autonomy in appearance, is the schema of freedom, to the degree that it reveals itself in nature" (SW 1/1, 249).

By integrating the causalities of freedom and necessity through an organic causality of life, Schelling rejects the limits Kant places on our use of the *Bildungstrieb* of nature's *nisus formativus*, by refusing to accept Kant's almost dogmatic claim that the integrative point of the intelligible and sensible must remain an "inexplicable" mystery, like the "supersensible substrate of nature" (AA 5, ix, 194). Far from being an otherworldly transcendent mystery, freedom is instead at work in varying degrees in the formative power of organization that, as Schelling writes in the *Weltseele*, when applied to "a theory of evolution" opens up a "path of possible explanation" that must be pursued scientifically (SW 1/2, 529). To understand our world and experience through the synchronic boundaries of a dual-plane metaphysics, with its accompanying mysteries of compatibilism and preestablished harmonies, not only fails to do justice to our experience, but places too great a limit on our investigation and understanding of nature. Schelling's alternative is a genetic method of philosophy driven by the generative interplay of these opposing forces of an expansive freedom and contractive necessity, understood as two parts of the whole of our self-organizing world. Thus, paradoxically perhaps, since "I am necessarily a *living* being" (SW 1/1, 249), I am necessarily free as long as I live.

The structural move Schelling makes here *inverts* Kant's architectonic, setting the dynamic categories of nature before those of mathematics. This inversion brings with it a host of systematic consequences. Perhaps the most notable makes the self-organizing dynamic of the organic foundational, and therewith sets the inexponible category of *Wechselwirkung* and *Gemeinschaft* as the primary category for understanding our world. The heart of this multivalent intersection of opposing causal forces betrays a chaotic rhythm, whose indeterminability finds each opposing yet complementary force superimposed in the other, each entangled in dynamic interaction as both cause and effect of the other. Kant recognizes this irreducibly nonmechanistic factor of reciprocal causation when, due to its resistance to being reduced to a series, he excludes this inexponible concept from the synthesis of the unconditioned (*KrV* A414/ B441). Inverting Kant, Schelling begins with this inexponible causal dynamic in which the linear relation of cause to effect is replaced by the reciprocal and thus simultaneous relations of causes determined by their effects. In articulating the disjunctive dynamic of how the opposing forces of cause and effect reciprocally determine one another, this category of self-organization suggests an organic system that, unlike a mechanistic system, holds open, by necessity, the possibility of its progressive development. This follows from his transcription of Newton's expansive and contractive forces into the Platonic pairing of the limited and unlimited, a move that justifies positing the expansive force as unlimited, thereby just slightly tipping the scale, providing the dynamic asymmetry required to catalyze and sustain progression. Within this frame, Schelling conceptualizes the possibility of new and original actions, resulting in what he calls the "individualization of matter" and the "dynamic evolution" of nature (SW 1/2, 520). Extended to encompass the system of our universe, Schelling sees its powers of self-organization, its power to be "both cause and effect of itself" (SW 1/2, 40), as indicating the possibility of articulating a freedom that does not depend on the noumenal-phenomenal divide. Instead, due to the stochastic dynamic of the iterative causality indicative of *Wechselwirkung*, all of nature "manifests the appearance of freedom," no matter how faint and seemingly chaotic (SW 1/5, 527).

Animating Leibniz's principle of indiscernibles, Schelling argues that "[e]ven within the same type, nature knows of a certain unmistakable freedom, which maintains a certain leeway for differentiation...so that no *individual* is ever absolutely equal to another" (SW 1/10, 378). By positing this low-level freedom in nature as a type of chaotic force that propels the evolutionary differentiation of life, Schelling generates the conceptual resources required to integrate freedom and necessity into a unified account of nature, in which both intertwine in an organic, and thus partially chaotic, process of self-differentiation that generates increasingly complex iterative systems. At some point a threshold of complexity is passed and human consciousness emerges, demonstrating how "the dynamic interaction of opposed yet complementary forces [lies] not only at the basis of matter, but of thinking as well" (SW 1/2, 360). Because of this, because our cosmos is animated and sustained by this disjunctive identity of oppositional forces, the principles that inform our thought are homologous with the principles that animate our world:

> These same principles are necessarily those of the sum total of nature and thus ultimately of the All itself, and according to these [principles] we would like to develop, as it were, symbolically in matter the entirety of the inner driving power of the universe and the highest *Grundsätze* of philosophy itself. (SW 1/2, 360)

These principles of which Schelling here writes are those that animate "the most sublime science," whose goal can only be "to present...the actuality, the presence, the living *Da-sein* of God in the entirety and particularity of all things," since as the power of life itself, "everything lives in him" (SW 1/2, 376).

Given this account of Schelling, and accepting his *Naturphilosophie* as the only source for a systematic account of romantic naturalism, I would have to modify Beiser's claim that the romantics shared Spinoza's position that "everything is simply a mode of God" to read instead that "everything is animated by the organizing principles of the divine life." Consequently, Beiser's claim that "God acts from the necessity of his nature" asserts nothing more than God's nature is life, which, according to Schelling, is the first predicate attributable to him. This is a position that not only deflates Beiser's claim that the romantics sacrificed their autonomy on the altar of naturalism, but more importantly, it is a *new* position that informs a way of thinking an organic philosophy that moves beyond the debilitating limits imposed by the dualism required by Fichte's radical freedom.

Refusing to begin with the certainty of the ego, Schelling begins with the inexponible unity of life as an organic system, whose organizing principles inform and animate its development. Given this interconnectedness of nature, of matter and mind being driven by the same principles of growth, we become faced with the prospect of what Schelling termed our *conscientia*, or *Mitwissenschaft* with nature. Refusing to accept the terms of "the skeptical problems that motivated Cartesian epistemology"—in Beiser's words, problems such as "how do we *know* that there is a nature or history beyond consciousness?" (*RI* 132)– Schelling reframes modernity's epistemological obsessions in accordance with the reciprocal dynamic of self-organizing systems and our status as an organ of knowing *within* this system. From this standpoint he contends that we can explain why we are capable of knowing with "direct certainty" that "there are things beyond us," even though this knowledge "refers to something quite different and opposed to us" (SW 1/3, 343). We are capable of knowing that which shows itself to be other than we are because we are "of this world," having been created through the very same dynamic organization that has brought our entire cosmos into being. What precedes and thus unifies knowing subject and known object is this underlying order of organic nature that bonds us with the phenomenal world in which we live. Our power to appreciate "the unfathomable intentionality, the unbelievable naiveté of nature in the achievement of its purposes," points to "the view of a true inner history of nature" in "whose formation humanity can look into as into that of a related being" (SW 1/10, 378; SW 1/10, 381). Most clearly demonstrated by the works of the scientific and artistic genius, our function in the autoepistemic structure of nature is that of an organ whereby nature comes to know herself.

From this embedded standpoint within creation Schelling's critique of the "dualism" that is a "necessary phenomenon of the modern world" becomes clear (SW 1/5, 273). Initiated by Descartes, formulated by Kant, and perfected by Fichte, modernity's subject denies the objective reality and intrinsic value of nature, since as "a product of the I," the world of nature becomes nothing more than a "*Gedankending*" to be posited by the thinking subject "when needed" (SW 1/5, 110). This devaluation of sensuous nature has its roots in modernity's promotion of the thinking subject to the rank of the absolute, in an inflation of the cogito that leads to the deification of the human subject at the subsequent cost of what Schelling presciently calls the "annihilation of nature":

> Descartes, who through the *cogito ergo sum* gave philosophy its first ori-
> entation to subjectivity, and whose introduction of philosophy (in his
> *Meditations)* is in fact identical with the later grounding of philosophy in
> idealism, could not yet present the orientations entirely separated—sub-
> jectivity and objectivity do not yet appear completely divided. But his real
> intention, his true idea of God, the world, and the soul he articulated more
> clearly in his physics than through his philosophy. In the comprehensive
> spirit of Descartes, his philosophy permitted the annihilation of nature,
> which the idealism of the above mentioned form [Fichte's] extols, just as
> truly and factually as it actually was in his physics. (SW 1/5, 274)

No longer the primary reality of our being, nature becomes something derivative, dependent for *its* being on the thinking subject. As the sole arbiter of what
is real in our world, the modern subject defines reality as the self-certainty of
the cogito, understood as its own reflective knowledge of self. Yet if what is real
and true can only be that which corresponds to this reflective self-certainty,
and can only be articulated through the predicates of discursive thought, then
the thinking of the unity of nature becomes impossible. The "living band" of
a transitive *being*, which as *natura naturans* connects humanity with nature,
is thereby dissolved into the discrete moments of *logos*, of the *relata* of subject
and predicate (SW 1/7, 100). Once this dissection has occurred, and we begin
philosophy with the certitude of the disembodied self, we find it impossible to
find the same quality of certitude in knowing the things of the embodied world;
an epistemological quandary that leads to questions that some still find philosophically important, such as "how do we *know* that there is a nature beyond
our consciousness?" (*RI* 132).

Capturing the absurdities of solipsism with admirable precision, Schelling
argues that if one begins with the dualism of a Fichte, and accepts the disembodied cogito as determinative, then "all knowledge" derived from this principle will remain trapped within an "insoluble circle" of its own fabrication,
with the result that the thinking subject, pressed up against the conceptual
lens of its own making, can only look out at the world of sensuous nature as if

it, the cogito, "did not also belong to the world" (SW 1/6, 144). This was precisely the point Schelling repeatedly attempted to get Fichte to understand in their last exchange of letters. Briefly, Schelling begins with a "Subject = Object" more original than Fichte's philosophizing subject, writing that the opposition between real and ideal does not lie in the self, "but in something higher," namely in an "objective...producing self" that "in this, its own producing, is itself nothing other than nature" (HKA 3/1, 295).[6] This is the organic unity of nature that, in preceding the disjunctive interaction of the opposing powers of the real (limiting) and the ideal (unlimited), is the organic root of our *conscientia* with nature.[7] Fichte could not accept that the powers of our cogito were manifestations of nature's power, insisting instead that Schelling, in arguing such a position, was himself guilty of the worst sort of circular reasoning, since any rational order or pattern we discern in nature has been put there by the philosophizing subject. This was, however, a line of argument that proved Schelling's point that Fichte was himself trapped within an "insoluble circle" of his own making, forever alienated from the world of sensuous nature as if it, his cogito, "did not also belong to the world." It was as if Fichte's philosophy was so wedded to the methodical order of the philosophizing subject's own reflected image that it dealt "with the world of lived experience just as a surgeon who promises to cure your ailing leg by amputating it."[8] But even then, once philosophy surgically removes the opaque firstness of real experience, it only finds itself trapped within the prison of its own success, unable to break free to become an engaged force in transforming the world.

Beyond the obvious, yet unfortunately too often overlooked fact that in destroying nature we harm ourselves, we can see that implicit in Schelling's critique of Descartes and Fichte's treatment of nature is the demand to extend Kant's kingdom of ends to all the kingdoms of nature. This follows clearly from his critique of the alienated subject of modernity, who values the gifts of nature only if they can be transformed into "beautiful houses and proper furniture" or "tools and household goods," since it is only then that "as a tool of his lust and desire" that the world of nature takes on meaning and value (SW 1/7, 111, 114). Cutting straight to the heart of modernity's early capitalist ambitions, Schelling demand that we stop exploiting nature by making it subservient to our immediate "economic-teleological ends" as if it had no inherent value in itself (SW 1/7, 17). Consistent with his contention that "the highest speculative concepts" must always be "simultaneously the most profound ethical concepts," the making absolute of the knowing cogito initiates an inversion of the ego's relationship to the physical world it inhabits, whereby the ego claims the right to remake the world in its own image (SW 2/3, 67). No longer subject to acts of nature, the modern subject can, emboldened by humanity's advances in the experimental sciences, as Kant put it, "constrain" and "compel" nature to make her subject to its needs (*KrV* B xiii). Fichte announces such a course of *Beherrschung* in his *Bestimmung des Menschen* (1800), declaring his intent to "invade the external world," where "I will be lord of Nature, and she shall be my servant. I will influence her according to the measure of my capacity, but she shall have no influence over me" (GA 1/6, 209f.). In Schelling's *Freiheitsschrift*, it is precisely this "exaltation of the self-will" that Schelling blames for destroying "the divine measure and balance" of the "nexus of living forces" of nature, which he argues sustain its continued health and productivity, flowing "together into one God-filled world" (SW 1/7, 365; SW 1/2, 377). Because of this sacred status, nature has inherent value for Schelling, resulting in his position that humanity's ordained role in creation is not one of subsumption and domination, but of reciprocity and stewardship, in which we engage as "co-poets" with this God-filled world, working together to create a culture capable of sustaining the balanced growth and development of all forms of life.[9]

The course modernity has taken, with its exaltation of the self, Schelling diagnoses in the *Freiheitsschrift* as an "evil" brought about "through a misuse of freedom" (SW 1/7, 366). We are free to elevate and inflate the self, to dominate nature and to make it serve humanity's "economic-teleological ends"; indeed, we are free to even "annihilate nature." But we are also at liberty to refuse freedom as *Herrschaft*, and instead to dethrone the self and return it to an integrated and balanced relationship of reciprocity with nature's nexus of living forces. Acting on this decision would then aim at the productive unity of self and nature, generating an understanding of freedom as the essence of life lived embedded in and informed by the oppositional interplay of nature's processes. Acting on this decision we might remove the cogito's self-imposed limitations that exclude not only the other of nature, but also omit the more familiar other of other human beings.

To do this is to begin to overcome our alienation from these other beings, and in this important sense Schelling claims that the overcoming of these limits through the realization of the unity and mutual dependency of self and nature will generate a knowledge that is, in fact, redemptive. Thus does "the most sublime science" of his *Naturphilosophie*, in seeking "to present the actuality" of "the living *Da-sein* of God in... all things" (SW 1/2, 76), seek to create an organic frame for conceptualizing and realizing the redemptive harmony of the *en kai pan*. The realization of this harmony, however, cannot be achieved by the parsing of logical possibilities in the parlor-game manner a Descartes or Hume doubts the existence of the world. It can only be grasped in an emphatic and experiential act of knowing, in which what comes to be known is of such importance that one could never be "indifferent (*gleichgültig*)" about it (SW 2/3, 26). Schelling injects an emotive force into his project, since if certainty is superseded by unity, freedom must then trump logical necessity, with the result that a motive cause is now required to channel freedom's power. As his organic strategy seeks to integrate the opposing realities of the intelligible and sensible, it follows that reason itself must reconcile with emotion, so that that which grounds and animates philosophy once again becomes infused with affective love of its desired wisdom.

The soteriological dimension emerges with the act of realizing our *conscientia* or *Mitwissenschaft* with nature, engendering an identification of our subject world with the object world of phenomenal being. This realized identity of human consciousness with nature—in which identity signifies the unity of the reciprocal interplay of our consciousness and nature—generates an unmediated understanding that can never be the *result* of a deliberative argumentation (SW 1/8, 200; SW 1/9, 221). It is instead the inescapable beginning of Schelling's organic way of thinking that Fichte could never grasp, since it situates the beginnings of our conscious freedom in an unconscious substrate of sensuous nature, whose necessary force limits and thus remains opaque to the logos of discursivity—an epistemological ground zero about which Schelling cites Aristotle's "fitting words" that "the starting point of thinking is not thinking, but something stronger than thinking" (SW 1/2, 217). This starting point discloses itself in the absolute of a living unity whose "symbolic presentation" is that towards which "every true philosophy strives, which is objective in religion, an eternal source of new intuitions, and a universal *Typus* of everything that is to become, in which human activity strives to express and cultivate the harmony of the universe" (SW 1/5, 115).

And with this, we begin to grasp Beiser's unease with the heretical nature of Schelling's philosophy, since it aspires not just to a theoretical knowing, but, more importantly, to the act of realizing a unity with nature, which as the manifestation of divine, means that Schelling's philosophy itself lives from what "is objective in religion," although "it is not in its principle religion." Rejecting "a knowledge of the absolute that emerges from philosophy as a result" (SW 1/5, 116), he instead demands the experience of this absolute as a precondition for expressing and cultivating an understanding of this unitive source through the discipline of philosophy. To do this, however, philosophy must become open to the other of logos, with its obscure language of mythos that speaks with the voice of nature as it "sensualizes truth" (*Plitt* 1, 37). This is a possibility that can only be entertained, however, if unity becomes the telos of philosophy, thereby challenging it to harness the disclosive powers of logos *and* mythos. Set into opposition, mythos binds together the discrete moments of logos, functioning organically as the inexponible whole that integrates and thus makes possible the unending expression of the *logoi*, generating the transformative power to further the development of our world. The loss of harmony and balance toward either extreme, however, leads to stagnation and regression, be it the result of the destructive fatalism of religious or scientific zealots or the compulsive skepticism of the tenured elite.

And it is precisely the absence of such a transformative myth that motivated the romantics then, and Manfred Frank today, to search for a way to provide a normative sanction to legitimize and orientate our social order—the central idea and concern that motivated his series on the topic of *The New Mythology*. In his lectures *Der kommende Gott* (1982), Frank argued that the contemporary problem of the estrangement of state from society results not only in the legitimacy of the state being undermined, but also in a general societal malaise and political fatalism.[10] Both of these concerns are symptoms of a deeper metaphysical challenge that has faced the West throughout the past century, namely how are we to sanction and thereby legitimize our social institutions and practices in the shadow of God's death. Moreover, as Frank has recently made clear, with the ever expanding reach of the neurosciences, last century's philosophical "death of the subject" may just be followed by this century's scientific reduction of consciousness itself to neurobiological brain states. The moral, legal, and societal consequences of this are almost unimaginable. Dancing around ways these challenges might be met, he points out in his *Kaltes Herz unendliche Fahrt* (1989) that "every myth and every religious worldview—whether Christian or not—protects the supreme moral convictions that ground the consensus of its members through the act *of sanction*."[11] *Sanctio*, however, not in the instrumental sense of a Rorty-like pragmatic hypothesis that we could change tomorrow, but in the profoundly numinous sense of a normative principle worth dying for—what Frank calls "an absolute value" and "justification" that can motivate and inspire people to risk their own self-interest for a higher cause.[12] Remaining true to the spirit of Kant's critical philosophy, the only support Frank can offer for such "quasi-religious justificatory claims" are counterfactual positions that speak only to that which is not yet, das *Seinsollende*. This is what he calls a "quasi-religious dowry" of the counterfactual, a practical hypothesis that is the necessary presupposition for moral action (*KM* 99). Such "practical beliefs," however, are not "the result of an argumentative discourse," since what rational discourse decides is always fallible (*KM* 101). And it is in this sense that Frank appears quite close to the position of the romantics who first diagnosed this problem, and whose prescribed cure could only be communicated in religious terms and symbols, specifically the idea of a new myth for a new religion.

The most captivating prescription to address this ill is the so-called "Oldest System Program of German Idealism" (1797), which announces the advent of a new religion whose text is nature, which, as living, provides the schema of our freedom.[13] Further developing his earlier writings in which he posits myth as the "schematism of nature" (SW 1/1, 472), Schelling posits a new mythology of nature, which in this new religion will usher in an era of harmony through the realization of the divine in nature. Connecting this new mythology with his *Naturphilosphie*, he argues in his *Philosophy of Art* (1803) that "in the philosophy of nature...the first, distant foundation has been laid for that future symbolism and mythology" (SW 1/5, 449). The content of this symbolism and mythology is "the world of ideas," which, however, "are not objects of speculation but of action, and to that extent objects of a *future* experience...something that should be realized in reality" (SW 1/5, 451; SW 1/1, 465). Such ideas are rather straightforward when Schelling considers Kant's regulative ideas of soul, world (freedom), and God, all of which aim at the unconditioned unity of human knowledge and action, but a quite different challenge arises when he widens his kingdom of ends to include all of nature. While acknowledging the problematic challenge of speaking to this possible future, Schelling suggests that this "new religion" will announce itself "in the rebirth of nature as the symbol of eternal unity," since "in nature the life of the newly arisen deity" will manifest itself (SW 1/5, 120). Although Schelling's substantive meaning here is far from clear, his words suggest Friedrich Christoph Oetinger's understanding of creation as the suffering body of Christ, whose "annihilation" at the hands of our "economic-teleologic" desires echoes Jesus's crucifixion on the cross. In a more speculative sense, we can see in Schelling's use of the future an echo of his idea that the *tense of the absolute* itself is the future—an understanding of a future that is not predetermined by its past, but rather offers unseen possibilities and thus an open-ended orientation to *what should be* (*das Seinsollende*). Embedded in the weaving of freedom into the very fabric of living nature, Schelling's teleology departs from the hindcasting of the Aristotelian model in which the telos is already prefigured in its formal cause. To say that futurity is the tense of the absolute is to acknowledge that the living absolute is, just like every self-organizing system, incessantly engaged in the process of stochastic development and further self-differentiation. As Schelling's account of creation in his early text on the *Timaeus* makes clear, it is precisely this incessant creating that is complete, and completeness in this process speaks to the possibility of the future as the arena in which *what should be* is realized as *what is*.[14] And it is in this sense that this new teleology might support what I would like to call *utopian thinking*.

The denigration of the utopian vision in our own society illustrates the values of our ruling order, which embraces not only the concrete and positivistic restrictions of the empirically real and politically powerful, but even the intelligentsia of the academy. Opting for the risk-free embrace of fragmentation in the face of the alleged totalizing dangers of Grand Narratives, the very scholars who should know better opt to repeat the mistakes of the last generation of intellectuals who faced the growing threats of political fascism. I am thinking of the criticism of nonaction Ernst Bloch directed at the Left of the Weimar years, which he attributed to their inability to understand and take seriously both the power of people's utopian longing and the power of myth to satisfy and direct that longing. Bloch's argument was that if the Nazis, however temporarily and deceptively, fulfilled real needs, there is no point in trying to conjure these needs away.[15] Since nature abhors a vacuum, if the contemporary Left does nothing on this level of meaning, then corporate interests and their parties become the only voices speaking to people's need for the mythic, as in the myth of Globalization or American exceptionalism. Determined as they are to reinforce current structures of power, such mythic narratives prove regressive as they retreat into the imaginary world of a golden era that never was.

To counter this, I suggest the idea of a utopian imperative that demands our world be measured according to principles and ideals, rather than utility and profits. It demands the cultivation of a "utopian conscience" that realizes the value and necessity of imagination and yes, even *illusion*, in creating a future different than our past by employing the power of the imagination to critically reject an inhibiting reality in favor of a vision of what *could* become a reality.[16] And indeed it is this dimension of irreality in the utopian vision that has a subversive and emancipatory power, and it is this anticipatory illumination of a reality not yet made real that is a fundamental category of a utopian philosophizing that appeared in the first years of romanticism.[17] And it is precisely this subversive power of utopian thinking that makes romanticism so important. Not only do we envy their learning and culture, we envy their strength and courage in daring to create alternative futures and to imagine a unified and integrated world of man and nature, of science and *Bildung*. The example of Schelling and his suggestive sketch of a "mythology of nature" would serve us well as a foil for considering how a utopian imagination might not only integrate religion and humanism, but also envision how symbols of a suffering god may be replaced by symbols of a suffering world—a challenge an orthodox Kantian might reject, but a challenge nonetheless to utopian fantasy to imagine not just a kingdom of ends that admits only rational beings, but a kingdom of ends that encompasses all of creation.

NOTES

1. Frederick Beiser, *The Romantic Imperative* (Cambridge, MA: Harvard University Press, 2002) (hereafter *RI*), 151.
2. Manfred Frank, Ulrich Schnabel, and Thomas Assheuer, "Ein Gespräch mit dem Tübinger Philosophen Manfred Frank über die Illusionen der Hirnforschung und ihre zweifelhaften politischen Folgen," *Die Zeit*, August 29, 2009. http://www.zeit.de/2009/36/Hirnforschung.
3. Letter of September 4, 1797, in which he also asks for further works of Ploucquet to aid his work on his *Von der Weltseele: eine Hypothese der höheren Physik* (1798). *Aus Schellings Leben*, in *Briefen*, ed. G. L. Plitt, 3 vols. (Leipzig: Herzel, 1869–70) (hereafter *Plitt*), vol. 1, 205ff.

4. Hanns-Peter Neumann and Franz Michael, eds., "Joseph Friedrich Schellings Dissertatio philosophica de simplicibus et eorum diversis speciebus von 1758. Einführung, Text und Übersetzung," in *Der Monadenbegriff zwischen Spätrenaissance und Aufklärung* (Berlin: Walter de Gruyter, 2009), 362. See his introduction to Ploucquet in the same work, 226.

5. Friedrich Christoph Oetinger (1702–82), an older colleague of Schelling Sr., insisted that the principle of freedom with all of its consequences extended throughout the natural world, defending the nonmechanical and nonrational forces that in engendering and sustaining life demonstrated their divine and sacred status. The principle of sufficient reason was not a universal law of our world, particularly when set in contrast to the many evils of this world. Perhaps the *Principio rationis sufficientis* obtained in the world of made things, but it failed to exhaustively explain the workings and purpose of life's multifarious systems. See Friedmann Stengel, "Theosophie in der Aufklarung," in *Offenbarung und Episteme: Zur europäischen Wirkung Jakob Böhmes im 17. und 18. Jahrhundert*, ed. Wilhelm Kühlmann and Friedrich Vollhardt (Berlin: Walter de Gruyter, 2012), 513–48.

6. Letter to Fichte, November 11, 1800.

7. "Poured from the source of things and the same as the source, the human soul has a co-knowledge (*Mitwissenschaft*) of creation" (SW 1/8, 200).

8. F. W. J. Schelling, *System der Weltalter: Münchener Vorlesung 1827/28 in einer Nachschrift von Ernst von Lasaulux*, ed. Siegbert Peetz (Frankfurt am Main: Klostermann, 1990), 92.

9. Novalis supplies a similar account in 1800 when he writes, "We will understand the world when we understand ourselves, since we and it are integrated halves. Children of god, divine seeds are we. One day we will be what our father is" (NS 2, 548).

10. Manfred Frank, *Der kommende Gott: Vorlesungen über die Neue Mythologie* (Frankfurt am Main: Suhrkamp, 1982), 11.

11. Manfred Frank, *Kaltes Herz unendliche Fahrt* (Frankfurt am Main: Suhrkamp, 1989), 53.

12. Manfred Frank, *Conditio moderna* (hereafter *KM*) (Stuttgart: Reclam, 1993), 94.

13. "The So-Called 'Oldest System Programme of German Idealism' (1796)," translated by Andrew Bowie, in *Aesthetics and Subjectivity* (Manchester: Manchester University Press, 1990), Appendix A, 266f. Contrary to Pöggler (see Otto Pöggeler, "Hegel, der Verfasser des ältesten Systemprogramms des deutschen Idealismus," *Hegel-Studien* 4 [1969]: 17–32) and others who see in this document both the penmanship and brilliance of Hegel, it is clear to those familiar with Hegel *and* Schelling—most notably Franz Rosenzweig, who discovered the text—that only the latter could have developed the ideas expressed in this fragmentary manifesto. Franz Rosenzweig, *Kleinere Schriften* (Berlin: Schocken, 1937), 230–77. Werner Beierwaltes makes a similar argument when he notes that "for Schelling the essential relation of philosophy and theology has, since his beginning in the *Systemprogramme*, never been questionable: true philosophy is simultaneously theology or philosophical religion." Werner Beierwaltes, *Platonismus und Idealismus* (Frankfurt am Main: Klostermann, 1972), 68.

14. But *complete* in this process of development does not mean the telos of this process is *completely determined*, a situation that for Schelling could only generate "complete boredom" (SW 1/1, 472).

15. Ernst Bloch, *Über Ungleichzeitigkeit, Provinz und Propaganda. Ein Gespräch mit Rainer Traub und Harald Wieser*, in *Gespräche mit Ernst Bloch* (Frankfurt am Main: Suhrkamp, 1975), 197ff.

16. Ibid., 14.

17. Ernst Bloch, *The Utopian Function of Art and Literature*, trans. Jack Zipes and Frank Mecklenburg (Cambridge, MA: MIT Press, 1993), xxxv.

PART FOUR

Science and Nature

12

Mathematics, Computation, Language, and Poetry

The Novalis Paradox

PAUL REDDING

Once, Georg Philipp Friedrich von Hardenberg, better known under the nom de plume "Novalis," had provided a handy stereotype for the nineteenth-century "romantic" poet—mystical, otherworldly, and fixated on death. Such a picture was largely constructed after his own death at the age of twenty-eight around a few episodes of his life, especially the death, at the age of fifteen, of his fiancée, Sophie von Kühn, an event reflected in his perhaps most well-known work, *Hymns to the Night*.[1] More recently, however, the complexity of the actual person has come to disrupt this nineteenth-century myth, and the interests, pursuits, and achievements of the hitherto "unknown Novalis" have come to be known and appreciated.[2] Among these are those interests shared with others in the circle of so-called Jena romantics—crucially, an intense involvement with the demanding philosophy of Immanuel Kant, occasioned by the influence of Karl Leonard Reinhold (1757–1823), the occupant of the chair of critical philosophy at the University of Jena between 1787 and 1794, and after that, with the philosophy of Johann Gottlieb Fichte, Reinhold's more prestigious successor at Jena.

Hardenberg had first encountered Reinhold after arriving at University of Jena in 1790 to study law, and although he moved from Jena to the University of Leipzig in 1792 (and then to Wittenberg, to finish his legal education) he remained connected to the philosophical culture of Jena via personal connections such as that to Friedrich Schlegel. Beyond these philosophical interests, however, and to some extent separating him from the more literary foci of other members of the circle, were Hardenberg's substantial interests in the sciences of his day, especially those developed during the formal scientific training he came to acquire in 1797 and 1798 at the Freiburg Mining Academy. These scientific studies themselves related to the practical dimensions of Hardenberg's short adult life, given that they were meant to equip him for a managerial position at the Saxon salt mines in Weissenfels, and yet they also fed into his philosophical interests, as can be seen in his unfinished notebook entries for a "romantic encyclopedia" written in late 1798.

Even when traditional stereotypes of the "romantic" have been corrected by the actual activities of the Jena romantics, there are still aspects of Hardenberg's interests and pursuits that can seem hard to reconcile with his status *as* a romantic, however. Broadly, the Jena romantics had taken Kant's critique of metaphysics as a cue to raise the stakes of areas of culture such as religion and art whose cognitive status had in many ways been threatened in modernity by, among other factors, the rise of the mathematized natural sciences. Following Kant they took it that metaphysics could not give us a theoretically determinate picture of the way the world was "in itself," but the human longing for this could be satisfied to some degree by the indirect presentations of the world and our place in it achievable within the arts and religion. This did not mean that the romantics had rejected the natural sciences, and distinctly "romantic" approaches to the sciences developed well into the first half of the nineteenth century, especially in relation to the emerging sciences of the living world. But romanticism, nevertheless, is usually understood as representing a reaction against the "disenchantment" of nature—that "reduction of circumambient nature to a mechanical system whose lineaments are provided by the immaterial forms of mathematical physics"—and part of the attraction of the "life sciences" consisted in the fact that they seemed to demand explanatory principles not reducible to mechanical ones.[3] However, seemingly at odds with this *anti*-mechanistic tenor to romanticism in general was Hardenberg's interest in the project of an *ars combinatoria*,[4] the project of a proto-*computationalist* approach to thought stretching back beyond Leibniz, but associated in Leibniz in particular with the idea of a universal language of science whose component concepts were able to be manipulated in mechanical ways.[5]

Leibniz's speculative combinatorial or computationalist approach to the workings of the mind, inspired by Hobbes,[6] is now commonly regarded as anticipating a number of distinctive scientific movements that started in the nineteenth century and gained momentum in the twentieth: the developments of symbolic logic and the formalization of proofs in mathematics and, in more practical domains, the foundational principles of contemporary disciplines of computer science and information theory and artificial intelligence and robotics.[7] Leibniz believed "in advance of Hilbert, that a consistent system of logic, language, and mathematics could be formalized by means of an alphabet of unambiguous symbols manipulated according to mechanical rules" and envisaged "a digital computer in which binary numbers were represented by spherical tokens, governed by gates under mechanical control."[8] In Hardenberg's hands, this combinatorial approach was viewed in a very different light as a means for the "poetization" and "romanticization" of science itself. Hardenberg's envisaged "machine" is to be played like a musical instrument: "Combinatorial analysis leads to numerical imaginings—and teaches the *art of the composition of numbers*—mathematical *basso continuo* (Pythagoras. Leibniz). Language is a musical instrument of ideas."[9] Indeed, Hardenberg is now associated with approaches to language and, more generally, semiotics that seem to anticipate broadly "structuralist" and "poststructuralist" approaches of recent times,[10] approaches that seem to be anathema to computationalist approaches to the mind and the generally "representationalist" assumptions on which they draw. How then are we to square these two opposing aspects of the object of his interest?

12.1. LOGIC, MATHEMATICS, AND THE IDEA OF MECHANIZED THOUGHT IN THE SEVENTEENTH AND EIGHTEENTH CENTURIES

In work that stretched from his early dissertation written at the age of nineteen, *Dissertatio de Arte Combinatoria* (1666), to his most mature thought, Leibniz had pursued ideas for a project for the application of mathematics to syllogistic logic, and thereby to the forms of discursive arguments whose forms syllogistic logic attempted to codify.[11] The *calculus of concepts* that Leibniz developed from this starting point is now seen as anticipating many of the features of the mid-nineteenth-century attempt to algebraicize logic found in the work of Boole and others, approaches that were crucial to the later development of information theory and ideas of "machine intelligence."[12] More than this, however, part of Leibniz's project was the construction of a "universal characteristic," the conception of which Gottlob Frege was to acknowledge as a precursor to his own "concept script" or *Begriffsschrift*, announced in 1879. Leibniz's project had been a complex one involving diverse aspects of his metaphysics and linking logic to an epistemology and a philosophy of mind, and at its heart was the idea of an *ars combinatoria* or universal characteristic—an "alphabet of human thoughts."[13] Somewhat like the way in which the idea of "analysis" functioned in the early years of analytic philosophy, the primitive concepts of Leibniz's universal characteristic were regarded as the ultimate termini of a process of analysis in which "clear and confused" ideas could be decomposed into their "clear and distinct" elements, represented in the universal characteristic in a way that showed their essential logical connections. Such analytic and synthetic transitions were determined by strictly definable mathematical rules of combination and transformation, resulting in a hierarchy of forms from simple to compound concepts to propositions and the inferential relations linking them. In this way, an inventory of all knowledge would eventually be able to be produced—a "rational encyclopedia."

The romantics were notoriously critical of system building, and of course it is difficult to appreciate the degree to which the envisaged systematicity of Leibniz's project could have been appreciated by anyone in the later eighteenth century, let alone a young polymath such as Hardenberg. Nevertheless, it is easy to exaggerate the invisibility of such issues associated with Leibniz's logic prior to the mid-nineteenth century. Hardenberg seems to have been introduced to the basics of Leibniz's plan by the work of the Leipzig philologist turned mathematician Carl Friedrich Hindenburg.[14] In fact, despite the unavailability of much of Leibniz's own technical papers, the basic dimensions and purport of this attempt to apply algebra to logic and language in general had been discussed within German scientific circles from about the mid-eighteenth century, especially following the publication of Johann Heinrich Lambert's *Neues Organon* (a work owned by Hardenberg) in which Lambert attempted to develop a Leibniz-inspired universal characteristic, applying it to contemporary science. Moreover, the publication of *Neues Organon* had been followed by a public dispute between Lambert and the Tübingen logician Gottfried Ploucquet over the question of precedence in the development of Leibniz's approach (Risser 1770, 277). The figure of Ploucquet is of particular relevance for the development of idealism and romanticism in the 1790s, as Hegel, Schelling, and Hölderlin had all become familiar with his logic and metaphysics while seminarians at the Tübingen Stift (Frank 2009, 36).

Thus in volume 2 of his *Science of Logic, Subjective Logic*, Hegel sets out the key features of the Leibniz-Ploucquet approach to the structure of judgment that allow the application of algebra to logic, associating it with the reduction of thought to a mechanical process.[15] Hegel's attitude to the Leibniz-Ploucquet mathematization of logic was critical but nuanced. The "mathematical syllogisms" represents the point of collapse of the traditional Aristotelian syllogistic, which is brought down under the negative effects of its *own* dialectic. As such this mathematical logic played a necessary but purely negative role in the dialectic of logical thought generally. The mathematical syllogism is a stage through which logical thought *must* progress, but taken as anything *other* than a purely negative moment of this progression and regarded as *itself* a model of thought, the mathematical syllogism was an absurdity, and had in turn to be overcome in the characteristic move of the "negation of negation."[16]

Despite his own criticisms of romanticism, Hegel's criticisms of Leibniz's and Ploucquet's project for the mathematization of thought here are, in many ways, typical of what might be expected of a romantic. For Hegel, logic is meant to capture the dynamics of spirit or cognitive *life*, but in the *characteristica universalis* and the combinatorial approach to syllogisms, all we find are the *dead remains* of living thought.[17] In ways analogous to Hegel, Hardenberg seems to have recognized the application of a Leibniz-inspired combinatoric as integral to the higher-level romantic "poeticization" of the world, and not simply antithetical to it. Thus he seems to have thought that the consistent application of the combinatorial approach would thereby serve to undermine the sorts of assumptions more conventionally associated with it. To understand Hardenberg's thinking here we need to understand both the broader context within which these ideas were being received in the late eighteenth century as well as the fate that the plan to mathematize thought must have had for Hardenberg given the fact of his basically *Kantian* sympathies in philosophy.

12.2. THE CONTEXT FOR HARDENBERG'S ENGAGEMENT WITH LEIBNIZ'S COMBINATORIALISM

The impact of Kant's philosophy in Jena from the late 1780s through the 1790s had been roughly paralleled by the growth of interest in the empirical studies of language with the attendant philosophical reflection that had constituted what has been described as a German "linguistic turn."[18] The issue of the significance of language for thought in relation to Kant's philosophy had first appeared in the context of J. G. Hamann's "Metacritique of the Critique of the Purism of Reason" of 1784, where Hamann referred to language as "the first, last, and only organon and criterion of reason."[19] The "language" in question here was not meant to refer to the type of speculative universal languages theorized about in the seventeenth century, or some inner "language of thought" found in medieval logical theorists such as Ockham. For Hamann, "language" is only found as the plurality of particular and diverse natural languages found operating within actual living communities. With this appeal to social and linguistic particularism, Hamann intended to undermine the universalism of Kant's conception of the "understanding" that was supposedly universal and necessary. In fact, the general theme of the role of language in human cognition had been popularized earlier by a former student of both Hamann and Kant, J. G. Herder, in his 1772 *Treatise on the Origin of Language*.[20] More generally, the idea of a "semiotic," already mentioned in Locke's *An Essay Concerning Human Understanding*, had been made the object of a thematic study by Lambert in *Neues Organon*, and had been developed in works such as Johann Christoph Hoffbauer's *Semiological Investigations*, another work known to Hardenberg.[21]

This question of the link of language or semiology more generally to thought had paired naturally to the theme of Reinhold's major revision of Kant in the context of his attempts to develop critical philosophy—the unsystematic and untheorized concept of "representation" (*Vorstellung*) that Kant seemed to simply presuppose in his *Critiques*. Reinhold's central "proposition of consciousness" stated that "in consciousness representation is distinguished through the subject from both object and subject and is referred to both."[22] In turn, Reinhold's representational account of conscious was attacked by the Humean skeptic Gottlob Ernst Schulze, writing under the name "Aenesidemus," who questioned how such a representation could be *known* to refer to the "object" to which it was supposed to refer, precipitating Fichte's now famous review.[23] In this, Fichte criticized Reinhold's uniformly *representationalist* account of consciousness that made his account open to Schulz's criticism, making the subject's own consciousness of *itself* a type of *direct* rather than *representational* affair.

Among the romantics, the nature of language was theorized at a high level of abstraction in the hermeneutic project associated with the practice of translation by Friedrich Schleiermacher, and an explicit attempt at a Kantian linguistics applied to the grammars of actual language was found in the work of Wilhelm von Humboldt.[24] Kant himself had suggested the analogy between the architectonic of the understanding and the grammar of a language,[25] although he had refrained from *identifying* the two. In this context it is natural that older conceptions of a language of thought as found in Leibniz and others would be revived, and from such a perspective the crucial question to be answered becomes whether the language *in which* one thinks is, following Hamann (and, perhaps, the later Wittgenstein), one's *particular language* or, following Humboldt (and, perhaps, Chomsky), some type of universal language implicit within each particular language. But Hardenberg, I will argue, undercut the assumption on which this dichotomy is based, the assumption that the mind is restricted to the processes of any internalized language itself. When talk of "mental representation" becomes mixed with that of linguistic representation Hardenberg avoids the Hamann-Humboldt dichotomy by denying the equation of mental content and linguistic sign, in a way that undermines the traditional view that linguistic signs somehow "express" a determinate conceptual psychological content. While for Hardenberg, traditional talk of inner concepts grasped *without* the capacity for use of linguistic signs is refused, this does not imply that thought itself was considered to be a type of inner speaking.

In his *Fichte Studies*, composed 1795–1796, Hardenberg introduces some initially confusing, but, I suggest, ultimately enlightening distinctions in relation to the nature of representations (*Vorstellungen*). One the one hand there is the *material* (*Stoff*) that is the substrate of the representation (*Vorstellung*) itself, but this must be distinguished from the *matter* (*Materie*) of "intuition"

(*Anschauung*).[26] This is immediately confusing because "intuition" is, in Kant's account, a *kind* of representation itself—a *mental* representation, the immediacy and singularity of which distinguishes it from the other relevant kind of mental representation, *concept*. But we might start here by thinking of "representation" for Hardenberg as referring primarily to an "external" representation, such as a word—an equation that seems justified by Hardenberg's other talk of "representation" in a explicitly linguistic context.[27] Reading in this way we can see Hardenberg as bringing into focus issues that have become thematic in various areas of inquiry in recent times.

External representations, such as words or, say, pictures, will count as representations because they have some kind of representational "content." A word "chair" will thus be thought to refer to worldly things, *chairs*, and often thought to so refer because it will be used to express some mental content, a concept, say (in this case, the concept "chair") that will *itself* refer to worldly entities (actual chairs).[28] This is a view found in Aristotle's *On Interpretation*, and has been referred to by Tyler Burge as the "traditional view."[29] But clearly, external representations such as words or pictures have properties that are not necessarily connected with the objects to which they refer or to the concepts that they express. The word type "chair" rhymes with that of "pear" although chairs and pears may have nothing particularly distinctive in common. This point is often made in terms of the idea that the meanings of *words* are "conventional." Sometimes this point is expressed in terms of the idea that such representations are not *intrinsically* representational, or that they can be individuated by properties *other than* their intentional or representational properties. And this brings into focus the peculiarities of the assumed *mental* contents involved, which, on the traditional view, *are* thought to be intrinsically representational, and so as having *no* properties other than their referential ones.[30] Aquinas had in this way drawn on this principle in an argument for the incorporeal nature of the soul with the claim that "whatever knows certain things cannot have any of them in its own nature; because that which is in it naturally would impede the knowledge of anything else."[31] That is, the mind cannot have properties like the properties of the particular things it *knows,* as this would interfere with its capacity for *general knowledge.*

12.3. POETRY AND LINGUISTIC COMPUTATIONALISM

It will not be surprising that a poet might take an interest in such nonrepresentational properties of words, such as those that allow them to carry the rhythms and rhymes that distinguish poetry as a form of speech.[32] If we then take Hardenberg's "material" to refer to such properties of external representations like word tokens, and take the "matter" of perceptual states ("intuitions") as their actual *intentional* content, then it seems uncontroversially true that the "materials" of such representations are distinct from the "matter" of that to which they refer. That the word "chair" resembles the word "pear" will be part of its *material*, and nothing like this resemblance is found between the concepts or their worldly extensions. But similarly, these nonrepresentational properties of words are going to be relevant to a "combinatory" or "computationalist" approach to language, as the types of "combinations and permutations" intended are meant to be applied *mechanically* to "uninterpreted" symbols. We can see how the interests of the poet and the computationalist might converge on this point, and a point of convergence can indeed be found in the strange case of the combinatorial poetics of Erycius Puteanus, a seventeenth-century humanist whose generation of multiple verses to the Virgin Mary from a single eight-word poem came to the attention of Leibniz and other theorists of mathematics and language.

An eight-word, one-line Latin hexameter—"Tot tibi sund doles, Virgo quot sidera caelo (Thou has as many virtues, O Virgin, as there are starts in heaven)"— published in 1615 by the Jesuit Bernard Bauhuis formed the base from which Puteanus generated 1,022 verse permutations (this number thought to be the actual number of stars in the firmament) in a work published two years later.[33] The number of *possible* permutations of the eight words is 40,320 (the number *8 factorial*) but of course not all of these permutations preserve the poem's meter, and various attempts were made by mathematicians during the seventeenth century to exceed Puteanus's number. The poem had been discussed in John Wallis's *Tractatus de Algebra*, and, although Wallis had not given a number for the possible hexametric permutations, one reviewer of that work had suggested 2,580. This reviewer is thought to have been Leibniz, who had discussed this and other examples of such "proteus verses" in *Dissertatio de Arte Combinatoria*.[34] Leibniz here, however, gave no indication of how this number had been estimated, and the issue was later taken up by Jacob Bernoulli, who estimated the number at 3,312 and showed how this number could be arrived at from the classical laws governing the prosodic structure of hexametric verse.[35] The problem of finding the principles for the generation of such proteus verses represents a clear example of the search for a "syntactic engine" that can generate an output of well-formed sentences according to entirely syntactic laws. Here the relevant properties of the units are not their semantic ones, but those nonsemantic ones that determine whether or not the "output" will *scan* in the appropriate way. The convergence of computational and poetic principles here is not coincidental.

Hardenberg clearly takes the mathematical-combinatorialist account of language seriously, and draws the conclusion that *qua language* its elements cannot be regarded as "expressing" a type of determinate mental content, as is seen in the 1798 fragment "Monologue." "Speaking and writing is a crazy state of affairs really; true conversation is just a game with words. It is amazing, the absurd error people make of imagining they are speaking for the sake of things; no one knows the essential thing about language, that it is concerned only with itself.... If it were only possible to make people understand that it is the same with language as it is with mathematical formulae—they constitute a world in itself—their play is self-sufficient, they express nothing but their own marvelous nature."[36] It is this, *seemingly* "postmodern" aspect of Hardenberg's approach that denies some extralinguistic referent that is apparent in his *Fichte Studies*, especially in relation to his criticism of Fichte's account of the "I."

In Kant, the concept "I" had been thought as a special type of concept that captures the "transcendental unity of apperception." It is a representation that in the form of "I think" accompanies *all* of my representations, and that is ultimately responsible for their unification into representations of a *single world*.[37] But the exact status of representations like this, Reinhold complained, had never been clearly spelled out in Kant. Reinhold, as we have seen, treated such mental "representations" as standing in a certain relation to both the subject and the object of consciousness. Schulze (Aenesidemus) had interpreted "representation" as referring to something like a sign or image—a typical *external* representation that can be individuated *without* appeal to its representational content. The skeptical question could then be put: how do we know that such representations refer to *any* objects in the external world? As Burge points out, this question cannot be posed in the "traditional view" as there mental representations have no extrarepresentational properties that would allow them to be individuated so that this question *could be* asked.[38] *Fichte's* response to Schulz was then to reassert the traditional idea of the transparency of a concept, at least for the case of the "I." A thinker can recognize her own thoughts *as* her own directly without any need for some intervening "sign." Self-consciousness does *not* depend on one's ability to represent oneself with the sign "I." But this is just the view that Hardenberg challenges in his *Fichte Studies*.

Hardenberg's notes here are nothing more than that, but the general drift of the thought is the thesis that all "signifieds" of signs, the mental contents *expressed* in signs, are, contrary to the traditional view, dependent for their identities on the signs expressing them. But at the same time, the signs themselves, it would seem, are identifiable *as the signs they are* only in that they express a mental content: "The relationship of the sign to the signified. Both are in different spheres that can mutually determine each another."[39] Given that Hardenberg's "sign" effectively translates what Ferdinand de Saussure was to later call "signifier," Hardenberg's picture here approaches Saussure's complex holistic and differential account of language where differences among signifiers and differences among signifieds determine each other, ruling out the idea of words expressing "concepts" as understood in the "traditional view."[40] Applied to Fichte's account of self-consciousness, this suggests that a being could only be determinately conscious of itself to the extent that it could expresses itself with the token "I," suggesting that to be capable of intentionality, of mental contents, the subject needs to be in some kind of communicative relation to *other* subjects. Over a decade later, Hegel was to draw a similar lesson from Fichte's starting point in his well-known "recognitive" theory of self-consciousness, while the romantics were to draw their own thesis concerning social existence as a condition of thought: all philosophy for them was necessarily "*sym*-philosophy."

It might be thought that with this Hardenberg has reverted to something like Hamann's idea that mental representations have the properties of "external" representations, *actual* language. However, Hardenberg's account is developed in ways that, seemingly paradoxically, *retain* elements of the traditional "transparency" view of mental content. The relation between sign and mental content (sign and "signified") will be different regarding *whose* mental state one is considering in a communicative event. The suggestion clearly seems to be that while for the *speaker, at least considered in a particular way*, the words somehow *do* directly express essentially *transparent* thoughts, this *cannot* be the case from the point of view of the person communicated *to*. "To the extent that the signifying person is *completely free* either in the effect of the signified or in the choice of signs, and not even dependent on his internally determined nature— to that extent, the two [sign and signified] are interrelated for the signifying person alone... [while] they are completely separate for a second signifying person."[41] What I take this to mean is that from the first-person perspective, speech must be considered as in the traditional view, with signs expressing thoughts (signifieds) that are themselves somehow transparent and directly in touch with the world, while for the other person this cannot be the case. For the interlocutor, signs uttered by the other must be regarded *first* as elements of a language, which has some sort of priority in the determination of the thought being communicated. From the external point of view, language has to be taken as a system in which the identity of each of the parts is determined by the way it functions *within* the system. Our inner states must be expressed in language to gain determinacy, but the determinacy found there can never be adequate to the *feel* of those inner states themselves.

This complex account in which both elements of the traditional view and its linguistic criticism are apparent in the later so-called logological fragments where Hardenberg makes this point explicit, distinguishing between concepts and words—a distinction that he describes as crucial for understanding the nature of metaphysics and logic, and for the difficulty in bringing these two disciplines together. Metaphysics, as the "pure dynamics of thinking" is "concerned with the soul of the philosophy of mind," and metaphysical concepts "relate to each other like *thoughts, without words*."[42] Hardenberg is clearly aware as to the metaphysical strain that the idea of such wordless thoughts commits one, as is revealed in the comment from the *Fichte Studies*: "What kind of a relation is knowledge? It is a being outside of being that is nevertheless within being....Consciousness is consequently an image of being within being." But then he corrects "image" with "sign," and the theory of signs must be a "theory of presentation, i.e., of not-being, within being, in order to let being be there for itself in a certain respect."[43]

The "signs" invoked here are, of necessity, characterized as "nonbeing"—that is, as having *no other* properties than their presentational ones. In the logological fragments, however, he notes that the concepts of logic, which is "concerned simply with the dead body of the philosophy of mind," "relate to each other as words do, without thoughts."[44] Clearly, the thesis of the overall dependence of thoughts (signifieds) on material signs would render pure metaphysical thinking, in the sense suggested above, impossible—a position that one would expect from a broadly Kantian starting point. But logic consists of "words without thoughts," that is, signs considered exclusively in terms of their *nonrepresentational* (or nonsemantic) properties. It is precisely this latter claim that he has learned from the combinatorialist tradition.

12.4. LEIBNIZ AND HARDENBERG, BEYOND HOBBES AND DESCARTES

We might thus see Hardenberg as bringing out the contradiction at the heart of attempts to divest the traditional view of its *immaterialism* by treating thought itself as a type of language understood on combinatorial or computational principles. The perceived contradiction is centered on the fact that the combinatorial approach itself must treat mental representations in an entirely "syntactic" way, putting out of play all the representational features of the "representations" themselves. Recently, Hilary Putnam has pointed to this problem facing "language of thought" or "lingua mentis" theories: The idea that thinking is about the manipulation of representations surely comes from our experience of the *use* of representations, but "none of the methods of representation that we know about—speech, writing, painting, carving in stone, etc.—has the magical property that there cannot be different representations with the same meaning."[45] That is, in *no such systems* do we find the "intrinsically" meaningful representations required by *thought*. But the problem seems to be deeper than that posed by Putnam. Given that qua objects to which syntactic processes apply, "mental" words must be considered as uninterpreted, it might be asked how *any* semantic features of thought are re-established? That this question is not *easily* answered in the present-day "language of thought hypothesis" (LOTH) is suggested by the entry for this hypothesis in the *Stanford Encyclopedia of Philosophy*.[46] The question of how the semantic content of propositional attitudes is inherited from that of the mental symbols computed can be asked at two levels: First, how do molecular symbols get their semantic content from their atomic components? And next, how do the atomic components represent what they do? Language of thought theorists have most to say about the former, but about the latter it is stated that "the official line doesn't propose any theory...but simply assumes that the first question can be answered in a naturalistically acceptable way. In other words, officially LOTH *simply assumes* that the atomic symbols/expressions in one's LOT have whatever meanings they have."[47]

As has been pointed out by Jaan Maat in a study of Leibniz's universal characteristic (Maat 2004), this is precisely the problem that Leibniz faced and struggled with, ultimately unsuccessfully: he assumed that permitted syntactic transformations preserve the *semantic* features of the elements of the characteristic, and that the "syntactic and semantic aspects of the project are two sides of the same coin,"[48] but then had to answer the difficult question of how the atomic elements gained these semantic features in the first place.[49] Indeed, the problem is signaled by his shifting between describing the characteristic sometimes as an *alphabet* and sometimes as a *language*: contrary to the way we think of words of a language, the individual elements of an alphabet, of course, do not by themselves *have* semantic properties. Historically we might view the tension as between two influences feeding in to Leibniz's project: Descartes's account of the contents of consciousness and Hobbes's computational approach to the mind.

In his fourth objection to Descartes, Hobbes had linked his computational approach to thought to a thoroughgoing materialist account of cognition and drawn from it radically nonrepresentationalist consequences. In the suggested picture, reasoning is conceived as a "joining together and linking of name and labels by means of the verb 'be.'" But such names and labels are established entirely conventionally, as there is no possible resemblance between the two that could establish anything here other than conventionally supported relationships. In this picture the mind is "nothing more than motion occurring in various parts of an organic body."[50] In his reply, Descartes insists that surely *reasoning* must deal with what is *signified* by the words, not just with the words themselves: "As for the linking together that occurs when we reason, this is not a linking of names but of the things that are signified by the names.... Who doubts that a Frenchman and a German can reason about the same things despite the fact that the words that they think of are completely different?"[51] That is, Descartes simply reasserts the traditional view of the "transparency" of mental contents: if we are to talk of mental representations, these representations must be the vehicles of a direct access to the world, and ultimately it is God that establishes this connection. The certainty with which we feel that ideas perceived "clearly and distinctly" present the world to us as it is, is grounded in God's goodness, which prevents the possibility of deception here.[52]

In 1677 Leibniz was to write a dialogue on this very dispute, accepting Hobbes's view of the existence of mental characters with no intrinsic similarity to what they signify, using the mathematical example of the lack of any resemblance between "0" and *nothing*.[53] But he wanted of course to avoid the type of semantic skepticism of which Descartes accused Hobbes, and used a version of Descartes's appeal to clear and distinct ideas, but now such that these coincided with the final products of logical decomposition. But as Maat has pointed out, Leibniz was himself troubled by doubts about the coherence of the notion of an essentially *thinkable* atomic terminus of analysis. If a notion, call it A, is essentially thinkable, then it would seem that it must be capable of further analysis: it must be able to be analyzed into a component specific to its being A, and the concept "thinkability" that it will have in common with all other concepts.[54] It would be considerations such as these that were behind later idealist critiques of what is now known as the "Myth of the Given" and that has its prototype in Kant's insistence, noted above, that all representations, in order to *be* representations, be accompanied by the concept "I," the concept of the thinker for whom they are representations.[55]

We might think of this as just another expression of the problem discussed above. Leibniz defines his ultimate atomic units both as those for which no further analysis is possible, and those that can be known "through themselves." But to think of some purported atomic ultimate "A" as something known "through itself" sounds like it is conceived as some ultimate phenomenal presence, like the empiricist's "sensory impression" or "sense-datum"—something known in terms of its phenomenal properties, its own "*Stoff*." But being regarded as essentially *thinkable* sounds as if it is to be regarded as intrinsically *representational*, and known through the "*Materie*" of its content.

Hardenberg's alternative to Leibniz's dilemma was to aestheticize Leibniz's picture by emphasizing the aesthetic "*stoffliche*" dimensions of the characteristic, thus, *seemingly*, giving up its purported representational dimension. Poems are not to "mean," just "be!" One is to *play* the machine like a musical instrument, the products of this play, like the notes of a melody, thus becoming "self-sufficient" in needing no reference *beyond* themselves. They "express nothing but their own marvelous nature."[56] But how, then, can this conception have any relevance for activities, like those of science, where surely *some* conception of their adequacy involves the relation of their products to the world?

It is true that certain of Hardenberg's formulations suggest this dichotomization of external signs and inner thought, but such a position is contradicted by those formulas offering a more "Saussurean" alternative. Hardenberg wants the elements of Leibniz's characteristic to be understood in terms of their "*Stoff*" so that the "machine" can be played like a piano to produce patterns in which the elements, as with the notes of a melody, are not organized according to any considerations beyond those of the system of language itself—their accuracy in reflecting nonlinguistic worldly structures, for example. But the elements are, nevertheless, *words*—that is, *signs*—and not mere sounds. Qua *stoffliche* entities, semantic considerations must enter into the identities of words and signs in that within a language differences in sound only *count* when they function to differentiate meaning.[57] As Hardenberg articulates the point in *Fichte Studies*, "sign" (or for Saussure, "signifier") and signified are "in different spheres that can mutually determine each another."[58] Signs do not have meaning in as much that they express "concepts" and thereby determinately apply to "things" in the world. They have meaning to the extent that *stoffliche* differences among them can determine differences within the realm of meaning and use. Such words can be "played" according to their identities as signifiers so as to transform the system of signifieds. Thus the idea of poetry as "meaningless" melody does not capture the sense in which the elements are words and not notes, elements that cannot be entirely stripped of semantic properties and have *only* a syntax. For this reason we might be skeptical of those (such as Dalhaus)[59] who place "Novalis" here in the tradition of other romantics, such as Ludwig Tieck and E. T. A. Hoffman, who are seen as pointing to a conception of poetry as aspiring "towards the condition of music" (as Pater later put it),[60] and a conception of music as "absolute music"—music totally freed from the constraints of language and representation.

The acceptance of nonrepresentational wordless music as the paradigm of art seems to be one consequence of the *skeptical* interpretation of the critique of the "traditional view" of the relation of speech to thought like that of Hobbes. Hardenberg, however, as we have seen, retains elements of the traditional view within his account of the speaker's attitude to her own thoughts: a speaker, it appears, has no alternative but to take her expression as transparently manifesting her own cognitive states understood as veridically disclosing the world. It is only from the point of view of the *hearer* that the linguistic vehicle of the expression is considered to have *stoffliche* properties that accrue from the fact that it is a fragment of a social and public language. But it cannot be that this external point of view simply "trumps" that of the immediate point of view of the speaker herself. It cannot be the source of any "real" meaning of the utterance that replaces the speaker's irreducibly private one, as it is not the source of any determinate meaning *at all*. We might say that what this external "aesthetic" point of view provides for is a constant source of challenge to the speaker's understanding as to what her words amount to—a constant possibility of provocation to the speaker to reflect on and re-evaluate the meaning of her expressions in the light of this "reflective," external point of view. In this sense Hardenberg's "mathematical" approach to language seems to point a way not only beyond Descartes's and Hobbes's opposed approaches to meaning, but beyond what is commonly taken to be the nature of "romanticism" itself.[61]

NOTES

1. Hardenberg's personal loss had been doubled by the death of a brother, Erasmus, a month later.
2. David W. Wood, "Introduction" to *Notes for a Romantic Encyclopaedia: Das Allgemeine Brouillon*, ed. David W. Wood (Albany: State University of New York Press, 2007).
3. J. M. Bernstein, "Introduction," in *Classic and Romantic German Aesthetics*, edited by J. M. Bernstein (Cambridge: Cambridge University Press, 2003), ix.
4. For a systematic treatment of this theme in the work of Novalis, see John Neubauer, *Symbolismus und symbolische Logik* (Munich: Wilhelm Fink Verlag, 1978).
5. In general, positive reception of Leibniz's work among the romantics had centered on its quasi-*vitalistic*, antimechanistic dimensions. Frederick Beiser, *The Romantic Imperative: The Concept of Early German Romanticism* (Cambridge, MA: Harvard University Press, 2003), 143–44. Those aspects of Leibniz's work celebrated by the proponents of contemporary computationalist approaches to the mind seem very different.
6. Thus Hobbes, in a work of 1656, declares that "by ratiocination, I mean *computation*. Now to compute, is either to collect the sum of many things that are added together, or to know what remains when one thing is taken out of another. ... all ratiocination is comprehended in these two operations of the mind, addition and subtraction." Hobbes, "Elements of Philosophy," in *The English Works of Thomas Hobbes of Malmesbury*, ed. Sir William Molesworth, vol. 1 (London: John Bohn, 1839), 3.
7. See George Dyson, *Turing's Cathedral: The Origins of the Digital Universe* (New York: Random House, 2012); Ronald Hausser, *Computational Linguistics and Talking Robots* (Berlin: Springer, 2011), and Martin Davis, *The Universal Computer: The Road from Leibniz to Turing* (New York: Norton, 2000).
8. Dyson, *Turing's Cathedral*, 103–4.
9. Novalis, *Notes for a Romantic Encyclopaedia: Das Allgemeine Brouillon*, trans. David W. Wood (Albany: State University of New York Press, 1997), 97.
10. See Boris Gasparov, *Beyond Pure Reason: Ferdinand de Saussure's Philosophy of Language and Its Early Romantic Antecedents* (New York: Columbia University Press, 2013).
11. Wolfgang Lenzen, "Leibniz's Logic," in *Handbook of the History of Logic*, vol. 3: *The Rise of Modern Logic from Leibniz to Frege*, ed. Dov. M. Gabbay and John Woods (Amsterdam: Elsevier, 2004).
12. Donald Knuth, *The Art of Computer Programming*, vol. 4, *Generating All Trees: History of Combinatorial Generation* (Upper Saddle River, NJ: Pearson Education, 2006); Paul J. Nahin, *The Logician and the Engineer: How George Boole*

and *Claude Shannon Created the Information Age* (Princeton: Princeton University Press, 2013).

13. Jaap Maat, *Philosophical Languages in the Seventeenth Century: Dalgarno, Wilkins, Leibniz* (Dordrecht: Kluwer, 2004), 292.

14. Hans Niels Jahnke, "Mathematics and Culture: The Case of Novalis," *Science in Context* 4 (1991): 279–95.

15. G. W. F. Hegel, *Science of Logic*, trans. A. V. Miller (Atlantic Highlands, NJ: Humanities Press, 1969), 685–86. Rather than, like Aristotle, thinking of the judgment as the joining of a universal-naming predicate to a substance-naming particular subject, Leibniz had suggested treating the subject term as *itself* a predicate, such that "S is P" could be read as *identifying* terms "S" and "P" predicable of some (singular) "third" *not* named in the judgment. This effectively allowed Leibniz to treat categorical judgments as hypotheticals, and regard individual propositions as having one of two values (true or false). As Leibniz had already regarded the system of numbers as reducible to a binary system, this allowed the idea of computation within arithmetic to be extended to logical relations among bivalent propositions. For a systematic reconstruction see Lenzen, "Leibniz's Logic."

16. This transformation resulted in the traditional syllogistic being completely reconfigured into what Hegel describes as the "syllogism of reflection," which becomes made up on *singular* judgments, which allow *inductive* inferences, which then become dependent on forms of *analogical* judgments, and so on. Hegel, *The Science of Logic*, 686–95.

17. Thus, in Leibniz "the rational is taken as a dead and non-rational thing" (Hegel, *The Science of Logic*, 685) because thought, having been reduced to the "notion-less material" of numbers, is taken to be the sort of process that can be performed by "calculating machines" (684). Hegel identifies Leibniz having reached the most extreme point in the logic of "the understanding" that works on "ossified material... already to hand" (575).

18. Christina Lafont, *The Linguistic Turn in Hermeneutic Philosophy*, trans. José Medina (Cambridge, MA: MIT Press, 1999).

19. Jere Paul Surber, ed. *Metacritique: The Linguistic Assault on German Idealism* (Amherst: Humanity Books, 2001), 58.

20. Questions of who influenced whom in these regards are complex and contested. See, for example, Katie Terezakis, *The Immanent Word: The Turn to Language in German Philosophy, 1759–1801* (New York: Routledge, 2007) and Michael Forster, *After Herder: Philosophy of Language in the German Tradition* (Oxford: Oxford University Press, 2010) and *German Philosophy of Language: From Schlegel to Hegel and Beyond* (Oxford: Oxford University Press, 2011).

21. See Johann Christoph Hoffbauer, *Semiological Investigations, or, Topics Pertaining to the General Theory of Signs*, ed. and trans. Robert E. Innis (Amsterdam: J. Benjamins, 1991 [1789]).

22. Karl Leonard Reinhold, "The Foundation of Philosophical Knowledge," in *Between Kant and Hegel: Texts in the Development of Post-Kantian Idealism*, ed. and trans. George di Giovanni and H. S. Harris (Albany: State University of New York Press, 1985 [1791]), 70.

23. J. G. Fichte, "Review of Aenesidemus," in di Giovanni and Harris, *Between Kant and Hegel*.

24. Forster, *After Herder* and *German Philosophy of Language*.
25. Immanuel Kant, *Prolegomena To Any Future Metaphysics* ed. and trans. Gary Hatfield (Cambridge: Cambridge University Press, 2004, §39
26. Novalis, *Fichte Studies*, ed. and trans. Jane Kneller (Cambridge: Cambridge University Press, 2003), no. 226.
27. Ibid., no. 249.
28. In Kant's account, the application of concept to thing is never direct but always mediated by an *intuition*.
29. Aristotle, *Categories* and *De Interpretatione* 1, 16a4–7; Tyler Burge, "Concepts, Definitions and Meaning," *Metaphilosophy* 24 (1993): 309–25.
30. Burge, "Concepts, Definitions and Meaning," 310.
31. Aquinas, *Summa Theologica* I, 75, 2.
32. Cf., "A poem should not mean / But be." Archibald MacLeish, *Ars Poetica,* in *Collected Poems 1917–1982* (Boston: Houghton Mifflin, 1985 [1926]), 106.
33. The work was, *Pietatis Thaumata in Bernardi Bauhusii e Societate Jesu Proteum Parthenium*.
34. Donald Knuth (*The Art of Computer Programming*) discusses this in the context of the evolution of computer science. Neubauer notes that Novalis was interested in the similar phenomenon of "Bouts-rimé" (Neubauer, *Symbolismus und symbolische Logik*, 140).
35. Bernoulli, *The Art of Conjecturing, Together with Letter to a Friend on Sets in Court Tennis*, trans. Edith Dudley Sylla (Baltimore: Johns Hopkins University Press, 2005); Knuth, *The Art of Computer Programming*.
36. Novalis, "Monologue," trans. Joyce P. Crick, in Bernstein, *Classic and Romantic German Aesthetics*, 214.
37. Kant, *Critique of Pure Reason*, B131–32.
38. Burge, "Concepts, Definitions and Meaning," 321.
39. Novalis, *Fichte Studies*, no. 11. Hardenberg's concept of "sign" effectively equates to what Saussure was to call the "signifier", i.e., the sign grasped in terms of its non-representational properties. The striking similarities between the views of Saussure and Hardenberg are pursued in Gasparov, *Beyond Pure Reason*.
40. Saussure, *Course in General Linguistics*, trans. Wade Baskin, ed. Perry Meisel and Haun Saussy (New York: Columbia University Press, 2011 [1916]).
41. Novalis, *Fichte Studies*, no. 113.
42. Novalis, *Philosophical Writings*, trans. and ed. Margaret Mahony Stoljar (Albany: State University of New York Press, 1997), 51.
43. Novalis, *Fichte Studies*, no. 2.
44. Novalis, *Philosophical Writings*, 51.
45. Hilary Putnam, *Representation and Reality* (Cambridge: MIT Press, 1988), 21.
46. Murat Aydede, "The Language of Thought Hypothesis," *The Stanford Encyclopedia of Philosophy* (Fall 2010 Edition), Edward N. Zalta (ed.), URL = <http://plato.stanford.edu/archives/fall2010/entries/language-thought/>.
47. Emphasis added.
48. Maat, *Philosophical Languages*, 313. Cf., "In Leibniz's view, the power of a symbolism does not reside in the individual symbols, but in the systematical relations the symbols have to each other and to the things they designate. Hence Leibniz's central

concern in his efforts to construct a philosophical language is to establish a perfect conformity between its semantic and syntactic aspects" (Maat, 309–10).

49. Maat, *Philosophical Languages,* sections 5.3.4–5.3.5.

50. Hobbes in Descartes, *The Philosophical Writings of Descartes*, vol. 2, trans. J. Cottingham et al. (Cambridge: Cambridge University Press, 1984), 125–26.

51. Ibid., 126.

52. Descartes opposition to the idea that "ideas" would have their own *nonrepresentational* properties is, of course, consistent with his mind-body dualism.

53. M. Lagerlund, "Leibniz (and Ockham) on the Language of Thought, or How the True Metaphysics is Derived from the True Logic," in *Categories of Being: Essays on Metaphysics and Logic*, ed. Leila Haaparanta and Heikki J. Koskinen (Oxford: Oxford University Press, 2012), 103–6; Maat, *Philosophical Languages,* section 5.4.2.

54. Maat, *Philosophical Languages*, 314.

55. Kant, *Critique of Pure Reason*, B131–32.

56. Novalis, "Monologue," 214.

57. For example, some languages such as English will distinguish word-types according to whether they start with the sounds distinguished in English as "p" and "b," but in other languages this "voicing" of the consonant will not differentiate meanings at all and so be *inaudible*.

58. Novalis, *Fichte Studies*, no. 11.

59. Carl Dalhaus, *The Idea of Absolute Music*, trans. Roger Lustig (Chicago: University of Chicago Press, 1989), 145.

60. Walter Pater, *The Renaissance: Studies in Art and Poetry* (Berkeley: University of California Press, 1980), 106.

61. I wish to thank Dalia Nassar for helpful feedback on an earlier version of this essay. My thanks also go to Frances Massey, with whom I have had many illuminating discussions on topics touched on here.

13

Friedrich Schlegel's Romantic Calculus

Reflections on the Mathematical Infinite around 1800

JOHN H. SMITH

[Mathematik] sollte jeder Gelehrte verstehn eben wie [Grammatik]?
[Every scholar should have an understanding of (mathematics) as well as
(grammar)?]

—F. SCHLEGEL *(KA 18, 360, no. 474)*

Just what *is* "unendliche Annäherung" ("infinite approximation" or "approaching to infinity")? We know it as the title of Manfred Frank's groundbreaking lectures interpreting the philosophical background and contributions of the early romantic movement. And so much of our understanding of romanticism is associated with the infinite longing and endless striving of "progressive Universalpoesie" (F. Schlegel). This essay provides a different interpretation of this fundamental romantic concept by exploring the significance, context, and consequences of discussions in the latter part of the eighteenth century around the "mathematical infinite." We can take as a point of departure a footnote at the beginning of chapter 2 of Salomon (often also Solomon) Maimon's 1790 *Essay on Transcendental Philosophy*. The first sentences read:

I am not ignorant of what can be said against the introduction of mathematical concepts of infinity into philosophy. In particular, since these concepts are still subject to many difficulties in mathematics itself, it might appear as if I wanted to explain something obscure through something yet more obscure. However, I venture to claim that these concepts in fact belong to philosophy and were taken from there over into mathematics; as well as that the great Leibniz came upon the discovery of the differential calculus through his system of the Monadology.[1]

As we shall see, by replacing Kant's radical distinction between the faculties of sensibility and understanding with a view of their infinitesimal difference, Maimon is not only attending to debates among mathematicians and philosophers about the status of continuity, divisibility, and the infinitely small, but also opening up new avenues for idealism and romanticism. In pursuing the relevance of these discussions for philosophy around 1800, this essay specifically deals with the mathematical conceptions *of that period*; the fact that the foundations of calculus have undergone dramatic reformulations (at least four, three in the nineteenth century thanks to Cauchy, Weierstrass, and Cantor, and one in the 1960s thanks to Robinson) is not relevant here because my interest strictly concerns the way the mathematical infinite was understood in the latter half of the eighteenth century.[2] My point is that precisely those conceptions, "wrong" or ambivalent as they may be for (some) mathematicians today, provided powerful tools for rethinking both reality and consciousness. In fact, the very ambivalence associated with the notion of the differential, or the infinitesimal increment of a variable—Were they actual quantities? Did they "exist" or were they nothing? Can they "add up" to anything if they are equivalent to zero?—made them particularly fruitful for philosophical speculations. Friedrich Schlegel's thought around 1800 is imbued with the paradoxes of the infinite as they had been explored by mathematicians and philosophers (especially Kant and Maimon). His concept of the infinite, which both embraces philosophical dualisms even as he empowers consciousness with the ability to approach their overcoming, owes much of its formulation to debates concerning the infinitesimal calculus.

13.1. THE STATUS OF THE INFINITE IN EIGHTEENTH-CENTURY CALCULUS

As is well known, the techniques of differential and integral calculus as introduced in different ways by Newton and Leibniz in the last part of the seventeenth century had a tremendous range of application in the sciences. They could be used to calculate the movements of the planets, the course of a projectile, or flows of water—in sum, anything that undergoes change. And yet, as Hegel himself noted, "On the one hand its introduction into mathematics has led to an expansion of the science and to important results; but on the other hand it is remarkable that mathematics has not yet succeeded in justifying its use of this infinite by the Notion" (Hegel 279). The unclear status of the infinite in calculus led to major suspicions (as in Berkeley's sharp critiques of "infinitesimals" or infinitely small magnitudes as "ghosts of departed quantities"). But the lack of justification for the basic concepts in calculus also meant that leading mathematicians were inclined to philosophize about the foundations of their methods (even as they continued expanding those methods) and philosophers were able to exploit the ambivalence in the use of the "mathematical infinite" to address problems of their own. At stake are a number of fundamental issues: Does it make sense to speak of infinite divisibility? Are infinite quantities, especially infinitely small quantities (differentials), equivalent to zero? What is the effect of introducing quantities that can be thought but neither intuited nor represented? Let us look at three influential mathematicians for the different, and ambivalent, positions circulating on these questions.

Leonhard Euler (1707–1783), considered one of the most gifted mathematicians of his age (and in general), argued vehemently in his *Briefe an eine deutsche Prinzessin über verschiedene Gegenstände aus der Physik und Philosophie* (*Letters to a German Princess concerning Different Matters in Physics and Philosophy*, 1768) against the Leibnizian and Wolffian systems in the name of a radical materialism.[3] The two ideas he rejects are (1) the notion of a gradation of consciousness, that is, all monads—and there must be an infinite number of them—have "only very obscure ideas, whereas we have clear and occasionally even distinct ideas/representations" (Euler 192) and (2) the claim "that each body is composed of such parts, which have no extension whatever" (Euler 189) since this claim entails the emergence of extension from a composite of (an infinite number of) extensionless entities—which he finds absurd. It will be precisely the issues of infinite gradations of representability and the adding up (integrating) of infinitesimal acts of consciousness that will play a role in post-Kantian philosophies.

To appreciate the conundrum that mathematicians faced consider the odd results that can be produced when working with the infinite. In his highly significant *Institutiones calculi differentialis* (*Foundations of Differential Calculus*) of 1755 Euler argued for a deep ambivalence: infinitesimals are both nothing and something. In the preface to his book he claims first:

[D]ifferential calculus is concerned not so much with vanishing increments, which indeed are nothing, but with the ratio and mutual proportion. Since these ratios are expressed as finite quantities, we must think of calculus as being concerned with finite quantities.[4]

And then claimed:

> To many who have discussed the rules of differential calculus, it has seemed
> that there is a distinction between absolutely nothing and a special order of
> quantities infinitely small, which do not quite vanish completely but retain a
> certain quantity that is indeed less than any assignable quantity.[5]

As Sandifer points out, Euler seems to want it both ways. Indeed, this was
the way differentials were often treated, for example, by Newton and Leibniz: as
existing quantities so that they could be manipulated in equations, but then
disregarded as equivalent to zero in order to produce the final results.

Lazarus Ben David (often also Bendavid, 1762–1832) comes down on the
side of Euler in seeing infinitesimal magnitudes as equal to zero but also grapples with the problem of representation and intuition.[6]Although he wrote on a
variety of philosophical topics, of particular interest here is his *Versuch einer
logischen Auseinandersetzung des mathematischen Unendlichen* (*Essay on the
Logical Analysis of the Mathematical Infinite*) of 1789. Maimon must have been
aware of it prior to its publication since, as we shall see, he responds to it already
in his own *Versuch*. Like so many others, Ben David addresses the awkwardness
of the situation in which a science like calculus rests on a concept that has no
clear definition. Indeed, the more successful calculus is, the greater the need to
understand its fundamental principles: "the greater the advantages are that calculus affords us, and the more its results concur with those that had been found
by other means, the more desirous we become to establish the principles out
of which this calculus and its results emerge."[7] The problem with the particular
concept of the infinite is that it cannot be intuited or represented, its *Evidenz* is
not constructed as in geometry; therefore it requires logical analysis (Bendavid
xxx–xxxi).[8] He proceeds by looking at the nature of numbers and defining them
as manifolds that are gathered in a unity (Bendavid §18). Whatever is finite
("endlich") can be measured, is "meßbar" (Bendavid §19). An infinite magnitude, therefore, is one for which no number can be found that can be a measure
for it, and he concludes that "the mathematician calls every magnitude, which
cannot be expressed through numbers, infinite" (Bendavid §18). Since neither
the infinitely small nor infinitely large "can be given in terms of number or
measure; and it cannot be represented using any means that we would otherwise use to make a magnitude intuitable, as by construction" (Bendavid §22), it
is, strictly speaking, nothing. That is: "The expression 'infinite' means nothing
other than nowhere and nothing everywhere where it is used" (Bendavid §24).
It can be only thought, but not represented. Hence the crowning "logical analysis" in the form of a syllogism:

A. Only zero can be thought absolutely as quantity.

B. The infinite must, as quantity, be thought absolutely; from which it follows directly that

C. The infinite is zero. (Bendavid §28)

The infinite has only the quality of being an immeasurable quantity, but is used *analogously* in calculations as if it were a quantity (Bendavid §44). The infinite is thus like an intensive magnitude that cannot be increased or decreased as such (although something else can be measured, like the rise of mercury in a thermometer) (Bendavid §48–49).

A somewhat different position was represented by one of the more widely read mathematicians—in part because of his textbooks—of the second half of the eighteenth century, Abraham Gotthelf Kästner (1719–1800).[9] He points out in his *Anfangsgründe der Analysis des Unendlichen* (*Foundations of the Analysis of the Infinite*) that the "mysteries" and "inconsistencies" that so many authors have produced around the concept of infinity arise "whenever one views an infinite magnitude as something really existing"; instead, one needs to conceive "magnitudes that grow or diminish [as] undetermined/indefinite [*unbestimmt*]" and thus, strictly speaking, as not a number.[10] And indeed he refers positively to Euler in the preface to the second edition of 1770 (Kästner xvi). In a manner that will lead in the nineteenth century to a formulation of the foundations of calculus that does away with infinitesimals altogether, he understands the infinitely small or large relationship between dx and dy in terms of limits (Kästner 52–54). However, he refers to Leibniz's expression "toleranter vera" (a tolerable truth) that *does* permit us to speak of "the infinite as something real" (Kästner 52). That is, Kästner is referring to the fact that although given his metaphysics of monads Leibniz had argued for the reality of infinitesimal magnitudes, he later came to see them as "necessary fictions." Thus, though using somewhat different arguments than Euler, Kästner also ends up revealing the paradox of the mathematical infinite—it exists and does not exist—which leads him to suggest accepting the "manner of speaking" ("Redensart") which is "tolerably true" ("erträglich wahr"): "The relationship between infinitely small magnitudes, which can be given in terms of finite magnitudes" (Kästner 54). The unrepresentable (infinitely small or large magnitudes) can be represented as necessary fictions and tolerable truths. [11]

13.2. THE MATHEMATICAL INFINITE IN PHILOSOPHY: MAIMON

Against this background of conflicting positions—the mathematical infinite is both something and nothing and it cannot be intuited or represented (like

geometric constructions) but only thought—we can understand the reason why Kant needs to address the "mathematical antinomies" that revolve
around notions of infinity. When reason grapples with the infinite, as it apparently must, it also gets drawn toward the conundrums of the infinite. In the
Prolegomena zu einer jeden künftigen Metaphysik (1784, *Prolegomena to Any
Future Metaphysics*) Kant introduces the Antinomies with a remarkable number of hyperboles: We see here, he writes, "the most striking phenomenon"
of reason, which "affects us most forcefully" and which has the power "to
awaken philosophy from its dogmatic slumber" (Kant, *Prolegomena* 101) such
that thanks to this "strangest phenomenon of human reason...the critical
philosopher...is forced into reflection and disquietude" (Kant, *Prolegomena*
103). However, whereas Kant strove to dissolve the contradictions that arise
when thinking of the power of the infinite and its ambivalences in mathematics, many post-Kantians and the romantics embraced them. Thus we read
a fragment by F. Schlegel: "*Consciousness of 1/0 is the root of all knowing.
Consciousness can only be thought as 1/0 and 1/0 only as consciousness*" (KA
18, 409, no. 1062).

But to see how Schlegel could make such an extraordinary claim, we should
return to Maimon, for his response to basic problems in Kant introduced
the mathematical infinite into consciousness itself. [12] Maimon's argument is,
indeed, very difficult to grasp at times, for he himself was aware of his limitations as an autodidact in philosophy and as a nonnative speaker of German
(since he came from a Jewish family in Lithuania). At its core, his argument
seems to be a rethinking of Kant with a commitment to the reality of the infinitesimal, and to the infinitesimal nature of reality for consciousness. We can
state it this way: the act of synthesizing that Kant had considered consciousness's contribution to the production of knowledge is interpreted by Maimon
in terms of the twin notions of the differential and the integral. While for Kant,
knowledge as experience comes about by the two steps of first subsuming the
manifold of sense data under the forms of intuition to make representations
and then subsuming these representations under the categories provided by
the understanding, Maimon argues in a way more consistent with Leibniz and
Wolff that there is an infinite *gradation* of consciousness. At the "lower end" of
the continuum—and it is a continuum in a mathematical sense—we have the
"primitive consciousness of a constituent part of a synthesis" (which he calls a
"presentation" [*Vorstellung*]) and at the "upper end" we have the "consciousness of the completed synthesis" (Maimon 181). These two are "limit concepts"
or "mere ideas" (Maimon 181) in that by definition there would be no object
of knowledge whatever if there were no consciousness, that is, if consciousness were reduced to zero; and likewise, only an "infinite consciousness" (God)
could possibly attain full knowledge of how any object could be synthesized

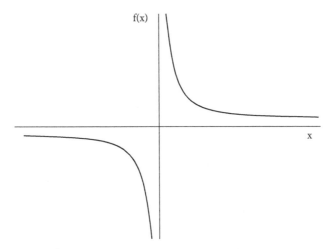

Figure 13.1. Asymptote of a curve is the line such that the distance between the line and the curve approaches zero as they tend to infinity.

with the totality of reality. He clearly has in mind something like the asymptotic function $y = 1/x$, where the x- and y-axes would be the "symbolic infinite," the "limits" that can never be reached (the asymptotes), while the infinitesimal difference that is "determinable yet undetermined" because it can always be made smaller, is the "intuitive" infinite (Maimon 181).[13]

If for Kant the infinite leads reason into antinomies, Maimon uses it in order to challenge the distinction between the faculties of sensibility and understanding, the radical nature of which Kant continually stressed.[14] Although Kant felt compelled to insist on an absolute difference between the faculty that subsumes data under the forms of intuition and the faculty that takes those "appearances" and unites them into objective judgments, this difference led to problems that forced him to introduce additional features, the "schematisms," in order to mediate between the two faculties if cognition is to occur. Maimon, however, points to the unbridgeability of the faculties in the Kantian model, realizes it threatens the critical enterprise, and asks: "Who will lead me out of this embarrassment?" (Maimon 204). Given the stark distinction, he views the question of the legitimacy of bringing them together (the issue of "quid juris?") as equivalent to the traditional mind/body dualism, "commercio animi et corporis" (Maimon 186). Maimon argues that the only way around the problem is not to accept the Kantian premise; he adopts, rather than breaks with, the Leibniz-Wolff position that these faculties are not different in kind, but only in degree. But because he has a mathematical notion of difference—the infinitesimal or differential—he can argue for the relationship between full consciousness and the apparent passivity of the senses as one of an infinite limit or, we

might say, "unendliche Annäherung." If the difference between sensible intuition and the understanding can be made infinitely small, that is, if faculties of
consciousness can be thought *in terms of* the infinite, then they do not need a
"bridge" between them.

Maimon's introduction of the mathematical infinite, what he himself refers to
as his "sublime" idea, not only "solves the greatest difficulties" (Maimon 38) that
Kant seems to face, but also transforms the very nature of reality as a product
of a finite consciousness working with the infinite. The task of consciousness is
to continually relate the differentials, symbolized as the infinitesimal increase
in the variables x and y as dx and dy, each of which may be considered = 0 but
in their relations have determinate values and thus give rise to the gradation
of experiences: "These differentials of objects are the so-called *noumena*; but
the objects themselves arising from them are the *phenomena*. With respect to
intuition = 0, the differential of any object in itself is $dx = 0$, $dy = 0$ etc.; however,
their relations are not = 0, but can rather be given determinately in the intuitions arising from them" (Maimon 21). Consciousness is constantly active in
constructing reality out of, or perhaps better, *as*, relations between perceptions.
The greater the conscious activity, the more we are aware of our contribution
to this construction. As consciousness diminishes or approaches zero we do
not recognize our own activity at the level of perception. While it is still a synthesis "in" us, it appears to come from the "outside"—a term that is not to be
understood spatially but as "not part of our consciousness," since the conscious
activity approaches zero. That sense of something "beyond" our consciousness
as a limit idea would be the "thing in itself." But because it makes no sense for us
to talk about our consciousness ever reaching that zero point, the perceptions
can always be "added up" (integrated) so that we become increasingly aware of
them. Maimon makes the comparison with physics and one of the primary uses
of calculus: "Just as, for example, with an accelerated movement, the preceding
velocity does not disappear, but ever joins itself onto the following ones, so
that an ever increasing velocity arises, so equally the first sensible representation does not disappear, but ever joins itself onto the following ones, until the
degree necessary for consciousness is reached" (Maimon 20–21). This "joining" of minimal sensations by consciousness is understood as the integrating of
an infinity of infinitesimal differential relations.[15] Maimon has thereby defined
consciousness as an entity that synthesizes a reality across a continuum ranging
between the limits of zero (receptivity) and infinity (totality of all relations in
thought), without ever reaching them. Although finite in nature, consciousness
nonetheless works *with* the infinitely small and infinitely large in paradoxical
yet powerful ways in order to produce conceptual knowledge. In a sense, consciousness is like the mathematicians who depend on notions of the infinitesimal and infinity to produce effective results even though, from the perspective

of their discipline around 1800, they cannot fully explain them in terms of their finite tools.

13.3. ROMANTICIZING THE MATHEMATICAL INFINITE

Recent studies have demonstrated the significance of mathematics, specifically aspects of calculus and the infinite, in the work of thinkers like Novalis and Kleist in the romantic tradition.[16]Given these studies, let me therefore focus on Friedrich Schlegel, for despite works exploring the infinite in his thought generally and his relation to other sciences, the role of mathematics has not been investigated with any thoroughness.[17] Now, while it is true that he never studied mathematics intensely (in comparison to his friend Novalis, from whom he undoubtedly heard a good deal about it), or delved deeply into calculus, or employed its concepts rigorously, we can see how it permeates and frames his thought.

The key problematic for Schlegel, namely the relationship of the absolute and the individual, is captured in his questions "on the answer to which everything depends": "*Why has the infinite come out of itself and made itself finite?—that* is in other words: *Why are there individuals?—Or: Why does the play of nature not run itself out in an instant, so that nothing would exist?*" (KA 12, 39).[18] He is in many ways *the* romantic thinker of the infinite, or, to state the inverse, the infinite is *the* key issue that he attempts to capture. While undoubtedly this concept enters into his thought via Spinoza and Fichte, we can hear clearly in these questions Leibniz, and with him then enters the mathematical infinite.[19] That is, the questions he is posing are versions of the debate about the continuous and the discrete, the infinitely large and the infinitely small, and the emergence of reality out of differentials, which seem to both exist and not exist at the same time. By considering the introduction of the mathematical infinite into philosophy not as a cause for reason's dialectic with itself but as an explanation of consciousness's construction of reality, we can understand how Schlegel can offer an answer to his questions: The infinite has entered into, or is always already within, the finite just as calculus employs differentials, infinitesimals, and their infinite integration in order to explore the world of constant change. The paradoxes of the ill-defined or at least highly ambivalent methods of the new mathematics resonate for Schlegel and make the infinite in his thought productive. It has consequences for his considerations of method, consciousness, the task of overcoming dualisms, and the nature of philosophy itself.

That Schlegel grappled with questions surrounding the mathematical infinite is clear from his voluminous fragments from the last years of the eighteenth century, where we encounter not only hundreds that address them, but also a variety of mathematical symbols, most commonly the paradoxical division by zero (see KA 18, 10, no. 66 for echoes of Ben David). While they clearly serve as a kind of shorthand, like Schlegel's use of Greek letters to abbreviate words, the use of symbols also points to a mode of thinking. Here we might recall his axiom: "All knowing is symbolic" (KA 12, 9), which itself echoes Maimon's discussion of symbolic cognition needed to deal with the nonrepresentable infinite. Schlegel never tires of representing anything absolute by putting it over 0, as in as in $\mu\alpha\theta/0$ or $\phi\upsilon/0$ for "absolute/infinite mathematics or physics" (KA 18, 154, no. 371) and he formulates a thought about the novel as follows: "Evidently the novel has the complete form from math, rhetoric, and music. From math, powers, progression of the $x/0$ irrational" (KA 18, 347, no. 311). Such mathemes become particularly prominent around 1800 (see the notebooks comprising KA 18, 408–22, nos. 1060–1231). He thinks through the problem of the I's relation to the Non-I, that is, the I's encounter with a limit in the ambivalent terms of the infinitesimal, a zero that is a productive nothing: "Limit = 0, but a becoming zero…Non-I = zero, a becoming or an only apparent zero" (KA 18, 408, nos. 1068, 1069). And immortality, the endless becoming, seems to be cast in terms of a differential between life and death, like the infinite tangents that make up a curve: "Symbol of immortality the curved line. Each part a play between two functions of the spirit" (KA 18, 410, no. 1084). And, of course, it would not be Schlegel if he didn't outdo the mathematicians, developing unique (and somewhat wild) formulas of his own: "The infinite not $1/0$ but $^{1/0}\sqrt{x^{1/0}/0}$" (KA 18, 491, no. 197), read, I suppose, as "the infinite root of the infinite power of x over 0" or "the infinite root of the infinite power of infinity."[20] Such references abound in his notes from the late 1790s.

It is, however, in Schlegel's main early effort to formulate a philosophical position, his lectures on transcendental philosophy held in Jena, winter 1800 to spring 1801, that we see the fruits of his grappling with the mathematical. It is thus not by chance that from the outset he aligns himself with thinking in mathematics (and physics): "The *method* according to which we proceed will be that of *physics* or *mathematics*. That is, our investigations will be an *experimenting*, as in physics, or a *constructing*, as in mathematics" (KA 12, 3). As with so much in these rich and thought-provoking lectures, Schlegel seems to be providing more of a program for a transcendental philosophy than a fully developed execution of one. That is, we are dealing with what he might mean by a *theory of* philosophical construction rather than by a philosophy that is actually produced by it. As is well known, Fichte and Schelling in the latter part of the 1790s were engaged in formulating their systems by means of (differing) notions of construction, and Schlegel was undoubtedly aware of them.[21] But I would propose that what Schlegel has in mind here differs dramatically because the model he is basing his method on is not geometry but the new mathematics of the infinite. The ideal of geometric construction is to grasp in an act of intuition how a theorem is proven, and the rise of the notion of "intellectual intuition" in this period speaks to the reliance on this ideal. One might think of a presentation of the Pythagorean theorem in one image that makes its proof immediately evident. In arithmetical construction, to the contrary, only a rule or process can be given; there is no intuitive act that can "see" the result. Schlegel states this principle explicitly in a fragment from the time of the lectures: "All numbers lie between 1 and 0 or 1/0 and 0/1. The prime numbers must be able to be constructed through a rule between them" (KA 18, 413; KA 5, 1109). Although he uses the example here of prime numbers, the notion of "construction [of a number] through a rule" comes closer to Maimon's understanding of the "symbolic cognition" required when dealing with the infinite. As Maimon writes in the appendix to his *Versuch*:

> So symbolic cognition extends to infinity… as with, for example, a circle viewed as a polygon with infinitely many sides, the asymptotes of a curved line, and the like. Although we cannot think the infinite as an object this is besides the point here, since we do not make use of infinity to think the object, but merely to think the way it arises. (Maimon 143)[22]

Schlegel's emphasis on both approximation and symbolism can thus be explained by the fact that the infinite cannot be grasped by intuition (intellectual or otherwise) but must be thought by a rule that can be extended (the simplest being $1 + 1 + 1 + 1 \ldots$ or a diminishing series like $1, \frac{1}{2}, \frac{1}{4}, \frac{1}{8} \ldots$). We find a number of fragments in close proximity to each other in his notebooks that bring these ideas together, namely the arithmetical (not geometrical) nature of construction, infinite synthesis, and unrepresentability: "*Numbers as well are constructed. Consciousness* = object + subject. The infinite = form + matter. These are the factors of the matter of idealism"; "The infinite is a One raised to powers [*eine potentirte Eins*]; consciousness is a never attained Zero [*eine nie zu vollendende Null*]"; and "Symbols are signs, representations of elements that can never be presented [*darstellbar*] in themselves" (KA 18, 406, no. 1030, KA 18, 418, no. 1173, and KA 18, 420, no. 1197). The radicality of Schlegel's mathematical infinite would demand a different notion of construction than the traditional one that relied on the intuitive basis of geometry.[23] While intellectual intuition is one moment of philosophy, it does not represent the "transcendental standpoint" (Schlegel says), which must be a "*knowing of a unique kind, an infinite knowing*" (KA 12, 24).

The reference to consciousness in the fragments just cited also allows us to understand the nature of Schlegel's idealism. Given that Schlegel praised Maimon as "the most significant among the new skeptics," even as he goes on to call for a move beyond skepticism to pure idealism (KA 12, 95; Frank 105), Schlegel's model of consciousness seems to develop Maimon's own interpretation of Kant. That is, the experience of consciousness is not a "subsumption" of representations under categories, but a synthesis along the continuum of mental faculties (intuition, perception, imagination, understanding) thanks to the gradation or integration of differentials. Since "continuity" is one of the "conditions" (*Bedingungen*) of the system (KA 12, 21), or, as he says in a fragment, "*Connection of all matter.* This *gradation* [*Gradazion*] and continuity [*Continuität*] is the essence of *progressivity* [*Progreßivität*]" (KA 18, 47, no. 291), it should not surprise us that the origin of reality for consciousness also emerges through a continuous synthesis.[24] "Consciousness is so to speak +a–a...a becoming and disappearing zero" (KA 12, 25). Out of an infinite series of infinitely graduated representations, each of which in itself approaches zero but which in their relations have definite (intensive) magnitude, the mind "integrates"—synthesizes—its sense of the real. The absolute (noumena) is not "elsewhere" in the sense of "outside" consciousness but always already in consciousness as the infinitesimal building blocks of experience. If we consider this synthesis a form-giving activity, then what is real is always formed by consciousness, even though as finite beings we cannot be fully aware of our own activity. As in Maimon's view, there is a gradation from infinitely approximating zero ("objectivity") to infinity (pure consciousness and form). Matter, Schlegel argues, should not be considered an "object" (*Gegenstand*) outside of consciousness since "only form can enter consciousness," or perhaps it would have been better to say that we can only be conscious of what has form (KA 12, 38). However, because the formative power of consciousness is in fact finite but extending without end in principle—"each form is infinite" (KA 12, 39)—we approach a condition of totalized form as the limit but never attain it, that is, "we cannot transform everything into form" (KA 12, 38). That remainder of our sythesizing/forming activity is matter. This is not to say that matter is a mere "given"; on the contrary, the necessity of matter (indeed, formless "chaos") "is brought forth in us" (KA 12, 38). Frank summarizes Schlegel's position in terms that likewise (unconsciously) exploit the language derived from the mathematical discussions of the late 1700s: "The absolute transverses the entire series in a way that generates continuity; and to this extent the series demonstrates...the synthetic activity of the absolute in its ostensible manifestation in relative (particular) syntheses" (Frank 933). In Schlegel's own words: "Mathematics must take as its point of departure *elements*, from which everything else must be produced. The elements of geometry would be the point (.) and the straight line (—). The elements of arithmetic would be 1 and 0" (KA 12, 15). In this infinite space between the 0 and the 1 consciousness unfolds over time, its two limit concepts being "chaos" and infinite knowledge, also called "allegory" (KA

18, 421, no. 1226) or the divine (*Gottheit*) (KA 12, 39). Just as a curved line could be conceived of as constructed or produced from the infinite number of infinitely small straight lines that make up the tangents at all points along its trajectory (as Newton conceived of movement), so, too, consciousness builds up the form of reality out of its syntheses. Perhaps it is in this light that we can understand Schlegel's fragment: "The schema for communication/transmission (*Mittheilung*) is to be sought in the doctrine of the curved line" (KA 18, 406, no. 1034).

If both being and consciousness, and their relationship, are constructed out of the infinite gradations of and between the zero and the one, this has consequences for the nature of philosophy itself. Thus, we encounter the dialectic of the one and the many in a familiar form. On the one hand, "All knowing is infinite. It is an indivisible totality." But on the other, "[Philosophy's] *divisibility is arbitrary*," by which he does not so much mean random as, rather, infinite, or, perhaps more precisely, indeterminate in degree (KA 12, 10). In a way that anticipates Hegel, Schlegel here does not so much "resolve" a Kantian antinomy as embrace it thanks to a turn to the mathematical infinite. The "one" of infinity can also be approximated by the infinite synthesis (integration) of infinitesimals. That he is indeed thinking in terms of "magnitudes" we can see from the otherwise odd formulation that philosophy is infinite in the sense of "*intensive as well as extensive*" (KA 12, 9). And this has the further consequence "that the most perfect/complete system can only be by *approximation*" (KA 12, 9). If philosophy is infinite, as knowledge is infinite, then we are also driven by an infinite skepticism (KA 12, 9; recall his praise of Maimon). The longing and striving for the infinite ("Streben" or "Sehnsucht nach dem Unendlichen," KA 12, 8, 11) that drive the philosopher and that the philosopher must awaken in others, is therefore closer to discussions of irrational numbers than antirational feelings.

Thus, for Schlegel the way to address the fundamental dualisms that preoccupy his, and indeed all post-Kantian, thought—dogmatism and empiricism, reality and consciousness, absolute and individual—is through the tools of mathematical thinking (not necessarily the rigors of mathematical proof). This conclusion is rooted in the nature of such thinking, for just before the previous quote on the elements of mathematics he states: "If one combines dualism and theory, a science would emerge that does not have phenomena as its point of departure but, rather, elements. This is mathematics. It is so to speak a *dualism a priori*" (KA 12, 15). Mathematical reasoning about the infinite is so important to him because it allows him to think through the dualism in its pure relationality. "All reality is the product of opposing elements" (KA 12, 8) in the sense of the infinitely small and the infinitely large that, then, converge with each other. Thus we can understand how Schlegel arrives at what he calls "our formula now from a positive perspective": "*the minimum of the I is equal to the maximum of nature; and the minimum of nature is equal to the maximum of the I. That is, the* smallest sphere of consciousness is equal to the largest of nature, and vice versa" (KA 12, 6). What might sound like a playful paradox coming from the philosopher of irony is rooted in the discussions around the antinomies associated with the infinitesimal. He formulates the task of idealism in terms that echo fully Maimon's uses of the differential relation to explain Kant's anticipations of perception and reality: "*The philosopher (idealism) deals with the minimum and the maximum, and physics with the finite members between reality and the elements of an infinite progression of proportions*" (KA 12, 17).

In thinking through the infinite in this way, Schlegel brings together a conception of a system that thinks through opposites. He formulates his own version of the fundamental antinomy: "the *thesis*, that *matter* [passes over] into *consciousness*; the *antithesis...that all form is infinite*" (KA 12, 36). But rather than flee the infinite or turn it into the merely indefinite, he makes it the task of philosophy to provide the "synthesis." Schlegel called for a final stage of philosophy that would introduce a crucial form of self-reflexivity. It would be the "philosophy of philosophy," a concept his age was in the process of "constructing" (*konstruieren*) (KA 12, 92). While Schlegel went on to dedicate himself to many other pursuits and thus did not devote himself exclusively to the task of this philosophical construction, he did contribute something crucial to its formation. For he recognized the need to introduce "a knowledge of the sciences that are connected to [the] whole, to the infinite [*eine Kenntnis der Wissenschaften, die sich auf (das) Ganze, Unendliche beziehen*]" (KA 12, 92). Because his conception of the infinite was radically paradoxical in that it had to be both the heart of philosophy and yet by definition unattainable, Schlegel's encyclopedic effort had to include that one science that itself embraced this paradox, infinitesimal calculus.

My project of connecting romantic "unendliche Annäherung" with specific discussions of the mathematical infinite is motivated in principle by David Foster Wallace's association between mathematics and metaphysics: "It is in areas like math and metaphysics that we encounter one of the average human mind's weirdest attributes, [namely] the ability to conceive of things that we cannot, strictly speaking, conceive of."[25] And with the romantics in mind, and Schlegel's conception of "progressive Universalpoesie," we could add poetry to these attempts to grasp the ungraspable. Indeed, there is an element of the poetic at the heart of the mathematical infinite, also as a result of its historical development.[26] One might even include Goethe in this rich body of mathematical, philosophical, and poetic literature, who said in a conversation with Riemer on March 27, 1814: "Numbers, like our poor words, are only attempts to grasp and express appearances, eternal unattainable approximations."[27]

What is particularly productive in Friedrich Schlegel's account was the way he united these elements—metaphysics, mathematics, and poetry—in the last years of the eighteenth century into a program centered on the infinite. For him, "unendliche Annäherung" was neither a forceful activity of the ego coming to grips with its other (nature) nor an emotional longing for the impossible akin to nostalgia. Rather, it marked a powerful paradox that lay at the heart of the calculus that had been developed during the previous century and which could be formulated as a series of antinomic propositions (the world is and is not infinitely divisible; the infinitesimal exists and is nothing). It was a paradox that could not be represented but could be thought. And it was a paradox that nonetheless made possible a powerful mathematical tool for grasping reality as change. Schlegel seized that paradox, following the lead of Salomon Maimon, used it to ground a new form of idealism that grasped the duality of consciousness and the infinite, and further to create a unity out of that dualism by locating the infinite as continuous synthesis within our finite consciousness. By definition, a philosophy and poetic practice based on this paradox could never become a completed system. Its relevance lies in its contrast to other approaches to the infinite, such as a (Kantian) critical practice that would impose limits on our thinking of the infinite, or a (Hegelian) idealism that would sublate it, or later nineteenth-century mathematical axiomatizations that would produce a grounding of calculus without the paradoxical infinitesimals.[28] The creative openness of Schlegel's philosophical thought is made possible by his insistence on the nonextinguishable difference that is the differential and infinite approximation, a difference lying at the heart of reality as constructed by consciousness. The next time this mode of philosophizing finds anything comparable (though without direct influence) comes with the similarly mathematically inflected "new thinking" of Franz Rosenzweig after the First World War, which departs from the neo-Kantian philosophy of mathematics of Hermann Cohen (as influenced by Maimon) and challenges the legacy of Hegelianism.[29] It was Friedrich Schlegel's romantic calculus that first opened up a way to conceive of the relation of mind, world, and God rigorously as infinite approximation.[30]

NOTES

1. Salomon Maimon, *Essay on Transcendental Philosophy*, trans. Nick Midgley, Henry Somers-Hall, Alistair Welchman, and Merten Reglitz (New York: Continuum, 2010), 19 n. 1. Hereafter cited as "Maimon" in the body of the text. In his *Logic* (1812) Hegel also argues for the significance of the mathematical infinite in terms that echo Maimon's: "But in a philosophical respect the mathematical infinite is important because underlying it, in fact, is the notion of the genuine infinite and it is far superior to the ordinary so-called *metaphysical infinite* on which are based the objections to the mathematical infinite." Georg Friedrich Wilhelm Hegel,

Wissenschaft der Logik, in *Werke in zwanzig Bänden*, ed. K. Michel E. Moldenhauer (Frankfurt am Main: Suhrkamp, 1969), 280. Hereafter cited as "Hegel" in the body of the text.

2. On the history of calculus, see I. Grattan-Guinness, ed., *From Calculus to Set Theory, 1630–1910* (London: Duckworth, 1980); Shaughan Lavine, *Understanding the Infinite* (Cambridge, MA: Harvard University Press, 1994); and David Foster Wallace, *Everything and More: A Compact History of Infinity* (New York: Norton: 2003).

3. Leonhard Euler, *Briefe an eine deutsche Prinzessin. Philosophische Auswahl* (Leipzig: Verlag Philipp Reclam jun., 1968). Hereafter cited as "Euler" in the body of the text. Swiss by birth, Euler spent most of his life in St. Petersburg, with an intervening twenty-five-year sojourn in Berlin at the invitation of Frederick the Great (1741–1766). Grattan-Guinness summarizes Euler's contributions: "The man who reshaped the Leibnizian calculus into a soundly organised body of mathematical knowledge was Leonard Euler....Euler's greatest influence on the calculus and on analysis in general was through his great textbooks, in which he gave analysis a definitive form, which it was to keep until well into the 19th century." Grattan-Guinness, *From Calculus to Set Theory*, 53.

4. Cited in C. Edward Sandifer, *How Euler Did It* (Washington, DC: Mathematical Association of America, 2000), 148.

5. Sandifer, *How Euler Did It*, 148.

6. Ben David, a respected Jewish supporter and propagator of Kant's philosophy, moved to Berlin in 1797 (after having been expelled with other foreigners from Vienna), where he was part of the circle around Marcus and Henriette Herz. The latter had a famous salon attended, among others, by Friedrich Schlegel and Friedrich Schleiermacher at the end of the century. Ben David also came to the financial aid of Maimon when he was having difficulties gaining entry into Berlin (as described in Maimon's autobiography). See Weissberg for biographical accounts. Frank mentions briefly the association between Bendavid and Maimon. Manfred Frank, *"Unendliche Annäherung." Die Anfänge der philosophischen Frühromantik* (Frankfurt am Main: Suhrkamp, 1997), 114 n. 2.

7. Lazarus Ben David, *Versuch einer logischen Auseinandersetzung über das mathematische Unendliche* (Berlin: Petit und Schöne, 1789), 23. Hereafter cited as "Bendavid" in the body of the text.

8. This discussion has remarkable parallels to sections of Moses Mendelssohn's winning response to the Academy question on whether metaphysical truths can have the same *Evidenz* as mathematical ones. In his *Essay on the Evidence of Mathematical Science* (*Abhandlung über die Evidenz der mathematischen Wissenschaft*), he compares them to the mathematics of "Fluxional-Rechung," which can be "begreiflich" but not "faßlich" (Moses Mendelsson, *Gesammelte Schriften*, vol. 2 [Leipzig: Brockh aus, 1843], 271.)

9. Kästner exerted considerable influence on the intellectual life of Germany through his teaching activities at the universities of Leipzig and Göttingen as well as through the prolific output of textbooks on mathematics and the physical sciences.

10. Abraham Gotthelf Kästner, *Anfangsgründe der Analysis des Unendlichen* (Göttingen: Im Verlag der Wittwe Vandenhoeck, 1761–70), x. Hereafter cited as "Kästner" in the body of the text.

11. This is just a very small sampling of the wealth of work done in these years on the topic. In addition to the separate textbooks, there was also the 1786 *Preisfrage* of the Prussian Academy to provide a clear and precise treatment of the mathematical infinite. Related to this issue was also the *Preisfrage* of 1782 to derive notions of calculus from Euclidean geometry. The concern there was the central one of whether the new notions of the infinite could be grasped with intuition (like geometry) or needed to be "constructed."

12. The contribution that Maimon made to the history of modern philosophy has been well documented over the last twenty years. Manfred Frank devotes over two lectures to him in his *Unendliche Annäherung* but he makes no mention of the mathematics in his otherwise excellent discussion. Beiser claims that Maimon's work is "of the first importance for the history of post-Kantian idealism," and he offers a brief discussion of the "difficult" theory of differentials. Frederick Beiser, *The Fate of Reason: German Philosophy from Kant to Fichte* (Cambridge, MA: Harvard University Press, 1993), 286. A number of Maimon scholars have argued that he be considered seriously in his own right and not just as a middle figure (S. H. Bergman, *The Philosophy of Solomon Maimon* [Jerusalem: Magnes, 1967]; Jan Bransen, *The Antinomy of Thought: Maimonian Skepticism and the Relation between Thoughts and Objects* [Dordrecht: Kluwer Academic Publishers, 1991]). However, few address why the notion of the mathematical infinite can shift our perspective on fundamental problems in philosophy. And while others address his use of the differential, no one has sought to locate him within the discussions of the period. Exceptions are recent discussions by Simon Duffy and Daniel W. Smith (in Sjoerd van Tuinen and Niamh McDonnell, eds., *Deleuze and the Fold: A Critical Reader* [New York: Palgrave Macmillan, 2010]), spurred by interest in Deleuze's work on Leibniz and mathematics. The one commentator to devote a monograph on Maimon and mathematics is Buzaglo, who offers a very brief discussion of the pertinent sections of Chapter 2 of the *Versuch*, only to claim that the notion of the differential is not relevant. See Meir Buzaglo, *Solomon Maimon: Monism, Skepticism and Mathematics* (Pittsburgh: University of Pittsburgh Press, 2002), 125. Freudenthal provides a very rich reading, recognizing at the outset that "Maimon's philosophy is imbued with mathematics." Gideon Freudenthal, "Maimon's Philosophical Program. Understanding versus Intuition," *Internationales Jahrbuch des Deutschen Idealismus/International Yearbook of German Idealism* 8 (2010), 83.

13. See also Freudenthal, "Maimon's Philosophical Program," 84, on asymptotes.

14. See Nuzzo's discussion of Kant's distinction between the faculties. Angelica Nuzzo, *Kant and the Unity of Reason* (West Lafayette, IN: Purdue University Press, 2005), 23–38. And according to Förster, "the claim that the faculty of sensibility differs in principle from conceptual abilities is Kant's own quite original position," although he then points to the passage where Kant himself says that these "two stems of human knowledge perhaps arise out of a common, but to us unknown root." Eckart Förster, *The Twenty-Five Years of Philosophy: A Systematic Reconstruction* (Cambridge, MA: Harvard University Press, 2012), 7 and 10. He cites Immanuel Kant, *Kritik der reinen Vernunft* A15/B28.

15. Given his position that the differential is an infinitely small quantum, which can never be zero but is only a "limit concept" of consciousness and the activity

of consciousness in constituting reality, it is not by chance that Maimon offers a spirited critique of his friend and supporter, Ben David, for mistakenly taking Euler's position that $dx = 0$. In the first part of the appendix to his *Versuch*, Maimon includes an essay "On Symbolic Cognition and Philosophical Language" (Maimon 139–72) that demonstrates the role of the mathematicians we have explored in his philosophical investigations. Differentials constitute a particular kind of "nothing that mathematicians nevertheless make into an object of their cognition because of the universality of their calculus" (Maimon 150). They must be thought of as infinitely small, "but this does not make them any less real" (Maimon 152). Ben David, in defining "the infinitely small = the infinitely large = 0" fails "to distinguish precisely these different types of nothing from one another" (Maimon 152). Instead, Maimon suggests, one should turn to another mathematician, for "it is only necessary to read a Kästner" (Maimon 150). See below on parallels between Maimon and Schlegel on such "symbolic cognition" of such nonrepresentables as infinitesimals. Furthermore, Maimon's argument makes use of Kant's later discussions in the *Critique of Pure Reason* of the "anticipations of perception" and reveals the power of the mathematical infinite beyond what Kant himself could see.

16. See Howard Pollack-Milgate's "Novalis and Mathematics Revisited," *Athäneum: Jahrbuch für Romantik* (1997): 113–40. In it, he provides a new reading that goes beyond Hamburger and Dyck. For Kleist, see Wolf Kittler on Kleist: "Falling after the Fall: The Analysis of the Infinite in Kleist's *Marionettentheater*," in *Heinrich von Kleist and Modernity*, ed. Bernd Fischer and Tim Mehigan (Rochester, NY: Camden House, 2011). By taking Kleist's knowledge of mathematics (via Kästner) seriously, Kittler offers a stringent critique of de Man's earlier reading. David Martyn looks at Kleist's understanding of the mathematics of probability. See "Figures of the Mean: Freedom, Progress, and the Law of Statistical Averages in Kleist's 'Allerneuester Erziehungsplan,'" *Germanic Review* 85 (2010): 44–62.

17. Brauers and Zeuch explore Schlegel and the infinite, also in relation to the Western tradition. Chaouli discusses Schlegel and chemistry. See Claudia Brauers, *Perspektiven des Unendlichen. Friedrich Schlegels ästhetische Vermittlungstheorie* (Berlin: Ernst Schmidt Verlag, 1996) and Ulrike Zeuch, *Das Unendliche: Höchste Fülle oder Nichts? Zur Problematik von Friedrich Schlegels Geist-Begriff und dessen geistesgeschichtlichen Voraussetzungen* (Würzburg: Königshausen und Neumann, 1991).

18. See Dalia Nassar, "Schelling und die Frühromantik: Das Unendliche und das Endliche im Kunstwerk," http://www.academia.edu/656856/Schelling_und_die_Fruhromantik_Das_Unendliche_und_das_Endliche_im_Kunstwerk (accessed April 20, 2013), for a discussion of Schlegel on the absolute in relation to Schelling and poetry.

19. Consider the footnote near the end of the introduction to his lectures: "Zwischen *Spinoza* und *Fichte* liegt *Leibnitz* in der Mitte" (KA 12, 30). Also John H. Smith, "Leibniz Reception around 1800: Monadic Vitalism and Harmony in Schleiermacher's *Reden über die Religion* and Schlegel's *Lucinde*," in *Religion, Reason, and Culture in the Age of Goethe*, ed. Elizabeth Kimmerer and Patricia Simpson (Rochester, NY: Camden House, 2013).

20. See also the many variation on this formula, such as: "$\sqrt{\chi\alpha}/0$ = Gott" (the square root of chaos divided by zero, i.e. infinite chaos; KA 18, 238, no. 540) or even wilder: "Gott = $^{1/0}\sqrt{\chi\alpha^{1/0}}/0$" (the infinite root of chaos to the infinite power divided by 0; KA 18, 277, no. 999). Or also: "Der Monolog ein $^{1/0}\sqrt{\text{Dialog}^{1/0}}$" (KA 18, 199, no. 34).

21. See especially Daniel Breazeale, "Men at Work: Philosophical Construction in Fichte and Schelling," http://www.europhilosophie.eu/recherche/IMG/pdf/ Plenar-Breazeale-beitrag.pdf (accessed April 20, 2013); and Helga Ende, *Der Konstruktionsbegriff im Umkreis des deutschen Idealismus* (Meisenheim am Glan: Anton Hain, 1973).

22. See also note 11 above.

23. Maimon goes so far as to "hold that geometrical propositions can be demonstrated far more powerfully through the *methodus indivisibilium*, or the differential calculus, than in the usual way" (Maimon 143). And consider Schlegel's fragment: "All geometry is cyclical and classical [*cyklisch und classisch*]—algebra is merely constructed [*construirt*] in itself and progressive [*progreßiv*]" (KA 18, 274, no. 954). Indeed, the notion of a rule to explain the way to generate an infinite (magnitude) that can only be represented symbolically seems here to be the very definition of the idea of "progression" that is the basis of romantic poetry.

24. See also the fragment from the time of the lectures: "Continuity is the character of all that is idealist [*alles Idealistischen*]" (KA 18, 363, no. 504).

25. Wallace, *Everything and More*, 22.

26. As Thiel reminds us: "In terms of the history of philosophy and of mathematics it is noteworthy that out of notions of the infinitesimal, which were often attacked as imprecise, a philosophy of the mathematics of the infinite arose in the eighteenth century, a 'metaphysics of infinitesimal calculus.' And a rich body of literature was produced that argued often in the style of its founders, like Leibniz, who....saw through infinitesimals as fictions and yet, rather than eliminate them, justified them by analogies." Christian Thiel, *Philosophie und Mathematik. Eine Einführung in ihre Wechselwirkungen und in die Philosophie der Mathematik* (Darmstadt: Wissenschaftliche Buchgesellschaft, 1995), 175–76.

27. Cited in Martin Dyck, "Goethe's Views on Pure Mathematics," *Germanic Review* 31 (1956): 59.

28. Robinson's nonstandard analysis did reintroduce infinitesimals, but with a new rigor that aimed to remove the paradoxes. See the discussion in John Bell, *The Continuous and the Infinitesimal in Mathematics and Philosophy* (Milan: Polimetrica, 2006).

29. See John H. Smith, "The Infinitesimal as Theological Principle: Representing the Paradoxes of God and Nothing in Cohen, Rosenzweig, Scholem, and Barth," *MLN* 127 (2012): 562–88.

30. I dedicate this essay to my friends, students, and colleagues at the University of Waterloo who provided a stimulating environment for me to write it. Research for the essay was supported by a UW/SSHRC Seed Grant.

14

The "Mathematical" *Wissenschaftslehre*

On a Late Fichtean Reflection of Novalis

DAVID W. WOOD

14.1. MATHEMATICS AND ROMANTIC PHILOSOPHY

There have been a number of important studies on Novalis's understanding of the mathematical sciences, revealing his technical competency in the field of pure mathematics.[1] This recognition has not always been present in Novalis scholarship. Not only in philosophy but also in the field of mathematics, Novalis has had to overcome the reputation of being a romantic dilettante. For example, in 1910, no less an authority than Wilhelm Dilthey dismissed Novalis's late reflections on mathematics as mere "hymns to mathematics," or as "unfruitful" instances of "conceptual mystical games."[2] Later studies have furnished a much more balanced and positive view of Novalis's mathematical thought and education. Any research completed in the last half-century has also had the benefit of the Historical-Critical edition of Novalis's works, which in its completeness, rearrangement, and reordering of the texts allows us to see his ideas and readings in context.[3] This edition demonstrates that Novalis's training in mathematics was exceedingly broad and up-to-date, with studies in combinatorial analysis, analytic functions, pure geometry, arithmetic, exponentiation, logarithms, and calculus.[4]

For a romantic figure, one could ask: why was Novalis interested in these abstract and complex fields of thought? As we will see with Fichte, the late fragments of Novalis show his interest to have been much more of a *philosophical* one, and he above all attempted to grasp the reciprocal interactions between the symbolic languages and methods of philosophy and mathematics. Or in the words of the historian of mathematics, Hans Niels Jahnke, it was mathematics as the "symbol of a higher unity of knowledge" that appealed to Novalis.[5]

Novalis's most in-depth study of mathematics took place in 1791–1793 at the University of Leipzig, where he attended courses on the combinatorial analysis of Carl Friedrich Hindenburg,[6] and in 1798–99 while at the Freiberg Mining Academy, where he indeed sought theoretical and systematic unity, not just in mathematics, but in all the sciences. This attempt achieved its most comprehensive expression in his "scientific Bible" of 1798–99, a romantic encyclopedia of the sciences written parallel to his mathematical studies.[7] According to Frederick Beiser, on account of its systematicity the encyclopedia project exhibits one of the clearest differences between the early and later notebooks of Novalis: "While Novalis was critical of almost all philosophical pretensions in his early notebooks, he continued to nurture systematic ambitions, which eventually grew into his project for the encyclopaedia of all the sciences. No less than Schelling and Hegel, Novalis was a systematic philosopher, whose goal was to show how all the sciences form a unity."[8] This positive evaluation of the power of philosophy in Novalis's later notebooks compared to his earlier ones such as the "Fichte-Studies" from 1795–96, raises the question of the status of idealism in philosophical romanticism—a question lying at the heart of a number of modern debates. Due to their inherent skepticism and rejection of a philosophy of first principles, Manfred Frank primarily situates the romantics outside the idealist stream; whereas on account of its rationality, Platonistic tendencies and systematic pretensions such as Novalis's encyclopedia, Beiser places philosophical romanticism within the idealist current.[9] Despite these interpretative differences, these debates have been fruitful insofar as they have led to a much closer examination of the philosophical texts of the early German romantics. However, they have also exposed certain lacunae, such as the lack of critical attention paid to the later philosophical writings of Novalis.

Although Novalis's encyclopedia project remained incomplete and was put aside in March 1799, its guiding philosophical idea of a single universal science can still be found in Novalis's postencyclopedia writings, including the 1799 essay "Christendom or Europe".[10] It is similarly present in 1800 toward the end of the final "Fragments and Studies", where philosophy only becomes "truly visible" within the finished system of all the sciences: "[Philosophy] is the undetermined science of the sciences—a mysticism of the drive for knowledge on the whole—the spirit of science as it were.… Thus all the sciences are interrelated—and philosophy will never be completed. Only in the perfect system of all the sciences will philosophy become truly visible" (NS 3, 666). This final systematic form of philosophy for Novalis is therefore a regulative ideal in the

Kantian sense, because we can approach it but never fully attain it. Or it can be conceived as similar to the Fichtean idea of a vocation (*Bestimmung*): philosophy can never be completed, nor can it ever appear *in concreto*. Hence in addition to the terms "romantic philosophy," or "magical idealism," Novalis's system of thought in these later fragments may also be characterized as a form of "encyclopedic philosophy." Comparing his idea with Fichte's goal to make the *Wissenschaftslehre* into a "science of the sciences" or with Hegel's *Encyclopaedia of the Philosophical Sciences* we see that Novalis likewise shares this striving for a system of universal knowledge with the German idealists.

A further point in which Novalis is intellectually aligned with the idealistic stream lies in the fact that he ascribes a special status to mathematical thinking. Mathematics plays a central role in his encyclopedic brand of philosophy, since it serves as an ideal model and standard of all scientific knowledge.[11] Specifically, entries 1006–1042 of the *Romantic Encyclopaedia*—most probably written in February–March 1799—are concerned with problem-solving and with and how mathematical methodology may shed light on scientific method. He writes, for instance, how it is not so much the content of this science that gives one the right to be called a mathematician, but the understanding of its cognitive methodology as the core of science method on the whole: "The mathematical method is the essence of mathematics. Whoever fully understands this method, is a mathematician. As the *scientific method in general* it is extremely interesting, and perhaps supplies us with the most accurate model for the classification of knowledge, or for the *faculty of experience*" (NS 3, 457). As we will see, this view of mathematics forms a direct parallel with Fichte's conception of philosophy developed one year later as a form of mathematical thought or scientific *mathesis*.

Unlike philosophy, which only becomes visible after the unification of all the sciences, mathematics is already a visible and useful instrument, because the objects of mathematics are initially found in the visible sense world. This concept is apparent in the group of about forty "mathematical fragments" of 1799–1800 (the ones labeled by Dilthey as "hymns to mathematics"). Nevertheless, what is mathematics itself? Here we once again approach the contentious issue of how to interpret Novalis's idealism in mathematics and philosophy: that is, whether or not it should be viewed as a form of absolute idealism in the rationalistic or Platonistic tradition, a reading supported by Beiser but resisted by Frank.[12] With respect to Novalis and mathematics, one could go further and say that there is not just a Platonic but even a Pythagorean undercurrent in his thought, when he reflects on the following interrelations between number and language: "The numerical system is the *model* for a genuine system of linguistic signs.—The letters of our alphabet shall become numbers, our language, arithmetic. What did the Pythagoreans really understand by the forces of numbers?"

(NS 3, 52). Novalis's conception of mathematics repeatedly argues in favor of a harmony between idealistic philosophy and the world of nature: "Mathematics is the most complete and valid testimony of the idealism of nature"; mathematics has the "internal connection, the sympathy of the universe, as its basis" (NS 3, 52). Or again: nature speaks the language of mathematics because nature herself is a supreme mathematician: "Nature incessantly adds, subtracts, multiplies, raises to a higher power etc. The applied mathematical sciences show us Nature as a mathematician" (NS 3, 52). To be sure, with Dilthey, one could interpret these fragments as an expression of the mysteriousness of mathematics and the mysticism of the German romantics.[13] Yet these fragments could also be placed in the scientific tradition of Galileo, in which mathematics is the language that nature herself speaks. Novalis adheres to an immanent view of nature and mathematics; mathematics is "*in*" nature, and we have to learn to read and decipher these outer mathematical symbols or language of nature in order to understand its inner meaning or workings.

Moreover, these late fragments recall Novalis's famous mathematical definition of romanticizing in the *Vorarbeiten* of 1798: "The world must be romanticized. This yields again its original meaning. Romanticizing is nothing else than a qualitative potentialization. In this operation the lower self becomes identified with a better self. Just as we ourselves are a qualitative potential series of this kind" (NS 2, 545, no. 105). Quantitative potentialization is the operation of exponentiation or raising to a higher power. However, in addition to the quantitative version of this mathematical operation, Novalis maintains that there is a qualitative version, but that this aspect is still unknown to researchers. On the one hand, this qualitative version of potentialization concerns the status of the self, where the romantic philosopher endeavors to raise his ordinary self up to a "better self." On the other hand it is an operation referring to the external world, for ordinary objects can likewise be raised to a higher degree, and "given a mysterious appearance."[14] Hence potentialization is a twofold intellectual operation, and this is the essence of romanticizing: in its quantitative version it is primarily a numerical operation in mathematics. This quantitative operation concerns the external or visible activities of measurement and counting the sensible objects of nature. Whereas in its qualitative version, this operation designates inner, moral, or intelligible operations, the activity of understanding or grasping our self and its place in the world.

14.2. THE *WISSENSCHAFTSLEHRE* AS MATHEMATICS?

In entry no. 429 of the *Romantic Encyclopaedia* Novalis writes: "There exists a philosophical, a critical, a mathematical, a poetical, a chemical, a historical

Wissenschaftslehre."[15] Or again in entry no. 464: "One could imagine a highly instructive series of specific presentations of the Fichtean and Kantian systems, for example, a poetical, a chemical, a mathematical, a musical etc."[16] Fichte's philosophical or critical *Wissenschaftslehre* is relatively well-known, and the mathematical aspects of Kant's system have been frequently examined, but what could a mathematical version of Fichte's system be?

Manfred Frank has convincingly demonstrated, particularly in his detailed reading of Novalis's "Fichte Studies", that Novalis and many of the other romantics had rejected the "fictional" and axiomatic starting point (*Grundsatz*) of the *Wissenschaftslehre* almost as soon as Fichte had arrived in Jena.[17] Notwithstanding, in the above entries from the 1798–99 encyclopedia, the poet-philosopher Novalis continues to make a number of positive remarks on Fichte after writing this text, and after his period of "Fichticizing" with Friedrich Schlegel in 1795–96.[18] If the early Novalis was skeptical of the Fichtean enterprise and rejected significant elements of it, how are we to understand his later positive remarks on Fichte, particularly those concerning a possible mathematical reading of the *Wissenschaftslehre*?

This question could be preceded by another one: did Fichte himself think the *Wissenschaftslehre* to be mathematical? One has to give an affirmative answer to this question. In fact, beginning with the discovery of the *Wissenschaftslehre* in the winter of 1793–94, where he saw himself as a sort of modern Euclid, right up until his final lectures in the winter of 1813–14, Fichte repeatedly argued for the *Wissenschaftslehre*'s close affinity and even at times its identity with mathematics.[19] Why did Fichte equate his philosophy with mathematics? This is because for him they shared a number of crucial "distinctions" or characteristics in common. First, he considered the first postulate of his system, like those in geometry, to be wholly self-evident to the unprejudiced thinker. Second, genuine intellectual intuition for him was similar to mathematical intuition because the act of thinking about oneself possesses a *universal* validity that holds for every rational being, regardless of the language, signs, or symbols we choose to use. The language or signs are only external assistances to arrive at an internal intuition of the self. Third, again like in Euclidean geometry, Fichte's starting point or first postulate was unprovable and therefore logically "irrefutable"; that is because for Fichte all refuting and disproving are confined to the sphere of *conceptual* operations.

Fichte's point of departure is a based on pure or intellection intuition. Intuition is not subject to conceptual proofs, but must be directly grasped or *seen* by each individual. In this sense the "proof" of his first principle cannot be fully demonstrated by means of sensible or linguistic propositions, or be drawn like ordinary lines or figures on a page. The latter are merely sensible manifestations of an *intelligible* act, in which every sensible element must ultimately be abstracted or stripped away, and where every rational person must inwardly carry out this intelligible act individually. The postulates of geometry state the possibility of carrying out certain spatial activities, expressed, for instance, in Euclid's first postulate concerning the act of drawing a line: "To draw a straight line from any point to any point." Fichte's postulate in the Second Introduction of 1797 likewise expresses the invitation to carry out an act; however, not that of drawing a line in space, but of a specific mental act. "And our first postulate would be the following: Think of yourself; construct the concept of yourself and take note of how you do this."[20] These parallels between self-evidence, intuition, and a postulate-based system led Fichte to explicitly equate his own philosophy with pure mathematics, in the small but controversial *Announcement* of 1801: "Because the *Wissenschaftslehre* is mathematics, it also has the distinctions of mathematics."[21] To this extent geometry and mathematics are propaedeutics for the Fichtean system. Thus, similar to Novalis's comments on the value of mathematics for philosophy, Fichte's views too could be placed in the Platonic tradition. Echoing the legendary words to the entrance of the Platonic Academy that no one could enter who had not properly studied geometry, Fichte would likewise write in THE *Announcement*: "Hence, I wish people had some knowledge of mathematics before embarking on a study of the *Wissenschaftslehre*; i.e. not without first obtaining a clear insight into the ground of the *immediate self-evidence* and *universal validity* of mathematical *postulates* and theorems."[22]

Apart from Kant and Spinoza, Fichte rarely compared his philosophy directly to other systems in philosophical history; yet on account of its similarly profound commitment to idealism, he saw Plato's philosophy as a forerunner to his own: "Among the Greeks, Plato was on this path to the *Wissenschaftslehre*.... among the ancient philosophers Plato may have had an inkling [of our view]" (GA 1/9, 73, 110). This Platonist component of Fichte's thought is particularly evident in his theory of "original" geometry from 1805, which is based on absolute, ideal, and infinite elements that have to be grasped in geometric intuition, and which he set in opposition to the "ordinary" geometry of Euclid.[23] Novalis was one of the first thinkers to detect this Platonist or Neoplatonist heritage in the Fichtean system, when in 1798 he briefly cited the "*idealistic* similarity" between Fichte and Plotinus.[24] Fichte's idealistic proximity to the Platonic stream was finally explained in convincing detail by the Swiss philosopher of mathematics Andreas Speiser in the middle of the twentieth century.[25]

In contrast to Novalis's remarks on Fichte's idealism and the possibility of a mathematical *Wissenschaftslehre*, the majority of Fichte's contemporaries, including Kant, Jacobi, Jakob Sigismund Beck, and even his own student Johann Friedrich Herbart, all either explicitly rejected or failed to see its mathematical pretensions. Friedrich Karl Forberg, Fichte's colleague at the University of Jena, who was later to play a prominent role in the atheism dispute, summed up the views of many of these contemporaries when he said in 1795: "What Fichte understands about mathematics is for the most part false, and he has not fared any better in this field than Maimon, who likewise wanted to deal with mathematics, but without any greater success."[26] In other words, Novalis's remarks are at odds with many of the other thinkers of the time. Again, this is not to say that Novalis did not harbor doubts about certain elements of Fichte's philosophy, such as the emphasis on a philosophy of first principles. He did harbor doubts, yet he was still able to recognize the mathematical aspects of Fichte's philosophy. If Novalis was not convinced of the self-evident geometric starting point of the *Wissenschaftslehre*, then what was mathematical about it for him? One way of answering this question is to see that Novalis and Fichte were interested in wholly different branches of mathematics, and this influenced their mathematical readings.

14.3. EXPONENTIATION AND PROBLEM-SOLVING

As we saw, when speaking of the relationship between the methods of mathematics and philosophy, Fichte particularly appeals to the Euclidean axiomatic system, that is to say, to indemonstrable first principles or postulates. His conception of mathematics is more of a synthetic or geometric one. Fichte is following Kant's lead insofar as the latter too especially chose examples from geometry to illustrate philosophical problems.[27] Fichte's theory of mathematics underscores the importance of geometrical *images* (*Bilder*) and the conscious *construction* of these images. He frequently resorts to the examples of drawing a line and the construction of triangles, in which the geometrical figures are sensible images for understanding intellectual activities such as the construction of the I or self. Novalis, by contrast, often has arithmetic, logarithms, exponentiation, or more analytic methods in mind, and selects his principal examples from the sphere of algebra, arithmetic, and calculus. In contrast to Fichte, Novalis seeks qualitative versions of quantitative mathematical operations, and wishes to find unknown variables by means of known numerical values and figures. This is most apparent in his famous definition of romanticism mentioned above, in which the chief operation is not a geometrical construction, but the quantitative algebraic operation of *exponentiation* (potentialization).

Paradoxically perhaps, it is precisely the more analytic problem-solving methods of algebra and calculus that Novalis finds related to the *Wissenschaftslehre*. In a sense, one could say that this provides further support for Manfred Frank's thesis of the romantics' rejection of *Grundsatz* philosophy. With regard to

Novalis, he rejected and was skeptical about Fichte's postulate-like first principle because he was less attracted to and convinced by axiomatic systems in
general. Nevertheless, he did not dismiss every mathematical aspect of the
Wissenschaftslehre, for he still discerned in it a problem-solving power similar to the operations found in algebra and calculus. He saw in the Fichtean
project an ideal meta-reflection on the activity of philosophizing that could be
applied back to an understanding of the nature of mathematical activity itself.
This is why three years after "Fichticizing" with Friedrich Schlegel he could
still write: "Fichte's demand for simultaneous thinking, acting and observing
is the ideal of philosophizing."[28] This reflective focus on joint volitional and
intellectual operations, as well as the reciprocal relationships between the disciplines of philosophy and mathematics, seems to have held an enduring appeal
for Novalis. Here the operation of exponentiation and its inverse once again
holds: the ideal system of philosophy may be viewed as a potentialization of
mathematics and vice versa: "In the end, mathematics is only *common, simple*
philosophy, and philosophy is higher mathematics in general."[29] Or again: "(Has
philosophy originated from the contemplation of mathematics?) Philosophy is
universal—or higher mathematics—the animating principle of mathematics—
poetic mathematics—or the substance, if mathematics is the form."[30]

It is interesting to note that Fichte too referred to the *Wissenschaftslehre* in
terms of the potentialization of mathematics. As we saw, he considers his system to be similar to geometry because it is based on intuition, self-evidence, and
construction, although it still does not possess the same authority. In terms of
knowledge or epistemology, he believed that the *Wissenschaftslehre* even stood
at a higher level than mathematics. While mathematicians carry out constructions or intuitions with their attention generally focused on the specific sensible
objects of their knowledge (their spatial constructions), the philosopher of the
Wissenschaftslehre abstracts away all these sensible aspects and focuses on the
pure activities of constructing and intuiting themselves: "The *Wissenschaftslehre*
is mathesis of the mind. In actual mathematics one only examines the *products*
of construction; here [in the *Wissenschaftslehre*], one examines the [activity
of] constructing itself" (GA 2/5, 344).[31] Fichte ultimately considers his philosophy to be a more universal science than mathematics, because the latter only contains limited and *particular* examples and instances of intuition,
self-evidence, and construction, whereas the *Wissenschaftslehre* aims to explain
the *universal* nature of intuition, self-evidence, and construction. Accordingly,
the *Wissenschaftslehre* should no longer simply be considered as mathematics
or "mathesis," but as a science of the nature of mathematical knowledge as such,
or "mathesis of mathesis."[32]

Of course, Novalis and Fichte realize there are limits to our problem-solving
abilities in mathematics and philosophy. The unknown is not always attained

from out of the known, and sometimes we fail to uncover the right answer, or a problem simply cannot be solved. We therefore need a science to consciously reflect on these methodological limits, whose origin lies in a reflection on the limits and nature of the activity of problem-solving itself. This is entirely in the spirit of Kant's critical philosophy, which is a science reflecting on the limits and boundaries of pure thought. This critical approach should be adopted with regard to mathematics, resulting in a discipline that takes over where ordinary mathematics leaves off, a transcendental or meta-discipline explaining why ordinary mathematics reaches and runs up against certain limits, as well as explaining the very conditions of its *possibility*. In other words, there is a necessity for a genuine philosophy of mathematics, a discipline that had not yet been sufficiently established during the idealistic and romantic period. With his cognitive reflections on the nature and possibility of mathematical activity it is obvious that Fichte considered the *Wissenschaftslehre* as being able to contribute to such a disciple. Fichte writes in 1804,

> Let the arithmetician as mere arithmetician tell me how he is able to generate a solid and fixed number one; or let the geometer explain what holds and keeps his space stationary for him while he draws his continuous lines in it;…. This is not in any way meant as a reproach to mathematics; because mathematics should and cannot be anything else. And it is certainly not our business to blur the boundaries of the sciences; but it should simply be recognized that this science [of mathematics], like all the other sciences, is not the first science, and it is not independent, but that the principles of its possibility lie in another, higher science. (GA 2/8, 47f)

Fichte's most detailed reflections on a philosophy of mathematics were to appear the following year in his 1805 course on logic in Erlangen.[33]

One could argue that what is particularly "Fichtean" about some of the late fragments of Novalis is that he seems to agree with Fichte that the methods of the *Wissenschaftslehre* could provide a framework for a kind of proto-philosophy of mathematics. Novalis here made a direct comparison between Fichte and the French mathematician Georges-Louis Le Sage, who was trying to introduce rigorous "speculative" and mechanistic models into physics: "The *Wissenschaftslehre* is nothing more than a proof of *the reality of logic*—its harmony with the rest of nature and [it is] completely analogous to mathematics with regard to its discoveries, its rectifications—and to what it can achieve. (Le Sage has accomplished something similar in mathematics)" (NS 3, 559). For Novalis, the *Wissenschaftslehre*'s method of inwardly directing one's attention to the activities of the mind during the constructing of the self could serve as a model for reflecting on the activities and constructions of mathematics, especially on its limits and failures, to render mathematics in turn more scientific. Such a discipline, according to Novalis, could be called the "*Wissenschaftslehre* of mathematics," as he outlines in entry 1015 of the *Romantic Encyclopaedia*:

> Attempt to prove and solve this [i.e., the functions of the analytic and synthetic methods in mathematics]—to construct what mathematics fails to prove or solve—the *Wissenschaftslehre* of mathematics. The application of problems and theorems—combining them—the *scientification of mathematics*. (NS 3, 175)[34]

Hence, among contemporary philosophers, it is above all Novalis who saw the *Wissenschaftslehre*'s potential for contributing to a scientific discipline reflecting on the problems, activities, and limits of mathematics. However, here one should keep in mind a number of other things. Firstly, one has to be careful about overinterpreting these late fragments on the need for a philosophy of mathematics, or attributing too much value to what are admittedly only scattered remarks on Fichte's mathematical *Wissenschaftslehre*. Novalis's ideas remain brief indications and are not fully developed.[35] Second, one should not forget Novalis's cutting criticisms of the presentation of Fichte's system in the late fragments: the *Wissenschaftslehre* is a "frightful convolution of abstractions" that is not yet "complete or presented precisely enough" and "absolutely unpoetic" (NS 4, 230).[36] Finally, Novalis's utterances on the deficiencies in the presentations of Fichte's system should not be taken in turn as rejections of the *Wissenschaftslehre* as a whole. For Fichte had made exactly the same criticisms about the presentation of his philosophy. He too was not satisfied with its external form, and continually revised and recast his system in an attempt to assist the understanding of his readers. As Fichte remarked to Reinhold in 1797: "Your evaluation of *my* presentation, as it has appeared so far, is much too favorable. Or perhaps the content has allowed you to overlook the deficiency of the presentation. I consider it to be most imperfect. Yes, I know that it gives off sparks of spirit; but it is not a *single* flame."[37]

14.4. THE RELEVANCE OF NOVALIS'S FINAL FRAGMENTS

How can one speak about the relevance of Novalis's final philosophical fragments today? One way would be to show how some of his insights are still fruitful because they help us to better understand certain aspects or phenomena. In addition to Novalis's indication of Fichte's affinity to Neoplatonism, I maintain that this is also the case with his views on the mathematicity of the

Wissenschaftslehre. For it was likewise only in the twentieth century that this aspect of Fichte's system was acknowledged as significant by a number of leading philosophers and mathematicians, such as Hermann Weyl and Jules Vuillemin. Neither of these later thinkers directly refers to Novalis's remarks on the mathematical nature of Fichte's philosophy, yet they too argue for a positive mathematical reading of the *Wissenschaftslehre.* Hence, like the above-mentioned example of Andreas Speiser's research on the Platonic elements of Fichte's thought, one could also consider the work of Weyl and Vuillemin to have provided an independent confirmation of some of Novalis's original insights. In conclusion, we will outline two specific instances of this.

First, the German mathematician and philosopher Hermann Weyl (1885–1955) seems to have especially valued Fichte's theory of construction and his art of conceptual distinctions. As Norman Sieroka has shown in great detail in his recent book *Umgebungen,* it was Fichte's 1812 lectures on transcendental logic that helped Weyl to better grasp the nature of logical antinomies, the understanding of which subsequently helped him to clarify certain elements of set theory and mathematical logic.[38] Already in his 1918 book *Das Kontinuum,* Weyl had proposed that Fichte's philosophy could be of benefit to philosophers of mathematics: "We cannot now proceed to the final explanation of the essence of a factual issue, judgment, object, and quality; this task would lead us into metaphysical depths. Here one has to receive advice from men whose names cannot be mentioned among mathematicians without eliciting a compassionate smile—Fichte, for example."[39] Moreover, with reference to the Pythagorean theorem, Sieroka explains how for both Weyl and Fichte the mathematical theory of self-evidence has its initial foundation in a "*feeling* for truth and certainty."[40] These are then combined with the hovering ("*Schweben*") of the imagination, allowing the mathematician to "construct" certain laws, principles, and operations. Weyl's emphasis on a clear analysis of the concept of operation and activity in mathematics also parallels a key mathematical concept in Novalis, as has been recently noted by Benoît Timmermans.[41] In any event, these particular elements of Fichte's theory were much more palatable to Weyl than the phenomenological theory of Husserl.[42]

A second example of the prescience of Novalis's remarks concerning the mathematicity of the *Wissenschaftslehre* may be found in the work of the late French philosopher of mathematics Jules Vuillemin (1920–2001). In his 1962 seminal study, *La philosophie de l'algèbre,* Vuillemin argues that Fichte's progression beyond Kant's theory of sensible intuition to an exact and reflective mode of intellectual intuition has a direct historical comparison with the algebraic methods developed by the French mathematician Joseph-Louis Lagrange in 1770. Philosophically, Vuillemin asserts two main points: first, the history of mathematics shows that revolutions in the methods of mathematics have repercussions on the methods of philosophy, which are only subsequently understood by philosophers. Thus, philosophers could learn a lot and make advances in their knowledge by studying the revolutions in mathematics.[43] Second, Vuillemin applies this to Fichte by demonstrating a significant parallel between the genetic method of the *Wissenschaftslehre* and Lagrange's abstracting method in algebra. Technically speaking, Lagrange had noticed how a posteriori methods for solving algebraic equations frequently reduced the problem by employing some kind of transformation to the solution of a certain auxiliary equation of a lower degree. Instead of merely obtaining particular solutions to particular equations, Lagrange discovered an a priori general method for solving cubic and quartic equations, that is, of the third and fourth degree. Lagrange's insight was to consider the roots (the particular numerical values) of an equation in a symbolic or wholly abstract manner, instead of (as his predecessors had done) as a numerical value. Thus, instead of achieving just particular solutions, Lagrange was able to proceed to a higher level of rational abstraction by examining problem-solving *methods* in general, and to explain why certain methods were successful and others were not. Lagrange's realization was the first step in an a priori and generalized method that would ultimately lead to the branch of mathematics called group theory—not with particular quantitative solutions, but a theory of their qualitative structures and laws.[44]

For Vuillemin, this revolution in mathematics sheds important light on the philosophical path from Kant to Fichte. He maintains that Fichte's *Wissenschaftslehre* is similar to the problem-solving power of Lagrange's algebraic method because it too makes the transition from sensible, particular cases and constructions, to abstracted and universalized considerations on the activity of constructing itself. Vuillemin sees this as one of Fichte's principal advances over Kant: the move beyond sensible intuition to intellectual intuition, and the focus on the nature of intellectual activities and *operations*.[45] Thus, an earlier progression in mathematical thought was later paralleled by a progression in philosophical thought. As we saw above, it is precisely the considerations on the operations and limits of problem-solving that also led Novalis to qualify the *Wissenschaftslehre* as "mathematical," for the latter not only seeks to obtain answers to particular, sensible questions, but also to abstract away and supply more universal and intelligible solutions. In the language of the romantic philosopher, the methodology of mathematics has become philosophically potentialized, for one has abstracted from the particular quantitative case to find a higher universal or *qualitative* case.[46]

14.5. CONCLUSION

To summarize: as we saw above, Novalis did not just write lovely poetic hymns to mathematics, but had also engaged in serious mathematical studies, which led him in turn to reflect on the relationship between this discipline and philosophy. Like Fichte, the late Novalis saw mathematics as a scientific ideal and argued for the need for a genuine philosophy of mathematics. Writing in the 1799 *Freiberg Natural-Scientific Studies*, Novalis remarks: "All the sciences should become *mathematics*. Up to now, mathematics has merely been the first and simplest expression or revelation of true scientific spirit.... *Poetics* of mathematics. *Grammar* of mathematics. *Physics* of mathematics. *Philosophy* of mathematics" (NS 3, 50).[47] Moreover, there are two kinds of mathematical operations for Novalis, the purely quantitative operations concerned with numerical facts and the measurement of external sensible nature, and a qualitative operation, concerned with the higher self or intelligible inner world of the human being. Novalis not only defined the latter qualitative operation as the method of romanticizing as such, but on account of their similar concerns with mathematical operations or *activity*, he also saw a link between this qualitative mathematical method and Fichte's *Wissenschaftslehre*, or what he called the "*Wissenschaftslehre* of mathematics." Finally, with their views on the propaedeutic value of mathematical thinking for idealistic philosophy, both Fichte and Novalis could be placed in the Platonic tradition. As Novalis remarks in his *Final Fragments* of 1800 on the relationship of mathematics to idealism: "Pure mathematics is the intuition of the intellect as a universe. Genuine mathematics is the actual element of the magician.... In music it appears formally, as revelation—as creative idealism" (NS 3, 593).

In the field of German philosophy the question is often asked: "Did the Romantics really understand Kant and Fichte?" With regard to the mathematical pretensions of the *Wissenschaftslehre* the first elements of an answer may now be provided. In contrast to the outdated view that Novalis had at most a "poetically inspired" grasp of Fichte's system, one could argue that he was only able to attain his insights on account of his extensive mathematical and philosophical studies. This background allowed him to actually *understand* the *Wissenschaftslehre* better than many of his contemporaries, and to perceive mathematical aspects in it which have only been grasped by more recent research. In terms of relevance it therefore seems that scholars of German idealism and philosophical romanticism can still benefit from a closer examination of Novalis's reflections on Fichte, especially those found in his final philosophical fragments.

NOTES

1. I would like to thank the Fritz Thyssen Stiftung for their generous assistance during the period of writing this essay. On Novalis and mathematics, see among others: Martin Dyck, *Novalis and Mathematics* (Chapel Hill: University of North Carolina Press, 1960); Käte Hamburger, "Novalis und die Mathematik," in *Philosophie der Dichter: Novalis, Schiller, Rilke* (Stuttgart: Kohlhammer, 1966),

11–82; Howard Pollack, "Novalis and Mathematics Revisited: Paradoxes of the Infinite in the Allgemeine Brouillon," *Athenäum: Jahrbuch für Romantik* 7 (1997), 113–140; and more recently, Benoît Timmermans, "Novalis et la réforme des mathématiques," in *Modernité Romantique*, ed. Augustin Dumont and Laurent van Eynde (Paris: Éditions Kimé, 2011), 73–88.

2. Wilhelm Dilthey, *Das Erlebnis und die Dichtung: Lessing, Goethe, Novalis, Hölderlin*, in *Gesammelte Schriften*, vol. 26 (Göttingen: Vandenhoeck & Ruprecht, 2005), 196.

3. The Historical-Critical edition was begun in 1960 and completed in 1988.

4. See especially NS 3, 50–53, 115–28, 593–94.

5. Hans Niels Jahnke, "Mathematik und Romantik," in *Disziplinen im Kontext*, ed. Volker Peckhaus and Christian Thiel (Munich: Wilhelm Fink Verlag, 1999), 172.

6. See Timmermans's remarks on Novalis and Hindenburg's theories, "Novalis et la réforme des mathématiques," 80–81.

7. For an English translation of this text see Novalis, *Notes for a Romantic Encyclopaedia: Das Allgemeine Brouillon*, ed. and trans. David W. Wood (hereafter *Romantic Encyclopedia*) (Albany: SUNY Press, 2007).

8. Frederick C. Beiser, *German Idealism: The Struggle against Subjectivism, 1781–1801* (Cambridge, MA: Harvard University Press, 2002), 410.

9. Cf. Manfred Frank's summary of his differences with Beiser in his *Auswege aus dem Deutschen Idealismus* (Frankfurt am Main: Suhrkamp, 2007), 16–19. See also Chapter 1 of this volume.

10. Here Novalis speaks of how philosophy can assist in the unification of the sciences. See "Christenheit oder Europa", 1799 (NS 3, 521).

11. Cf. Dyck, *Novalis and Mathematics*, 75–77.

12. Cf. Beiser's criticisms in *German Idealism*, 354–355.

13. On Novalis's view of the "mysterious" function of mathematics, see Pollack, "Novalis and Mathematics Revisited," 139f.

14. Ibid.

15. *Romantic Encyclopaedia*, 66.

16. Ibid., 78.

17. Cf. Manfred Frank, *"Unendliche Annäherung." Die Anfänge der philosophischen Frühromantik* (Frankfurt am Main: Suhrkamp, 1998), 816–22, 849–53.

18. See Friedrich Schlegel's letter to Novalis, May 5, 1797 (NS 4, 482). On this romantic notion, see my "From 'Fichticizing' to 'Romanticizing': Fichte and Novalis on the Activities of Philosophy and Art," *Fichte-Studien* 42 (2013): 249–80.

19. For more details of this, see David W. Wood, *"Mathesis of the Mind": A Study of Fichte's Wissenschaftslehre and Geometry* (hereafter *"Mathesis of the Mind"*) (New York: Rodopi, 2012).

20. See Fichte's "Second Introduction," in J. G. Fichte, *Introductions to the Wissenschaftslehre and Other Writings*, ed. and trans. Daniel Breazeale (Indianapolis: Hackett, 1994), 41.

21. J. G. Fichte, "Announcement," in *The Philosophical Rupture between Fichte and Schelling: Texts and Selected Writings* (hereafter *Philosophical Rupture*) (Albany: SUNY Press, 2012), 89.

22. Ibid.

23. For a discussion of Fichte's theory of original geometry and its relation to Platonism, as well as a translation into English of the key text, see my *"Mathesis of the Mind,"* esp. 79–120, 275–90.

24. As he also did with Kant. See Novalis to Friedrich Schlegel, December 10, 1798 (NS 4, 269). Cf. Werner Beierwaltes, *Platonismus und Idealismus* (Frankfurt am Main: Klostermann, 1972; reprint 2004), 84–85.

25. See Andreas Speiser, *Ein Parmenideskommentar—Studien zur platonischen Dialektik*, 2nd ed. (Leipzig: K. F. Koehler, 1959), 73–106; and "Die Grundlagen der Mathematik von Plato bis Fichte," *Eranos Jahrbuch* 14 (1946): 11–38.

26. Cf. *J. G. Fichte im Gespräch*, vol. 1, ed. Erich Fuchs (Stuttgart-Bad Cannstatt: Frommann-Holzboog, 1978), 241.

27. Cf. Lisa Shabel, *Mathematics in Kant's Critical Philosophy* (New York: Routledge, 2003), 115.

28. *Romantic Encyclopaedia*, 107, 189; *Vorarbeiten* (NS 2, 524).

29. *Romantic Encyclopaedia*, 86.

30. Ibid., 133.

31. Cf. *Philosophical Rupture*, 102.

32. See *Philosophical Rupture*, 87.

33. See *"Mathesis of the Mind,"* 33–78.

34. The relation of "Fichte's *Wissenschaftslehre*" to problem-solving, "*connecting*—and *higher* science" or "universal system," is again intimated in the so-called "Mathematische Fragmente" of the *Freiberg Natural Scientific Studies* (see NS 3, 127; translated in "Appendix" to *Romantic Encyclopaedia*, 207).

35. Cf. Jahnke, "Mathematik und Romantik," 175.

36. See *Romantic Encyclopaedia*, 164.

37. J. G. Fichte to K. L. Reinhold, March 21, 1797, in *Fichte: Early Philosophical Writings*, ed. and trans. Daniel Breazeale (Ithaca: Cornell University Press, 1988), 417.

38. See Norman Sieroka, *Umgebungen: Symbolischer Konstruktivismus im Anschluss an Hermann Weyl und Fritz Medicus* (Zurich: Chronos, 2010), 57–59.

39. Hermann Weyl, *Das Kontinuum* (Leipzig: Veit & Comp., 1919), 2.

40. See Norman Sieroka, *Umgebungen*, 102–4.

41. Cf. Timmermans, "Novalis et la réforme des mathématiques," 84–85.

42. See Sieroka, *Umgebungen*, 175–79.

43. See Jules Vuillemin, *La philosophie de l'algèbre* (Paris: PUF, 1962, reprint 1993), 116.

44. Ibid., 99–120.

45. Ibid., 59–60, 102–22.

46. Regarding Novalis's mathematical ideas and later parallels in the development of group theory, see Timmermans, "Novalis et la réforme des mathématiques," 78–80.

47. See *Romantic Encyclopaedia*, 195.

15

Irritable Figures

Herder's Poetic Empiricism

AMANDA JO GOLDSTEIN

I want to begin by emphasizing this chapter's once improbable premise: there *is* "romantic" philosophy of science, whether we capitalize "Romantic" to name a historically bounded cultural movement, or leave it small to hold open, at the same time, the possibility of a recurrent position, style, or mode. In a tenacious nineteenth-century caricature that begins at last to give way, romanticism has frequently been defined *against* natural scientific curiosity, as the inward-turning, imaginative backlash against a (symmetrically caricatured) Enlightenment, out to master nature through reason and experiment. But the romantic era in fact confronts us with the as yet unfinished emergence of the very opposition between literature and science upon which such assessments have relied: a process of field differentiation that was neither complete nor inevitable during the period in question. This process would ultimately transform the meaning of "literature" from learning in general to a prestige feature of a certain kind of text; it would polarize the vocations of artist and scientist; and it would circumscribe poetry, formerly one mode of expressing anything important, to a special discourse of subjective universality that ceded the task of representing natural realities to a host of professionalizing scientific discourses.[1] But at work in the romantic period were not only arguments and impulses that contributed to the now deep-seated division of labor between scientific and literary production but also those that contested, ignored, did not accept, or did not know that division—positions of which the period's many apparently hybrid, amorphous, or even "monstrous" projects are the sign.[2]

It is my premise that such projects were not necessarily philosophically naive, although their ontological, epistemological, and ethical ground has frequently slipped from view. If the organization of Kant's monumental third *Critique* into aesthetic and natural philosophical halves predicted the nineteenth-century consolidation of the "Two Cultures," rival romantic philosophies presumed, proposed, or defended other possible orders of knowledge. Period philosophies of science, then, merit our attention both for their role in the emergence of lasting separations between the natural and human sciences *and*, more provocatively, for their richness as a reservoir of neglected alternatives to that division. Such lapsed possibilities renew their relevance at our own historical moment: it is at last abundantly clear that the field divisions we have inherited from the nineteenth century not only fail to resolve but also help to produce, the ecological, bio-political, and economic crises that chronically evade their grasp.

From the historical reconstruction of romantic era philosophies of science, we might begin to delineate as "romantic" a kind of provocation that also precedes and follows the period bearing the name: recurrent challenges to what twentieth-century philosophers of science have come to call the "criteria of demarcation" distinguishing science from nonscience. It is romantic to experiment upon the constitutive exclusions that divide scientific rationality from its purported opposites at a given historical moment—fiction, for instance, or theology, or feeling. When it came to the protocols of experimental science emergent after the scientific revolution, romantics were above all intent to query what counted as a relevant "experience" or trial. On revision, the eighteenth- and nineteenth-century movement's notorious "irrationality"—its preoccupations with states of reverie, infancy, primitivity, ecstasy, madness, illness, intoxication, and *Rausch*—can be seen as as the systematic solicitation of forms of sensory experience excluded from contemporary protocols of empirical accounting. Such gestures, as Robert Richards, John H. Zammito, and Frederick Beiser have each amply proved, do not only or always reject outright the Enlightened aspiration to know the natural world through the testimony of the senses. Romantic writers also elaborate and radicalize this project, carrying it into unexamined corners of experience and subjecting its methods to unforeseen renovation.[3]

Under particular, and particularly romantic, pressure in this essay will be the line of demarcation between science (*Wissenschaft, scientia*) and poetry (*poesis*, production), as well as the fate of stimuli so plural and so slight that they hardly cross the threshold into sensation. I will explore the subversion of that line of demarcation and the fate of those obscure stimuli in two essays by Johann Gottfried Herder (1744–1803), one that argues for the physiologically *poetic* relation between sensation and thought, and another for the veracity of poetic figures.

Herder's "On the Cognition and Sensation of the Human Soul [*Vom Erkennen und Empfinden der menschlichen Seele*]" (1778) and "On Image, Poetry, and Fable [*Über Bild, Dichtung, und Fabel*]" (1787) anticipate many of the challenges that have come to define "postpositivist" problems in the philosophy of science: the interimplication of history and philosophy, the instability of the "fact/value" distinction, the "theory-ladenness" of observation, and the constitutive role of linguistic and technological apparatus in the "discovery" and representation of scientific facts and theories.[4] Herder develops an empiricist epistemology profoundly sensitive to the historicity, social-situatedness, and asymmetrical relations of power inherent in the process of studying nature through experimental enquiry—and yet, as I will try to argue, this philosophy of science *does not* issue in sheer linguistic or social constructivism, as some of its postmodern analogues seem to do. Here the ineradicable contingency and anthropomorphism of the knowledge humans make neither derealizes the objects of scientific inquiry nor severs that knowledge finally from the world of (other) things. For Herder, I will argue, the "all too human" contingency of knowledge in fact describes its scientifically indispensable zone of contact with other natures. And Herder moreover rehabilitates poetry—specially understood as the joint product of observer and observed—as the mode of representation adequate to this contact: a neglected resource for a science capable of resisting radical skepticism in both its empiricist and idealist flavors.[5]

"Not ashamed to run after images," as he puts it, Herder' revalues poetry for, or better, *as* natural science in unapologetically figurative style (CS 189). Drawing on contemporary physiology to explore the relays required to transform "obscure irritations" into something as polished and unitary as a conscious sensation, Herder concludes that our sense organs are constantly "translating," "allegorizing," and "schematizing" (CS 189–90, IPF 359). He thus sees poetic tropes as intrinsically linked to the physical activity of sensory experience, and proceeds to advocate figurative language as sensory knowledge's fittest mode of expression. Yet this is *not* tantamount to discrediting empirical knowledge as a "mere" verbal construct. The physiology of figure at issue in Herder entails neither the linguistic production of the natural body, nor the naturalization of language as inborn or "hardwired" biological fact. Instead, he confronts us with a premise now strange in the extremity of its naturalism: human figurative work on words is just one species of the tropic activity that propels natural bodies in general. Human metaphorics derive from, and depend upon, forms of non- and pre-verbal transport that precede it phylogenetically, ontogenetically, and in each act of sensation. To write in tropes, then, as poets do, may be less to obscure the simple evidence of sense than to practice maximum fidelity to it.

Isaiah Berlin once designated the polymathic philosopher, theologian, poet, and literary critic, Johann Gottfried Herder, with Kant, as one of the two "true fathers of romanticism."[6] Yet Kantian critical philosophy, its transformation at Jena, and its refracted dissemination in English romantic aesthetics, persistently overshadows the naturalist, historicist, and anti-dualist romantic strain that Herder prolifically advocated. Herder's writings furnish an alternative set of philosophical premises that help us to recognise and account for, features of the English and German romantic literary canons that do not square with the subjectivist and idealizing trends long thought to define romantic aesthetic and natural philosophy (the physiology-saturated poetics of John Keats, William Blake, Novalis, and Georg Büchner, for example). That invoking Herder for "romanticism" brings the dates and motives of that classification into dizzying overlap with many others (Enlightenment [*Aufklärung*], Counter-Enlightenment, Sturm und Drang, the culture of sensibility) is true to the best new insights of interdisciplinary scholarship on what many are calling "the long eighteenth century." At stake are more diverse, nuanced, and skeptical Enlightenment cultures—and more scientifically and socially engaged romantic ones—than we have previously been called upon to explain.[7]

In this essay's first part, "Revisionary Empiricism and the Science of Sensation," I take a step back in order to set out how Herder's philosophy of science derives and departs from the legacies of New Scientific experimentalism and classical empiricist psychology, as well as to touch on its engagement with the emergent sciences of life. In the second, longer part, "The Physiology of Tropes," I delve deeper into the irritable fibers of Herder's romantic observer, exploring how his provocative account of the physiology of sensation as a seriously *figurative* process serves to valorize poetry as a privileged technique of empirical inquiry and representation.

15.1. REVISIONARY EMPIRICISM AND THE SCIENCE OF SENSATION

As intimated above, Herder's philosophy of science exemplifies a strain of revisionary, romantic empiricism that cannily sophisticates the empiricist and experimentalist project of knowing the world through the testimony of the senses. Herder's revisionary empiricism, like that of Goethe, Erasmus Darwin, William Wordsworth, and William Blake, demands that practitioners confront bewildering intricacies of human sensoria—their multiplicity, historicity, and social formation—in order to comprehend and cultivate their limits and potentials as instruments of experimental inquiry. Like these thinkers, Herder delves with freshly voluptuous natural scientific curiosity into the obscurity, confusion, and complexity that prior empiricisms had sought to eliminate from sensuously derived knowledge.

Jonathan Crary has influentially posited the *camera obscura* as the epitome of classical empiricist protocol: presuming both a "pre-given world of objective truth" and an autonomous subject capable of observing this world from the sequestered space of his own interiority, this optical apparatus figured knowledge as a "kind of *askesis*" through which the observer purified and regulated the world's disorderly advance.[8] At the beginning of the nineteenth century, Crary argues, the science of vision abandoned these pristine mechanics of light and descended into the observer's complex physiology: the visible "escaped from the timeless order of the camera obscura" to "lodg[e] in another apparatus...the unstable physiology and temporality of the human body."[9] Crary's sketch is broad-brush, but Herder wittily affirms the caricature (albeit two decades earlier than Crary's periodization scheme would allow). The author of "On the Sensation and Cognition of the Human Soul" describes his own essay as a descent into the body that would have made prior philosophers blush: "Often there lie under the diaphragm causes which we very incorrectly and laboriously seek in the head...in the face of this sort of deep abyss of obscure sensations...our bright and clear philosophy is horrified" (CS 196). Herder delights to ridicule those abstemious philosophers, "standing firm and secure," in "happy ignorance" of the uncouth abyss of "obscure forces and irritations" from which their luminous ideas actually arise (201).

To argue that classical empiricist psychologies had decorporealized thought curiously minimizes those philosophies' signature provocation, which had been to redescribe selves and their thoughts as aggregates of sense impressions without innate or transcendent source. But if Crary and Herder tend to underestimate prior empiricisms' rich exploration of the linguistic and historical contingencies that afflict sense-based knowledge, this is because, in that prior philosophical discourse, such problems had intruded above all at the secondary level of "association" *between* "simple ideas of sense," rather than at the level of sensation itself. In Locke, sense impressions are as "*simple*" as ideas come; though shorn of any transcendental guarantee, they nonetheless constitute the least problematic building blocks for knowledge. "[T]he ideas [things] produce in the mind," Locke affirms, "enter by the senses simple and unmixed," and "nothing can be plainer to a man than the clear and distinct perception he has of those simple ideas."[10] Famously, these "simple ideas of sensation" impress a self of correspondent uniformity and simplicity: "white paper, void of all characters, without any ideas," and Locke explicitly declined to examine "by what motions of our spirits or alterations of our bodies we come to have any *sensation* by our organs, or any *ideas* in our understandings."[11] Herder, then, and Crary after him, is astute to notice that the rise of experimental physiology, a science precisely devoted to how "we come to have any *sensation* by our organs," has the potential to transform empiricist psychology. For better or worse, this science could restore the "body full of sensations, full of irritations" to the "vaporous skeleton" common to both rationalist metaphysics and empiricist philosophy (CS 182).

From Herder's physiologically informed point of view, it is quite futile to posit an "idea of sense" as "simple" or "uncompounded." He argues that any sensation attaining to consciousness represents a belated sum of innumerable and nameless interactions: an "aggregate of all the obscure wishes [*sie ein Aggregat sind alle der dunklen Wünsche*]" emanating from "each little thicket of life" in a creature's "diverse, thousandfold organized body" (192 [335], 182). Discrete sense impressions, impressions that fall neatly into the five acknowledged categories of sight, sound, smell, taste, and touch, are reductive approximations of the panoply of subliminal and multisensory co-operations that make up a person's felt state:

At the very moment that he sees, he also hears, and unconsciously enjoys, through all the organs of his manifold machine, external influences that, though they remain largely obscure sensations, nevertheless secretly cooperate on the sum of his whole condition at all times. He floats in a sea of impressions of objects, in which one wave laps against him softly, another more perceptibly. (IPF 357, trans. mod.)

Zu eben derselben Zeit, da er siehet, höret er auch und genießt unvermerkt durch alle Organe seiner vielartigen Maschine Einflüsse von außen, die zwar größtenteils dunkle Empfindungen bleiben, jederzeit aber auf die Summe seines ganzen Zustandes ingeheim mitwerken. Er schwimmt in einem Meer von Eindrücken der Gegenstände, wo Eine Welle leiser, die andre fühlbarer ihn berühret. (633)

Ideas of sense are late glosses on the "sea of impressions" registered within the thousand-fold weave of his body. Moreover, the whole method of distillation that an individual unconsciously performs—the method of producing sensations from "obscure forces and irritations," and cognitions from sensations—is a work of cultural history (CS 201).

That is, regardless of sensory stimulus, Herder argues, "we would grope about in deep night and blindness if instruction [*Unterweisung*] had not early on thought *for us* and, so to speak, imprinted in us ready-made thought-formulas [*fertige Gedankenformeln uns eingeprägt hätte*]" (CS 212 [358]). We require the prosthetic of instruction—"the support of staffs that were reached to us in earliest childhood"—to bind sensations to cognitions and, indeed, to sense coherently at all. In an important formulation, Herder writes that familial and cultural indoctrination forge an armature of "secret bonds [*geheime Bände*]" through which any "object *has* to come to us," if it is to take sensible shape at all (212 [358], emphasis added). The present members of any given society have their very eyes "accustomed, tied, limited" to the "viewpoint" characteristic of their context; any sensed object arrives by way of prepared and permissible paths.[12] For Herder, then, it is not particularly fruitful, even heuristically, to conceive of sensation as simple or the self in originary blankness: "Man is such a complex, artificial being [*ein so zusammengesetztes, künstliches Wesen*] that despite every effort he can never achieve a wholly simple state" (IPF 357 [633]). Herder instead exposes philosophical pretenses of purity and autonomy as attempts to suppress the real "birth of our reason" in circumstances of physical and psychic dependency (CS 212). Dependency on *women*, no less: from the very womb forward, Herder points out embryonic philosophers float in a maternal matrix of communicated "impressions and irritations" (CS 207); "the nursemaids who form our tongues are our first teachers of logic" (F 48); the best human inventions emerge from "the husks of human need, in a cradle of childhood, in swaddling clothes" (F 55); and "in this matter women are our philosophers, not we theirs" (CS 207).

Extraordinary in these passages, from a present-day perspective, is the single gesture with which Herder performs what would now seem to be ideologically opposed operations, "naturalizing" *and* "historicizing" human knowledge at once. Thought is coextensive with the biological body, worked up from "the longing yearning, with which each little thicket of life in our body [*jeder kleine Lebensbusch unsres Körpers*] thirsts for satisfaction [*Befriedigung*]" (CS 192 [335]). Yet this very assertion enables Herder to describe that body's necessary and consequential incorporation of social forms. At issue is a notion of natural (or biological, or organic) life that is neither determined in advance nor purely auto-poetic, but unfinished, needy, pliant, and resourceful. Such a life incorporates, from the outset, the helps on offer, even to attain basic physical development—even to be able to see.

What Herder strikingly calls the "sense of an alien which imprints itself in us [*dieser Sinn eines Fremden, der sich in uns einprägt*]" thus shapes our profoundest interiority and is perpetuated in each instance of movement, sensation, or thought (CS 212 [359]). Illusions of subjective autonomy ironically reveal the relational nature of human life, for only an animal equipped to interweave "alien" stays so early, necessarily, and easily into its frame could mistake these "*bonds*" for its own creations. One begins to see just how tactically powerful naturalism could be, in the late eighteenth century, as a means to articulate natural life as a process of sociohistorical conformation. Herder shows how a collection of norms that precede our coming scaffold "the deepest self *in us*": a self, therefore, "not as autonomous, voluntarily choosing, and unbound as is believed [*nicht so eigenmächtig, willkürlich, und los, als man glaubet*]" (CS 212 [359]).

Having sketched the way Herder's thought intensifies its classical empiricist inheritance by bringing historical contingency to bear at the level of sensation, I want to underscore a second, characteristically romantic revision of that legacy. Perpetuating the Cartesian truth criteria of "clarity and distinctness," previous empiricist psychology had emphasized the obscurity and heterogeneity inherent in sensuously derived knowledge primarily in order to target such imperfections for elimination. Herder and like-minded romantics viewed sensory impurity less as an epistemic impediment (whose removal would adequate knowledge to truth) than as a neglected cache of true experience (awaiting transformation into knowledge by philosophically unorthodox means). Thus Herder inverts the philosophical virtue of clarity and distinctness with mischievous precision: "what," he asks, "does that clear, luminous, encompassing cognition *lack* so that it is not and does not become sensation?"[13] Here, the distillation of sensation into "so called *pure thinking*" enforces a *loss* of information and accuracy prior philosophy splendidly "reveals the unity in everything...but does it also reveal as distinguishingly the eachness in each thing?" (CSd 180, CS 242). Herder regrets that a "broad region of sensations, drives, affects...gets called *body, obscure ideas, feelings*"—and systematically ignored. He therefore sets out to track and redeem the "rich traces [*reiche Spuren*]" of bodily interaction with the world that thinking must bear, "despite all distillation [*Trotz aller Destillation*]" (CS 181, 242 [392]).

For such revisionary empiricism, the mixed "abyss" of "obscure forces and irritations" that do not cross the threshold into discursive clarity constitutes a critical, corporeal register of interactions with the objects of scientific curiosity (CS 201). Its "rich traces" are essential to any empirical effort to document these objects' efficacy and ours. Attending to the subtle, divergent, near-imperceptible impressions, impressions that "touch him softly," "whose sounds get lost in each other more obscurely," will advance the description of nature, without and within (CS 192).

Clearly such a project requires enhanced self-scrutiny on the part of the observer, vigilantly attuned to "the most complexly woven sensations and passions of our so composite machine [*unsrer so zusammengesetzten Maschine*]" (190 [333]). But we ought no longer assume that such romantic self-scrutiny relinquishes natural curiosity in favor of the purely introspective work of subjective genius. Indeed, Herder dismisses as "puerile hysteria" and "abstract egoism" the contemporary cult of genius that was pressing philosophy—natural, aesthetic, and moral—towards idealism: "inspiration; creative force; originality; heaven-aspiring, independently self-developing original power; and so forth" (239, 209, 235). The "soul"—which Herder's essay invites us to interpret as the "nerve structure" personified, if not the power of nerves to conjure up our very sense of personhood—"spins, knows, cognizes nothing *out of itself*...it must use the irritations, the senses, the forces and opportunities which became its own through a fortunate, unearned inheritance" (209). Like the natural body, from which it ought no longer be separated, the psyche resourcefully assimilates chance materials that condition its coming.

"In my modest opinion," comments Herder, "no *psychology* is possible which is not in each step determinate *physiology*" (196). As I suggested at the outset of this section, "On the Cognition and Sensation of the Human Soul" aims to fulfill this antidualist agenda, bringing empiricist psychology into step with the new sciences of the animal life. These sciences, then, are the final context to thicken before turning in detail to Herder's own poetic physiology. Herder's essay is, among other things, a rhapsody on the groundbreaking experimental physiology of Albrecht von Haller. Haller's work on the "irritability" and "sensibility" of bodily fibers and nerves redescribed the once quasi-mechanical animal body as nervous, responsive, productive, and communicative; his research provided a physiological dimension to the eighteenth-century culture of sensibility.[14] Despite Haller's own dualist theological commitments, many of his contemporaries took his reactive corporeal conduits as evidence that the "higher" powers of sentience and cognition were firmly rooted in the body's "soft marrow" (198). Herder's essay thus openly aspires to raise "*Haller's* physiological work" to the level of "psychology" in a way that Haller himself was loathe to do (196).[15]

The physiology of sensation thus expresses one aspect of that controversial "epistemological rupture" in eighteenth-century culture that Michel Foucault, Georges Canguillhem, and François Jacob famously posited for the twentieth-century historiography of modern science. Their theses argued the unprecedented appearance of "life" as a discrete and autonomous concern around 1800, a special category of being that, now seeming to merit its own research program, catalyzed widespread transformation in the traditional domains of natural, aesthetic, and moral philosophy.[16] Though the temporality of "rupture" has been nuanced, elongated, and backdated, few historians contest the pan-cultural "vitalization of nature" in the course of the eighteenth century: research into the forms of motion, reactivity, force, and power purportedly unique to *living* beings flourished, and active matter displaced inert, Newtonian stuff as the basic material of the cosmos and the most alluring target of experimental and philosophical inquiry.[17]

The rise of experimental physiology goes some way toward explaining the bewildering crossing of subjects and objects of experimental observation, and indeed of methodological essays and experimental findings, in the texts of the romantic period. With biological life under scrutiny, the living observer, no less than the live animals subject to inspection (embryonic chicks, freshwater polyps, microscopic animalculae), becomes an object of interest and a physiological variable at the scene of empirical investigation.[18] It is perhaps Goethe, writing in his journal *On Morphology*, who provides the most economical gloss on this conundrum and the prospects for turning it to advantage: "Every new object, well seen, opens up a new organ in us [*Jeder neue Gegenstand, wohl beschaut, schließt ein neues Organ in uns auf*]."[19] Revisionary empiricism is abbreviated in this astonishing phrase, which transforms "us" from observing subject to observed object, and back again: keen observers of metamorphosis, Goethe suggests, cannot but metamorphose in the act of observation; we cannot but open an "organ" adjusted to the metamorphic object that occasioned this opening, ourselves the objects of a transformative process whose outcome is to produce us as observing subjects once again. Sensation is here understood as a process of bilateral physical transformation, and the living "metamorphoses" that are the object of life scientific enquiry begin to implicate observing subjects and their empirical methods, as well.

In the next section, we will see Herder splendidly elaborate the other end of this rigorous confusion between the subjects and objects of live observation, exploring the way the observer's sensorium transforms objects to fit its habits and needs. Clearly needful, in the romantic period, were forms of empiricism that would confront, and even cultivate, the methodologically untidy likelihood that neither subject nor object emerges unchanged from the scene of sensory observation. Both, Herder will suggest, are transfigured in a way that only poetic *figures* can mark.

15.2. THE PHYSIOLOGY OF TROPES

As we have seen, the kind of sidelined corporeal experience that Herder sets out to vindicate for knowledge in "On the Sensation and Cognition of the Human Soul" resists "clear and distinct" representation. In place of this, Herder's philosophy proposes something extraordinary from a present-day point of view: the form of representation scientifically adequate to sensory experience is *figuration*—image, metaphor, allegory, personification. And this is not because here Herder parts ways with the aims and methods of natural science in order to initiate a linguistic turn that would forgo reference to nondiscursive realities, or a subjectivist one that would strive to represent imagined experience by unapologetically fictional means. Instead, Herder pioneers a point that Nietzsche would make famous a century later: sensation, the basis of all knowledge from an empiricist point of view, is literally, physiologically, *poetic* (in the root sense of "making"), *figurative* (in the root sense of "fashioning"), and *metaphoric* (in the root sense of "carrying-over" [*Übertragung*]).[20]

And since for Herder, as we will see, the sensory basis of empirical knowledge is poetic down to its very nerves and fibers, the epistemological status of poetic *language* changes: the tropes, figures, images, and metaphors formerly thought to veil the simple evidence of experience may instead manifest underappreciated forms of veracity. Herder concedes that any truth communicated in such poetic science will be "human truth, certainly," ineluctably anthropomorphic in shape (CS 188). But for him, this condition, though necessary, is neither tragic nor debilitating for knowledge.[21] Instead, the contingencies that delimit human knowledge also demarcate its points of contact with other natures.[22] Indeed, part of what makes Herder's stance so difficult to re-inhabit today is his thoroughgoing attempt to philosophize not *about* nature, but *as* one nature among others, one body among many bodies—without letting go his prescient grasp on the historicity and the species-specificity (to speak redundantly), of this effort.

"Our whole life," Herder argues in "On Image, Poetry, and Fable," "is to a certain extent *poetics.*" It turns out that "life" here is physiologically meant, and that Herder sees sensation as the primary site of coextension between life and poetics. No neutral register of the influx of the external world, Herder presents sensation as the active and selective process through which we "separat[e] objects from others," "giving them outline, dimension, and form [*Umriß, Maß und Gestalt*]" (IPF 358 [635]). Receptive only to those aspects of an "infinite" object that approach in a specific medium—and, as we have seen, by socially sanctioned paths—our sense organs parse and transform "the interwoven tangle of obscure irritations [*zusammen geflochtner Knäuel dunkler Reize*]," into the consistent and manageable phenomena of a "world-structure [*Weltgebäude*]" (CS 202–3 [348]).

Explaining life's "poetics," Herder argues that any sensation attaining to minimal awareness needs to be understood as a perceptual artwork utterly, transformed by its passage "through the eye":

[W]e do not see, rather we create images for ourselves [*wir sehen nicht, sondern wir erschaffen uns Bilder*]....For the image that is projected on the retina of your eye is not the idea that you derive from its object; it is merely a product of your inner sense, a work of art created by your soul's faculty of perception [*ein Kunstgemälde der Bemerkungskraft deiner Seele*]. (IPF 358, trans. mod. [635])

Here again, in Herder, we come upon a basic physical "datum" of sensation—the retinal image—redescribed as the product of a prior relay, an unnoticed act of re-presentation among the functions of the animate body. But true to his scorn for the idealist notion that a soul "should dream a world *out of itself*" (CS

208), he quickly takes pains to prevent readers from mistaking his notion of sensory poetics for ex nihilo creation:[23]

> In real and absolute terms, the human being can neither poeticize nor invent, for otherwise in doing so he would become the creator of another world. What he can do is conjoin images and ideas, designate them with the stamp of *analogy*, thus leaving his own mark on them;...For everything that we call image in Nature becomes such only through the reception and operation of his perceiving, separating, composing, and designating soul. (IPF 365)

> Eigentlich und absolut kann der Mensch weder dichten, noch erfinden; er würde damit der Schöpfer einer neuen Welt. Was er tun kann, ist, Bilder und Gedanken paaren, sie mit dem Stempel der *Analogie*, insonderheit aus sich selbst, bezeichnen;...Denn alles was Bild in der Natur heißt, wird solches nur durch die Empfängnis und Wirkung seiner bemerkenden, absondernden, zusammensetzenden, bezeichnenden Seele. (645)

The "stamp of *analogy*" invoked in this passage and its cognates—"stamp of our consciousness," "stamp of my inner sense"—recur frequently in Herder in order to defamiliarize the image of an object, to reveal its appearance "in Nature" as the outcome of a prior assimilation. At stake in sensation is a "reception and operation" between observer and observed for which the image must be understood not as the raw or simple datum but the final "mark."

With his emphatically figurative figure of an appropriating "stamp [*Stempel*]" or "seal [*Siegel*]" of analogy, Herder rewrites the inherited notion of a simple sense "impression [*Eindruck*]" printed on the passive mind. Here, in a word, the senses press back, intervening consequentially—transfiguratively—between things and ideas. The wrought or figured contours of a finished sensation in Herder—its "outline, dimension, and form"—bear witness to an active, bilateral process that conforms the entering object to the capacities, needs, and habits of the perceiver's sensorium. Thus, Herder likens diverse sensory apertures to customs offices: "pass[ing] though the gates of a different sense," an object is "given a different stamp, in keeping with the different customs prevalent there and the different use to which it is put" (IPF 359). Again, revisionary empiricism points out the activity of culture, convention, and even state power, within the most primary and miniscule of physiological processes. And even as Herder attributes active, shaping power to the organs of sense, he does not render sensation a unilateral imaginative act: as we saw above, the very capacity to sense in this way, to fashion sensory experience into coherent subjectivity (one's "own mark"), is contingent upon the ingress of "an alien which imprints itself in us."

One asset of this account of "sensuous cognition," a feature that would appeal to Nietzsche and to Foucault, is that it brooks no illusion of a sensory transaction that does not leave its mark, no pretense at impartial observation (aesthetic or scientific) uncontaminated by relations of power and appropriation. "Only a fool," Herder explains, "forgets the *having* [*das Haben*]" in thinking, severing thought from the needy and desirous, "receiving and giving," body that "draws in and exudes" (CS 213 [359], 191). Both the consequential ingress of the object into the body of the observer, and the selecting and assimilating force, which, like a customs officer, conditions that "reception," are openly expressed through Herder's "stamp of analogy," a figure of assimilation that renders the object perceptible, licit, legitimate, but only by occulting or excluding aspects of its difference from the perceiving self.

Perhaps acknowledging that something of perceiver and perceived is risked and lost in this transaction, Herder writes of the irritations that excite sensation as a kind of "gentle violence [*sanfte Gewalt*]": "nature does him gentle violence, and he nature" (CS 191 [335]). But the modifier "gentle" suggests that such violence poses no real threat to life; instead, it merely jeopardizes philosophical confidence in the integrity of subjects and their objects, a confidence at risk whenever embodied sensation is taken seriously. The media of light, scent, and sound, "flow into [the] senses and bring the objects into them," such that "a way is already opened up for cognition *outside us*" (CS 202–3). "Sensation" for Herder, is really and ineradicably relational: the "*circle of thinking and sensing*," like the "deepest self *in us*," is coconstituted with other beings and thereby exceeds the scope of our own skin (188 [330], 212 [359]).

Sensation, as we have seen, is a bilateral act of *figuration* (from the Lat. *fingere*) in the material sense of to fashion, form, or shape: sense organs physically fashion "obscure irritations" into assimilable images, sounds, or scents. But as he uncovers the "image" and "analogy" producing capacities of the sense organs, Herder connects this physical meaning of *figure* to its other, rhetorical meaning: the deviation from proper use and arrangement usually reserved for a work on words. Stressing the radical differences between the "chaos" of sensible objects and the fibrous irritations they induce, between those irritations and visible images they occasion, between those visible images and thoughts to which they are yoked by "*secret bonds*," and between the different sensory systems that simultaneously admit an object, Herder describes the activity of sensuous perception as *allegorizing, schematizing, translating* work. He thus insists that the tropic operations typically consigned to verbal ornamentation are moving non- and pre-verbally within the very physiology of sensation:

Hence it follows *that our soul, like our language, allegorizes constantly* [*beständig allegorisiere*]. When the soul sees objects as images, or rather

when it transforms them into mental images [*in Gedankenbilder verwan-
delt*], according to rules that are imprinted [*eingeprägt*] on it, what is it doing
but translating [*übersetzen*], *metaschematizing* [metaschematisieren]? And
if the soul now strives to illuminate these mental images—which are its work
alone—through words, through signs [*Zeichen*] for the sense of hearing, and
thereby to express them to others, what is it doing once again but translating,
alloisizing [alläosieren]? (IPF 359 [635–36])

A careful reading makes it clear that here the work of sensation is a poetic work
that is "like our language," but not exclusive to it. The "translation" that finally
produces "words" in this passage is but the latest in a series of transfigurative
relays that render the object differently, "*alloisizing*" or "othering" it at each
turn. The passage's subtle shift from the soul *allegorizing*, "speaking otherwise
than one seems to speak," to the more general *alloisizing*, "changing, altering,"
encapsulates our point about a poetics not limited to words: Herder etymo-
logically revises the figural action from "other-*speaking*" to a broader sensory
"*othering*" of which verbal language would be but one outcome and instance.
Herder does not further explain the emphatic term "*metaschematizing*" upon
which the above passage's account of sensation and speech seems to hinge.[24] But
to prefix *meta* to "*schema*"—Greek for form and shape, which Latin translated
to *figura*—drives home the central Herderian insight that any word or image
that attains to consciousness, let alone to language, is already a *meta*-figure that
glosses a complex of preverbal figurative events: "cloth[ing]," as Herder puts it
elsewhere, "a thousand beings with one robe *for me*" (CS 203).

The passage proceeds to further underscore the heterogeneity internal to any
sensorium, reframing the figurality of sensation (which we initially examined
as a poetics of assimilation, a poetics of making *mine* exemplified by the "stamp
of analogy") from the perspective of an *alloisis* that stresses instead the discrep-
ancies that enable and motivate such assimilating movements:

The object has so little in common with the image, the image with the
thought, the thought with the expression, the visual perception with the
name, that they, as it were, touch one another only by virtue of the sensibility
of our complex organization, which perceives *several things* through several senses *at the same time*. Only the *communicability* among our several
senses... [constitutes] the so-called perfectibility of man. If we had but one
sense and were connected with Creation only by a single aspect of the world,
as it were, there would be no possibility of converting objects into images
and images into words or other signs. Then we should have to bid farewell to
human reason! (IPF 359 [636])

Herder's astonishing final claim is this: the advanced semiotic practice distinctive of "human reason" stems from the copresence of *plural* sensory systems
within the confined space of the human body, where their divergent, modes of
"converting objects" overlap. Tropological communications within a body that
senses "a thousandfold and a thousandfold differently" set the pattern, and condition the possibility, for the verbal version of "language" as we usually mean
it. Such language, then, must be conceived fundamentally as metaphor (*meta*,
over/beyond + *pherein* to bear or carry) and its near synonym, translation, both
figures of transport that deviate as they represent.

Remarkably, Herder declares the poetic quality that marks sensuous experience not a symptom of fictitiousness, but a "seal of truth [*Siegel der Wahrheit*]"
(CS 189 [331]). This figured mark is truthful in at least two ways: it attests,
first, to the fact of real, physical contact between perceiver and perceived, and
it makes plain, second, the anthropomorphic shape that any fact perceived by
a human truth-seeker will bear. For Herder, the kind of truth that manifests
this figurative "seal," that is, the kind of truth that neither conceals its "*analogy to the human being*," nor pretends to transcendent validity, is the best
possible truth:

> Human truth [*Menschliche Wahrheit*], certainly, and as long as I am a
> human being I have no information about any higher [truth]. I am very little
> concerned about the superterrestrial abstraction which places itself beyond
> everything that is called "*circle of our thinking and sensing*" onto I know not
> what throne of divinity. (CS 188 [330])

This unabashedly figural truth—truth transfigured and sealed in the act of
observation—is thus, in Herder, the mark of philosophy's epistemological
modesty *and* its realism. Thought, Herder insists, is "*present* in the universe
through action and reaction on this body full of sensations, full of irritations"
(CS 181–82), and figuration precisely manifests this physicality, this corporeal-
ity, of thought. To eschew the poetic confines and resources of "this body" is
not only impossible but also undesirable for knowledge: it is as a body that we
come into transfigurative contact with the bodies we wish to know (181–82).
Deflationary for metaphysicians, the poetics of the senses might be a resource
for physicians, physicists, and poets, all concerned to register the subtle interactions at work within and between embodied beings.

From this perspective, the purportedly modest Kantian prohibition against
projecting our own thinking onto "things in themselves" veils a greater
hubris: the presumption that our thinking is independent of other things and
that thought (or what matters of it) owes nothing to natural bodies, ours or others'. Herder's revisionary empiricism thus marks out the vast distance between

the epistemologically modest recognition that the truth gleaned by humans will be inflected by our partial, personal, and species limitations, and the conclusion that within this *"circle of thinking and sensing,"* we can know nothing with certainty other than the workings of our own minds (CS 188). For Herder, the knowledge that sensation bears is indeed *partial*, even doubly so: both incomplete and biased towards the human form, each human sense *"abstracts from created beings as much as this portal can receive, but leaves to them everything else, their whole infinite abyss* [das so viel von den Geschöpfen abreißt als diese Pforte empfangen kann, alles übrige, ihren ganzen unendlichen Abgrund, ihnen aber lässet]" (CS 202 [347]). Yet this partiality does not render the senses' transmissions invalid—and certainly not invented. "Poetic" is the perfect way to describe their manifest impropriety and their truth.

Again, if the very portals of empirical experience are poetic, poetic *language* might be doing the work of high-resolution representation, rather than inessential adornment. Indeed, Herder praises poetic language in terms we frequently reserve for the scientific and journalistic prose genres that now monopolize objective description. Poetry excels in "accuracy," "faithfulness," "truth" and "minor detail":

> Our inner poetic sense is able to bind together the manifold features of the sensation so faithfully and accurately [*so wahr und genau zusammen zu knüpfen*] that in its artificial world [*Kunstwelt*] we feel once more the whole living world, for it is precisely the minor details [*kleinen Umstände*]—which the frigid understanding might not have noticed… [or] omits as superfluous [*als Überfluß wegstreichet*]—that are the truest lineaments [*wahresten Striche*] of the peculiar feeling, and that precisely because of this truth, therefore, possess the most decided efficacy [*dieser Wahrheit wegen von der entschiedensten Wirkung*]. (IPF 362 [641])

Above all, poetry is the "truest" representation of the panoply of noticed and unnoticed interactions that amount to a given sensation; its empirical truth consists in unstinting reproduction of all *"the diversity of that which we felt all at once"* upon sensing an object ("der Mannigfaltigkeit dessen, was wir beim Genuß dieses Gegenstandes damals auf Einmal fühlten" (IPF 362 [640–41]). Such a reproduction rejects no detail as "superfluous," and therefore presents a thorough record of both the perceiver's sensibility and the manifold "efficacy" of the perceived (IPF 362).

Might poetic and fictional texts, then, provide access to those "rich traces" of embodied experience unavailable to science while "clarity and distinctness" remain the criteria of sound knowledge? By now it will come as no surprise that Herder's essays answer this question with multiple "yeses" and a flurry of metaphors. That Shakespeare "is no *physiologist*," he writes, "no one could say who had seen *Hamlet* and *Lear*": "without knowing it, he depicts the passion right down to the deepest abysses and fibres from which it sprouted" (CS 199). The logical complement to this view is equally important to Herder. Scientific discovery, he argues, is disavowed poetics:

> *Newton* in his system of the world became a poet contrary to his wishes [*wider Willen en Dichter*], as did *Buffon* in his cosmogony… for the most part it was *a single* new image [*Bild*], *a single* analogy [*Analogie*], *a single* striking metaphor [*auffallendes Gleichnis*] that gave birth to the greatest and boldest theories. The philosophers who declaim against figurative language [*Bildersprache*], and themselves serve nothing but old, often uncomprehended, figurative idols [*unverstandnen Bildgötzen*], are at least in great contradiction with themselves. (CS 188 [330])

At stake is an observation akin to the one that would open Hans Blumenberg's "Prospect for a Theory of Non-Conceptuality" (1960) some two hundred years later. Metaphors, Blumenberg observes, form the cutting edge of "experimental theoretical conceptions," preceding and leading the consolidation of technical terminology.[25] But more than mere placeholders for incipient concepts, metaphors demonstrate a theoretical efficacy that attests to their "authentic way of grasping…connections with the life-world"—connections that, for Blumenberg, form "the constant motivating support (though one that cannot be constantly kept in view) of all theory" (81). For Herder, too, figures issue from couplings with the world that conceptual philosophy is structurally ill-equipped to see; in his case, from the subtle, opaque, and erotic interactions that define our physiological being: "in the face of this sort of deep abyss of obscure sensations our bright and clear philosophy is horrified" (CS 196). Expressing real-physical interactions that conceptual decorum needs to leave unknown, metaphors know more than knowledge cares to acknowledge.

In the context of a given conceptual system, then, this form of poetic and theoretical expression can easily take on the elevated, prophetic, and mystified character of genius (CS 199). Herder will ground it firmly in terrestrial experience instead. In an extraordinary passage, he likens poetics to animal instinct, deriving the prophetic power of each from their link to the "unknown region" of physiological irritation. Here the "it" in question refers to the irritation induced by an unanticipated object:

> It is a new *experience* [Erfahrung], which… does not exactly follow from our system now [*nicht eben aus unserm System jetzt folget*]. It is a new, prophetic

drive [*weissagender Trieb*] which promises us enjoyment, makes us intuit this obscurely [*dunkel ihn ahnden läßt*], jumps over space and time [*Raum und Zeit überspringet*], and gives us a foretaste of the future [*uns Vorgeschmack gibt in die Zukunft*]. Perhaps that is how it is with the instincts of the animals. They are like instrument strings [*Saiten*] which a certain sound of the universe stirs…connected with the element [*Sie hangen mit dem Element*]…with the unknown region of the world [*mit der unbekannten Weltgegend*] whither they speed; invisible bonds [*unsichtbare Bande*] pull them in that direction, whether they arrive there or not. (CS 200 [345])

Indeed, provided as an elaboration on the physiological insightfulness of poetry, the above passage makes clear that the "drives" increasingly attributed to living matter in the new life sciences are another name for the practice that poets call "metaphor," that transport whose movement discloses an unforeseen link between apparently dissimilar entities and actions. This movement is audible, in the above passage, when the drive "jumps over" the limits of the present knowledge at the instigation of "invisible bonds."

Here Nietzsche's strikingly Herderian essay, "On Truth and Lying in a Non-Moral Sense [*Über Wahrheit und Lüge im außermoralischen Sinne*]," aids interpretation.[26] After affirming that preverbal sensation is already metaphor—"The stimulation of the nerve is first translated into an image: first metaphor!"—Nietzsche explains metaphor exactly in terms of a leaping motion between "spheres" of being: "each time there is a complete leap from one sphere into the heart of another, new sphere" (144). Echoing Herder's "drive to make analogies," Nietzsche designates "the drive to form metaphors [*Trieb zur Metapherbildung*]" as the "fundamental human drive" (150).[27] For Nietzsche here, as Sarah Kofman has argued, metaphoric activity "is not just a drive like any other; it could be called the general form of all drives."[28]

Herder's easy oscillation between the prophetic transports of poetry and those of fibrous irritation seems to agree that to speak of a metaphor-forming drive is nearly tautological. Indeed, Andrea Christian Bertino has argued in this context that the fundamentally relational notion of a "drive" signals a movement *towards* something not contained or containable in its concept: drives in Herder and Nietzsche advert to their own conceptual limits and even, he argues, to "the uncontrollable necessity of metaphorical carrying-over."[29] Terms like "drive" and "irritability" are not typical concepts; with them, Herder recognized in experimental physiology not only the potential to speak more poetically (and therefore more truthfully) about natural bodies, but also, as we have seen, the potential to recognize among natural bodies (including, but not limited to our own) forms of metaphoric activity more basic and more general than our works on words. For Herder, then, the "uncontrollable necessity of metaphorical carrying-over" betokened in the physiology "of force, irritation, efficacy," is of interest precisely because it is *not* given as exclusive to human language. Rather, it opens onto a notion of natural bodies in general as instinct with tropic, transfigurative movement. Here, for instance, is how Herder is wont to describe a botanical body, rife with tropic ("turning"), assimilating, and mimetic activity: "Observe that plant, that beautiful structure of organic fibers! How it twists, how it turns... [it] purifies alien juice into parts of its more subtle self... [and] produces living off-prints of itself, leaves, germs, blooms, and fruits" (CS 192).

So we might close by stressing again how Herder's interest in the poetic quality of empirical knowing and representing does *not* aim, as Nietzsche's essay does, primarily to uncover our role as *"artistically creative subjects,"* unwitting linguistic producers of the world that our science purports to "discover" (148). At stake instead is a now unfamiliar understanding of physical bodies as fundamentally tropic, enmeshed in a multitude of figurative transactions and displacements of which human rhetoric is but one outcome and instance. Indeed, from his prize-winning essay *On the Origins of Human Language* (1772) forward, Herder strenuously advocated a *natural* origin for human language, synecdoche in the period for a naturalism so thoroughgoing that it would account for even the most intellective, apparently immaterial aspects of the universe (languages) without recourse to divine causes.[30]

In asserting the figurative status of human sensation and language, then, Herder does not subordinate "nature" to our verbal metaphorics, but renders those metaphorics derivative of a broader category transfigurations and transports already and everywhere underway. Similarly, when Herder notices that metaphors and organic drives share a formal structure, his aim is not to unmask physiological theory as "mere" metaphor, "mere" product of human speech. Like many of his contemporaries, Herder finds in Haller's "irritable" fibers—"these obscure stamens of irritation towards sensation" (CS 190 [133])—scientific confirmation that material nature tends *towards* changes of shape, form, and figure, and the metaphoric leaping between levels of which language is only the most flagrant example. Irritation, an effect akin to mechanical expansion and contraction, nonetheless tends *"towards* sensation," effecting a transport that shuttles "dead nature" toward animate life, physics toward physiology, bodily toward mental activity. In Herder's hands, irritations and drives participate in the epochal shift towards a naturalistic conception of life's origins: the conviction that "life in swift flight" could spring up from inert materials was necessary both to evolutionist accounts of phylogeny and to epigenetic accounts of ontogeny (CS 194).[31]

In "On the Cognition and Sensation of the Human Soul," poets and scientists demonstrate a conspicuously reciprocal ignorance of the fact that "for

us all of physics remains a kind of *poetics* for our senses," a fact that, as we
have seen, Herder regards as both ineluctable and fortuitous for knowledge. Shakespeare was a "physiologist" "without knowing it," Newton a poet
despite himself. Herder's is romantic philosophy of science insofar as it seeks
the knowledgeable form of representation that would result if we could cultivate the poetic aspect of scientific representation as a key source of its truth,
and the scientific aspect of poetic representation as a key source of its pleasure. "Oh, what a work of strangely fine developments and observations," he
muses, could a "thinking and feeling physiologist" write: it would capture "this
noble string-play in its structure, in its conducting and knotting, entwining
and subtilizing" (206). And what an unvarnished "offprint of a living human
soul [*Abdruck einer lebendigen Menschenseele*]" could be produced by a poet
who cultivated his writing's function as "betrayer" of "how he received images,
how he ordered and adjusted them and the chaos of his impressions" (217–19
[366]). The assumption that literature has no science and science no poetics,
Herder thinks, inhibits the truth and efficacy of each.

NOTES

1. Robin Valenza, *Literature, Language, and the Rise of the Intellectual Disciplines*
   (Cambridge: Cambridge University Press, 2009), 1–33; Raymond Williams, *Culture
   and Society, 1780–1950* (New York: Columbia University Press, 1983), 30–48;
   Lorraine Daston and Peter Galison, *Objectivity* (New York and Cambridge: Zone
   Books and MIT Press, 2007), 37, 242–47.
2. For a pithy, like-minded account of the alternative Herder posed to the (ultimately victorious) formation of the disciplines, and of the frequent misprision of
   this alternative in historical retrospect, see Eva Knodt, "*Hermeneutics and the End
   of Science: Herder's Role in the Formation of Natur- and Geisteswissenschaften*," in
   Johann Gottfried Herder: Academic Disciplines and the Pursuit of Knowledge,
   ed. Wulf Koepke, (Columbia, SC: Camden House, 1996), 1–12. Notice how
   the characterization "monstrous" arises in works as diverse as Denise Gigante's
   Life: Organic Form and Romanticism (New Haven: Yale University Press,
   2009) and Bruno Latour's *We Have Never Been Modern* (Cambridge, MA: Harvard
   University Press, 1993). After decades of careful scholarship on the scientific "contexts" of romantic-era literature, as well as new histories of romantic-era science,
   it is now safe to conclude that natural scientific reading, writing, and research
   were the rule, rather than the exception, among even the most canonically *literary* romantics, productive of the texts, not just the contexts, of romantic era
   literature. Fine emblems of this now vast bibliography include Jocelyn Holland,
   *German Romanticism and Science: The Procreative Poetics of Goethe, Novalis, and
   Ritter* (New York: Routledge, 2009), Noel Jackson, *Science and Sensation in British
   Romanticism* (Cambridge: Cambridge University Press, 2008), and Safia Azzouni,
   *Kunst als praktischer Wissenschaft: Goethes "Wilhelm Meisters Wanderjahre" und
   die Hefte Zur Morphologie* (Köln: Böhlau Verlag, 2005).

3. Beiser, *The Romantic Imperative: The Concept of Early German Romanticism* (Cambridge, MA and London: Harvard University Press, 2003), 1–5; Richards, *The Romantic Conception of Life: Science and Philosophy in the Age of Goethe* (Chicago: University of Chicago Press, 2002), xvii–xix; Zammito, "Teleology then and now: The question of Kant's relevance for contemporary controversies over function in biology."

4. Herder, "On the Cognition and Sensation of the Human Soul," in *Herder: Philosophical Writings*, ed. and trans. Michael N. Forster (Cambridge: Cambridge University Press, 2002), 187–243; and "On Image, Poetry, and Fable," in *Selected Writings on Aesthetics: Johann Gottfried Herder*, ed. and trans. Gregory Moore (Princeton, NJ and Oxford: Princeton University Press, 2006), 357–82. These two essays are abbreviated CS and IPF in what follows. Citations from the German, when given, refer to HW 4, 329–93 and 633–77; page references to this edition appear in square brackets. My summary of cruxes in postpositivist philosophy of science is heavily indebted to Zammito, *A Nice Derangement of Epistemes: Post-positivism in the Study of Science from Quine to Latour* (Chicago: University of Chicago Press, 2004).

5. See Beiser, *The Fate of Reason: German Philosophy from Kant to Fichte* (Cambridge, MA: Harvard University Press, 1993).

6. Berlin, *The Roots of Romanticism*, ed. Henry Hardy (Princeton, NJ: Princeton University Press, 1999), 57.

7. See, for instance, Zammito, *Kant, Herder, and the Birth of Anthropology* (Chicago: University of Chicago Press, 2002), Peter Hanns Reill, *Vitalizing Nature in the Enlightenment* (Berkeley: University of California Press, 2005), Anne C. Vila, *Enlightenment and Pathology: Sensibility in the Literature and Medicine of Eighteenth-Century France* (Baltimore, MD: Johns Hopkins University Press, 1998), Kevis Goodman, *Georgic Modernity and British Romanticism* (Cambridge: Cambridge University Press, 2004), and Maureen McClane, *Romanticism and the Human Sciences: Poetry, Population, and the Discourse of the Species* (Cambridge: Cambridge University Press, 2000).

8. Jonathan Crary, *Techniques of the Observer: On Vision and Modernity in the Nineteenth Century* (London: October/MIT Press, 1990), 39.

9. Ibid., 70.

10. John Locke, *An Essay Concerning Human Understanding*, 2 vols., ed. Alexander Campbell Fraser (New York: Dover, 1959), vol. 1, book 2, 2.1, 144.

11. Ibid., 2, 1.2, 121; Intro., 2, 26.

12. Herder, "Fragments on Recent German Literature," in Forster, *Herder: Philosophical Writings*, 33–64, 50. Abbreviated F hereafter. See Forster's illuminating discussion of Herder's "quasi-empiricist" theory of language in *After Herder: Philosophy of Language in the German Tradition* (Oxford: Oxford University Press, 2010), esp. 70–74 and 132–37. Forster argues that Herder agrees with Locke and Hume that concepts originate in sensation, but innovates upon them to argue that the acquisition of language "transforms the nature of a person's sensations" (71). I depart from Forster's further argument that Herder thinks we can also "achieve concepts which are in a way non-empirical...by means of a sort of metaphorical extension from the empirical ones" (72). As I argue in the next section, such metaphorical

extensions are not necessarily "non-empirical" because, (1) for Herder, metaphors occur *within* nonverbal processes of sensation, and (2) metaphors function by virtue of their contact with unnoticed physical and sensory stimuli.

13. "On Cognition and Sensation, the Two Main Forces of the Human Soul," a 1775 draft of Herder's published essay; in Forster, *Philosophical Writings*, 178–86, 180. Abbreviated CSd hereafter.

14. See Anne C. Vila, *Enlightenment and Pathology*, and Shirley A. Roe, *Matter, Life, and Generation: 18th-Century Embryology and the Haller-Wolff Debate* (Cambridge: Cambridge University Press, 1981).

15. See Zammito's excellent account of the importance of Herder's strategic misappropriation of Haller's physiology in *Kant, Herder, and the Birth of Anthropology*, 309–45, esp. 326–332.

16. Canguilhem, *La connaissance de la vie* (Paris: J. Vrin, 1965); Jacob, *The Logic of Life: A History of Heredity*, trans. Betty E. Spillman (New York: Pantheon, 1973), 19–129; Foucault, *The Order of Things: An Archaeology of the Human Sciences* (New York: Vintage Books, 1994), 226–32. See also Roe's excellent overview of the epigenesis controversy in *Matter, Life, and Generation* and Charles T. Wolfe, "Why Was There No Controversy over Life in the Scientific Revolution?" in *Controversies within the Scientific Revolution*, eds. V. Boantza and M. Dascal (Amsterdam: John Benjamins, 2011), 187–221.

17. For a most lucid and nuanced account of this process that, in my view, opens up continuities between "high and late Enlightenment" and "romantic" sophistications of early Enlightenment rationalism and mechanism, see Reill, *Vitalizing Nature in the Enlightenment*. Because idealist *Naturphilosophie* exemplifies romanticism for Reill, however, he positions the two movements as radically distinct, and treats the poetic science of the "Schwärmer" Herder as *surprisingly* typical of Enlightenment thought (in "Herder's Historical Practice and the Discourse of Late Enlightenment Science," *J.G. Herder: Academic Disciplines*, 13–21).

18. See Crary, *Techniques of the Observer*, 70–74.

19. Goethe, "Bedeutende Fördernis durch ein einziges geistreiches Wort," *Zur Morphologie* 2.1, in MA 12, 306.

20. Nietzsche, "On Truth and Lying in a Non-Moral Sense," in *The Birth of Tragedy and Other Writings*, ed. Raymond Guess and Ronald Speirs, trans. Speirs (Cambridge: Cambridge University Press, 1999), 139–53.

21. On Herder's comfort with the inexorable sensuousness and contingency of human knowledge, an orientation that enabled him to position images (*Bilder*) at the origin of thought, rather than to attempt, like Kant, to purify analytical concepts of that which belongs to sensation, see Tilman Borsche, "Bildworte. Vom Ursprung Unserer Begriffe," in *Zwischen Bild und Begriff: Kant und Herder zum Schema*, ed. Ulrich Gaier and Ralf Simon (München: Wilhelm Fink, 2010), 55–69, esp. 63. On the consequences of his refusal to distinguish ontologically between man and nature, see Knodt, "Hermeneutics," 3–7.

22. As per their shared Latin etymon *con* + *tangere*, to touch together.

23. Notice how starkly this contradicts a variety of epistemological modernity emergent in Herder's lifetime and quite hegemonic in ours, according to which the truth in poetry inheres in its status as self-productive and self-referential language. As

Phillipe Lacoue-Labarthe and Jean-Luc Nancy put it in their seminal poststructuralist interpretation of the *Athenaeum* fragments, romantic literary philosophy aspired towards a notion of *poesis* as utterly self-authorizing truth, *"production, absolutely speaking...* in which the literary thing produces the truth of production in itself... the truth of the production *of itself"* (*The Literary Absolute*, 12). This interpretation in fact reflects the consolidation of a division of labor and prestige between science and literature that some romantic oeuvres fundamentally contest. See Lacoue-Labarthe and Nancy, *The Literary Absolute: The Theory of Literature in German Romanticism*, trans. Philip Barnard and Cheryl Lester (Albany, NY: SUNY Press, 1988) and Beiser's rebuttal in *The Romantic Imperative*.

24. See, however, Ulrich Gaier, "Metaschematisieren? Hieroglyphe und Periodus," in Gaier and Simon, *Zwischen Bild und Begriff*, 19–53, for a thorough interpretation.

25. Hans Blumenberg, "Prospect for a theory of Nonconceptuality," in *Shipwreck with Spectator*, trans. Steven Rendall (Cambridge, MA: The MIT Press, 1997), 81–102. See Hans Dietrich Irmscher's indispensible study of *Witz* and *Analogie* in Herder as technologies for the discovery of new fields of knowledge, "Witz und Analogie als Instrumente des entdeckenden Erkennens," in *"Weitstrahlsinniges" Denken: Studien zu Johann Gottfried Herder von Hans Dietrich Irmscher*, ed. Marion Heinz und Violetta Stolz (Würzburg: Königshausen & Neumann, 2009), 206–35, and his "Der Vergleich im Denken Herders," in *J.G. Herder: Academic Disciplines*, 78–96.

26. Nietzsche, "On Truth and Lying in a Non-Moral Sense," in *The Birth of Tragedy and Other Writings*, ed. Raymond Guess and Ronald Speirs, trans. Speirs (Cambridge: Cambridge University Press, 199), 139–153 On Niezsche's debts to Herder on the question of the tropic origin of thought, see Andrea Christian Bertino, *"Vernatürlichung": Ursprünge von Friedrich Nietzsches Entidealisierung des Menschen, seiner Sprache und seiner Geschichte bei Johann Gottfried Herder*, (Berlin: De Gruyter, 2011), esp. 170–203. See also Borsche, "Bildworte," 63–64.

27. Bertino, *Vernatürlichung*, 170–72.

28. Kofman, *Nietzsche and Metaphor*, trans. Duncan Large (Stanford, CA: Stanford University Press, 1993), 25.

29. Bentino, *Vernatürlichung*, 172. I disagree that Herder uses the notion of figurative drive as a "non-biological" heuristic: Bertino bases this conclusion on the assertion that this drive surfaces in discussions of poetry and language, rather than in biological natural scientific contexts—but the "Sensation and Cognition" essay is biological indeed.

30. See Beiser, *The Fate of Reason*, 130–35.

31. Ibid., 328.

16

Romantic Empiricism after the "End of Nature"

Contributions to Environmental Philosophy

DALIA NASSAR

It has been almost two decades since the publication of Bill McKibben's book, *The End of Nature* (1989), which, as the title proclaims, announced the end of that which we have, for many centuries, called nature. McKibben's claim is that the increasing influence of human activity on the natural environment has led not only to unprecedented transformations in an extremely short amount of time, but also to the complete elimination of a reality that is outside of or independent of the sphere of human activity. "The idea of nature," he writes, "will not survive the new global pollution—the carbon dioxide and CFCs and the like.... We have changed the atmosphere, and we are changing the weather. By changing the weather, we make every spot on earth man-made and artificial.... The world, the whole world, is touched by our work even when that work is invisible."[1]

Over the last decade, McKibben's claim that nature has come to an end has been reiterated and, in many cases, reconfigured. Thus, although environmental philosophers have generally agreed with the view that the idea of nature is problematic or implausible, their reasoning often differs from McKibben's. Timothy Morton is a case in point. In his recent book, *Ecology without Nature* (2007), Morton argues that ecology and ecological thought must rid itself of the idea of nature. This is not, however, because we have destroyed nature such that it no longer exists. Rather, Morton's claim is that nature is an idealized reality—an idea—that does not describe material reality or specify phenomena.

The idea of nature, he argues, "hinders authentic ecological politics, ethics philosophy and art" because it is "transcendental term in a material mask."[2]

In agreement with Morton's view, recent work in environmental theory has similarly argued that the idea of nature, as Kate Rigby puts it, "is a metaphysical construct borne of a particular intertextual history and projected onto certain kinds of stuff in a variety of contexts, with a range of potentially very material effects."[3] Rigby claims that the emergence of the abstract concept of nature coincides with the emergence of human culture. In the Western tradition, it is when human beings achieved a fully formed alphabetical writing and theorized the purely intelligible world of ideas in classical Greece that an opposing notion of nature—whether as cosmic whole or as indwelling principle or as virgin territory or as mother—emerged.[4] Thus, from the beginning, she argues, the idea of nature both assumes and implies a problematic and false opposition or dualism between nature and culture, natural product and human product.

Alongside these critiques of the idea of nature, a number of studies have appeared that consider (and in part reintroduce) the environmental contributions of romantic thought. These works, which largely focus on the British poetic tradition, seek to offer a reappraisal of romanticism as proto-ecological. Thus although the term "ecology" was not coined until 1866 by Ernst Haeckel, a number of scholars (primarily literary critics) have traced the origins of ecology back to romantic ideas circulating in the late eighteenth and early nineteenth centuries.[5]

This recent interest in the environmental appraisal of romanticism is not surprising. After all, the movement that we now identify as "romanticism," and which spanned several decades and transcended national boundaries, was united in its critique of the instrumentalization of reason and industrialization—which it considered to be symptomatic of a deeply problematic relationship to nature. Furthermore, the romantics challenged the dualistic view—which underlay and legitimized modern science—of the mind as opposed to and distinct from nature. Instead, the romantics contended that mind and matter are two sides of the same reality. Or, as Schelling put it in one of his earliest writings on the philosophy of nature: "Nature should be spirit made invisible, spirit the invisible nature" (HKA 1/5, 107).

What is surprising, however, is that the rise of interest in romanticism occurred alongside—and partly in dialogue with—the critique of the idea of nature.[6] The interest in romanticism thus seems out of place, given that the romantics were *the* modern thinkers who ascribed to nature a special significance. In both their philosophical and their poetic works, the romantics did not simply conceive of nature as a mysterious entity whose secrets must be (through the work of experimentation or mathematization) uncovered, but as the fundamental and underlying reality (principle) of all things—including the human being. In other words, for the romantics, *nature*—not ecology, the environment, or, to use Morton's most recent term, the "coexistence" of things—was the most significant and central concern.

In light of the critiques of the idea of nature, the interest in romanticism seems perplexing and perhaps even problematic. Does the romantic idea of nature not also suffer from the kinds of problems that McKibben and Morton point out? In fact, Morton's rejection of the idea of nature begins with a critical assessment of romanticism, and it is precisely the romantic view of and approach to nature that he considers to be the source of the problem. Nonetheless, one is left to wonder whether the (or a) romantic conception of nature can contribute to contemporary debates, and whether the critical challenges to the idea of nature have either *overlooked* or *misunderstood* certain aspects of romanticism.

In the following, I offer an environmental reappraisal of romanticism, which takes account of the recent critiques of the idea of nature. My goals are historical and systematic. First, I seek to assess the validity of Morton's critique of romanticism by distinguishing different traditions or strands within romantic thought. Thus I aim to shed light on the various conceptions of nature within romanticism, and challenge the view that romanticism offers only one account of nature, which is implausible or problematic in the contemporary context. I argue that within romanticism, we find a tradition that emphasizes empirical experience, careful observation, and methodological inquiry, and offers a conception of nature that cannot be criticized as an idealized or abstracted transcendental entity.[7] Second, I consider the systematic significance of this "romantic empiricism," and argue that while an abstract or idealized notion of nature is indeed problematic, a concrete conception that is achieved through the mutually supportive work of observation and reflection is *essential* for environmental thought. In particular, I contend that it is only on the basis of the kind of careful empirical observation and rigorous ontological account of nature that we find in the work of Johann Wolfgang von Goethe that an environmental ethic is possible. In Goethe's approach, we find a notion of epistemological responsibility or obligation that offers the necessary first step toward developing a sustainable environmental ethic.

16.1. GERMAN ROMANTICISM AND NATURE

As Jonathan Bate has clarified, a key difference between the British and American romantics concerns their understanding of nature. While the British romantics were interested in specific places and the ways in which these places could affect and vitalize the human spirit, the Americans were concerned with the vastness of nature, and understood nature as pristine wilderness.[8] In contrast to both, the German romantics were concerned, above all, with exploring the relation between nature and culture, understanding the way in which the two can enhance or destroy one another, and developing an ethical ideal for the relation between the human being and the natural world. They did this by observing cultural differences in varying geographies (Herder, Alexander von Humboldt), explicating the relation between natural organisms and artifacts (Herder, Schelling, Goethe), outlining a comprehensive theory of mind (Schelling), and elaborating how the destruction of nature would lead to the destruction of culture (A. von Humboldt). For the German romantics, nature was never thought of as a particular landscape or a vast expanse, but as a dynamic reality in which human beings dwell and to which they contribute.

In Jena, Weimar, and Berlin, the generation of philosophers after Kant was concerned with overcoming the various oppositions that resounded throughout his corpus: the opposition between sensibility and the understanding (intuition and intellect), noumena and phenomena, necessity and freedom, matter and mind, passivity and activity. Although in the *Critique of Judgment* (1790) Kant promised to bridge the gulf between these distinct domains, his concluding claim that nature and freedom can only be unified in a hypothetical and unknowable "supersensible substrate" did not ultimately achieve this end. So long as the unity between nature and freedom (matter and mind) remained hypothetical, there was no way by which to establish the connection necessary for, on the one hand, overcoming skepticism, and, on the other, developing an adequate philosophy of nature.[9] At this time, I will not delve into the specific difficulties of Kant's position, or the criticisms it received.[10] Rather, I will only briefly mention the romantic response to the Kantian project.

The romantics challenged the mind-matter dualism on two fronts: ontologically and epistemologically. In the first instance, they contended that human beings participate in natural processes both directly and indirectly. Growth and sexual reproduction (which by the late eighteenth century had become *the* central concern of natural philosophers) in addition to mounting evidence of morphological continuity between animal and human bodies illustrated a direct and immanent relationship between human beings and a larger (more than human) world. In turn, the study of different (primarily non-European) cultures and increased knowledge of geography illustrated the influence of natural surroundings and habitats on human culture (including human language). In significant ways, Herder's call for a "new world of knowledge," which would bring together various scientific disciplines and show the influences of heat and cold, electricity, chemistry, and the climate on "the mineral and vegetable kingdoms, and on men and animals," played a key role in motivating the romantic project.[11]

From an epistemological perspective, the romantics maintained that knowledge is only possible if the known object (nature) is not ultimately beyond or distinct from the knowing subject. As Schelling puts it in his 1800 *System of Transcendental Idealism*, knowledge rests upon the "coincidence" of subject and object, such that the primary aim of philosophy must be the demonstration of this coincidence (HKA 9/1, 32). Thus in the wake of Kantian philosophy, and the premise that the thing-in-itself is infinitely unknowable, the romantics argued that the very possibility of knowledge and philosophy depends on a unity between self and world, the human mind and nature.

Yet, even within the larger German romantic tradition, one finds distinctive directions with diverse methods and perspectives. Schelling is exemplary in his attempt to *construct* a "system of nature." This construction begins by positing an original premise, an absolute or necessary first principle. This principle, however, contains a contradiction, a duality, which must be resolved. The resolution of this duality occurs in the so-called process of construction, in which one intuition is generated after the other, until finally, an "absolute synthesis" is achieved. That is, a synthesis of all the previous intuition is realized in one culminating insight—an insight that also demonstrates the validity of the original premise.[12] In the philosophy of nature, the different intuitions that are successively generated through the internal contradiction of the first premise are nothing other than the stages of natural development: from magnetism and electricity, to chemistry and organisms, and, finally, to the specific evolutionary relationships between different organisms, Schelling constructs the history of nature.[13] While Schelling undertook experiments and emphasized the significance of experience for the adequate construction of a system of nature, his method and aims were determined by his systematic ideals. More specifically, his goal was to establish the *theoretical foundations* of a system of nature.

In contrast to Schelling's systematic construction of nature, Herder, Goethe, and eventually Alexander von Humboldt were concerned with developing a new empiricism—what Schiller described as "rational empiricism," and what I call "romantic empiricism." The juxtaposition of *romantic* and *empiricism* is—to most minds—highly unlikely and even contradictory. The romantics are, after all, known for their abstract systematic ideals, which appear to strongly contrast with an empiricist approach grounded in phenomena and concerned with the observation of nature. Thus, to speak of a romantic empiricism is to speak of the "unknown romanticism." What differentiates this strand of romanticism is an interest in nature as a phenomenon to be observed (and not merely theorized or systematically constructed), and a concern with investigating and transforming our capacity to observe and grasp the natural world.

In what follows I investigate this understudied empiricist approach *within* romanticism, and consider its relevance for contemporary environmental theory. Due to lack of space, I will focus on the romantic whose work most clearly exemplifies this approach, namely Goethe.

16.2. GOETHE'S ROMANTIC EMPIRICISM

In a letter to Goethe from January 19, 1798, Schiller describes Goethe's scientific method as a "rational empiricism." "Only *rational empiricism*," he writes, "can penetrate the pure phenomenon" (MA 8/1, 499). Rational empiricism, Schiller continues, must be a true wedding of both empiricism and rationalism: "only the most perfect activity of the free powers of thought with the purest and most expansive activity of sensible perception [*Wahrnehmungsvermögen*] lead to scientific knowledge." In what ways was Goethe's method both rational and empirical, and what are the implications of this method?

Goethe's interest in nature and the natural sciences commenced during his tenure as an administrator in Saxe-Weimar Eisenach. One of his first tasks in Weimar was the reopening of the mines in Ilmenau, which led him to the study of minerals and the development of his own mineral collections.

During this time, Goethe began to study botany, reading Carl Linneaus, working with the Jena professor August Johann Batch, and developing a garden for his research. For Goethe, reading Linneaus was both exciting and disappointing. Linneaus had attempted to organize the world; however, Goethe surmised, not one of his attempts was a success. Linneaus's system led to a fragmentary and superficial taxonomy because it was based on a few visible parts. In contrast, Goethe argued that knowledge must seek to grasp and present the *unity* of the phenomena—that is to say, discern how the different parts and stages of development participate in the phenomenon as a *whole*. Only by grasping the integrated character of the plant, he maintained, can we go on to recognize it as a member of a particular species or kingdom (a plant *as* plant, an animal *as* animal). The question for Goethe, then, was not *whether* plants exhibit a distinctive unity, but rather *what* this unity involves, and *how* it can be recognized and articulated.

In his essay "Intuitive Judgment" ("Anschauende Urteilskraft") Goethe takes to task Kant's claim that natural ends or organic unities cannot be cognized. While he expresses sympathy with Kant's project, Goethe also emphasizes his disagreement with the latter's premises and methodology.[14] By setting limits to knowledge, Goethe argues, Kant was also, and necessarily, transgressing them. He writes,

> In my effort to utilize, if not actually master, the Kantian doctrine, it sometimes occurred to me that the worthy man was proceeding roguishly and ironically, at one point appearing to set narrow limits for our cognitive

capacity and at another beckoning us furtively beyond them.... Our master thus restricts his thinkers to reflective and expository judgment, sternly forbidding determinative judgment; but after driving us sufficiently into a corner and even bringing us to despair, he suddenly decides in favor of the most liberal interpretations and allows us to make what use we will of the freedom he has in some measure vouchsafed for us. (MA 12, 98)[15]

Goethe's critique, which Hegel also leveled against Kant's methodology, applies most directly to Kant's claim that knowledge of natural ends or organisms is beyond our cognition. How, Goethe asks, was Kant able to draw these limits if *he* (Kant) did not have any access to what is beyond them? This was not, however, the only reason that Kant's framework appeared perplexing to Goethe. The very thing that Kant had denied—cognition of organic beings—Goethe believed himself to have achieved. Thus, he goes on, "had I myself not ceaselessly pressed forward to the archetype, though at first unconsciously, from an inner drive; had I not even succeeded in evolving a method in harmony with Nature? What then was to prevent me from courageously embarking upon the adventure of reason, as the old gentleman of Königsberg himself calls it?" (MA 12, 99).

In Kant's writings, Goethe found much to praise; yet he felt compelled to go beyond the limits that Kant had set—at first without realizing it because he was unfamiliar with Kant's work, and then later, after studying critical philosophy, by giving more thought to methodological and epistemological questions. Nonetheless, for Goethe, the Kantian problems were largely, although not exclusively, theoretical. His own methodology, in contrast, was not developed purely theoretically, but through continued scientific practice and observation (something with which Kant was less concerned, as his primary concern was with the possibility of offering an *explanation* of the phenomena).

Goethe agreed with Kant that there is always a "gap" between idea and experience. For Kant, this gap is due to an incongruity between the singularity of the perceived (the individual *this*) and the generality or universality of concepts. This incongruity, according to Kant, results in a "contingency" in our knowledge: "our understanding is a faculty of concepts, i.e., a discursive understanding, for which it must of course be contingent what and how different might be the particular that can be given to it in nature and brought under its concepts" (AA 5: 406). For Goethe, by contrast, the gap between idea and experience is specifically temporal, and concerns the temporal and spatial character of experience and the nontemporal and nonspatial character of ideas. He describes the gap as follows:

this difficulty of *uniting* idea and experience presents obstacles in all scientific research: the idea is independent of space and time, while scientific research is bound by space and time. In the idea, then, simultaneous elements are intimately bound up with sequential ones, but our experience always shows them to be separate; we are seemingly plunged into madness by a natural process that we are to conceive of in idea as both simultaneous and sequential. (MA 12, 99—100)

While in the idea, successive and simultaneous are "intimately connected," in experience they are "always separated." But what exactly do these terms mean, and how is it possible—if at all—to overcome the gap between idea and experience? To answer these questions, it is important to understand the problem that underlies them, and this requires investigating Goethe's project in some detail.

In 1786, Goethe travelled to Italy with the aim of immersing himself in the visual arts and learning about plant physiology. It was during this time that he arrived at his idea of an "*Urpflanze*" or archetypal plant. In the garden in Palermo, he was struck by both the diversity and unity of what he observed. He writes: "I was confronted with so many kinds of fresh, new forms, I was taken again by my old fanciful idea: might I not discover the *Urpflanze* amid this multitude? Such a thing must exist after all! How else would I recognize this or that form as being a plant, if they were not all constructed according to one model?" (MA 15, 327). What is it, Goethe asks himself, that enables him to recognize the manifold varieties of plants as plant. Or, what is the unifying principle of plants? Importantly, he does not seek it outside of the multiplicity, but "amid the multitude."

In a letter to Herder, dated exactly one month following his visit to the garden, Goethe writes that he has come very near to comprehending "the secret of plant generation and organization" (MA 15, 393). He has realized, he reports to Herder, that the unity he is after is inherently connected to growth and generation. It was not until July of 1787, however, that Goethe more clearly articulated his discovery. In a report in which he includes the two passages quoted above, he adds the important conclusion: "it has become apparent to me that in the plant organ we ordinarily call the leaf a true Proteus is concealed, that can hide and reveal itself in all formations. From top to bottom, a plant is all leaf, united so inseparably with the future bud that one cannot be imagined without the other" (MA 15, 456). What distinguishes a plant, what makes it recognizable as a plant, are the formative relationships between its parts: the way in which each of the parts appears to anticipate what comes after it and the plant as a whole—or, as Goethe put it, each part anticipates "the future bud." Thus, by claiming that "all plant is leaf," Goethe is not reducing the plant to the leaf, but rather recognizing a *morphological continuity* between the parts, wherein each part is a formative manifestation ("*bildende Kraft*")[16] of the "true Proteus," that is, of an underlying ideal that determines the parts and their relations in developmental terms. In other words, what unifies the plant is not simply its *structure*, but its structure *as* its *formative unity*, that is, *as* the developmental relations between the parts, *as* the way in which each part realizes the plant's continued development.

In his *Essay on the Metamorphosis of Plants* (1790) Goethe presents this insight in greater detail. An observation of plants, he writes, reveals "that certain of their external parts sometimes undergo a change and assume, either entirely or in greater or lesser degree, the form of the parts adjacent to them" (MA 12, 29, no. 1). This is most evident, he explains, in what might be called intermediate parts, cases where stem leaves have taken on attributes of the calyx, or where the calyx is tinted with the color of the blossom, or where petals show resemblances to stamens and so on. In other words, if the plant's parts are perceived alongside one another, one begins to recognize morphological continuity between the parts, and it becomes clear that each part assumes a form that is a modification or progression of the other parts.

The various parts of the plant thus appear as moments in a continuum of formation—particular manifestations of the transformation that the plant undergoes from seed to fruit (or seed). This transformation, Goethe goes on, is the bringing forth of "one part through the other," which presents "the most diverse forms through modification of a single organ" (MA 12, 29, no. 3). Further observation of the plant reveals that plant metamorphosis occurs in two complementary ways. First, it is apparent that every part of the plant is a moment of either expansion or contraction. While the seed is the first contraction, the stem leaves are the first expansion. The calyx is a contraction, and the petals are an expansion. The sexual organs are once again a contraction, while the fruit is the "maximum expansion" and the seed within it is the "maximum concentration." Alongside this development, is a second development—that of progression or intensification (*Steigerung*). Each of the parts comes progressively closer toward reaching the goal of growth, attained in the final parts of the plant, the reproductive organs (MA 12, 44, no. 50; MA 12, 65, no. 113).

By observing the plant's development and discerning morphological continuity along an axis of contraction and expansion, as well as progression, Goethe arrived at the of idea of the plant: the internal unity and coherence that makes the plant, plant. His claim is that this unity is inseparable from the distinctive form of each of the plant's parts, that is, the way in which each part is both a response to what precedes it and an anticipation of what is to come. Each part, one can say, reflects the *history* of the plant and thereby contains within it the whole plant. The unity of the plant is thus inherently connected to its growth, and development, such that each part is a physical manifestation of a stage of metamorphosis. It is a unity that emerges in time, and is realized in and through the plant's growth and transformation.

But how is such a unity to be grasped and articulated? More specifically, what kind of temporal structure underlies and makes this unity possible, and how does it differ from the structure of experience? Goethe had remarked that while in the idea, successive and simultaneous are "intimately connected," in experience they are "always separated." The question thus is: how can one grasp the plant's organizing principle if its temporal structure is contrary to the structure of experience?

Observation, Goethe explains, always begins by distinguishing or delimiting the different stages or parts of a living being. One sees the stem, then the leaf, then the bud, and so on. The relations between the parts and the continuity between them are thus not immediately perceived. In an organism, however, the parts do not develop in isolation of one another, nor are their forms (morphological forms) or functions independent of one another. Rather, the development of the different parts of living beings occurs in both sequential and simultaneous relation to one another. In the plant, for instance, the leaf develops through the stem, the flower through the calyx, and so on. Each of the parts, as we have seen, emerges in relation to what precedes it (and in relation to what is to come after it). In addition, Goethe explains, development or formation occurs simultaneously. A stem does not first grow to full length, and is then followed by a leaf. Rather, leaves develop simultaneously with the stem.

Thus, the very fact that organic beings *grow* and their parts represent stages of development means that the different stages presuppose and anticipate one another. That is, the possibility of future stages is already at work in earlier ones. For example, just as the formation of the flower presupposes the formation of the stem, so the *possibility* of the flower is already at work in the development of pistil and stem. The structure of the organism can be thus distinguished from the structure of casual observation in three ways. First, the parts grow in relation to one another, and not independently of one another. Second, this development reveals an anticipation of the future, such that the possibility of "the future bud," as Goethe put it, is already at work in the present. Finally, the parts develop simultaneously (they grow *together* or *at once*).

Given the fact that, when we perceive, we see the parts independently of one another, and, moreover, experience a temporal structure in which the past *alone* determines the present, how are we to grasp the organizing principle that underlies plant development? The answer to this question lies in our ability to perceive and grasp the continuity and relatedness between the different stages, so as to be able to see the *simultaneous and the successive as one*.[17] How is this to take place?

The transitions, after all, are not given immediately to sensibility. For this reason, Goethe surmises, the only way by which to grasp them is by visualizing them in memory—and for this the imagination is necessary. Through the imagination I recreate in my mind what takes place in nature, and thereby present to the *mind's eye* what remains imperceptible to the physical eye. To achieve this, Goethe writes, I must "consider all phenomena in a certain developmental sequence and attentively follow the *transitions* forwards and backwards. Only in this way do I finally arrive at the living view of the whole, from which a concept is formed that soon will merge with the idea along an ascending line" (LA 1/8, 74).

This involves two steps. First, I must discern the transitions between the parts, and thereby see how each part relates to the one that precedes and the one that follows it. Second, I must grasp these transitions as they occur simultaneously. After all, the goal is not simply to arrive at an understanding of the continuity between the parts and see how each part is a metamorphosis of the one that preceded it, but also to grasp the unified activity of the plant. For only in this way can one see all the parts as interrelated members of a living process. But what does it mean to grasp the unified activity, or the *underlying unity* of the distinctive parts? For Goethe this means nothing less than transforming what is given to perception and imagination into an idea. He explains this transformation as follows:

> If I look at the created object, inquire into its creation, and follow this process back as far as I can, I will find a series of steps. Since these are not actually seen together before me, I must visualize them in my memory so that they form a certain ideal whole.
>
> At first I will tend to think in terms of steps, but nature leaves no gaps, and thus, in the end, I will have to see this progression of uninterrupted activity as a whole. I can do so only by dissolving the particularity without destroying the impression itself. (WA 2/6, 303–4)[18]

The idea that is grasped in this way is not a static or abstract concept that is divested of difference and particularity. Nor is it something that is imposed upon the sensibly given by the understanding. Rather, it emerges out of an engagement with the sensibly given, and thus provides, as Goethe puts it, an impression of the whole that does not destroy the particular. The idea must enable insight of the different parts and their relations—the continuity between them—and thus present the differences *within* the unity. Only in this way can I grasp the unity of a living organism, that is, an internally differentiated unity.

Goethe's claim is that perception must be transformed through imagination so that what is perceived more accurately presents what occurs in nature. Only in this way does the idea (as the organizing principle of an internally differentiated unity) emerge, such that there is no "gap" between idea and experience. This is in deep contrast to the method that commences with ideas, applies them onto some particular given, and then concludes that ideas (precisely because they are the abstract starting point) cannot depict these singular empirical givens. For, unlike Kant, Goethe begins with a particular experience and asks what is involved in it—what makes this experience possible—and in this way arrives at the idea (at the implicit organizing principle). He agrees with Kant's view that the distinctive character of a living organism is its growth and reproduction, and with his claim that an organism is both "cause and effect of itself" (AA 5: 370).[19] Thus, Goethe emphasizes that the key to grasping a living being is grasping its growth, more specifically, the *causal* or *temporal* structure that underlies and determines this growth. This did not mean, however, offering an abstract explanation of the mechanism of growth, but rather overcoming the gap that emerges in the first moment of observation, that is, the temporal gap between experience and the actual structure of an organism. In other words, *understanding* means above all *remaining with what is perceived and seeking to make it meaningful and coherent.*

From an epistemological or methodological perspective this means that to grasp the distinctive character of organic unity (what makes a plant, plant), to grasp the idea that underlies it, it is imperative that one immerse oneself in the phenomena and seek the unity therein. For this reason, Goethe recommends to anyone who wishes to observe nature to "seek nothing behind the phenomena: they are themselves the theory" (MA 17, 824).[20] Goethe's empiricism is rational, then, because it does not remain on the level of observation and eliminate theory. Rather, it seeks to make conscious or explicit the idea that is *implied* in what is observed. As he put it in the preface to the *Theory of Color*, "we labor in vain to describe a person's character, but when we draw together his actions, his deeds, a picture of his character will emerge" (MA 10, 9).

Goethe's approach has significant implications. First, it implies both the necessity and possibility of transforming thinking and perceiving, such that they are no longer incongruous, or in Kant's words "contingent." As he puts it, "my perception itself [becomes] a thinking, and my thinking a perception" (MA 12, 306). Only in this way, he maintains, do we achieve a necessary "plasticity" in our thinking. For, he elaborates, "if we want to arrive at a living intuition of nature, we must become as flexible and quick as the examples that nature gives us" (MA 12, 13).

Second, his approach implies that knowledge involves the attempt to become identical with the thing known. Goethe described his method as a "delicate empiricism, which makes itself utterly identical with the object" (MA 17, 823). This identity requires a transformation in the knower—a transformation that takes place on two levels. On the one hand, the knower actively seeks to make her thinking identical with her perceiving—and thus shifts the balance in her cognition, so that concepts do not determine and grant meaning to inchoate sensibly given data, but rather, thought and ideas emerge from and in light of what is perceived. On the other hand, perceiving must itself strive to become identical with what is before it; it too must achieve a certain plasticity, so as to be able to grasp the organism as an integrated unity. This double transformation leads to what Goethe calls the "eye of the mind," that is, a thinking that emerges out of and is identical with perception.[21]

Goethe's emphasis on phenomena, and his refusal to think of nature as an abstract, transcendent entity, places him in great proximity to contemporary environmental philosophers and theorists. Yet Goethe differs from the majority of contemporary theorists in that his objections to philosophical abstractions were articulated alongside a positive account of natural phenomena and scientific methodology. Thus Goethe's views on nature and philosophical knowledge were not simply critical, but offered a concrete method, developed through continuous engagement with the phenomena and a serious commitment to the practice of science. It is his particular approach, and his insistence on remaining with the phenomena, rather than merely theorizing about them, that makes Goethe particularly relevant in environmental debates today. However, before considering the extent to which his views can offer insights or solutions to contemporary questions, it is important first to turn to a brief examination of the state of environmental thought and examine the prospects of environmental philosophy "after the end of nature."

16.3. ENVIRONMENTAL PHILOSOPHY AFTER NATURE

The origins of the environmental movement were in conservation, whose goal, as the name belies, were to conserve or protect. These origins are significant because they reveal the underlying assumption of environmentalism, namely that there is *something* that should be conserved or protected. In other words, environmental thought is based on the idea that there is a "nature" or "environment" that carries some normative value and should be protected. If there were no such entity (nature or environment), then environmentalism would find itself in a difficult situation, in which there is no clear object of concern or self-evident goal, and must therefore justify not only its goals, but also its very existence. If there is no nature, then we must ask the question: what is environmental action and theory for?[22]

As a substitute for the concept of nature and in order to answer this question, several thinkers have developed new concepts or employed old ones in new ways. Morton, for instance, speaks of the "coexistence" of things, and argues that we should strive to exist *with* things.[23] Coexistence, according to Morton, describes a "pre-ontological level of 'existence,'" in which we cannot speak about distinct ontological beings, but rather the "intimacy of all life forms." What he means, however, is never made clear. For one, he refuses to distinguish between living and nonliving things, and at no point does he explain what he means by "life forms." Yet he often includes nonliving entities into his schema of "coexistence." Although Morton's notion of coexistence has the positive intention of offering an inclusive conception of reality, it ends up doing exactly what Morton finds problematic in the idea of nature: it is a vague and abstract *concept that is imposed on the phenomena*. It is, furthermore, a concept that does not offer a concrete approach to the phenomena or disclose the phenomena in their particularity: it does not tell us anything other than that things stand next to one another. *What* they are, *how* they stand next to one another, and *what their relations* are remain unclear. Thus, rather than seeking to understand a phenomenon, the notion of coexistence eclipses phenomena in, as Morton puts it, the "constant flux."

Biodiversity is another idea that has been put forth as a replacement for the notion of nature and is connected with the disappearance or extinction of certain types. While Morton distinguishes his notion of coexistence from the idea of biodiversity, where the goal is to save or maintain as many kinds of beings as possible, in both cases the decisive idea is that of the existence or continuation of existence—that is, the preservation of something that exists now. Biodiversity rests on the idea that we must strive to maintain the greatest number of kinds. Number, however, is not self-evidently healthy. Thus kinds must be understood in accordance to their diverse and complex functions within an ecological niche. This means that we must investigate and understand these niches, and to simply speak in terms of the concept of "biodiversity" is just as vague and abstract as the concept "nature." Furthermore, the notion of biodiversity alone fails to offer a concrete approach to the phenomena. Instead, just like the notion of "coexistence," it relies on a vague idea of preservation and continuity, which does not provide adequate ways of discerning differences, recognizing similarities, and drawing judgments. The unquestioned assumption in both is that because all things are part of the general flux (coexist), they must continue to exist.

Thus both concepts—coexistence and biodiversity—lack the grounded and concrete approach that Morton and others have called for. As they have rightly argued, it is only on the basis of such an approach, an approach that regards things in their particularity or specificity, that a convincing environmental ethic can be developed. However, rather than delivering this approach, they have resorted to the same abstractions that they criticize. If we do not develop ways by which to discern differences, and thereby recognize different kinds of processes—process that are affected by human activity and those that remain unaffected (such as bird flight); processes that can be described as complex mechanisms, and those that are not reducible to mechanical principles—then we not only find ourselves in a state of ignorance, but also, I think, in a state of ethical immobility—that is, an inability to make adequate judgments.

16.4. GOETHE'S ENVIRONMENTAL ETHICS

Following the various declarations of the end of nature, thinkers have found it necessary to posit some idea to play the role that nature (as that which is to be preserved or investigated) has traditionally played. However, these ideas not only lack epistemological and ontological rigor, but also appear to be more abstract than the idea of nature. In other words, in spite of their critical objections to nature as an idea, theorists have not offered viable substitutes that can ground and justify the environmental movement.

Although Goethe was no critic of nature, he was a critic of philosophical abstractions. However, alongside his objection to philosophical constructs that had little to do with empirical observation, Goethe offered a positive account of natural phenomena, based on careful methodological considerations.

My thesis is that Goethe and specifically his method offer a viable solution to the lacuna in contemporary environmental theory. His approach to the natural world allows him to discern differences, without however undermining or overlooking similarities. For his goal was to grasp the unity in the multiplicity, and thereby recognize the distinctive singularity of each thing through its relations and place within a larger context. His *Urpflanze*, or archetypal plant, was indeed an idea. As such, however, it was not separable from the phenomena of the plants; it was neither an arbitrary abstraction derived from some apparent commonalities between a set of plants, nor a purely mental construct generated through an intellectual intuition. Rather, as an idea, the *Urpflanze* was *achieved* through empirical investigation; it was verified through its ability to disclose the distinctive character of plants, or as Goethe put it, the "secret of plant generation and organization." Thus, in Goethe we find an idealism that does not imply antirealism, nor does it involve a shutting out of empirical phenomena. The opposite is the case. As I have shown, for Goethe, knowledge can emerge only through careful and arduous observation coupled with theoretical and methodological consideration. The idea is never divorced from the phenomenon, but rather *is* the phenomenon in the most immanent sense.

Furthermore, Goethe's epistemology and his approach to nature carry some significant consequences for environmental ethics. His view that the knowing subject must *transform* herself in order to grasp the phenomenon adequately challenges two widespread conceptions of the character of knowledge. On the one hand, it challenges the idea that knowledge is purely representation or construction, in which the known object (nature) is considered to be no more than inert and passive, receiving forms imposed upon it by an active knowing subject. On the other hand, Goethe's view implies that the act of knowing is never morally neutral, but always already involves a specific ethical *demand*, namely the demand to remain open to being transformed by what is known. The knower, in other words, stands in a relation of obligation to what she seeks to know: an obligation to know it in the right way. This in turn implies that the knower must be open to transforming herself in order to intimate properly that which is before her. Thus, the act of knowledge is always already an act that carries with it an obligation to what is known, an obligation that specifically pertains to the knower. This obligation, importantly, cannot be thought apart from the particular phenomenon, for it is only in seeking to understand it *in the right way* that one is compelled to transform her- or himself. In other words, to know responsibly, and to transform oneself for the sake of knowledge, is only possible if there is an ontological reality (a particular entity) that demands to be known in a particular way. That is to say, the epistemological act is not separable from the ontological reality, and the two are ultimately connected to a specific ethical demand and responsibility.

The act of knowledge thus rests on an honest engagement with reality, with the phenomena. While this is not a thorough and comprehensive environmental ethics, the claim that we are under an epistemological obligation to what is before us provides the first step in that direction. This obligation falls entirely on the side of the knower, and, importantly, does not involve the ethicist in the vicious circle of having to assume values or rights—precisely what she or he seeks to justify.[24]

NOTES
1. Bill McKibben, *The End of Nature* (London: Viking, 1990), 54 and 56.
2. Timothy Morton, *Ecology without Nature: Rethinking Environmental Aesthetics* (Cambridge, MA: Harvard University Press, 2007), 14.
3. Kate Rigby, "Writing after Nature," *Australian Humanities Review* 39–40 (2006). www.australianhumanitiesreview.org/archive/Issue-September-2006.rigby.html.
4. Ibid.
5. See for instance, Jonathan Bate, *Romantic Ecology: Wordsworth and the Environmental Tradition* (London: Routledge, 1991); Karl Kroeber, *Ecological Literary Criticism: Romantic Imagining and the Biology of Mind* (New York: Columbia University Press, 1994); James McKusick, "Coleridge and the Economy of Nature," *Studies in Romanticism* 35 (1996): 375–92.
6. This is all the more astonishing when one sees that the key critics of the idea of nature are also scholars of literary romanticism. This includes Timothy Morton and Kate Rigby. Rigby's book on European romanticism significantly assesses the relevance of romantic thought for environmental philosophy. She remains uncomfortable, however, with what she sees as an overarching (and anthropocentric) holism

in romanticism. See *Topographies of the Sacred: The Poetics of Place in European Romanticism* (Charlottesville, VA: University of Virginia Press, 2004). In this paper, I seek to emphasize a specific romantic legacy—what I call "romantic empiricism"—that Rigby also discusses, but does not specifically consider in relation to contemporary environmental thought.

7. Amanda Jo Goldstein's chapter in this volume similarly traces the empiricist tradition of romantic thought in the work of Herder. See chapter 15.

8. Bate, *Wordsworth and the Environmental Tradition*, 39.

9. Shortly after the publication of the *Critique of Pure Reason* (1781), Kant's first critics accused him of skepticism. If things-in-themselves could not be known, then how could we be sure that our knowledge actually reflects truth and is not merely illusory? (The first review of the *Critique*, coauthored by Johann Georg Heinrich Feder and Christian Garve, published in 1782 and known as the "Göttingen Review" or the "Feder/Grave Review," leveled precisely this critique, arguing that Kantian philosophy was a full-blown idealism). Or, how can a priori forms agree with or correspond to a posteriori matter? (This is the principle critique of Salomon Maimon in his *Versuch über die Transcendentalphilosophie* [1789].) Or, given Kant's basic premises, how can we know that sensibility was indeed receptive, and that things-in-themselves existed at all? (This was the essence of Jacobi's argument, in which he claimed that Kant inconsistently argued that objects are the causes of our representations.) For a complete account of the skeptical attacks on Kant's philosophy, see Frederick C. Beiser, *The Fate of Reason: German Philosophy between Kant and Fichte* (Cambridge, MA: Harvard University Press, 1987). In turn, the possibility of a philosophy of nature depends on the unification of two irreconcilable principles: the mechanism that underlies nature "as the sum of all appearances," and the teleology that is presumed (and is thus only regulative) to explain those entities that are inexplicable on mechanical principles. Although Kant seeks to reconcile these two principles in the Antinomy of Teleological Judgment, it is difficult to see how exactly his solution achieves reconciliation. For a comprehensive and illuminating analysis of the difficulty of the task at hand, see Eric Watkins, "The Antinomy of Teleological Judgment," *Kant Yearbook* 1 (2009): 197–222.

10. See my *The Romantic Absolute: Being and Knowing in German Romantic Philosophy 1795–1804* (Chicago: University of Chicago Press, 2013).

11. Johann Gottfried Herder, *Outlines of a Philosophy of the History of Man*, trans. T. Churchill (London: J. Johnson, St Paul's Churchyard, 1803), 24.

12. For an explication of how the first premise determines the development of the system, see my *The Romantic Absolute*, Part 3.

13. For an account of Schelling's derivations, see Eckart Förster, *The Twenty Five Years of Philosophy: A Systematic Reconstruction*, trans. Brady Bowman (Cambridge, MA: Harvard University Press, 2012), 233–34.

14. For a more complete account of Goethe's relation to Kant's conception of organisms, and his methodology, see my "Sensibility and Organic Unity: Kant, Goethe and the Plasticity of Cognition," *Intellectual History Review* (forthcoming 2014).

15. One of the more difficult aspects of the *Critique of Judgment* has to do with the apparent distinction that Kant draws between our experience of organisms and our cognition of them (as ends of nature or as purposive). For it seems that, on

the one hand, organisms "appear" to us in experience—such that we are able to distinguish them from nonorganic beings and make claims about their structure—while, on the other hand, they are deemed as ultimately incomprehensible (see for instance, Peter McLaughlin, *Kant's Critique of Teleology in Biological Explanation* [Lewiston: Edwin Mellen Press, 1990], 56). For Goethe, the kind of difference that Kant seems to want to draw between experience and knowledge does not make sense—for insofar as a phenomenon *appears*, then it is *knowable*.

16. In his work on animal morphology, Goethe describes the relations between the parts of an animal as developing "according to a certain scheme, formed [*umgeformt*] differently through the formative force [*bildende Kraft*] in the most steady manner" (FA 24, 280).

17. See Förster, *The Twenty-Five Years*, 261.

18. See also FA 1/24, 102.

19. The causal structure of an organism thus appears to challenge or contradict the structure of efficient causality in which the cause is distinct from (and precedes) the effect. Goethe realized this and for this reason focuses on the temporal incongruity between our *experience* of organisms and their *actual structure*.

20. In the same remark in *Maxims and Reflections* Goethe also states that "the most important thing to grasp is that all fact is already theory" (MA 17, 824).

21. On the transformative or plastic nature of cognition according to Goethe, see Eckart Förster, "Goethe and the 'Auge des Geistes,'" *Deutsche Vierteljahrsschrift für Literaturwissenschaft und Geistesgeschichte* 75:1 (2001): 87–101 and Frederick Amrine, "The Metamorphosis of the Scientist," *Goethe Yearbook* 5 (1990): 188–212.

22. It should be noted that this is a problem that specifically plagues thinkers who claim that the idea of nature is incoherent and philosophically unjustifiable (Morton, for instance). McKibben's take, in contrast, is that nature *once was* but *no longer is*, such that he is able to demand environmental activism that is inspired by this historical reality. In other words, the idea of nature (although no longer a reality) has a normative status in McKibben's thought.

23. Timothy Morton, "Coexistence and Coexistents: Ecology without a World," in *Ecocritical Theory: New European Approaches* (Charlottesville: University of Virginia Press, 2011), 168–80. In this context, Morton criticizes the notion of a lifeworld or lifeworlds, which have been used (at least since Heidegger) to distinguish the domain of living beings and, more recently, justify an environmental ethic.

24. The research and writing of this paper was supported by the Australian Research Council Discovery Early Career Research Award (DE120102402).

WORKS CITED

TEXTS BY AUTHORS FROM THE ROMANTIC ERA

German

Diez, Immanuel Carl. *Briefwechsel und Kantische Schriften. Wissensbegründung in der Glaubenskrise Tübingen-Jena (1790–1792)*. Edited by Dieter Henrich. Stuttgart: Klett-Cotta, 1997.

Fichte, Johann Gottlieb. *J. G. Fichte: Gesamtausgabe der Bayerischen Akademie der Wissenschaft*. Edited by R. Lauth, H. Jacob, and H. Gliwitsky. Stuttgart-Bad Cannstatt: Frommann-Holzboog, 1964–2012.

Forberg, Friedrich Karl. *Fragmente aus meinen Papieren*. Jena: J. G. Voigt, 1796.

——. "Briefe über die neueste Philosophie." *Philosophisches Journal* 6 no. 5 (1797): 44–88.

Friedrich, Caspar David. "Äußerungen bei Betrachtung einer Sammlung von Gemählden von größtentheils noch lebenden und unlängst verstorbenen Künstlern." In *Kritische Edition der Schriften des Künstlers und seiner Zeitzeugen*, edited by Gerhard Eimer in collaboration with Günther Rath. Frankfurt am Main: Kunstgeschichtliches Institut der Johann Wolfgang Goethe-Universität, 1999.

Fries, Jakob Friedrich. *Reinhold, Fichte und Schelling*. Leipzig: Reineicke, 1803.

Goethe, Johann Wolfgang von. *Goethes Werke* (Weimarer Ausgabe). Edited by P. Raabe et al. Weimar: Hermann Böhlau, 1887–1919.

——. *Die Schriften zur Naturwissenschaft*. Edited by D. Kuhn et al. Weimar: Hermann Bölhaus Nachfolger, 1947.

——. *Über die Gegenstände der bildenden Kunst*. Zurich: Artemis Verlag, 1961–66.

——. *Sämtliche Werke nach Epochen seines Schaffens* (Münchner Ausgabe). Edited by K. Richter et al. Munich: Carl Hanser, 1985–98.

——. *Sämtliche Werke* (Frankfurter Ausgabe). Edited by H. Birus et al. Frankfurt am Main: Deutscher Klassiker Verlag, 1985–1999.

Hardenberg, Friedrich Leopold von [Novalis]. *Novalis Schriften*. Edited by R. Samuel, H. J. Mähl, and G. Schulz. Stuttgart: Kohlhammer, 1960–88.

Hegel, Georg Wilhelm Friedrich. *Werke in zwanzig Bänden*. Edited by K. Michel and E. Moldenhauer. Frankfurt am Main: Suhrkamp, 1969–71.

Herder, Johann Gottfried. *Werke.* Edited by Ulrich Gaier et al. Frankfurt am Main: Deutscher Klassiker Verlag, 1985–2000.

Hölderlin, Friedrich. *Sämtliche Werke: Kleine Stuttgarter Ausgabe.* Edited by Friedrich Beißner. Stuttgart: J. G. Cottasche Buchhandlung Nachfolger, 1944.

Jacobi, Friedrich Heinrich. *Ueber die Lehre des Spinoza in Briefen an Herrn Moses Mendelssohn.* Neue vermehrte Auflage. Breslau: Löwe, 1789.

——. *Werke,* vols. 1/1 and 1/2: *Schriften zum Spinozastreit.* Edited by Klaus Hammacher and Irmgard-Maria Piske. Hamburg: Meiner; Stuttgart-Bad Cannstatt: Frommann-Holzboog, 1989.

Kästner, Abraham Gotthelf. *Anfangsgründe der Analysis des Unendlichen.* Göttingen: Im Verlag der Wittwe Vandenhoeck, 1761–70.

Kant, Immanuel. *Gesammelte Schriften.* Edited by Preußischen Akademie der Wissenschaft. Berlin: de Gruyter, 1900–.

Mendelssohn, Moses. *Gesammelte Schriften.* Leipzig: Brockhaus, 1843.

Niethammer, Friedrich Immanuel. "Von den Ansprüchen des gemeinen Verstandes an die Philosophie." *Philosophisches Journal* 1, no. 1 (1795): 1–45.

——. *Korrespondenz mit dem Herbert- und Erhard-Kreis.* Edited by Wilhelm Baum. Vienna: Turia + Kant, 1995.

Ploucquet, Gottfried. *Logik.* Edited and translated into German by Michael Franz. Hildesheim: Olms, 2006.

Reinhold, Karl Leonard. *Versuch einer neuen Theorie des menschlichen Vorstellungsvermögens.* Prague: C. Widtmann & J. M. Mauke, 1789.

——. *Beyträge zur Berichtigung bisheriger Mißverständnisse der Philosophen, Erster Band, das Fundament der Elementarphilosophie betreffend.* Jena: Michael Mauke, 1790.

——. *Allgemeine Literatur-Zeitung* 53 (May 1792): 425–27.

——. "Ueber den Unterschied zwischen dem gesunden Verstande und der philosophierenden Vernunft in Rücksicht auf die Fundamente des durch beyde möglichen Wissens." In *Beyträge zur Berichtigung bisheriger Mißverständnisse der Philosophen,* vol. 2, *Die Fundamente des philosophischen Wissens, der Metaphysik, Moral, moralischen Religion und Geschmackslehre betreffend.* Jena: Johann Michael Mauke, 1794.

Schelling, Friedrich Wilhelm Joseph von. *Sämmtliche Werke.* Edited by K. F. A. Schelling. Stuttgart: Cotta, 1856–61.

——. *Aus Schellings Leben: In Briefen.* Edited by G. I. Plitt. 3 vols. Leipzig: Hirzel, 1869–70.

——. *System der Weltalter: Münchener Vorlesung 1827/28 in einer Nachschrift von Ernst von Lasaulux.* Edited by Siegbert Peetz. Frankfurt am Main: Klostermann, 1990.

——. *Joseph Friedrich Schellings Dissertatio philosophica de simplicibus et eorum diversis speciebus von 1758.* Edited, translated into German, with an introduction by Michael Franz and Hanns-Peter Neumann. In *Der Monadenbegriff zwischen Spätrenaissance und Aufklärung,* edited by Hanns-Peter Neumann, 339–99. Berlin: Walter de Gruyter, 2009.

——. *Werke: Historisch-Kristiche Ausgabe.* Edited by H. M. Baumgartner, W. G. Jacobs, and H. Krings. Stuttgart-Bad Cannstatt: Frommann-Holzboog, 1976–.

Schelling, Friedrich Wilhelm Joseph von, and Johann Gottlieb Fichte. *Fichte-Schelling Briefwechsel.* Edited with an introduction by Walter Schulz. Frankfurt am Main: Suhrkamp, 1968.

Schiller, Friedrich. *Werke. Nationalausgabe.* Weimar: Hermann Böhlaus Nachfolger, 1943–.

Schlegel, Friedrich von. *Friedrich Schlegels philosophische Vorlesungen aus den Jahren 1804 bis 1806.* Edited by C. J. H. Windischmann. Bonn: Eduard Weber, 1846.

——. "Philosophie der Philologie." In "Friedrich Schlegels 'Philosophie der Philologie' mit einer Einleitung herausgegeben von Josef Körner." *Logos 17* (1928).

——. *Kritische Friedrich-Schlegel-Ausgabe.* Edited by E. Behler, J. J. Anstett, and H. Eichner. Paderborn: Schöningh, 1958–.

Schleiermacher, Friedrich Daniel Ernst. *Sämmtliche Werke.* Edited by O. Braun and J. Bauer. Berlin: G. Reimer, 1835–64.

——. *Hermeneutik und Kritik.* Edited by Manfred Frank. Frankfurt am Main: Suhrkamp, 1977.

——. *Kritische Gesamtausgabe.* Edited by Günter Meckenstock et al. Berlin: de Gruyter, 1980–2005.

Schmid, Carl Christian Erhard. *Empirische Psychologie.* Jena: Cröker, 1791.

——. "Rezension von Reinholds Fundament des philosophischen Wissens." *Allgemeine Literatur-Zeitung* 92–93 (April 1792): 49–60.

——. "Bruchstücke aus einer Schrift über die Philosophie und ihre Principien." *Philosophisches Journal einer Gesellschaft Teutscher Gelehrten* 3, no. 2 (1795): 95–132.

English Translations

Fichte, J. G. "Review of Aenesidemus." In *Between Kant and Hegel: Texts in the Development of Post-Kantian Idealism.* Edited and translated with introductions by George di Giovanni and H. S. Harris. Albany: State University of New York Press, 1985.

——. *Fichte: Early Philosophical Writings.* Edited and translated by Daniel Breazeale. Ithaca: Cornell University Press, 1988.

——. "Second Introduction." In *Introductions to the Wissenschaftslehre and Other Writings.* Edited and translated by Daniel Breazeale. Indianapolis: Hackett, 1994.

——. "Announcement." In *The Philosophical Rupture between Fichte and Schelling: Texts and Selected Writings.* Albany: State University of New York Press, 2012.

Hegel, Georg Friedrich Wilhelm. *Science of Logic.* Translated by A. V. Miller. Atlantic Highlands, NJ: Humanities Press, 1989.

——. *Lectures on the History of Philosophy*, vol. 3, *Medieval and Modern Philosophy.* Translated by E. S. Haldane and Frances H. Simson. Lincoln: University of Nebraska Press, 1995.

Herder, Johann Gottfried. *Outlines of a Philosophy of the History of Man.* Translated by T. Churchill. London: J. Johnson, St Paul's Churchyard, 1803.

——. *Herder: Philosophical Writings.* Edited and translated by Michael N. Forster. Cambridge: Cambridge University Press, 2002.

——. *Selected Writings on Aesthetics: Johann Gottfried Herder.* Edited and translated by Gregory Moore. Princeton: Princeton University Press, 2006.

Hölderlin, Friedrich. *Essays and Letters on Theory.* Edited and translated by Thomas Pfau. Albany: State University of New York Press, 1988.

——. *Selected Poems and Fragments.* Translated by Michael Hamburger. London: Penguin, 1998.

——. *Odes and Elegies.* Translated by Nick Hoff. Middletown, CT: Wesleyan University Press, 2008.

Kant, Immanuel. *Critique of Pure Reason.* Translated and edited by Paul Guyer and Allen W. Wood. Cambridge: Cambridge University Press, 1998.

——. *Critique of the Power of Judgment.* Edited by Paul Guyer and translated by Paul Guyer and Eric Matthews. Cambridge: Cambridge University Press, 2000.

——. *Prolegomena to Any Future Metaphysics.* Translated by Gary Hatfield. Cambridge: Cambridge University Press, 2004.

Novalis. *The Novices of Sais.* Translated by Ralph Manheim. New York: Curt Valentin, 1949.

——. *Fichte Studies.* Edited and translated by Jane Kneller. Cambridge: Cambridge University Press, 2002.

——. *Notes for a Romantic Encyclopaedia: Das Allgemeine Brouillon.* Edited and translated by David W. Wood. Albany: State University of New York Press, 2007.

Reinhold, Karl Leonard. "The Foundation of Philosophical Knowledge." In *Between Kant and Hegel: Texts in the Development of Post-Kantian Idealism,* edited and translated by George di Giovanni and H. S. Harris. Albany: State University of New York Press, 1985.

Schlegel, Friedrich von. *Lectures on the History of Literature.* London: Bell and Daldy, 1873.

——. "Philosophy of Philology." In "Friedrich Schlegels 'Philosophie der Philologie' mit einer Einleitung herausgegeben von Josef Körner." *Logos 17* (1928).

——. *Friedrich Schlegel: Dialogue on Poetry and Literary Aphorisms.* Edited with an introduction by Ernst Behler and Roman Struc. University Park: Pennsylvania State University Press, 1968.

——. *Friedrich Schlegel's "Lucinde" and the "Fragments."* Translated by Peter Firchow. Minneapolis: University of Minnesota Press, 1971.

Schleiermacher, Friedrich Daniel Ernst. "On the Different Methods of Translation." In *German Romantic Criticism,* edited by A. L. Wilson. New York: Continuum, 1982.

——. *Hermeneutics: The Handwritten Manuscripts.* Edited by J. Duke and J. Forstman. Atlanta: Scholars Press, 1986.

——. *On Religion: Speeches to Its Cultured Despisers.* Translated by Richard Crouter Cambridge: Cambridge University Press, 1988.

——. *Hermeneutics and Criticism.* Edited and translated by A. Bowie. Cambridge: Cambridge University Press, 1998.

——. *The Christian Faith.* Edited by H. R. Mackintosh and J. S. Stewart. Translated by D. M. Baillie et al. London: T&T Clark, 1999.

——. *Essay on a Theory of Social Behavior.* Translated by Peter Foley. In Peter Foley, *Friedrich Schleiermacher's Essay On a Theory of Social Behavior (1799): A Contextual Interpretation.* Lewinston, NY: Edwin Mellen Press, 2006.

OTHER TEXTS AND SECONDARY LITERATURE

Adorno, Theodor W. *Ästhetische Theorie.* Frankfurt am Main: Suhrkamp, 1973.

——. *Negative Dialektik.* Frankfurt am Main: Suhrkamp, 1975

——. *Noten zur Literatur.* Frankfurt am Main: Suhrkamp, 1981.

Alexander, Werner. *Hermeneutica Generalis. Zur Konzeption und Entwicklung der allgemeinen Verstehenslehre im 17. und 18. Jahrhundert*. Stuttgart: M&P Verlag für Wissenschaft und Forschung, 1993.

Ameriks, Karl. *Kant and the Historical Turn: Philosophy as Critical Appropriation*. Oxford: Clarendon Press, 2006.

——. *Kant's Elliptical Path*. Oxford: Clarendon Press, 2012.

——. "History, Idealism, and Schelling." *Internationales Jahrbuch des Deutschen Idealismus/International Yearbook of German Idealism* 10 (forthcoming).

Amrine, Frederick. "The Metamorphosis of the Scientist." *Goethe Yearbook 5* (1990): 188–212.

Arndt, Andreas. *Dialektik und Reflexion. Zur Rekonstruktion des Vernunftbegriffs*. Hamburg: Meiner, 1994.

——. "Geselligkeit und Gesellschaft. Die Geburt der Dialektik aus dem Geist der Konversation in Schleiermachers 'Versuch einer Theorie des geselligen Betragens.'" In *Salons der Romantik. Beiträge eines Wiepersdorfer Kolloquiums zu Theorie und Geschichte des Salons*, edited by Hartwig Schultz, 45–61. Berlin: Walter de Gruyter, 1997.

Arendt, Hannah. "Berlin Salon." In *Essays in Understanding, 1930–1954*. New York: Harcourt Brace & Company, 1994.

Atterbom, Per Daniel. *Reisebilder aus dem romantischen Deutschland. Jugenderinnerungen eines romantischen Dichters und Kunstgelehrten aus den Jahren 1817 bis 1819*. Berlin, 1867; reprint Stuttgart: Steingrüben, 1970.

Austin, J. L. "A Plea for Excuses." In *Philosophical Papers*, edited by J. O. Urmson and G. J. Warnock. Oxford: Oxford University Press, 1979.

Aydede, Murat. "The Language of Thought Hypothesis." In *The Stanford Encyclopedia of Philosophy* (Fall 2010 Edition), edited by Edward N. Zalta, http://plato.stanford.edu/archives/fall2010/entries/language-thought/.

Azzouni, Safia. *Kunst als praktische Wissenschaft: Goethes Wilhelm Meisters Wanderjahre und die Hefte Zur Morphologie*. Cologne: Böhlau Verlag, 2005

Bate, Jonathan. *Romantic Ecology: Wordsworth and the Environmental Tradition*. London: Routledge, 1991.

Bate, W. Jackson. *The Burden of the Past and the English Poet*. Cambridge, MA: Harvard University Press, 1970.

Behler, Ernst. *German Romantic Literary Theory*. Cambridge: Cambridge University Press, 1993.

Behler, Ernst, and Roman Struc. "Introduction." In *Friedrich Schlegel: Dialogue on Poetry and Literary Aphorisms*, edited by Ernst Behler and Roman Struc. University Park: Pennsylvania State University Press, 1968.

Beierwaltes, Werner. *Platonismus und Idealismus*. Frankfurt am Main: Klostermann, 1972.

Beiser, Frederick. *The Fate of Reason: German Philosophy from Kant to Fichte*. Cambridge, MA: Harvard University Press, 1993.

——. *German Idealism: The Struggle against Subjectivism, 1781–1801*. Cambridge, MA: Harvard University Press, 2002.

——. *The Romantic Imperative: The Concept of German Romanticism*. Cambridge, MA: Harvard University Press, 2003.

——. *Diotima's Children: German Aesthetic Rationalism from Leibniz to Lessing.* Oxford: Oxford University Press, 2009.

Bell, John. *The Continuous and the Infinitesimal in Mathematics and Philosophy.* Milan: Polimetrica, 2006.

Ben David, Lazarus. *Versuch einer logischen Auseinandersetzung über das mathematische Unendliche.* Berlin: Petit und Schöne, 1789.

Bergman, S. H. *The Philosophy of Solomon Maimon.* Jerusalem: Magnes, 1967.

Berlin, Isaiah. *The Roots of Romanticism.* Edited by Henry Hardy. Princeton, NJ: Princeton University Press, 1999.

Berman, A. *L'épreuve de l'étranger.* Paris: Gallimard, 1984.

Berman, Russell A., Christina Crosby, Frederick L. de Naples, et al. "Why Major in Literature? What We Say to Our Students." *PMLA* 117, no. 3 (2002): 487–521.

Berner, Christian. *La philosophie de Schleiermacher. Herméneutique. Dialectique. Ethique.* Paris: Les Éditions du Cerf, 1995.

Bernoulli, Jacob. *The Art of Conjecturing, Together with Letter to a Friend on Sets in Court Tennis.* Translated by Edith Dudley Sylla. Baltimore: Johns Hopkins University Press, 2005.

Bernstein, J. M. "Introduction." In *Classic and Romantic German Aesthetics*, edited by J. M. Bernstein. Cambridge: Cambridge University Press, 2003.

Bertino, Andrea Christian. *"Vernatürlichung": Ursprünge von Friedrich Nietzsches Entidealisierung des Menschen, seiner Sprache und seiner Geschichte bei Johann Gottfried Herder.* Berlin: De Gruyter, 2011.

Biedermann, Flodoard Freiherr von. *Goethes Gespräche.* Edited by Wolfgang Herwig. 5 vols. Munich: Deutscher Taschenbuchverlag, 1998.

Bloch, Ernst. *Über Ungleichzeitigkeit, Provinz und Propaganda. Ein Gespräch mit Rainer Traub und Harald Wieser.* In *Gespräche mit Ernst Bloch.* Frankfurt am Main: Suhrkamp, 1975.

——. *The Utopian Function of Art and Literature.* Translated by Jack Zipes and Frank Mecklenburg. Cambridge, MA: MIT Press, 1993.

Bloom, Harold. *The Anxiety of Influence.* Oxford: Oxford University Press, 1973.

Blumenberg, Hans. "Prospect for a Theory of Nonconceptuality." In *Shipwreck with Spectator*, translated by Steven Rendall, 81–102. Cambridge, MA: MIT Press, 1997.

Borsche, Tilman. "Bildworte. Vom Ursprung unserer Begriffe." In *Zwischen Bild und Begriff: Kant und Herder zum Schema*, edited by Ulrich Gaier and Ralf Simon, 55–69. Munich: Wilhelm Fink, 2010.

Bowie, Andrew. *Aesthetics and Subjectivity from Kant to Hegel.* Manchester: Manchester University Press, 2003.

Boyle, Nicholas. *Goethe, the Poet and the Age.* vol. 2, Oxford: Oxford University Press, 2000.

Breazeale, Daniel. "Men at Work: Philosophical Construction in Fichte and Schelling." Accessed April 20, 2013. http://www.europhilosophie.eu/recherche/IMG/pdf/Plenar-Breazeale-beitrag.pdf.

Brandom, Robert. *Making It Explicit: Reasoning, Representing, and Discursive Commitment.* Cambridge, MA.: Harvard University Press, 1998.

Brandt, Reinhard. "Zur Metamorphose der Kantischen Philosophie in der Romantik. Rhapsodische Anmerkungen." In *Kunst und Wissen. Beziehungen zwischen Ästhetik und Erkenntnistheorie im 18. und 19. Jahrhundert*, edited by Astrid Bauereisen, Stephan Pabst, and Achim Vesper, 85–101. Würzburg: Königshausen & Neumann, 2009.

——. "Caspar David Friedrich. Landschaftsmalerei als Seelenführung." In *Kunst und Religion. Ein kontroverses Verhältnis*, edited by Markus Kleinert, 31–55. Mainz: Chorus, 2010.

Bransen, Jan. *The Antinomy of Thought: Maimonian Skepticism and the Relation between Thoughts and Objects*. Dordrecht: Kluwer Academic Publishers, 1991.

Brauers, Claudia. *Perspektiven des Unendlichen. Friedrich Schlegels ästhetische Vermittlungstheorie*. Berlin: Erich Schmidt Verlag, 1996.

Bubbio, Diego Paolo and Paul Redding, ed. *Religion after Kant: God and Culture in the Idealist Era*. Newcastle upon Tyne, UK: Cambridge Scholars Press, 2012.

Budick, Sanford. *Kant and Milton*. Cambridge, MA: Harvard University Press, 2010.

Burge, Tyler. "Concepts, Definitions and Meaning." *Metaphilosophy* 24 (1993): 309–25.

——. *Truth, Thought, Reason: Essays on Frege*. Oxford: Oxford University Press, 2005.

Busch, Werner. *Caspar David Friedrich. Ästhetik und Religion*. Munich: C. H. Beck, 2003.

Buzaglo, Meir. *Solomon Maimon: Monism, Skepticism and Mathematics*. Pittsburgh: University of Pittsburgh Press, 2002.

Cahen-Maurel, Laure. *L'art de romantiser le monde. Caspar David Friedrich et la philosophie romantique*, PhD thesis, Universität München/Université Paris IV, October 2013.

Canguilhem, Georges. *La connaissance de la vie*. Paris: J. Vrin, 1965.

Cavell, Stanley. *Claim of Reason: Wittgenstein, Skepticism, Morality, and Tragedy*. Oxford: Oxford University Press, 1979.

——. *In Quest of the Ordinary: Lines of Skepticism and Romanticism*. Chicago: University of Chicago Press, 1988.

——. *Must We Mean What We Say? Updated Edition*. Cambridge, MA: Harvard University Press, 1969.

——. "The *Investigations*' Everyday Aesthetics of Itself." In *The Literary Wittgenstein*, edited by John Gibson and Wolfgang Huemer. London: Routledge, 2004.

Chaouli, Michel. *The Laboratory of Poetry: Chemistry and Poetics in the Work of Friedrich Schlegel*. Baltimore: Johns Hopkins University Press, 2002.

Clarke, Thompson. "The Legacy of Skepticism." *Journal of Philosophy* 69, no. 20 (1972): 754–69.

Cohen, Hermann. *Die Infinitesimalrechnung und ihre Geschichte*. Berlin: F. Dümmler, 1883.

Conant, James. "Stanley Cavell's Wittgenstein." *Harvard Review of Philosophy* 13, no. 1 (2005): 51–65.

Constantine, David. *Hölderlin*. Oxford: Oxford University Press, 1988.

Corngold, Stanley. "Implications of an Influence: On Hölderlin's Reception of Rousseau." In *Romantic Poetry*, vol. 7, edited by Angela Esterhammer. Amsterdam: John Benjamins Publishing Company, 2002.

Crary, Jonathan. *Techniques of the Observer: On Vision and Modernity in the Nineteenth Century*. London: October/MIT Press, 1990.

Critchley, Simon. "Cavell's 'Romanticism' and Cavell's Romanticism." In *Contending with Stanley Cavell*, edited by Russell B. Goodman, 37–54. Oxford: Oxford University Press, 2005.

——. *The Faith of the Faithless: Experiments in Political Theology*. New York: Verso, 2012.

Crone, Rainer, and Alexandra Von Stosch. *Anish Kapoor*. London: Prestel, 2008.

Crouter, Richard. "Introduction." In Friedrich Schleiermacher, *On Religion: Speeches to Its Cultured Despisers*, edited and translated by Richard Crouter. Cambridge: Cambridge University Press, 1996.

Currie, Gregory. *The Nature of Fiction*. Cambridge: Cambridge University Press, 1990.

Dalhaus, Carl. *The Idea of Absolute Music*. Translated by Roger Lustig. Chicago: University of Chicago Press, 1989.

Danto, Arthur C. *The Transfiguration of the Commonplace: A Philosophy of Art*. Cambridge, MA: Harvard University Press, 1981.

——. *The Philosophical Disenfranchisement of Art*. New York: Columbia University Press, 1984.

Daston, Lorraine, and Peter Galison. *Objectivity*. New York: Zone Books; Cambridge, MA: MIT Press, 2007.

Derrida, Jacques. *The Post Card: From Socrates to Freud and Beyond*. Translated by Alan Bass. Chicago: University of Chicago Press, 1980.

——. "White Mythology: Metaphor in the Text of Philosophy." In *Margins of Philosophy*, 207–72. Translated by Alan Bass. Chicago: University of Chicago Press, 1985.

——. *Glas*. Translated by John P. Leavey and Richard Rand. Lincoln: University of Nebraska Press, 1990.

Descartes, René. *The Philosophical Writings of Descartes*. 2 vols. Translated by J. Cottingham, R. Stoothoff, and D. Murdoch. Cambridge: Cambridge University Press, 1984.

Diamond, Cora. "Losing Your Concepts." *Ethics* 98, no. 2 (1988): 255–77.

Dilthey, Wilhelm. *Schleiermacher's Hermeneutical System in Relation to Earlier Protestant Hermeneutics*. Translated by Theodore Nordenhaug. In *Selected Works*, vol. 4, *Hermeneutics and the Study of History*. Edited by Rudolf A. Makkreel and Frithjof Rodi. Princeton, NJ: Princeton University Press, 1996.

——. *Das Erlebnis und die Dichtung: Lessing, Goethe, Novalis, Hölderlin*. In *Gesammelte Schriften*, vol. 26. Göttingen: Vandenhoeck & Ruprecht, 2005.

Dyck, Martin. "Goethe's Views on Pure Mathematics." *Germanic Review* 31 (1956): 49–69.

——. *Novalis and Mathematics: A Study of Friedrich von Hardenberg's "Fragments on Mathematics" and Its Relation to Magic, Music, Religion, Philosophy, Language, and Literature*. Chapel Hill: University of North Carolina Press, 1960.

Dyson, George. *Turing's Cathedral: The Origins of the Digital Universe*. New York: Random House, 2012.

Eichner, Hans. *Friedrich Schlegel*. New York: Twayne Publishers, 1970.

——. "Germany/Romantisch—Romantik—Romantiker." In *'Romantic' and its Cognates/The European History of a Word*, edited by Hans Eichner. Toronto: University of Toronto Press, 1972.

Eldridge, Richard. *Leading a Human Life: Wittgenstein, Intentionality, and Romanticism*. Chicago: University of Chicago Press, 1997.

——. *The Persistence of Romanticism*. Cambridge: Cambridge University Press, 2001.

Eldridge, Hannah Vandegrift. "The Influence of Anxiety: Poetology as Symptom." *German Quarterly* 86, no. 4 (Fall 2013): 443–62.

Ende, Helga. *Der Konstruktionsbegriff im Umkreis des deutschen Idealismus*. Meisenheim am Glan: Anton Hain, 1973.

Escoubas, Eliane. "Kant or the Simplicity of the Sublime." In *Of the Sublime: Presence in Question*, edited by Jean-François Courtine, translated by Jeffrey S. Librett, 55–70. Albany: State University of New York Press, 1993.

———. "La tragédie du paysage: Caspar David Friedrich." In *L'espace pictural*, 69–90. Paris: Les Belles Lettres, 2011.

Euler, Leonhard. *Briefe an eine deutsche Prinzessin. Philosophische Auswahl*. Leipzig: Verlag Philipp Reclam, 1968.

———. *Foundations of Differential Calculus*. Translated by John D. Blanton. New York: Springer Verlag, 2000.

Feagin, Susan. "Imagining Emotions and Appreciating Fiction." In *Emotion and the Arts*, edited by Mette Hjort and Sue Laver, 50–62. New York: Oxford University Press, 1997.

Fiesel, E. *Die Sprachphilosophie der deutschen Romantik*. Tübingen: J. C. B. Mohr, 1927.

Fohrmann, Jürgen, and Wilhelm Voßkamp, eds. *Wissenschaft und Nation. Studien zur Entstehungsgeschichte der deutschen Literaturwissenschaft*. Munich: Wilhelm Fink, 1991.

———. *Wissenschaftsgeschichte der Germanistik im 19. Jahrhundert*. Stuttgart: Metzler, 1994.

Foley, Peter. *Friedrich Schleiermacher's "Essay on a Theory of Sociable Behavior" (1799): A Contextual Interpretation*. Lewiston: Edwin Mellon Press, 2006.

Förster, Eckart. "Goethe and the 'Auge des Geistes.'" *Deutsche Vierteljahrsschrift für Literaturwissenschaft und Geistesgeschichte* 75 (2001): 87–101.

———. *Die 25 Jahre der Philosophie: Eine systematische Rekonstruktion*. Frankfurt am Main: Klostermann, 2011.

———. *The Twenty-Five Years of Philosophy*. Translated by Brady Bowman. Cambridge, MA: Harvard University Press, 2012.

Forster, Michael. *After Herder: Philosophy of Language in the German Tradition*. Oxford: Oxford University Press, 2010.

———. *German Philosophy of Language: From Schlegel to Hegel and Beyond*. Oxford: Oxford University Press, 2011.

———. "Herders Beitrag zur Entstehung der Idee *romantisch*." In *Die Aktualität der Romantik*, edited by M. N. Forster and K. Vieweg. Berlin: LIT, 2012.

———. "The German Romantic Re-Thinking of Ancient Tragedy" (forthcoming).

Foucault, Michel. *The Order of Things: An Archaeology of the Human Sciences*. New York: Vintage Books, 1994.

Frank, Hilmar. *Aussichten ins Unermessliche*. Berlin: Akademie Verlag, 2004.

Frank, Manfred. *Das individuelle Allgemeine. Textstrukturierung und Textinterpretation nach Schleiermacher*. Frankfurt am Main: Suhrkamp, 1977.

———. *Das Sagbare und das Unsagbare*. Frankfurt am Main: Suhrkamp, 1989.

———. *Der kommende Gott: Vorlesungen über die Neue Mythologie*. Frankfurt am Main: Suhrkamp, 1982.

———. *Was ist Neostrukturalismus?* Frankfurt am Main: Suhrkamp, 1984.

———. *Einführung in die frühromantische Ästhetik*. Frankfurt am Main: Suhrkamp, 1989.

———. *Kaltes Herz unendliche Fahrt*. Frankfurt am Main: Suhrkamp, 1989.

———. "Wittgensteins Gang in die Dichtung." In *Wittgenstein. Literat und Philosoph*, edited by Manfred Frank and Gianfranco Soldati, 7–72. Pfullingen: Neske, 1989.

———. *Stil in der Philosophie*. Stuttgart: Reclam, 1992.

———. *Conditio moderna*. Stuttgart: Reclam, 1993.

——. *"Unendliche Annäherung." Die Anfänge der philosophischen Frühromantik.* Frankfurt am Main: Suhrkamp, 1997.

——. *Selbstgefühl. Eine historisch-systematische Erkundung.* Frankfurt am Main: Suhrkamp, 2002.

——. *Auswege aus dem deutschen Idealismus.* Frankfurt am Main: Suhrkamp, 2007.

——. "Schelling's Late Return to Kant: On the Difference between Absolute Idealism and Philosophical Romanticism." *Internationales Jahrbuch des Deutschen Idealismus / International Yearbook of German Idealism: Romanticism* 6, edited by Karl Ameriks and Fred Rush. Berlin: Walter de Gruyter, 2009.

——. "'Religionslose Kathedralen im ewigen Winter'—Der Moderne Caspar David Friedrich im frühromantischen Kontext." In *Szenen des Heiligen*, edited by Cai Werntgen, 112–60. Berlin: Insel Verlag, 2011.

Frank, Manfred, and Gerhard Kurz, eds. *Materialien zu Schellings philosophischen Anfängen.* Frankfurt am Main: Suhrkamp, 1975.

Frank, Manfred, Ulrich Schnabel, and Thomas Assheuer. "Ein Gespräch mit dem Tübinger Philosophen Manfred Frank über die Illusionen der Hirnforschung und ihre zweifelhaften politischen Folgen." *Die Zeit*, August 29, 2009. http://www.zeit.de/2009/36/Hirnforschung

Freudenthal, Gideon. "Maimon's Philosophical Program. Understanding versus Intuition." *Internationales Jahrbuch des Deutschen Idealismus / International Yearbook of German Idealism* 8 (2010): 83–105.

Friedman, Michael. "Kant—Naturphilosophie—Electromagnetism." In *Hans Christian Ørsted and the Romantic Legacy in Science: Ideas, Disciplines, Practices*, edited by Robert Brian, Robert Cohen, and Ole Knudsen, 135–58. Dordrecht: Springer, 2007.

Gabriel, Gottfried. "Literarische Form und nicht-Propositionale Erkenntnis in der Philosophie." In *Literarische Formen der Philosophie*, edited by Gottfried Gabriel and Christiane Schildknecht, 1–25. Stuttgart: Metzler, 1990.

——. *Zwischen Logik und Literatur. Erkenntnisformen von Dichtung, Philosophie und Wissenschaft.* Stuttgart: Metzler, 1991.

Gadamer, Hans-Georg. *Wahrheit und Methode.* Tübingen: Mohr, 1990.

——. *Truth and Method.* Translated by Joel Weinsheimer and Donald G. Marshall. New York: Continuum, 2003.

Gaier, Ulrich. "Metaschematisieren? Hieroglyphe und Periodus." In *Zwischen Bild und Begriff: Kant und Herder zum Schema*, edited by Ulrich Gaier and Ralf Simon, 19–53. Munich: Wilhelm Fink, 2010.

Gasparov, Boris. *Beyond Pure Reason: Ferdinand de Saussure's Philosophy of Language and Its Early Romantic Antecedents.* New York: Columbia University Press, 2013.

Girard, René. "Conversion in Christianity and Literature." In *Mimesis & Theory: Essays on Literature and Criticism, 1953–2005*, edited by Robert Doran, 263–73. Stanford: Stanford University Press, 2008.

Gibson, John. *Fiction and the Weave of Life.* Oxford: Oxford University Press, 2007.

——. Wolfgang Huemer, and Luca Pocci, eds. *A Sense of the World: Essays on Fiction, Narrative, and Knowledge.* New York: Routledge, 2007.

Gigante, Denise. *Life: Organic Form and Romanticism.* New Haven: Yale University Press, 2009.

Gipper, H., and P. Schmitter. *Sprachwissenschaft und Sprachphilosophie im Zeitalter der Romantik*. Tübingen: Gunter Narr, 1985.

Gjesdal, Kristin. *Gadamer and the Legacy of German Idealism*. Cambridge: Cambridge University Press, 2009.

Glock, Hans-Johann. "Schopenhauer and Wittgenstein." In *The Cambridge Companion to Schopenhauer*, edited by Christopher Janaway, 422–58. New York: Cambridge University Press, 2000.

Goodman, Kevis. *Georgic Modernity and British Romanticism*. Cambridge: Cambridge University Press, 2004.

Gorodeisky, Keren. "(Re)encountering Individuality: Schlegel's Romantic Imperative as a Response to Nihilism." *Inquiry* 54, no. 6 (2011): 567–90.

Gould, Timothy. *Hearing Things: Voice and Method in the Writing of Stanley Cavell*. Chicago: University of Chicago Press, 1998.

Graff, Gerald. *Professing Literature. An Institutional History*. Chicago: University of Chicago Press, 1989.

Grattan-Guinness, I., ed. *From Calculus to Set Theory, 1630–1910*. London: Duckworth, 1980.

Grave, Johannes. *Caspar David Friedrich und die Theorie des Erhabenen*. Weimar: VDG-Verlag, 2001.

Hamburger, Käte. *Philosophie der Dichter: Novalis, Schiller, Rilke*. Stuttgart: Kohlhammer, 1966.

Hamburger, Michael. "The Sublime Art: Notes on Milton and Hölderlin." In *Contraries: Studies in German Literature*. New York: E. P. Dutton, 1957.

Hansen, Frank-Peter. *Das älteste Systemprogramm des deutschen Idealismus. Rezeptionsgeschichte und Interpretation*. Berlin: de Gruyter, 1989.

Hartmann, Nicolai. *Die Philosophie des deutschen Idealismus*. Berlin: de Gruyter, 1923.

Hausser, Ronald. *Computational Linguistics and Talking Robots*. Berlin: Springer, 2011.

Haym, Rudolf. *Die romantische Schule*. Berlin: Gaertner, 1882.

Hazony, Yoram. *The Philosophy of Hebrew Scripture*. Cambridge: Cambridge University Press, 2012.

Heidegger, Martin. *Gesamtausgabe*. 2/52. Frankfurt am Main: Klostermann, 1982.

———. *Vorträge und Aufsätze*. 10th ed. Stuttgart: Klett-Cotta, 2004.

Heise, Ursla. *Nach der Natur. Das Artensterben und die moderne Kultur*. Frankfurt am Main: Suhrkamp, 2010.

Henrich, Dieter. "Hölderlin über Urteil und Seyn: Eine Studie zur Entstehung des Idealismus." *Hölderlin-Jahrbuch* 14 (1965–66): 73–96.

———. *Fichtes ursprüngliche Einsicht*. Frankfurt am Main: Klostermann, 1967.

———. "Hölderlin in Jena." In *The Course of Remembrance and Other Essays on Hölderlin*, edited by Eckart Förster, 90–118. Translated by Taylor Carman. Stanford: Stanford University Press, 1997.

———. *Konstellationen: Probleme und Debatten am Ursprung der idealistischen Philosophie (1789–1795)*. Stuttgart: Klett-Cotta, 1991.

———. *Der Grund im Bewußtsein. Untersuchungen zu Hölderlins Denken*. Stuttgart: Klett-Cotta, 1992.

———. *Grundlegung aus dem Ich. Untersuchungen zur Vorgeschichte des Idealismus Tübingen-Jena (1790–1794)*. Frankfurt am Main: Suhrkamp, 2004.

Higginbotham, James. "Conceptual Competence." *Philosophical Issues* 9 (1998): 149–62.

Hobbes, Thomas. "Elements of Philosophy." In *The English Works of Thomas Hobbes of Malmesbury*, edited by Sir William Molesworth, vol. 1. London: John Bohn, 1839.

Hoffbauer, Johann Christoph. *Semiological Investigations, or, Topics Pertaining to the General Theory of Signs.* Edited, translated, and with an introduction by Robert E. Innis. Amsterdam: J. Benjamins, 1991 (1789).

Hofstetter, Michael J. *The Romantic Idea of a University: England and Germany, 1770–1850.* New York: St. Martin's Press, 2001.

Holland, Jocelyn. *German Romanticism and Science: The Procreative Poetics of Goethe, Novalis, and Ritter.* New York: Routledge, 2009.

Hühn, Helmut. "Bilder des Lebendigen. Zur Erkenntnisfunktion der dichterischen 'Mythe' im Werk Hölderlins." In *Darstellung und Erkenntnis*, edited by Brady Bowman, 117–33. Paderborn: Mentis, 2007.

Huyssen, Andreas. *Die frühromantische Konzeption von Übersetzung und Aneignung.* Zurich: Atlantis, 1969.

Irmscher, Hans Dietrich. "Witz und Analogie als Instrumente des entdeckenden Erkennens." In *"Weitstrahlsinniges" Denken: Studien zu Johann Gottfried Herder von Hans Dietrich Irmscher*, edited by Marion Heinz and Violetta Stolz, 206–35. Würzburg: Königshausen & Neumann, 2009.

Jackson, Noel. *Science and Sensation in British Romanticism.* Cambridge: Cambridge University Press, 2008.

Jacob, François. *The Logic of Life: A History of Heredity.* Translated by Betty E. Spillman. New York: Pantheon, 1973.

Jaeschke, Walter. *Hegel-Handbuch.* Stuttgart: Metzler, 2003.

Jahnke, Hans Niels. "Mathematics and Culture: The Case of Novalis." *Science in Context* 4 (1991): 279–95.

——. "Mathematik und Romantik." In *Disziplinen im Kontext*, edited by Volker Peckhaus and Christian Thiel. Munich: Wilhelm Fink Verlag, 1999.

Jamme, Christoph, and Hans Schneider, eds. *Mythologie der Vernunft. Hegels ältestes Systemprogramm des deutschen Idealismus.* Frankfurt am Main: Suhrkamp, 1988.

Jusdanis, Gregory. "Two Cheers for Aesthetic Autonomy." *Cultural Critique* 61 (2005): 22–54.

Kapoor, Anish. "'I Don't Know Where I'm Going.'" Interview with Alastair Sooke, *The Telegraph*, September 26, 2006. http://www.telegraph.co.uk/culture/art/3655568/I-dont-know-where-Im-going.html

Kim, Jaegwon. "Multiple Realization and the Metaphysics of Reduction." In *Supervenience and Mind: Selected Philosophical Essays.* New York: Cambridge University Press, 1993.

——. *Mind in a Physical World: An Essay on the Mind-Body Problem and Mental Causation.* Cambridge: MIT Press, 2000.

Kirchner, Erwin. *Philosophie der Romantik.* Jena: Diederichs, 1906.

Kittler, Wolf. "Falling after the Fall: The Analysis of the Infinite in Kleist's *Marionettentheater*." In *Heinrich von Kleist and Modernity*, edited by Bernd Fischer and Tim Mehigan, 279–94. Rochester, NY: Camden House, 2011.

Kneller, Jane. *Kant and the Power of Imagination.* Cambridge: Cambridge University Press, 2007.

——. "Feminism." In *Oxford Handbook to German Idealism*, edited by Michael Forster and Kristin Gjesdal. Oxford: Oxford University Press, forthcoming.

Knuth, Donald E. *The Art of Computer Programming, vol. 4, Generating All Trees: History of Combinatorial Generation*. Upper Saddle River, NJ: Pearson Education, 2006.

Kofman, Sarah. *Nietzsche and Metaphor*. Translated by Duncan Large. Stanford: Stanford University Press, 1993.

Korff, H. A. *Geist der Goethezeit*. Leipzig: Koehler und Amelang, 1964.

Koselleck, Reinhart. "The Status of the Enlightenment in German History." In *The Cultural Values of Europe*, edited by Hans Joas and Klaus Wiegandt, 253–64. Liverpool: Liverpool University Press, 2008.

Kroeber, Karl. *Ecological Literary Criticism: Romantic Imagining and the Biology of Mind*. New York: Columbia University Press, 1994.

Kuzniar, Alice. *Delayed Endings: Nonclosure in Novalis and Hölderlin*. Athens: University of Georgia Press, 1987.

Kvanvig, Jonathan. *The Value of Knowledge and the Pursuit of Understanding*. Cambridge: Cambridge University Press, 2003.

Lacoue-Labarth, Philippe, and Jean-Luc Nancy. *The Literary Absolute: The Theory of Literature in German Romanticism*. Translated by Philip Barnard and Cheryl Lester. Albany: State University of New York Press, 1988.

Lafont, Christina. *The Linguistic Turn in Hermeneutic Philosophy*. Translated by José Medina. Cambridge, MA: MIT Press, 1999.

Lagerlund, Henrik. "Leibniz (and Ockham) on the Language of Thought, or How the True Metaphysics Is Derived from the True Logic." In *Categories of Being: Essays on Metaphysics and Logic*, edited by Leila Haaparanta and Heikki J. Koskinen, 99–108. Oxford: Oxford University Press, 2012.

Lamarque, Peter. "Learning from Literature." In *A Sense of the World: Essays on Fiction, Narrative, and Knowledge*, edited by John Gibson, Wolfgang Huemer, and Luca Pocci, 13–23. New York: Routledge, 2007.

Lambert, Johann Heinrich. *Neues Organon oder Gedanken über die Erforschung und Bezeichnung des Wahren und dessen Unterscheidung vom Irrthum und Schein*. Leipzig: Johann Mendler, 1764. http://www.kuttaka.org/~JHL/L1764a.html.

Larmore, Charles. *The Romantic Legacy*. New York: Columbia University Press, 1996.

——. "Hölderlin and Novalis." In *The Cambridge Companion to German Idealism*, edited by Karl Ameriks, 141–60. Cambridge: Cambridge University Press, 2000.

Latour, Bruno. *We Have Never Been Modern*. Cambridge, MA: Harvard University Press, 1993.

Lavine, Shaughan. *Understanding the Infinite*. Cambridge, MA: Harvard University Press, 1994.

Leibniz, G. W. *Logical Papers: A Selection*. Translated and edited by G. H. R. Parkinson. Oxford: Oxford University Press, 1966.

Lenzen, Wolfgang. "Leibniz's Logic." In *Handbook of the History of Logic*, vol. 3, *The Rise of Modern Logic from Leibniz to Frege*, edited by Dov. M. Gabbay and John Woods, 1–84. Amsterdam: Elsevier, 2004.

Locke, John. *An Essay Concerning Human Understanding*. Edited by Alexander Campbell Fraser. 2 vols. New York: Dover, 1959.

Losonsky, M. "Leibniz's Adamic Language of Thought." *Journal of the History of Philosophy* 30 (1992): 523–643.

Lovejoy, Arthur. "On the Discriminations of Romanticism." *Proceedings of the Modern Language Association* 39 (1924): 229–53. Reprinted in Lovejoy, *Essays in the History of Ideas,* 228–53. New York: Capricorn, 1960.

——. "Schiller and the Genesis of German Romanticism." In *Essays in the History of Ideas,* 207–27.

Maap, Jaap. *Philosophical Languages in the Seventeenth Century: Dalgarno, Wilkins, Leibniz.* Dordrecht: Kluwer, 2004.

Maatsch, Jonas. *"Naturgeschichte der Philosopheme." Frühromantische Wissensordnungen im Kontext.* Heidelberg: Winter Verlag, 2007.

MacLeish, Archibald. "Ars Poetica." In *Collected Poems, 1917–1982.* Boston: Houghton Mifflin, 1985 (1926).

Maimon, Salomon. *Essay on Transcendental Philosophy.* Translated by Nick Midgley, Henry Somers-Hall, Alistair Welchman, and Merten Reglitz. New York: Continuum, 2010.

de Man, Paul. "The Image of Rousseau in the Poetry of Hölderlin." In *The Rhetoric of Romanticism.* New York: Columbia University Press, 1984.

Martyn, David. "Figures of the Mean: Freedom, Progress, and the Law of Statistical Averages in Kleist's 'Allerneuester Erziehungsplan.'" *Germanic Review* 85 (2010): 44–62.

McClane, Maureen. *Romanticism and the Human Sciences: Poetry, Population, and the Discourse of the Species.* Cambridge: Cambridge University Press, 2000.

McKibben, Bill. *The End of Nature.* London: Viking, 1990.

McKusick, James. "Coleridge and the Economy of Nature." *Studies in Romanticism* 35 (1996): 375–92.

McLaughlin, Peter. *Kant's Critique of Teleology in Biological Explanation.* Lewiston, ME: Edwin Mellen Press, 1990.

Meckenstock, Günter, ed. *Schleiermachers Bibliothek.* Berlin: de Gruyter, 1993.

Millán, Elizabeth and John H. Smith, eds. *Goethe Yearbook.* vol. 18 (2011).

Millán-Zaibert, Elizabeth. "The Revival of Frühromantik in the Anglophone World." *Philosophy Today,* Spring 2005: 96–117.

——. *Friedrich Schlegel and the Emergence of Romantic Philosophy.* Albany: State University of New York Press, 2007.

Millikan, Ruth. *Language, Thought, and Other Biological Categories.* Cambridge: MIT Press, 1984.

——. *Language: A Biological Model.* Oxford: Oxford University Press, 2005.

Marcuse, Herbert. *The Aesthetic Dimension.* Translated by Herbert Marcuse and Erica Sherover. Boston: Beacon Press, 1977.

Marion, Jean-Luc. *The Idol and Distance: Five Studies.* New York: Fordham University Press, 2001.

Moore, G. E. *Philosophical Papers.* London: Allen and Unwin; New York: Macmillan, 1959.

Moran, Richard. "The Expression of Feeling in Imagination." *Philosophical Review* 103, no. 1 (1994): 75–106.

Morton, Timothy. *Ecology without Nature: Rethinking Environmental Aesthetics.* Cambridge, MA: Harvard University Press, 2007.

——. "Coexistence and Coexistents: Ecology without a World." In *Ecocritical Theory: New European Approaches,* edited by Axel Goodbody and Kate Rigby, 168–80. Charlottesville: University of Virginia Press, 2011.

Nahin, Paul J. *The Logician and the Engineer: How George Boole and Claude Shannon Created the Information Age*. Princeton, NJ: Princeton University Press, 2013.

Nassar, Dalia. *The Romantic Absolute: Being and Knowing in German Romantic Philosophy, 1795–1804*. Chicago: University of Chicago Press, 2013.

——. "Schelling und die Frühromantik: Das Unendliche und das Endliche im Kunstwerk." Accessed April 20, 2013. http://www.academia.edu/656856/Schelling_und_die_Fruhromantik_Das_Unendliche_und_das_Endliche_im_Kunstwerk.

——. "Sensibility and Organic Unity: Kant, Goethe and the Plasticity of Cognition." *Intellectual History Review* (forthcoming 2014).

Neubauer, John. *Symbolismus und symbolische Logik*. Munich: Wilhelm Fink, 1978.

Nietzsche, Friedrich. "Über Wahrheit und Lüge im außermoralischen Sinn." In *Kritische Gesamtausgabe*. Edited by G. Colli and M. Montinari. Berlin: Walter de Gruyter, 1975.

——. "On Truth and Lying in a Non-Moral Sense." In *The Birth of Tragedy and Other Writings*, edited by Raymond Guess and Ronald Speirs, translated by Ronald Speirs, 139–53. Cambridge: Cambridge University Press, 1999.

Norman, Judith. "The Work of Art in German Romanticism." *Internationales Jahrbuch des Deutschen Idealismus / International Yearbook of German Idealism* 6 (2008): 59–79.

Nuzzo, Angelica. *Kant and the Unity of Reason*. West Lafayette, IN: Purdue University Press, 2005.

O'Regan, Cyril. "Aesthetic Idealism and its relation to theological formation: reception and critique." In *The Impact of Idealism. The Legacy of Post-Kantian German Thought, vol. 4: Religion*, edited by Nicholas Adams, 142-66. Cambridge: Cambridge University Press, 2013.

Pater, Walter. *The Renaissance: Studies in Art and Poetry*. Berkeley: University of California Press, 1980 (1893).

Pinkard, Terry. "Subjects, Objects, and Normativity: What Is It Like to Be an Agent?" *Internationales Jahrbuch des Deutschen Idealismus / International Yearbook of German Idealism* 1 (2003): 201–19.

Plantinga, Alvin, and Nicholas Wolterstorff. *Faith and Rationality*. Notre Dame, IN: University of Notre Dame Press, 1983.

Pöggeler, Otto. *Hegels Kritik der Romantik*. Bonn: Friedrich Wilhelms-Universität, 1956.

——. "Hegel, der Verfasser des ältesten Systemprogramms des deutschen Idealismus." *Hegel-Studien* 4 (1969): 17–32.

Pollack-Milgate, Howard. "Novalis and Mathematics Revisited." *Athäneum: Jahrbuch für Romantik* 7 (1997): 113–40.

Prager, Brad. "Kant in Caspar David Friedrich's Frames." *Art History* 25 (2002): 68–86.

Putnam, Hilary. *Representation and Reality*. Cambridge, MA: MIT Press, 1991.

Redding, Paul. *Continental Idealism: Leibniz to Nietsche*. London: Routledge, 2009.

Reill, Peter Hanns. *Vitalizing Nature in the Enlightenment*. Berkeley: University of California Press, 2005.

Richards, Robert. *The Romantic Conception of Life: Science and Philosophy in the Age of Goethe*. Chicago: University of Chicago Press, 2002.

Richter, Gerhard. "Aesthetic Theory and Nonpropositional Content in Adorno." *New German Critique* 97 (2006): 119–35.

Ricoeur, Paul. "Schleiermacher's Hermeneutics." *The Monist* 60, no. 2 (1977): 181–97.

Rieger, Reinhold. *Interpretation und Wissen. Zur philosophischen Begründung der Hermeneutik bei Friedrich Schleiermacher und ihrem geschichtlichen Hintergrund.* Schleiermacher-Archiv, vol. 6. Berlin: Walter de Gruyter, 1988.

Rigby, Kate. *Topographies of the Sacred: The Poetics of Place in European Romanticism.* Charlottesville: University of Virginia Press, 2004.

——. "Writing after Nature." *Australian Humanities Review* 39–40 (2006). www.australianhumanitiesreview.org/archive/Issue-September-2006.rigby.html

Risser, Wilhelm. *Die Logik der Neuzeit, vol. 2, 1640–1780.* Stuttgart-Bad Cannstatt: Frommann, 1970.

Roe, Shirley A. *Matter, Life, and Generation: 18th-Century Embryology and the Haller-Wolff Debate.* Cambridge: Cambridge University Press, 1981.

Rosenblum, Robert. *Modern Painting and the Northern Romantic Tradition: Friedrich to Rothko.* New York: Harper & Row, 1975.

Rosenzweig, Franz. *Kleinere Schriften.* Berlin: Schocken, 1937.

Rush, Fred. Review of Elizabeth Millán-Zaibert's *Philosophical Foundations of Early German Romanticism. Notre Dame Philosophical Review*, December 9, 2004. http://ndpr.nd.edu/news/23011-the-philosophical-foundation-of-early-german-romanticism.

Sandifer, C. Edward. *How Euler Did It.* Washington, DC: Mathematical Association of America, 2000.

Santner, Eric. "Chronology." In Hölderlin, *Hyperion and Selected Poems.* New York: Continuum, 2002.

Saussure, Ferdinand de. *Course in General Linguistics.* Edited by Perry Meisel and Haun Saussy. Translated by Wade Baskin. New York: Columbia University Press, 2011.

Schalkwyk, David. "Fiction as 'Grammatical' Investigation: A Wittgensteinian Account." *Journal of Aesthetics and Art Criticism* 53, no. 3 (1995): 287–98.

——. *Literature and the Touch of the Real.* Newark: University of Delaware Press, 2004.

Schefer, Olivier. *Résonances du romantisme.* Brussels: La Lettre volée, 2005.

Schildknecht, Christiane. *Sense and Self: Perspectives on Nonpropositionality.* Paderborn: Mentis Verlag, 2002.

——. "'Ein seltsam wunderbarer Anstrich'? Nichtpropositionale Erkenntnis und ihre Darstellungsformen." In *Darstellung und Erkenntnis*, edited by Brady Bowman, 31–43. Paderborn: Mentis, 2007.

Scholtz, Gunter. *Ethik und Hermeneutik. Schleiermachers Grundlegung der Geisteswissenschaften.* Frankfurt am Main: Suhrkamp, 1995.

Schopenhauer, Arthur. *Werke in fünf Bänden.* Edited by Ludger Lütkehaus. Zurich: Haffmans, 2006.

Searle, John. *The Rediscovery of the Mind.* Cambridge: MIT Press, 1992.

Seyhan, Azade. "What Is Romanticism, and Where Did It Come From?" In *Cambridge Companion to German Romanticism*, edited by Nicholas Saul, 1–20. Cambridge: Cambridge University Press, 2009.

Shabel, Lisa. *Mathematics in Kant's Critical Philosophy.* New York: Routledge, 2003.

Sieroka, Norman. *Umgebungen: Symbolischer Konstruktivismus im Anschluss an Hermann Weyl und Fritz Medicus.* Zurich: Chronos, 2010.

Smith, John H. *Dialogues between Faith and Reason: The Death and Return of God in Modern German Thought.* Ithaca: Cornell University Press, 2011.

——. "Living Religion as Vanishing Mediator: Schleiermacher, Early Romanticism, and Idealism." *German Quarterly* 84:2 (2011): 137–158.

——. "The Infinitesimal as Theological Principle: Representing the Paradoxes of God and Nothing in Cohen, Rosenzweig, Scholem, and Barth." *MLN* 127 (2012): 562–88.

——. "Leibniz Reception around 1800: Monadic Vitalism and Harmony in Schleiermacher's *Reden über die Religion* and Schlegel's *Lucinde*." In *Religion, Reason, and Culture in the Age of Goethe*, edited by Elizabeth Kimmerer and Patricia Simpson. Rochester, NY: Camden House (forthcoming).

Speiser, Andreas. "Die Grundlagen der Mathematik von Plato bis Fichte." *Eranos Jahrbuch* 14 (1946): 11–38.

——. *Ein Parmenideskommentar—Studien zur platonischen Dialektik*. 2nd ed. Leipzig: K. F. Koehler, 1959.

Stengel, Friedmann. "Theosophie in der Aufklarung." In *Offenbarung und Episteme: Zur europäischen Wirkung Jakob Böhmes im 17. und 18. Jahrhundert*, edited by Wilhelm Kühlmann and Friedrich Vollhardt, 513–48. Berlin: Walter de Gruyter, 2012.

Stolnitz, Jerome. "On the Cognitive Triviality of Art." *British Journal of Aesthetics* 32, no. 3 (1992): 191–200.

Surber, Jere Paul, ed. *Metacritique: The Linguistic Assault on German Idealism*. Amherst, NY: Humanity Books, 2001.

Szondi, Peter. *Schriften I*. Frankfurt am Main: Suhrkamp, 1978.

——. "Schleiermacher's Hermeneutics Today." In *On Textual Understanding and Other Essays*. Translated by Harvey Mendelsohn. Minneapolis: University of Minnesota Press, 1986.

——. *Introduction to Literary Hermeneutics*. Translated by Martha Woodmansee. Cambridge: Cambridge University Press, 1995.

Terezakis, Katie. *The Immanent Word: The Turn to Language in German Philosophy, 1759–1801*. New York: Routledge, 2007.

Thiel, Christian. *Philosophie und Mathematik. Eine Einführung in ihre Wechselwirkungen und in die Philosophie der Mathematik*. Darmstadt: Wissenschaftliche Buchgesellschaft, 1995.

Thielke, Peter. "Recent Work on Early German Idealism, 1781–1801." In *Journal of the History of Philosophy* 51, no. 2 (2013): 149–192.

Thompson, Scott J. "Friedrich Hölderlin: A Chronology of His Life." http://www.wben-jamin.org/hoelderlin_chron.html.

Timmermans, Benoît. "Novalis et la réforme des mathématiques." In *Modernité Romantique*, edited by Augustin Dumont and Laurent van Eynde, 73–88. Paris: Éditions Kimé, 2011.

Trabant, J. *Apeliotes oder der Sinn der Sprache. Wilhelm von Humboldts Sprachbild*. Berlin: Akademie Verlag, 1986.

Tuinen, Sjoerd van, and Niamh McDonnell, eds. *Deleuze and the Fold: A Critical Reader*. New York: Palgrave Macmillan, 2010.

Unger, Richard. *Hölderlin's Major Poetry: The Dialectics of Unity*. Bloomington: Indiana University Press, 1975.

Valenza, Robin. *Literature, Language, and the Rise of the Intellectual Disciplines*. Cambridge: Cambridge University Press, 2009.

Venuti, L. *The Translator's Invisibility: A History of Translation*. London: Routledge, 1995.

Vila, Anne C. *Enlightenment and Pathology: Sensibility in the Literature and Medicine of Eighteenth-Century France*. Baltimore: Johns Hopkins University Press, 1998.

Virmond, Wolfgang. "Neue Textgrundlagen zu Schleiermachers früher Hermeneutik. Prolegomena zur kritischen Edition." In *Schleiermacher-Archiv*, vol. 1, part 2, *Internationaler Schleiermacherkongreß 1984*, edited by Kurt-Victor Selge et. al. Berlin: Walter de Gruyter, 1985.

Vuillemin, Jules. *La philosophie de l'algèbre*. Paris: PUF, 1993.

Waibel, Violetta. *Hölderlin und Fichte, 1794–1800*. Paderborn: Schöningh, 2000.

Wallace, David Foster. *Everything and More: A Compact History of Infinity*. New York: Norton: 2003.

Walton, Kendall. "Fearing Fictions." *Journal of Philosophy* 75 (1978): 5–27.

——. *Mimesis as Make-Believe: On the Foundations of the Representational Arts*. Cambridge, MA: Harvard University Press, 1990.

——. "Spelunking, Simulation, and Slime: On Being Moved by Fiction." In *Emotion and the Arts*, edited by Mette Hjort and Sue Laver, 37–49. New York: Oxford University Press, 1997.

Wach, Joachim. *Das Verstehen. Gründzüge einer Geschichte der hermeneutischen Theorie im 19. Jahrhundert*. 3 vols. Tübingen: J. C. B. Mohr, 1926–33.

Walzel, Oskar. *German Romanticism*. New York: Putnam, 1932.

Watkins, Eric. "The Antinomy of Teleological Judgment." *Kant Yearbook* 1 (2009): 197–222.

Weber, Max. "Science as a Vocation." In *The Vocation Lectures*, 1–31. Indianapolis: Hackett, 2004.

Weissberg, Liliane. "Fußnoten. Zum Ort der ästhetischen Erfahrung in Lazarus Bendavids Selbstbiographie." In *Berliner Aufklärung*, edited by Ursula Goldenbaum and Alexander Koženina, 231–53. Berlin: Wehrhahn Verlag, 1999.

——. "Lazarus Bendavid." Lexikon deutsch-jüdischer Literatur, edited by Andreas Kilcher. 48–50. Stuttgart: J. B. Metzler Verlag, 2000.

Weyl, Hermann. *Das Kontinuum*. Leipzig: Veit & Comp., 1919.

Williams, Raymond. *Culture and Society, 1780–1950*. New York: Columbia University Press, 1983.

Wittgenstein, Ludwig. *Culture and Value*. Edited by G. H. von Wright in collaboration with Heikki Nyman. Translated by Peter Winch. Chicago: University of Chicago Press, 1980.

——. *Remarks on the Philosophy of Psychology*. Vol. 1. Edited by G. E. M. Anscombe and G. H. von Wright. Translated by G. E. M. Anscombe. Oxford: Blackwell, 1980.

——. *Philosophical Investigations*. Translated by G. E. M. Anscombe. Oxford: Blackwell, 1997.

——. *Tractatus Logico-Philosophicus*. London: Routledge, 2001.

Witzel, E. J. Michael. *The Origins of the World's Mythologies*. Oxford: Oxford University Press, 2012.

Wolfe, Charles T. "Why Was There No Controversy over Life in the Scientific Revolution?" In *Controversies within the Scientific Revolution*, edited by V. Boantza and M. Dascal, 187–221. Amsterdam: John Benjamins, 2011.

Wood, David W. Introduction to *Notes for a Romantic Encyclopaedia: Das Allgemeine Brouillon*, edited by David W. Wood. Albany: State University of New York Press, 2007.

——. *"Mathesis of the Mind": A Study of Fichte's Wissenschaftslehre and Geometry*. New York and Amsterdam: Rodopi, 2012.

———. "From 'Fichticizing' to 'Romanticizing': Fichte and Novalis on the Activities of Philosophy and Art." *Fichte-Studien* 42 (2013): 249–80.

Wordsworth, William."Preface to *Lyrical Ballads*." In *Selected Poems and Prefaces*. Edited by Jack Stillinger. Boston: Houghton Mifflin, 1965.

Yeo, Richard R. *Defining Science: William Whewell, Natural Knowledge, and Public Debate in Early Victorian Britain*. New York: Cambridge University Press, 1993.

Zammito, John H. *Kant, Herder, and the Birth of Anthropology*. Chicago: University of Chicago Press, 2002.

———. *A Nice Derangement of Epistemes: Post-Positivism in the Study of Science from Quine to Latour*. Chicago: University of Chicago Press, 2004.

———. "Teleology then and now: The question of Kant's relevance for contemporary controversies over function in biology." *Studies in History and Philosophy of Biological and Biomedical Sciences* 37 (2006): 748–770.

Zeuch, Ulrike. *Das Unendliche: Höchste Fülle oder Nichts? Zur Problematik von Friedrich Schlegels Geist-Begriff und dessen geistesgeschichtlichen Voraussetzungen*. Würzburg: Königshausen & Neumann, 1991.

Ziche, Paul. "Naturforschung in Jena zur Zeit Hegels. Materialien zum Hintergrund der spekulativen Naturphilosophie." *Hegel-Studien* 32 (1997): 9–40.

———. "Gehört das Ich zur Natur? Geistige und organische Natur in Schellings Naturphilosophie." *Philosophisches Jahrbuch* 108 (2001): 41–57.

Ziche, Paul, and Olaf Breidbach, eds. *Naturwissenschaften um 1800. Wissenschaftskultur in Jena-Weimar*. Weimar: Hermann Böhlaus Nachfolger, 2001.

Ziolkowski, Theodore. *German Romanticism and Its Institutions*. Princeton: Princeton University Press, 1990.

INDEX

absolute idealism. *See* idealism
absolute, the,
  epistemological ground of, 24
  experience of, 213, 250
  definition of, 130–131
  in Hölderlin, 130, 131–132, 136–137,
    139–140
  irrepresentability
    as antinomial attempt, 150
    as endless striving, 18, 28–29 (*see*
      also infinite striving)
    and gap between finite and
      infinite, 190
    and limits of language, 170, 173
    magnitude, questions of, 188–189
  and reason, 36
  in relation to the subject, 210, 247
  in Schlegel, F., 170
  temporality of, 247
Adorno, Theodor W., 150, 159n14
aesthetics
  creativity in, 41
  and *Naturphilosophie*, 41
  romantic, 39
  and the truth of art, 41
  See also beauty; sublime
"annihilation of nature," 203, 210, 215
antifoundationalism, 5, 23–25, 30, 37–38,
    150. *See also* Schlegel, Friedrich von
Aquinas, Saint Thomas, 227
archetype, theory of, 33, 193, 302
Arnim, Achim von, 191

Athäneum (journal), 2, 9n2, 10n6, 10n7, 114
Austin, J. L., 179

Bate, Jonathan, 298
beauty
  in art and nature, 122
  as completion of science, 154–155
  as harmony of parts, 162n42
  as intuition of perfection, 40
  in Kant's Copernican Revolution, 39
  Neoplatonic vs. Kantian, 189
  sublime, as opposed to, 188
  truth, as not equivalent to,162n39
  See also sublime
being
  and consciousness, 27, 251
  and identity, 19, 22
Beiser, Frederick
  on freedom, 203–206
  on Novalis, 259
  Romantic Imperative, The, 202–203, 209,
    210, 213
  romanticism
    interpretation of, 2–3, 259–260, 264–265
    and politics, 205
    and religion, 213
    and Spinoza, 209
Ben David, Lazarus, 242–243
Berlin, Isaiah, 276
Bildung
  alternative conceptions of, 93, 105–106
  definition of, 92